Governing Natural Resources for Africa's Development

Bringing together some of the world's leading thinkers and policy experts in the area of natural resource governance and management in Africa, this volume addresses the most critical policy issues affecting the continent's ability to manage and govern its precious resources. The narrative of the book is solutions-driven, as experts weigh on specific issues within the context of Africa's natural resource governance and offer appropriate policy recommendations on how best to manage the continent's resources. This is a must-read for government policy makers in industrialized economies and, more importantly, in Africa and emerging economies, as well as for academic researchers working in the field, extractive companies operating on the continent, extractive industry and trade associations, and multilateral and donor aid institutions.

Hany Gamil Besada is Regional Advisor, African Minerals Development Centre, United Nations Economic Commission for Africa; Non-Resident Senior Research Fellow, United Nations University Institute for Natural Resources in Africa; Senior Fellow, University of Ottawa; Research Professor, Carleton University; and also Senior Governance Expert with ACT for Performance in Ottawa, Canada.

The International Political Economy of New Regionalisms Series
Series Editor: Timothy M. Shaw

The International Political Economy of New Regionalisms Series presents innovative analyses of a range of novel regional relations and institutions. Going beyond established, formal, interstate economic organizations, this essential series provides informed interdisciplinary and international research and debate about myriad heterogeneous intermediate-level interactions. Reflective of its cosmopolitan and creative orientation, this series is developed by an international editorial team of established and emerging scholars in both the South and North. It reinforces ongoing networks of analysts in both academia and think-tanks as well as international agencies concerned with micro-, meso- and macro-level regionalisms.

Most recent titles

1. Crisis and Promise in the Caribbean: Politics and Convergence
   Winston Dookeran

2. Contemporary Regional Development in Africa
   Kobena T. Hanson

3. Eurasian Regionalisms and Russian Foreign Policy
   Mikhail A. Molchanov

4. Africa in the Age of Globalisation: Perceptions, Misperceptions and Realities
   Edward Shizha and Lamine Diallo

5. Governing Natural Resources for Africa's Development
   Edited by Hany Gamil Besada

Governing Natural Resources for Africa's Development

Edited by Hany Gamil Besada

LONDON AND NEW YORK

First published 2017
by Routledge
2 Park Square, Milton Park, Abingdon, Oxon OX14 4RN

and by Routledge
711 Third Avenue, New York, NY 10017

Routledge is an imprint of the Taylor & Francis Group, an informa business

© 2017 Hany Gamil Besada

The right of the editor to be identified as the author of the editorial material, and of the authors for their individual chapters, has been asserted in accordance with sections 77 and 78 of the Copyright, Designs and Patents Act 1988.

All rights reserved. No part of this book may be reprinted or reproduced or utilised in any form or by any electronic, mechanical, or other means, now known or hereafter invented, including photocopying and recording, or in any information storage or retrieval system, without permission in writing from the publishers.

Trademark notice: Product or corporate names may be trademarks or registered trademarks, and are used only for identification and explanation without intent to infringe.

British Library Cataloguing in Publication Data
A catalogue record for this book is available from the British Library

Library of Congress Cataloguing in Publication Data
Names: Besada, Hany, editor.
Title: Governing natural resources for Africa's development / [edited by] Hany Gamil Besada.
Description: Abingdon, Oxon; New York, NY: Routledge, [2016] | Series: The international political economy of new regionalisms series; 5 | Includes bibliographical references and index.
Identifiers: LCCN 2016011596 | ISBN 9781138200517 (hardback) | ISBN 9781315514253 (ebook)
Subjects: LCSH: Natural resources–Government policy–Africa. | Mines and mineral resources–Africa. | Economic development–Africa.
Classification: LCC HC800.Z65 G684 2016 | DDC 333.7096–dc23
LC record available at https://lccn.loc.gov/2016011596

ISBN: 978-1-138-20051-7 (hbk)
ISBN: 978-1-315-51425-3 (ebk)

Typeset in Times New Roman
by Out of House Publishing

Printed and bound by CPI Group (UK) Ltd, Croydon, CR0 4YY

Contents

List of figures — viii
List of tables — ix
Contributors — x
Foreword 1: governing natural resources for Africa's development — xv
MAHMOUD MOHIELDIN

Foreword 2: the African state and natural resource governance in the 21st century — xviii
DR. NGOZI OKONJO-IWEALA

Introduction — 1
HANY GAMIL BESADA AND KENDRA EYBEN

PART I
African content — 11

1 The Africa Mining Vision as a model for natural resource governance in Africa — 13
ANTONIO M. A. PEDRO

2 Capacity development for natural resource management: findings from the 2013 Africa Capacity Indicators Report — 39
KOBENA T. HANSON

3 The other resource curse: extractives as development panacea — 64
CHRIS W. J. ROBERTS

PART II
Governance aspects   93

4 Natural resources, global economic volatility, and
   Africa's growth prospects   95
   GEORGE KARARACH AND WALTER ODHIAMBO

5 Natural resources, volatility, and African development
   policy: some agenda for action   137
   GEORGE KARARACH AND WALTER ODHIAMBO

6 Local content policies, natural resource governance, and
   development in the Global South   156
   JESSE SALAH OVADIA

7 When nature becomes a resource: spaces of
   environmental protection, land management, and
   development issues in francophone Africa   171
   CRISTINA D'ALESSANDRO

PART III
Land management   195

8 Sustainable development of mineral commodities in
   Africa: challenges and policies   197
   PAULO DE SA

9 Future land-grab solutions? The evolution and potential
   impact of public and private governance initiatives at
   the global level   220
   KATHRYN ANNE BRUNTON, ANNI-CLAUDINE BÜLLES, AND
   MATTHEW GAUDREAU

10 Winners and losers: contestation over land in the
   advent of oil exploration in Uganda   243
   WINIFRED ALIGUMA, ROBERTS MURIISA, MEDARD TWINAMATSIKO,
   AND PAMELA K. MBABAZI

PART IV
Foreign policy 261

11 Canada and China: accepting Africa's rise? 263
    JOSEPH K. INGRAM

12 Russia's geostrategic vision of African natural resources 284
    LEONID FITUNI

   Index 312

Figures

2.1	Policy environment/efficiency of instrument.	52
2.2	Legitimacy and incentives of NRM policy.	52
2.3	Dialogue and social inclusion on natural resource governance (percentage of countries).	53
2.4	Key linkages and sequencing of NRM in post-conflict/fragile vs. stable countries.	55
3.1	Four governance and regulatory levels of analysis.	68
3.2	Conflicting objectives of extractive industry regulations.	69
3.3	EI upstream, downstream and sidestream linkages.	72
3.4	Extractives value pyramid.	74
4.1	Real GDP and per capita growth of African countries.	97
9.1	Breakdown of hectares in land-grab deals in SSA by country of origin.	223
11.1	China's imports, by country of origin.	266
11.2	Africa is outperforming the United States and Western Europe in productivity gains.	268
11.3	Percentage change in share of world exports for G20 countries, 2000–2010.	272

Tables

1.1	Policy responses to a minerals-driven cycle	21
1.2	The AMDC result areas	29
2.1	ACI 2013 – country percentage by cluster and level of capacity	49
2.2	ACI-NRM 2013 – resource-endowed countries	50
3.1	Contemporary extractives milestones for SSA	77
3.2	SSA regulatory revisions in mining/oil and gas 2010–2013	87
4.1	Classification of commodities	98
4.2	Africa's simplified commodity current account (2008–2009)	99
4.3	Definitions of variables	132
4.4	Descriptive statistics (1990–2012)	132
4.5	Correlation coefficients	133
4.6	Pooled OLS regression	134
4.7	Pooled OLS regressions with country and year dummies	135
4.8	Instrumental-variables regressions	136
8.1	Growth rates in resource-rich countries	199
9.1	Land-grab-related private governance initiatives	229
12.1	Russia's mineral resource shortage and potential of Africa's mining sector	299
12.2	Major Russian investment projects in African natural resources (1992–2013)	307

Contributors

Cristina D'Alessandro is a Senior Fellow at the Centre on Governance of the University of Ottawa (Canada) and a Professor at the Paris School of International Affairs (France). Previously she served as a Knowledge Expert at the African Capacity Building Foundation in Harare (Zimbabwe) and as a professor at the University Lumière Lyon 2. As an international scholar with experience in Africa, Europe, and America, she holds a number of board positions and serves as an advisor for international organizations/institutions.

Winifred Aliguma works with Mbarara University of Science and Technology and holds a Master's Degree in Local Governance & Planning and a Bachelor's Degree in Information Technology, both from Mbarara University. Her research interests include: governance issues, community development planning, decentralization, and grass root participation.

Hany Gamil Besada is Senior Fellow with the Centre on Governance at the University of Ottawa (Canada). He is also Regional Advisor, African Mineral Development Centre (AMDC) at the United Nations Economic Commission for Africa (UNECA), Non-Resident Senior Research Fellow with the United Nations University Institute for Natural Resources in Africa (UNU-INRA), and a Research Professor, Institute of African Studies, Carleton University (Canada). Until very recently, he was Theme Leader: Governance of Natural Resources at the North-South Institute (NSI) in Ottawa, Canada, and Research Specialist on the United Nations High Level Panel Secretariat-Post 2015 Development Agenda, United Nations Development Programme (UNDP) in New York. Previously, Prof. Besada was Program Leader and Senior Researcher at the Centre for International Governance Innovation (CIGI) in Waterloo, Canada. Prior to that, he was the Principle Researcher: Business in Africa at the South African Institute of International Affairs (SAIIA) in Johannesburg, South Africa. Prof. Besada has worked as Policy Advisor for the South African Ministry of Local and Provisional Government

Kathyrn Anne Brunton is a research consultant whose work focuses on land governance, food security, and human rights. She currently serves on the Board of Directors for the Coalition for Equitable Land Acquisitions and Development in Africa (CELADA) and has most recently worked with the Canadian federal government and UNESCO's International Institute for Educational Planning. She holds a Bachelor of Commerce from the University of British Columbia and a Master of Arts in Globalization and International Development from the University of Ottawa.

Anni-Claudine Bülles has a Master of Arts in Globalization and International Development from the University of Ottawa, Canada. Her research focused on minority rights and majority interests in the context of development-induced displacement in India. In collaboration with the North-South Institute, she has published a report and policy brief on policy coherence and development effectiveness in Canada. Professionally, she has worked with Aboriginal communities across Canada on economic development and good governance projects.

Kendra Eyben is a candidate in the joint J.D.-M.A. program in International Affairs hosted at the University of Ottawa's Faculty of Law and the Norman Patterson School of International Affairs at Carleton University.

Leonid Fituni, Dr.Sc., is Professor and Director, Centre for Strategic and Global Studies, and Deputy Director, Institute for African Studies, Russian Academy of Science. He is also President of the Independent Centre for Documentation on Liberty, Democracy and Justice (Moscow, Russia). He is the author of eighteen books on international economic relations, developing economies, global security, sustainable development, and justice.

Matthew Gaudreau is a doctoral candidate at the Balsillie School of International Affairs, University of Waterloo. His research pertains to the global political economy of food and agriculture, while his dissertation focuses on China's relationship to the global seed industry. He has carried out and designed research projects in China, Europe, and Canada, with publications in the *Journal of Environment and Development* and *Canadian Food Studies*, as well as a chapter in the book *Facing China as a New Global Superpower*.

Kobena T. Hanson is founder/CEO of Strategic Outlooks, and a faculty member at the Ghana Institute of Management and Public Administration, Ghana. He previously was Head – Knowledge, Evaluation and Learning Department, African Capacity Building Foundation, Zimbabwe. He is widely published on issues of leadership in higher education, natural resource governance, regional development, and public policy. His most recent publication, *Contemporary Regional Development in Africa* (2015), is by Ashgate. He holds a Ph.D. from Queen's University, Canada.

Joseph K. Ingram is the former President of Canada's The North-South Institute and a former World Bank Special Representative to the United Nations and the World Trade Organization (WTO). During a 30-year career in the World Bank he resided in and directed Bank-supported programs in West and Central Africa, Bosnia and Herzegovina, the former Yugoslavia and in North Africa and the Middle East. He is a former Deputy Director of the World Bank Institute. His early career included work with the International Development Research Center, and teaching in the Ivory Coast. He has served as a consultant to the WTO on issues relating to trade facilitation in francophone Africa. He currently chairs the advisory board of a South African based company advising equity investors.

George Kararach is an Economic Affairs Officer, Macroeconomic Policy Division, UN Economic Commission for Africa, Addis Ababa, Ethiopia and Senior Consultant, Statistics Department, African Development Bank, Abidjan, Côte d'Ivoire. His most recent books include: *Development Policy in Africa: Mastering the Future?* (Palgrave Macmillan, 2014), *Development in Africa: Refocusing the Lens after the Millennium Development Goals* (Policy Press, with H. Besada and T. M. Shaw (eds), 2015), *Economic Management under Hyperinflationary Environment: The Political Economy of Zimbabwe, 1980–2008* (Oxford University Press, with Raphael Otieno (eds), 2016).

Pamela K. Mbabazi is a Professor of Development Studies and is currently an independent researcher and consultant. Her research interests include the changing nature and character of the state in Africa, the political economy of oil, electoral governance, land governance and peace studies.

Mahmoud Mohieldin is the World Bank Group Senior Vice President for the 2030 Development Agenda, UN Relations and Partnerships. He has previously held numerous senior positions in the government of Egypt, including as Minister of Investment. He also served on several boards of directors, including the Central Bank of Egypt and in the banking, corporate, and academic sectors. He is also Professor of Economics and Finance at Cairo University and Honorary Professor at Durham University.

Roberts Muriisa is an Associate Professor at Mbarara University of Science and Technology and holds a Ph.D. from the University of Bergen, Norway. His research interests are in the area of land governance, public policy planning, decentralization, and rural development.

Walter Odhiambo is a Development Economist at the Strategy and Policy Department of the African Development Bank. He has previously worked for the Agriculture and Agro-industry Department of the same bank and has extensive experience in natural resource management issues. He also has extensive experience in policy research and analysis at both international and national levels. His areas of research include natural resources management, agricultural trade and poverty analysis. Walter Odhiambo is a Kenyan national with a Ph.D. in agriculture and rural development from the University of Hohenheim, Germany, and an M.A. in economics from the University of Nairobi, Kenya.

Ngozi Okonjo-Iweala is a Senior Advisor at Lazard and Chair of GAVI. She was previously the Minister of Finance in Nigeria (August 2011 to May 2015). Prior to this, she was Managing Director of the World Bank (2007 to 2011). Dr. Okonjo-Iweala also held the positions of Finance Minister and Foreign Affairs Minister of Nigeria between 2003 and 2006. Dr. Okonjo-Iweala is the recipient of numerous awards, including honorary doctorates from Yale, UPenn, Brown, Colby. She has received many distinctions, including being named one of the World's 50 Greatest Leaders by *Fortune* in 2015 and one of the 100 most influential people in the world by *TIME* in 2014. She is also the author of several books and articles, including *Reforming the UnReformable: Lessons from Nigeria*.

Jesse Salah Ovadia is Lecturer in International Political Economy at Newcastle University. His research focuses on local content policies as creating linkages between oil and gas in sub-Saharan Africa and industrial development/economic growth in the non-oil economy. His new monograph is entitled *The Petro-Developmental State in Africa: Making Oil Work in Angola, Nigeria and the Gulf of Guinea*. He is also co-editor of the recently published *Energy, Capitalism and World Order: Toward a New Agenda in International Political Economy*.

Antonio M. A. Pedro is a geologist with over thirty years of broad experience in development issues and management at national, sub-regional and continental levels. He is currently Director of the Office for Eastern Africa at the United Nations Economic Commission for Africa. He has been at the forefront of mineral policy analysis and formulation. Of special relevance was the leading role he played in the formulation of the Africa Mining Vision adopted by the African Union in February 2009.

Chris W. J. Roberts is an instructor in the Department of Political Science at the University of Calgary (Canada) and President of African Access Consulting. He has over twenty years of consulting and operational experience with private firms, business associations, think-tanks, government agencies, and international organizations mostly related to aspects of Canada–Africa business development, trade and investment, and risk analysis. His scholarly research interests include extractive industries and the political economy of African development, and security.

Paulo de Sa is the Practice Manager of the Energy and Extractives Global Practice at the World Bank, where he coordinates and leads the Bank's oil, gas, and mining activities in more than fifty countries. He also heads three global programs and partnerships: the Extractive Industries Transparency

Initiative (EITI), the Global Gas Flaring Reduction (GGFR), and the Extractive Industries Technical Advisory Services (EI-TAF). Prior to that he was a Lead Operations Officer for the Latin America region of the World Bank.

Medard Twinamatsiko is a senior researcher with the Institute of Tropical Forest Conservation in Bwindi. He holds a Master's Degree in Development Studies from Mbarara University and is completing his Ph.D. at the same university. His research interests include resource governance, conflict prevention, and community development planning.

Foreword 1
Governing natural resources for Africa's development

Mahmoud Mohieldin

World Bank Group Corporate Secretary and President's Special Envoy

Governance of natural resources for Africa's development is one of the most important topics concerning Africa's economic future. Natural resource wealth, if managed well, offers opportunities for structural transformation, leading to a more sustainable and inclusive path for growth.[1]

First, Africa is growing. Africa's Pulse, released at the 2013 IMF-World Bank Annual Meetings, noted that economic growth in sub-Saharan Africa is likely to reach more than 5 percent on average in 2013–2015. Africa's growth numbers are largely due to high commodity prices worldwide and strong consumer spending on the continent. This growth could be harnessed to improve governance, the growth of a middle class and space for more people-centered policies.

Second, Africa is exceptionally well endowed with natural resources, boasting 15 percent of the world's oil reserves, 40 percent of its gold, and about 80 percent of the platinum group of metals. At the country level, Guinea alone has over 8 percent of total world bauxite production. The Democratic Republic of Congo and Zambia have a combined share of over 6 percent of total world copper production. Ghana and Mali together account for close to 6 percent of total world gold production. Every other week, news and headlines speak to the spate of new discoveries of oil, gas, and other minerals that have the potential to generate a wave of significant mineral wealth.

The collective challenge is to mobilize this wealth for economic prosperity and poverty-ending activities such as increasing food production and fighting the illiteracy and disease that blight the everyday lives of Africans, particularly the poorest. Africa's resources *could* be transformational for the continent and its people.

To recall the guiding principles contained in the Natural Resource Charter.

Precept 1 states: The development of a country's natural resources should be designed to secure the greatest social and economic benefit for its people.

This requires a comprehensive approach in which every stage of the decision chain is understood and addressed.

Precept 2 states: Successful natural resource management requires government accountability to an informed public.

With these two precepts, the profound nature of the challenge – and the opportunity – for improving governance of natural resources in Africa is apparent. From long experience, it is widely understood that translating natural resources wealth into broad-based development is generally difficult and has been particularly so in Africa. Harnessing the economic benefits of natural assets is typically subject to the "weakest link" problem – if any one link is broken the whole development enterprise can be jeopardized.

In negotiating resource-extraction contracts, resource-rich African nations have often failed to negotiate the best possible deals. Successful contract negotiations require African governments to be at least as well informed about technical details and geological endowments as the oil, gas, or mining companies who negotiate with the help of highly paid lawyers and skilled technical staff.

Countries need a level playing field with the extracting industries. Work in natural resource governance shows that in many cases, there are large asymmetries with regard to information and legal expertise between governments and extractive industries. Left untended, opaque contracts, inadequate and perfunctory consultations, and an overall lack of transparency, will result in poor people being left out of the full and fair benefits of resource extraction. Support for increasing African capacities will be critical for helping negotiate the best possible deals so that natural resources wealth can be invested in inclusive, green, sustainable growth.

The literature is replete with examples where local populations suffer the environmental damage and development neglect of extraction, while the benefits – and profits – end up far away. This must be reversed. There is no dearth of keen analytical input in this domain.

These include procyclical government expenditure patterns, rules-based stabilization funds, conversion of natural resources into income-generating financial and physical assets, effective negotiation of tax and fiscal regimes, and, last but not least, the importance of strong institutions that promote transparency and good governance. This is certainly not a simple list of things to do. All of these must be backed by government will and effective engagement of people and broader civil society.

So for these compelling reasons, the World Bank has just launched a new fund, the Africa Extractive Industry Trust Fund, to help countries on the continent level the playing field and ensure equitable deals in their natural resource contracts with international companies.

Tribute must also be paid to the very large number of initiatives by civil society organizations – Publish What You Pay, Revenue Watch, Extractive Industries Transparency Initiative and the Natural Resources Charter have all helped boost greater accountability and transparency in the extractives sector. They have provided an excellent set of tools for policy makers, civil society, and industry, and helped shed light on some of the most important steps to be taken to improve the management of natural resources.

As previously highlighted, the central tenets for improving governance in the extractives sector are fairly straightforward: fair contracts, responsible conduct of mining operations, and optimal use of resource wealth for people-centered development projects, such as agriculture, education, health, and nutrition, and investment in income-generating financial and/or physical assets such as infrastructure, which in turn are necessary to fuel economic activity and growth.

Commodity markets have played a significant role in shaping Africa's economic destiny. There is a sense of urgency; the opportunities offered by the commodities boom and historic high commodity prices should not bypass Africa. Much of the contemporary debate on the extractives sector has focused on the central role of the mining industry. Thus there is a critical and beneficial role that a responsible corporate sector can and should play in promoting good governance in the natural resources sector.

A joint 2011 African Union Commission and UN Economic Commission for Africa paper, "Minerals and Africa's Development" by the International Study Group Report on Africa's Mineral Regimes speaks to the power of corporate social responsibility (CSR) for greater development effectiveness.

It is instructive to recall the Africa Mining Vision's view, which states that "as CSR approaches could be voluntary or legislated, it is important to entrench CSR in any policy framework in a manner that is clear about the responsibilities of mining companies and government." In fact, what is really needed is to go beyond limited understandings of CSR to a broad, deep, and meaningful partnership between government, business, and civil society – one that results in socially, economically, and environmentally sustainable investment.

The Vision places the onus of responsibility on both the mining companies and governments. One without the other is a recipe for the resource curse and all its adverse impacts. In fact, good corporate and public governance go hand in hand: Governments need to attract the finest companies to invest and grow if they are to meet their development goals; and companies must have a deep stake in improving governance if their business interests depend on a healthy and stable medium- to long-term business environment and investment climate.

I hope that this book will contribute to the understanding of important issues, generating consensus, strengthening existing partnerships, and forging new alliances. We can all join in the effort to help African countries manage their valuable resources prudently and effectively.

Note

1 Foreword adapted from keynote speech May 9th 2013 for North-South Institute's Governing Natural Resources for Africa's Development in Ottawa, Canada.

Foreword 2
The African state and natural resource governance in the 21st century

Dr. Ngozi Okonjo-Iweala
Minister of Finance, Nigeria (2003–2006, 2011–2015)
Managing Director, World Bank (2007–2011)

The subject of governance in resource rich countries is becoming an important topic for policy-makers and the investment community – both in Africa and abroad.

Although African economies are now slowly but gradually diversifying away from the extractive industries, natural resources still account for a significant part of economic growth and can play an important role in financing development goals. In the past decade, the natural resource map in Africa has changed significantly. New oil deposits have been discovered in Ghana, Uganda and Kenya. In East Africa, Tanzania and Mozambique are also developing offshore gas deposits, which are likely to be some of the largest in the world. For other solid minerals, explorations are continuing in countries such as Guinea, Zambia and Democratic Republic of Congo.

Foreign interest in natural resource investments are highly encouraging for the development of the continent, but also raise challenges for policy-makers in developing countries as well as for foreign mining firms.

For policy-makers in host countries, I would argue that there are three main challenges:

The first challenge involves macroeconomic management. For the macroeconomist, natural resource revenues raise challenges because commodity prices tend to be volatile, and also because resource endowments are depleting and exhaustible assets. As a result, many resource-dependent countries tend to have high macroeconomic volatility and low growth. The recommended policy solution is to decouple public expenditures from commodity revenues, in order to limit the transmission of commodity price volatilities into the national budget.

In 2003 we adopted this policy advice in Nigeria to manage our oil revenues. We implemented an oil-price based fiscal rule where revenues accruing above a reference benchmark oil price are saved in a special account, "The Excess Crude Account". The introduction of this fiscal rule has enabled us to reduce the macroeconomic volatility that previously plagued the Nigerian economy. In addition, we also increased the public savings in our Excess Crude Account. This limited the impact of the oil price shocks of 2008 where oil prices fell by more than 70 percent in the last 6 months of the year. We had up to $22 billion saved in the Excess Crude Account, and this served as a fiscal buffer to the price shocks. Furthermore, we also launched a Sovereign Wealth Fund for Nigeria, with an initial capitalization of about $1 billion.

A second challenge for policy-makers in developing countries is the need to ensure transparency and good governance in the management of their natural resources. They must ensure transparency both in the award of mining concessions and contracts, and also in the utilization of resource revenues. Civil society groups in Africa have become more vocal, and are seeking greater transparency and accountability in resource management. Now, more than ever before, African leaders are standing up to the challenges of managing their natural resources.

For the purposes of handling natural resource revenues, following management frameworks such as the Natural Resource Charters and the Extractive Industries Transparency Initiative (EITI) can be very helpful. The Natural Resource Charters, developed by Prof. Paul Collier and his colleagues, provides 12 principles that encompass the key economic and social dimensions of natural resource exploitation. By working through this framework, governments, businesses and civil society in resource-dependent economies can engage more actively with the challenges of natural resource extraction. We had some initial benchmarking work done by a panel of experts who applied the Natural Resource Charter framework to Nigeria. We also made some progress in developing institutions to manage our oil revenues – although this remains a constant challenge. During my first tenure as Minister of Finance, we made progress in introducing institutions such as the Nigerian Extractive Industries Transparency Initiative (NEITI) to improve the audits of Nigeria's hydrocarbon reserves and financial flows. Today, more than twenty African countries have signed on to these principles. Investors and mining firms also benefit from the EITI guidelines on how to conduct transactions transparently and legally.

In Nigeria, we also introduced the practice of publishing monthly revenues distributed from our government coffers to the Federal, State and Local Governments. This publication quickly became a bestseller – a boring bestseller – and has provided factual evidence for civil society groups to challenge their elected leaders on the use of public revenues.

Finally, the third challenge for developing countries arises in the negotiation of fiscal terms for mining contracts. In many instances, there tends to be wide information asymmetries between foreign contractor firms and host government officials, such that contract negotiations tend to be on uneven playing fields. Developing country governments would thus be well advised to invest more in building technical capacities, improving their negotiation skills and researching international best practices before signing off on agreements.

Departing from host country governments, there remains a series of challenges for foreign firms operating in Africa's extractive sectors as well. How should they think about their engagement with the host governments and their host communities? This is a subject which foreign investors and policymakers need to take seriously, given their large investments in the mining sector in Africa and other developing regions.

I would suggest five key principles to guide foreign firms in making smart and responsible investments in the natural resource sectors in African countries.

a. *Align your investments with host countries' development priorities.* It is important for firms to ensure that their investments fit within the broader development agenda of their host countries. For many African countries today, job creation is the number one concern of policy makers. There is a pending demographic bulge, and our youth are looking for apprenticeships and employment. In such a setting, if mining firms want to align with the host countries' priorities, then they may consider employing local technicians, rather than bringing in foreign craftsmen.

b. *Practice transparency.* It is important for foreign firms to ensure transparency in the negotiation of their mining contracts. For example, the recent practice of exchanging natural resource licenses for infrastructure projects is inherently difficult to evaluate, and will thus be perceived as non-transparent. We will only generate hostility from local communities if contract negotiations and tax payments by foreign firms are believed to be mired in secrecy. There are also several instances when foreign firms collude with corrupt local officials in African countries to win lucrative mining licenses or related contracts. In my book, *Reforming the Unreformable,* I described the story of how a foreign consortium TSKJ (comprised of France's Technip, Italy's Snamprogetti, Haliburton's subsidiary Kellogg Brown & Root, and Japan's JGC) made secret payments in excess of $180 million to Nigerian officials in order to win multi-billion dollar oil services contracts. The era of foreign businessmen bribing local officials for lucrative contracts in Guinea, in DRC, in Nigeria or elsewhere must cease.

c. *Add value.* In contrast to the previous colonial practice of simply extracting and shipping out raw commodities, today, foreign firms investing in developing countries must add value to the raw materials. This will ensure greater economic spillovers to the local economy, by creating employment and developing skills.

d. *Pay what is due and do what is right.* Foreign investor firms need to pay their taxes and ensure sound accounting practices. Developing countries need the tax revenues to invest in infrastructure and to provide public services for their citizens. These investments would improve the business environment for mining firms operating in their countries. But for these public investments to happen, practices such as transfer pricing and other clever accounting tricks must stop. An editorial in the Financial Times estimated that Zambia loses about $2 billion annually due to tax avoidance. Moreover, in spite of all their mining, DRC and Guinea also have tax revenue to GDP ratios of about 8 percent, compared to the IMF benchmark of 15 percent of GDP.

e. *Engage with local communities*. It is important for natural resource firms to engage more closely with their host communities, by investing in social infrastructure (such as schools and hospitals) in these communities. Many firms in Africa would be operating in challenging environments – whether in Katanga province in the DRC or in the Niger Delta in Nigeria. It is important that host communities understand that firms have a shared and vested interest in their economic development, and are aware of the environmental impact of business activities. In Nigeria, dysfunctional relationships between the local community and oil companies led to disruptions in operations in the Niger Delta. These disruptions cost the Government Treasury a lot of money, but it also raised costs for mining firms due to security concerns. Good corporate social responsibility would remain important for good business.

The natural resource sector has great potential in contributing to Africa's economic development. But we must get the governance of the sector right – both on the government side, and also on the side of the mining firms. We as policymakers must work hard to manage our resource revenues and also ensure transparency in the utilization of our resource revenues.

While it is impossible to fully explore the intricacies of good governance in one book, I believe that this volume will provide valuable insight into how to manage these various interests, while leveraging Africa's natural resources for economic development in a sustainable way.

Introduction

Hany Gamil Besada and Kendra Eyben

The global political economy is in a period of profound restructuring and reordering, exacerbated by the simultaneous rise of the BRICS countries (Brazil, Russia, India, China and South Africa) and decline of the PIIGS of the euro zone (Portugal, Italy, Ireland, Greece and Spain), which have now been joined by Cyprus. Jan Nederveen Pieterse (2012, 2–3) indicates that "twenty-first century globalization is markedly different from twentieth century globalization ... New trends in the twenty-first century are the rise of the global South, the growth of South–South relations in trade, energy and politics, and the growing role of emerging societies and sovereign wealth funds." In early 2013, PricewaterhouseCoopers suggested "China is projected to overtake the US as the largest economy by 2017 in purchasing power parity terms and by 2027 in market exchange rate terms. India should become the third "global economic giant" by 2050, a long way ahead of Brazil, which we expect to move up to 4th place ahead of Japan" (PwC 2013, 1). Hence the focus of the latest *Human Development Report* by the United Nations Development Programme – the rise of the South (UNDP 2013).

In 2011, participants at the first Ottawa Forum hosted by the North-South Institute (NSI) in Ottawa, Canada, started with such assumptions to analyze and anticipate multilateral development cooperation in a changing global order. Then NSI president and CEO Joseph Ingram (2011, 10) highlighted several evident "paradigm shifts," among them economic and power shifts toward emerging economies, growing public debates on the respective roles of public and private sectors in generating sustainable growth, and the unprecedented growth in demand for natural resources. Two years later, given the BRICS countries' continuing impact on the demand for and price of energy and minerals, international discourse evolved around the myriad development issues surrounding the governance of natural resources, particularly for Africa's development. Chatham House recently produced a telling report titled *Resources Futures*, which asserted that "collaborative governance is the only option": "Investment in the environmental and social resilience of developing economies will be critical to long-term resource security ... [E]merging economies such as China, India and Brazil must become partners with the OECD ... New modes of engagement also become critical as the centres of key decision-making on resources become diffused beyond traditional powers" (Lee et al. 2012, 8–9).

Africa is set to grow faster than any other region for at least the rest of this decade, facilitated by burgeoning foreign direct investment (*The Economist* 2013). The expanding literature on African agency is downplaying inherited dependency (Brown and Harman 2013) and indicating that the currently emerging economies will become dominant by mid-century (Ward 2012). Canada, on the other hand, is one of the global leaders in natural resources, including energy and agriculture, identified by Chatham House (Lee et al. 2012). As these and other key players move forward, the governance of natural resources is becoming increasingly transnational rather than intergovernmental (VanDeveer 2013).

Mining and extractive sectors constitute significant and progressively more important generators of exports and tax revenues for many African countries, as demonstrated by a March 2013 special report in *The Economist* titled "Emerging Africa: A Hopeful Continent" (2013). These sectors hold enormous potential to finance the rapid infrastructure development and private-sector-led socio-economic development projects that are needed for sustainable broad-based economic growth and poverty reduction. Hence the advocacy for "developmental states" by the United Nations Economic Commission for Africa, which has so far led to the articulation of the evolving Africa Mining Vision that was adopted by heads of state at a 2009 African Union summit and is linked to the Mining Policy Framework presented to the United Nations Commission on Sustainable Development in 2011 by the 48-member Intergovernmental Forum on Mining, Minerals, Metals and Sustainable Development (UNECA 2011). The Africa Mining Vision and its associated Action Plan form the most complete framework for collaborative governance on a continent with fifty-four national governments and abundant natural resources.

Africa is endowed with some of the most sought-after natural resources in the world. It has 300 million hectares of potential land for rain-fed agriculture (Ahlenius 2006) and eighty transboundary rivers and lake basins, including seventeen large catchment areas exceeding 100,000 square kilometers each. With respect to minerals, the continent holds roughly 60 percent of the world's diamonds, 40 percent of its phosphate, and 30 percent of its cobalt reserves, to name just a few. From 2000 to 2011, natural resource extraction constituted a major component of real gross domestic product growth in over fifteen resource-rich African countries, including over half of all growth in Equatorial Guinea, Ghana, and the Democratic Republic of the Congo (IMF 2012, 65). With high commodity prices and the rise of emerging economies, in particular the BRICS countries, driving multinational mining companies to implement more ambitious investment strategies, increased attention in African countries, Canada, and elsewhere is now being directed to harnessing Africa's resources for development (*The Economist* 2013).

Many countries have netted rewards from harnessing the wealth of natural resources. Benefits notwithstanding, over the past decade there has been an increase in detrimental events linked to the extraction of natural resources in both developed and developing countries. The unprecedented growth in global demand for natural resources driven by the emergence of a new global middle class, combined with an abundance of natural resources in Africa, has given rise to historic levels of growth and investment, but also to chaotic and wasteful practices; to the depletion of resources on which the economic livelihoods of societies are based; and, in some cases, to increased levels of violence. Countless rounds of dialogue and round-table discussion among the various stakeholders – governments, unions, local committees and companies – have contributed to a growing debate around governance and management of natural resources.

The debate has largely coalesced around the creation of clear and concrete regulations and mining codes; fiscal, monetary and budgetary discipline; pro-poor public–private partnerships; building skills and capacities in government departments; encouraging open dialogue between government and civil society; as well as around the transparency and accountability of the parties involved. All these issues point to the urgent need for an improved governance system in the natural resources sector. Reflecting this need, 2011 saw the formulation of the *Natural Resources Charter*, designed by Paul Collier, as well as the African Union's *Africa Mining Vision*, both of which produced a proliferation of new knowledge and ideas, as well as an increased awareness of the need for improved governance of natural resources.

Africa's leaders have also come to recognize that the manner in which the continent's resources are overseen and exploited is fundamental to their ability to enhance both state and human security, to contribute to sustainable development, as well as to their achievement of the Millennium Development Goals and of importance to their fundamental role in the post-2015 development agenda. With increased investment in the mining sector, and the growing frequency of violence associated with such activity, governments and civil society organizations have been paying increasing attention to the socio-economic impact of these investments on local communities as well as on the national economies. Given the relative importance of extractives as a component of economic growth, both the positive and negative effects have come to be recognized as having a particular bearing on political stability and social cohesion. Policy debates on the continent therefore center increasingly on how best to manage the exploitation of natural resources so that they produce benefits for all concerned.

In Africa in particular, an abundance of natural resources could be the key factor to poverty alleviation and lasting prosperity. Since the mid-1990s, more than forty African countries have substantially changed their mining legislation in order to attract more foreign direct investment. These changes have helped facilitate the deregulation and privatization of natural resource sectors. However, poor resource management can result in wasteful use of human capital, the exploitation of the resources on which societies' livelihoods are based, and, in extreme cases, political instability and violence at both national and regional level (Buckles 1999). Additionally, with the rise of the BRICS countries as significant investors in Africa, climate change, population growth, and often competing public and private sector interests, the continent is experiencing heightened competition for its land, water, oil, and mineral resources (Brown and Harman 2013).

A consistent and continually evolving innovative and inclusive approach to the governance of natural resources is required if foreign investment and private-sector activities are to support sustainable development and contribute to peace, security, and political stability in Africa. Clear objectives for all stakeholders must include the improvement of transparency and accountability, promotion of free, prior, and informed consent protocols, reinvestment of natural resource revenues into social services, poverty reduction for local mining communities and the larger populations of host countries, and diversification of economic development in resource-rich African countries. Given the scope of the challenges and the complexity of the underlying issues, an improved analytical framework for understanding the changing linkages between traditional and emerging private sectors, local communities, corporate social responsibility (CSR) and free, prior, and informed consent practices and host governments is necessary. This timely volume can help delineate such an approach, these objectives, and this analytical framework.

From the perspective of African stakeholders, effective natural resource governance is increasingly regarded as the key determinant of Africa's economic growth and future investment opportunities, especially if official development assistance volumes continue to decline. The Africa Mining Vision stands as a continental policy response to collectively improve natural resource governance. African leaders have come to recognize that the manner in which the continent's resources are managed and extracted fundamentally affects their abilities to mobilize more domestic resources, contribute to sustainable economic and social development, and enhance both state and human security. Given a changing global order distinguished by growing South–South relations, an understanding of Africa's governance of natural resources and the way in which this governance is likely to evolve is of greater importance than ever – especially for emerging economies seeking to invest in the continent.

It is important to distill from the growing body of knowledge and experience associated with natural resource extraction those practices which can best produce positive outcomes for all key stakeholders – local communities, extractive investors and host governments. In-depth analysis based on sound research and careful review of global experience is what produces best-practice policy outcomes. The book highlights the perspectives of key players – those who are engaged in implementing current initiatives for the governance of natural resources. It is organized around the following topics: current and future roles of multilateral and domestic institutions engaged in resource management; the role, priorities, and activities of the private sector and social development institutions in Africa; the involvement of emerging economies in natural resource management; free, prior and informed consent protocols in affected local communities; and the effectiveness of CSR principles in ensuring responsible corporate behavior.

The key objectives sought from this book are to identify best-practice policy options for natural resource governance based on knowledge and experience. The intention is to reflect both the needs and aspirations of host governments, mining investors and local communities, while at the same time addressing how available skill sets and knowledge at the local level can best be integrated in practice. This volume serves as a basis on which to begin building consensus, at a global level, on what constitutes the best-policy option for responsible resource governance in a diverse African context. It hopes to leave readers with a deeper appreciation of the current challenges and possible solutions facing African institutions, global investors, and, in particular, local communities.

This book emerged from the discussions held at the North-South Institute's *Governing Natural Resources for Africa's Development* conference in Ottawa, Canada, in May 2013 and following debates over the past eighteen months. The conference brought together African and Canadian policy makers, extractive industry representatives, civil society members and academics. Many presenters are represented in this book through chapter contributions. Others have consequently added their voices to the ongoing debate.

The framework

The book is organized according to key themes of the conference: African perspectives, governance issues, land management, and foreign policy. The three chapters by Pedro, Hanson, and Roberts come first and are grouped together since they both deal with African-led initiatives on the issue of global resource governance. The emergence of more voices from the African continent is a theme and a trend that we wish to encourage. After that, Chapters 4 through 7 deal with general issues of governance in the natural resource sector. They are a broad overview of the topic and address issues such as global economic volatility, local content and regionalism. The next three chapters are grouped together because they all deal specifically with issues of land management. Land management and natural resource governance are intimately linked, and the number of chapters that were submitted on the issue warranted a separate section. Finally, the last two chapters by Ingram and Fituni address foreign policy aspects of land management and illustrate how non-African countries are influencing the extractives sectors.

Chapter summaries

There are two forewords, one from a representative of a multilateral institution and the other from an African government official. The first is a speech from

Dr. Mahmoud Mohieldin, a World Bank special envoy, given at the opening of the Ottawa Conference. Dr. Mohieldin reflects on the possibilities offered to the African continent from its resource wealth. His optimism is tempered with pragmatism – the opportunities afforded the continent from its abundance of natural resources and the commodity booms are not guaranteed. Nigerian Finance Minister, Her Excellency Dr. Ngozi Okonjo-Iweala, writes the second speech in this collection. In her speech, she discusses the main issues facing both policy makers and mining firms. The challenges she outlines for policy makers focus on how to maximize the benefits of natural resource endowments. Natural resource extraction can lead to great economic benefits – but only if policy makers make smart decisions. For mining firms, she outlines five principles to guide their investment choices. The principles focus around making responsible and ethical decisions, and she stresses that the old colonial model of resource extraction is no longer acceptable.

Our first chapter by Mr. Antonio Pedro covers how the Africa Mining Vision can be used as a model for natural resource governance in Africa. The African Union adopted the Vision in 2009, and it serves as a key continental framework for resource governance. As Mr. Pedro illustrates, the Vision calls for a complete transformation of the minerals sector. This transformation is necessary since despite Africa's vast riches, it is still suffering from pervasive poverty. The Vision itself is unique since it represents a wholly African solution to the issues in resource governance. In his chapter, Mr. Pedro outlines the key tenets and challenges of the Vision and explains how the Vision has the flexibility to adapt to a varied and complex continent. He also outlines the key factors necessary to meet the ambitious goals of the Vision.

Dr. Kobena Hanson authors the second chapter. In the chapter, Dr. Hanson discusses the 2013 findings from the Africa Capacity Indicators Report. Capacity – which encompasses aptitudes, resources, relationships and facilitating conditions to act effectively – is crucial in the extractives sector. The extractive sector is complex, particularly in Africa. Hanson's findings suggest that the old resource management landscape is transforming and that models for capacity development should keep pace with those transformations. Some of the changes he identifies include the growth of social responsibility programs, the exposure of the "missing revenues" problem and the mobilization of community interests. He also points to a new normative environment in the resource-extraction industry, as evidenced by the emergence of various guiding policy documents, such as the Africa Mining Vision.

The third chapter is written by Dr. Chris Roberts, who discusses what he calls the "other resource curse," which is the common assumption that natural resources straightforwardly provide a revenue stream for public goods and socio-economic transformation. However, the linkage between economic development and natural resource richness is not as clear as many assume. Dr. Roberts explores analytical frameworks and conceptual tools that aid in understanding the regulatory environment around extractives in Africa. He also looks at why certain resources are exploited over others, and how the potential for economic development depends on which resource is developed. The chapter then outlines the successive eras that have characterized resource governance and regulations. Finally, Dr. Roberts concludes with a discussion on how the extractive sector can be turned from a panacea into a catalyst to cultivate institutions and processes that are beneficial to economic development.

The following chapters address governance aspects. The section starts with a chapter by Dr. George Kararach and Dr. Walter Odhiambo entitled "Natural resources, global economic volatility and Africa's growth prospects." This fourth chapter is concerned with the implications of global economic volatility in the extractive sector on GDP per capita growth and development. Extractive sector investment and development is a long-term strategy for revenue, and it is crucial that policy makers consider the risks of a fluctuating market. The authors strongly suggest that volatility must be managed based on common sense, to reduce risks and transactions costs. Their commonsense approach to volatility management is based on research conducted on seven main aspects where the relationship between volatility, economic growth and commodities is most evident. These aspects include the "Dutch disease," the resource curse, and the death of industrialization.

The fifth chapter is a continuation of the fourth chapter's discussion. Drs Kararach and Odhiambo build on their previous discussion on volatility and propose an agenda for action. The authors review stabilization policies in Africa, then provide a variety of tools that can be used in future policy making. To name a few, these tools include indexing delivery contracts to world prices, hedging export proceeds on futures markets and denominating debt.

Our sixth chapter is devoted to local content policies. Dr. Jesse Ovadia argues that these policies are a valuable tool to ensure the sustainability of resource-driven development. Local content policies are important, since there are few ways for the extractive sector to add value to a country's economy. However, local content policies are one way to link an extractive sector industry to the wider economy. The chapter gives an overview of these policies, particularly how they are used in the oil and gas sector. The author notes the dual aspect of local content policies: although they are useful in development they can also be a mechanism for elites to capture rents. Dr. Ovadia illustrates his points by using Nigeria and Ghana as case studies.

Dr. Cristina D'Alessandro contributes the seventh chapter on the impact of regional integration on capacity development for the post-Millennium Development Goal agenda. Her chapter investigates the continental processes taking place in Africa and attempts to establish which one would be the most beneficial for development. The author ultimately focuses on the benefits of sector-specific integration.

The eighth chapter, by Dr. Paulo de Sa, addresses the issue of the resource curse. He starts by outlining the recent economic performance and accomplishments in sub-Saharan Africa concerning resource governance, before turning to a more concrete discussion of how to avoid the "resource curse." He argues that despite the progress, more must be done to integrate resource extraction with downstream opportunities within African countries. The pure fiscal contribution of extracting resources cannot solely be relied upon if development is desired.

Ms. Kathryn Anne Brunton, Ms. Anni-Claudine Bülles and Mr. Matthew Gaudreau contribute the ninth chapter to the book. This chapter marks the shift in focus to issues concerning land rights. The three authors discuss the various public and private governance initiatives that have occurred to address the issue of so-called "land grabs." Land grabs have become increasingly common on the African continent, and they pose an interesting challenge due to the governance gap. The authors build upon work done by Mayer and Gereffi on determinants for successful private governance. Although the model is found to be solid, the authors suggest two additional hypotheses to address the shortfalls of private governance that Mayer and Gereffi do not cover in their framework. This theoretical base is then used to evaluate land-grab governance in sub-Saharan Africa.

The tenth chapter takes a look at land acquisition in Uganda. Ms. Winifred Aliguma, Dr. Roberts Muriisa, Mr. Medard Twinamatsiko and Professor Pamela Mbabazi describe the current situation in Ugandan land deals now that oil has been discovered in the south of the country. Local conflicts have started to emerge around land rights as investors and the government displace local populations. The authors argue that the Ugandan government has been very opaque in its land deals, and that occupants are often denied their rights. Part of this denial of rights stems from the fact that local populations are often uniformed and unaware of the laws governing land tenure and therefore cannot effectively protect their rights. Meanwhile, buyers and sellers of land often disregard constitutional laws that would protect local populations.

The final two chapters address foreign policy issues associated with the governance of natural resources. Mr. Joseph Ingram contributes the eleventh chapter in which he looks at Canada's and China's foreign policy approach to the new realities in sub-Saharan Africa. He chooses these two countries since they are both active players in the extractive industry. China and Canada are, however, confronted by different political realities and have differing strategies towards the African content and the natural resource sector. China's presence in Africa is driven by economics and a thirst for resources. Meanwhile, Canada oscillates between an economic and a development approach to the continent. Canada's priorities and strategy are significantly less clear than China's. The question remains, however, whether either China or Canada is actually responding to the needs of African countries.

Dr. Fituni contributes the twelfth chapter in this book. He looks at how the Russian Federation has approached its Africa policy with respect to natural resources. The Russian Federation is caught in the paradox of wanting to play a significant role in global governance, particularly in the natural resource sector, while also jealously guarding sovereign rights. Dr. Fituni reviews Russian policy towards Africa, and suggests how the new race for resources has impacted its long involvement with the continent.

References

Ahlenius, Hugo. 2006. "Current and Potential Arable Land Use in Africa." United Nations Environment Programme/GRID-Arendal. www.grida.no/graphicslib/detail/current-and-potential-arable-land-use-in-africa_a9fd.

Brown, William, and Sophie Harman, eds. 2013. *African Agency in International Politics*. Abingdon: Routledge.

Buckles, Daniel, ed. 1999. *Cultivating Peace: Conflict and Collaboration in Natural Resource Management*. Ottawa: International Development Research Centre.

The Economist. 2013. "Emerging Africa: A Hopeful Continent." Special Report. March 2.

IMF (International Monetary Fund). 2012. *Regional Economic Outlook: Sub-Saharan Africa; Sustaining Growth amid Global Uncertainty*. World Economic and Financial Surveys. Washington, DC: IMF.

Ingram, Joseph K. 2011. "Foreword." In *Canadian Development Report 2011; Global Challenges: Multilateral Solutions*. www.nsi-ins.ca/wp-content/uploads/2012/11/2011-CDR.pdf.

Lee, Bernice, Felix Preston, Jaakko Kooroshy, Rob Bailey, and Glada Lahn. 2012. *Resources Futures*. London: Chatham House.

Pieterse, Jan Nederveen. 2012. "Twenty-First Century Globalization: A New Development Era." *Forum for Development Studies* 39(3): 1–19.

PwC (PricewaterhouseCoopers). 2013. *World in 2050; The BRICS and Beyond: Prospects, Challenges and Opportunities*. London: PwC.

UNECA (United Nations Economic Commission for Africa). 2011. *Minerals and Africa's Development: The International Study Group Report on Africa's Mineral Regimes*. Addis Ababa: UNECA.

VanDeveer, Stacy D. 2013. *Still Digging: Extractive Industries, Resource Curses, and Transnational Governance in the Anthropocene*. Washington, DC: Transatlantic Academy.

Part I
African content

1 The Africa Mining Vision as a model for natural resource governance in Africa

Antonio M. A. Pedro

Introduction

In February 2009, the Assembly of the African Union Heads of State and Government adopted the Africa Mining Vision (AMV or "the Vision") as the key continental framework to "transform the extractive sector away from its colonially-created enclave features" (UNECA 2011: 9) – in which the ownership of mines and operations was foreign, minerals were exported in raw form, and mining inputs were imported from abroad (UNECA 2011: 151) – and, through linkages, "integrate it more coherently and firmly into the continent's economy and society."

The adoption of the AMV came out of the realization that despite Africa's huge endowments in minerals, the majority of Africans still lived in pervasive poverty, a paradox of plenty. The AMV is therefore the embodiment of Africa's aspiration to promote "transparent, equitable and optimal exploitation of mineral resources to underpin broad-based sustainable growth and socio-economic development" on the continent.

This chapter provides detailed information on the AMV construct and modalities, threats and opportunities for its successful implementation, both within and outside Africa.

The chapter is organized as follows:

- The genesis of the Africa Mining Vision (AMV)
- The AMV key tenets
- AMV strategies
- The AMV challenges
- The path towards good policy responses
- The AMV Theory of Change
- The AMV priority actions
- A word on implementation
- The next leg: country mining visions
- Staying the course when commodity prices are low: a daunting challenge
- The AMV success factors

The genesis of the Africa Mining Vision (AMV)

Africa contains some of the world's most significant mineral reserves and is one of the few remaining regions in the world which still has vast areas of land largely unexplored. By some estimates, the continent ranks first or second in quantity of global mineral reserves of diamonds, platinum group minerals (PGM), bauxite, phosphate rock, vermiculite, cobalt, zirconium, manganese, and vanadium.[1] It is also a global leader in the production of PGMs, phosphate, gold, vanadium, cobalt, diamonds, and aluminum. However, while opportunities for value addition in the mineral sector exist, most of Africa's minerals are still exported as ores, concentrates, or metals without significant downstream processing to add value, a feature inherited from colonial times. Then and now, Africa's export concentration on primary commodities is very high, a reflection of the continent's weak industrial base (UNECA 2013: 74). The insatiable demand in the 2000s for commodities from emerging economies, which fueled a commodity price boom, exacerbated the problem, for there was increased pressure to export ores and concentrates for quick wins.

By nature, mining is inherently unsustainable in that the life of a mine is limited and will eventually come to an end. However, its sustainability can be ensured by the linkages (downstream, upstream, sidestream, physical, and financial) it forms with other sectors of the economy (UNECA 2011: 101–114). This understanding is becoming part of mainstream mineral policy. In several mineral jurisdictions in developing countries and beyond, there are increased calls for greater local content and value addition in the extractive sector. Africa is no exception. There is also an increased awareness that value addition encompasses more than mineral processing and includes all aspects of the mineral value chain, such as local inputs and services into the mineral sector. Further, there is the realization that skills and technology acquisition, supported by a strong research and development and science and technology foundation, are the basis for creating value-added in the minerals sector. Much of this thinking is informed by experiences from countries such as Finland, Norway, and Sweden that have successfully made the transition from resource-based to knowledge-driven economies, where "the natural resources sector evolved from a position of low technology based on low-cost labour to one characterized by highly-skilled, knowledge-intensive and export-oriented activities" (UNECA 2004c: 13).

Following a long period of decline in the 1980 and 90s, beginning in 2002, mining investment experienced a boom and mineral commodity prices reached historical highs on the strength of strong demand for commodities, driven mainly by the rapid pace of industrialization taking place in large developing economies, particularly China (Morris et al. 2012). This trend is projected to continue for some time, despite the price corrections of 2008 and 2011. The current dispensation is also characterized by global concerns with security of supply and access to raw materials (HCSS and TNO 2010), coupled with strong competition for mineral acreage.

The 2000s were characterized by a massive explosion of soft regulation to earn a social license to operate. Through bodies such as the International Council on Mining & Metals (ICMM), the extractive industry – especially the so-called majors – has been repositioning itself and developing tools to equip mining companies to better mainstream sustainable development principles and practices in their business operations and to enhance mining's economic and social benefits (ICMM 2011). This period witnessed the emergence of development-oriented captains of industry such as Mark Cutifani, CEO of AngloAmerican. During the same period, the world faced the global economic meltdown and financial crisis of 2008. It has been argued that the crisis opened up more policy and fiscal space for developmental policies, as neoliberal fundamentals of the era of globalization were being criticized. Accordingly, and as a reflection of the times, Africa witnessed the rebirth of development planning and a narrative on economic structural transformation started to gain increasing ground and traction (UNECA, AUC 2013, 2014). The continent has also witnessed governance gains, as reflected by the growing strength of African civil society organizations (CSOs), which are increasingly contributing their views on how to shape important mineral policy processes.

It was against this background that the AMV was conceived. However, even though the AMV was formulated in 2009, during the age of the social license to operate, it is not a result of the euphoria of the 2000s commodity price boom. The Vision reflects the long-term aspiration of African countries to maximize value out of their mineral resource endowments. This aspiration fueled the nationalization spree in the 1960–70s and informed the formulation of many policy and strategy documents on the continent. These include the 1979 Monrovia Declaration on the "guidelines and measures for national and collective self-reliance in economic and social development for the establishment of a new international order"; the 1980 Lagos Plan of Action for the Economic Development of Africa, which manifested disquiet with Africa's overdependence on the export of raw materials and lack of linkages, and highlighted the importance of sectoral cooperation as a means to advancing regional integration (UNECA 2011: 182–184); the 1984 SADC Mining Sector Programme; and the 1991 Abuja Treaty, which stressed the importance of establishing the African Economic Community and recognized the need for incremental sector-based regional economic integration and harmonization of national policies in key sectors, including the extractives (UNECA 2011: 141–150). The AMV is also in line with the outcomes of the 2007 Big Table on "Managing Africa's Natural Resources for Growth and Poverty Reduction," which noted that Africa's liberal mineral regimes formulated during the mineral policy reforms of the 1980–90s, including John Strongman's 1994 "Strategies to Attract New Investment for Africa Mining," had not managed to change the enclave nature of Africa's extractive sector, and neither had they yielded significant development outcomes (UNECA 2015: 15–20).

The Vision is anchored in the belief that to overcome the historical structural deficiencies and enclave legacy of its extractive industry, and augment the share of mining-derived returns and social-economic benefits, the continent needs to speak in one voice through one common blueprint, the AMV. There was an equal understanding that the 2000s explosion of soft regulation and the global wealth shifts which catapulted China to the world stage offered Africa a unique window of opportunity to shift mineral policy from its rent-seeking and export-oriented approach to accommodate wider demands for broader long-term development goals and industrialization. In this new dispensation, the continent had a better chance to capitalize on the value of its natural resource endowment with a view to promoting inclusive economic and social structural transformation (UNECA 2011).

The AMV positions the debate on minerals for development in line with the Latin American debates on alternative development, extractivism, neo-extractivism and post-extractivism. As defined by Acosta (Lang and Mokrani 2013: 61–85) "extractivism refers to a type of an enclave economic model that is dependent on the large-scale removal (or extraction) and export of natural resources that are not processed (or are processed only to limited degree)." He notes that extractivism is a colonial and neo-colonial construct which generates very few benefits for the exporting countries. He argues for a transition from an anthropocentric model to a sustainable exploitation of natural resources, where environmental and social values are respected and economic diversification is pursued, anchored in strong institutions and credible public participation processes.

The AMV was drafted by a technical taskforce jointly established by the African Union Commission (AUC) and the United Nations Economic Commission for Africa (UNECA). It also included representatives from the African Development Bank (AfDB), the United Nations Conference on Trade and Development (UNCTAD), and the United Nations Industrial Development Organization (UNIDO). It was endorsed by the 1st Ordinary Session of the African Union (AU) Conference of Ministers Responsible for Mineral Resources Development in October 2008 and later approved by the AU Summit of Heads of State and Government held in February 2009 in Addis Ababa, Ethiopia.

The AMV key tenets

The AMV advocates for "transparent, equitable and optimal exploitation of mineral resources to underpin broad-based sustainable growth and socio-economic development" (African Union 2009: v). The Vision statement (Annex 1) begins with the notion that Africa's comparative mineral advantage would build competitive advantages and unleash structural economic transformations toward "knowledge-driven" economies. The AMV is anchored on the understanding that, if well managed and governed, mineral resources are an essential part of Africa's stock of natural capital that through appropriate social and economic linkages can propel the continent to transformational development and industrialization.

The AMV is founded on the following key tenets:

- creation of a sustainable and well-governed, transparent and accountable mineral sector that effectively garners and deploys resource rents to promote broad economic and social development;
- development of a comprehensive knowledge of Africa's mineral endowment;
- creation of a minerals sector that is knowledge driven and is a key component of a diversified, vibrant, and globally competitive African industrial economy;
- harnessing of the potential of small-scale mining to advance integrated and sustainable rural socio-economic development;
- promotion of a mineral sector that is inclusive and appreciated by all stakeholders, including surrounding communities;
- fostering of sustainable development principles based on environmentally, socially, and materially responsible mining, which is safe and appreciated by all stakeholders and surrounding communities;
- establishment of a minerals sector that catalyzes and contributes to broad-based growth and development through upstream, downstream, sidestream, and infrastructure linkages;
- building of human and institutional capacities towards a knowledge economy that supports innovation, research, and development.

These tenets have informed the formulation of the AMV Action Plan and the African Mineral Development Centre (AMDC) Business Plan, to be discussed later.[2]

AMV strategies

Because minerals are non-renewable assets, the core strategic approach that informs the AMV is the need to transform transient mineral wealth into other forms of lasting capital which outlive the currency of mining. The opportunities to achieve this transformation can be discerned if the minerals industry is unbundled to identify entry-points for (i) increasing local upstream support (supplier/input industries) sectors; (ii) enhancing downstream industries based on increased local beneficiation and value addition of goods; (iii) facilitating lateral migration of mining technologies to other industries; (iv) using mineral wealth to increase social, human, knowledge, and institutional capital (which can be used in other sectors); (v) promoting the development of sustainable livelihoods in mining communities; and (vi) creating small-and medium-sized enterprises and a more balanced and diversified economy with greater multiplier effects and potential to create employment.[3]

The principal resource endowment opportunities to realize the Vision (African Union 2009: 13) are therefore:

- resource rents: the use of resource differential and windfall rents to improve physical, social, and human capital and infrastructure;
- physical infrastructure: the multiple access to and collateral use of the high-rent resource infrastructure to open up, especially in the so-called development corridors, other resource potential (such as agriculture, forestry, and tourism) and to access zones of economic potential with lower returns (e.g. agriculture) that cannot afford their own requisite infrastructure;
- downstream value addition: the use of the locational advantage of producing crude resources to establish resource-processing industries (beneficiation) that could then provide the feedstock for manufacturing and industrialization;
- upstream value addition: the use of the relatively large resources sector market to develop a competitive resource supply/inputs sector (capital goods, consumables, services);
- technology/product development: resource-exploitation technologies generally need adaptation to local conditions (e.g. climate, mineralogy, terrain), which provide opportunities for the development of niche technological competencies in the resource inputs sector. This knowledge base and competencies can be used in other sectors of the economy.

Consistent with the seven value dimensions of the World Economic Forum (WEF) Minerals Value Management (MVM) Framework,[4] the Vision recognizes the centrality of mineral revenue, but underscores that other equally important benefits can be derived through employment generation, procurement of goods and services, entrepreneurial development, skills and knowledge creation, technology transfer, and infrastructure expansion.

The Vision calls for more fiscal space and responsive taxation to allow host countries to better capture windfalls and to encourage value addition and linkages. Modeled on the Alaska Permanent Fund, the AMV acknowledges the importance of establishing natural resource funds or stabilization funds as a means to sterilize excess mineral-derived liquidity in the economy and account for inter-generational equity (African Union 2009: 24–25). Nevertheless, countries should be aware that the establishment of such funds is not a panacea. To guarantee success, it is important to appoint good-quality administration of the funds and insulate it from political interference (Pedro 2006: 13). The existence of independent oversight bodies would strengthen overall accountability.

On mineral licensing, the AMV suggests that, where relevant, innovative licensing schemes, particularly auctioning systems or competitive tendering, can realize better value for mineral terrains than "the first come first served" principle. Competitive tendering would be easier to apply in mineral districts with known geology (e.g. the Copperbelt in Zambia, the Merensky Reef in South Africa, the Moatize Basin in Mozambique, to name a few) and a history of mining or with existing or abandoned mining sites. In these districts, exploration risks would be significantly lower than in virgin terrains. The bidding variables or factors could include a minimum work program, volume of capital expenditure, fiscal or revenue targets (as defined by the applicable royalty rate, income tax, state equity share, up-front cash payment), local procurement of goods and services, employment creation, infrastructure development, local processing and value addition, level of CSR investments, and other empowerment measures. The success of auctions would certainly depend on the quality of the design process, management of the invitation to bid, the number of participants in the auction, and the quality of the assessment process, which should be completely transparent and objective (UNECA 2011: 206–210).

The AMV challenges

The central argument in the AMV is that mineral resources can play a transformative role in Africa's development, based on the creation of appropriate social and economic linkages. However, mining in Africa has inherited severe structural deficiencies, which limit the extent to which greater value can be unlocked in the sector. Achieving this represents a daunting challenge for policy makers and other stakeholders (UNECA 2004b: 30–40). The following are the principal challenges.

Legacy and capacity dearth

To start with, many mining operations on the continent are enclaves in which most inputs are externally sourced and mining products externally consumed. The continent's inadequate level of technical skills, R&D infrastructure, and science and technology capabilities are another deterrent to the realization of the AMV key value proposition.

The regulatory dilemma

An important challenge also arises from the difficult balancing act that governments must perform to mainstream a linkages agenda in policy instruments and be responsive to domestic pressures that call for greater equity and local retention of mineral wealth, as well as to remain a competitive mining investment destination with an efficient and predictable legal and regulatory framework, which creates and sustains mineral wealth and benefits for all. This is particularly difficult because the most feared legal risk of mining investors is an adverse change of law and alterations in governmental requirements (Bastida et al. 2005: 80). In current times, this is called resource nationalism.[5] In particular, many countries fear that introducing linkages and local content provisions in their regulatory package would make them less competitive. After all, during the 1980s to the early 2000s, most African countries were locked in fierce competition with each other to offer the best possible incentives to attract foreign direct investment (FDI) to their respective extractive industry sector. This triggered a "winner's curse" for host countries that resulted in a "race to the bottom," where the extent of deregulation and the magnitude of favorable fiscal regimes and other legal and regulatory incentives contributed to a lesser local retention, if any, of mineral wealth. More disturbing was the fact that "policy options to organize a more dynamic long-term growth path in tandem with what the AMV now articulates, were foregone" (UNECA 2011: 15–19). Breaking this cycle is not easy.

Sharing mineral wealth and benefits with equity

Policy makers also find it difficult to formulate strategies and frameworks that ensure the effective use of non-renewable resources, such as minerals, to create assets that benefit all, including future generations. Once mineral wealth is created, investing transient mineral revenues wisely to ensure lasting wealth (the investment challenge) and/or distributing it fairly while balancing and managing conflicting local and national-level concerns and interests are difficult propositions (UNECA 2004b: 30–40). This is especially so in an environment where countries do not have adequate capacity (at national, sub-national and local levels) to administer the sector, plan appropriately (especially for a post-mining future), understand the Dutch disease, manage the vagaries and the conundrum of commodity price fluctuations and exogenous shocks, curb corruption and rent-seeking, ensure adequate public participation in decision making (UNECA 2004a; Pedro 2006), and manage expectations.

The path towards good policy responses

The exploitation of mineral resources does not always subject countries to a resource curse or expose them to the Dutch disease. Fortunately, there are good examples of successful management of mineral wealth to learn from and emulate, even in Africa. Botswana is often mentioned as one of those success stories. It has been argued that the country's ability to utilize diamond-derived revenue to promote economic growth and development is based on the strength of its leadership and institutions, clear vision and purpose, political stability and continuity, rule of law, anti-corruption practices, a conducive environment for business development, and good governance overall (Iimi 2006). Backed by a capable bureaucracy, the country pursued a disciplined and precautionary savings and investment policy. Investments on human and social capital formation were favored over consumption.

Inspired by such success cases, the AMV offers a continental framework to support the formulation of policy responses to address the challenges outlined above. However, the choice of policies in a given jurisdiction is context specific and should be mindful of (i) development paradigms (there is a window of opportunity now); (ii) the learning curve and stage of development of the country in a minerals cycle; (iii) the country's bargaining power; (iv) external dynamics (e.g. constraints arising from international law and trade and investment treaties, the state of the world economy, as well as geopolitics and the political economy of resource extraction); and (v) local context, especially the strength of the social movement, local power dynamics, the institutional environment, and the capacity of formal and informal institutions to contribute to the formulation and implementation of policies and to advocate for and implement change. Ultimate success hinges on promoting good governance and in creating strong and capable institutions (Pedro 2006), as well as platforms for enhanced collaboration and multi-stakeholder collaboration toward the implementation of a shared vision – the country mining vision.

Richard Auty developed a useful typology (Table 1.1) of policy responses to minerals-driven cycles which takes into consideration whether the economy is at a nascent, youthful, early-mature, or late-mature stage of the cycle. The need for differentiated responses is consistent with the AMV Theory of Change being developed.

Table 1.1 Policy responses to a minerals-driven cycle

Stage	Character	Macro effects	Policy response
Nascent	Mineral investment flow	Exchange-rate pressure	Create rent tax Build capital funds Establish revenue stabilization funds Grant central bank independence
Youthful	Rapid mineral expansion	Exchange-rate appreciation Dutch disease effects	Sterilize windfall rents Expand domestic absorptive capacity
Early-mature	Slowdown of output mineral	Growing tax and foreign exchange constraints	Substitute new tax sources Encourage domestic saving Promote sectoral diversification
Late-mature	Decline in mineral output	Persisting tax and foreign exchange shortages Rising unemployment	Depreciate real exchange rates Boost skills acquisition

Source: Macroeconomic policy for mineral economies, Richard Auty (www.commdev.org/files/1417_file_Marcoeconomic_Policy.pdf, Table 6).

The AMV Theory of Change

The AMV Theory of Change is being formulated as a game plan aimed at identifying the challenges and threats that can hamper the realization of the Vision; mapping opportunities to scale up its implementation; scanning stakeholders and boundary partners with relevant competencies and comparative advantages; and suggesting an optimal division of labor for the key protagonists in the operationalization of the AMV. The African Minerals Development Centre (AMDC), which was officially launched on December 16, 2013 in Maputo, Mozambique, at the margins of the Third African Union Conference of Ministers Responsible for Mineral Resources Development plays a core role in the AMV game plan.[6]

The AMDC is a joint project of the AUC, UNECA, the AfDB, and the United Nations Development Programme (UNDP) and will serve as a one-stop center of excellence to coordinate the realization of the Vision. The AMDC Business Plan is a source document for the game plan. It should be noted that even though the AMDC will play a vital function in rolling out the AMV, it cannot and will not be able to implement the Vision on its own. Instead, the Vision will become a reality only through the collective and individual contribution of a multitude of stakeholders at continental, regional/sub-regional, and national levels, and beyond Africa. These include governments, regional economic communities (RECs), CSOs and non-governmental organizations (NGOs), private sector, labor, and development partners, shareholders and institutional investors, international organizations, academia, and think-tanks.

At national level, the success of the AMV will be measured by the degree to which state and non-state actors mainstream and domesticate its key tenets into national processes, through country mining visions and/or other similar instruments and initiatives.

The AMV priority actions

As articulated earlier, the premise of the AMV is that, if well managed and governed, Africa's mineral resource endowments can catapult the continent to transformational development. Realizing this goal will require at least five crucial intervention points.

Strengthening domestic accountability and managing expectations

The AMV has identified seven building blocks for an effective governance of the mineral resources sector on the continent. These are: peace, security, and political stability; clear, transparent, predictable, and efficient legal and regulatory frameworks to ensure mineral wealth creation; fair and equitable fiscal regimes to facilitate equity in the distribution of benefits; credible public participation to enhance ownership and shape shared development outcomes; transformational leadership and followership to harness mineral wealth with a view to building resilient, diversified, and competitive economies; strong institutions to ensure effective management of the sector; and adequate infrastructure, including advanced human development to ensure that the extractive sector remains competitive and countries can build a future beyond mining.[7]

At the country level, the effort to strengthen domestic accountability and deepen the impact of the Vision with the view to ensuring that mineral resource exploitation generates benefits for all will be anchored in the existing African Peer Review Mechanism (APRM).[8] The APRM encourages public discussion with all stakeholders through an inclusive, participative, and consultative process that has the potential of creating a real and robust social compact between governments and their citizens, represented by different interest groups. It takes a comprehensive view of all aspects of a country's governance system, identifies and measures governance deficiencies, verifies the adoption, consolidation, and prescription of appropriate policies for the achievement of the socio-economic and political objectives of the New Partnership for Africa's Development (NEPAD). In addition, the APRM country review processes are evidence-based and include comprehensive fact finding and first-hand information gathering at the ground level. Each review process is different and customized to fit the local context and socio-political environment. The exercise contributes to the strengthening of transparency and mutual accountability, helps policy dialogue, builds capacity, and boosts compliance by monitoring a member state in respect to agreed governance standards and principles.

Up to 2012, the APRM country review processes were relatively silent on governance issues confronting the extractive sector. This was due to the non-existence of dedicated questions on matters of governance in the extractive industry. The comprehensive exercise initiated in 2010 to streamline the APRM Country Self-Assessment Questionnaire addressed this glaring omission. On July 14, 2012, the 17th Summit of the Committee of Participating Heads of State and Government of the APRM[9] adopted the Revised Country Self-Assessment Questionnaire for the African Peer Review Mechanism.[10] The new questionnaire includes specific questions and indicators on the governance of extractive industries captured in Chapters 4 (Economic Governance and Management) and 5 (Corporate Governance) of the document. This is a major development given the importance of mineral resources to many African countries and the complex governance challenges associated with the sector.

The domestic accountability agenda can also benefit from governance gains at the global level. In this respect, African countries are encouraged to adhere to initiatives such as the Extractive Industry Transparency Initiative (EITI) and ensure that key provisions in the EITI and from other global transparency standards such as Section 1504 of the Dodd-Frank Consumer Protection Act and the new Accounting Transparency Directive of the European Union are domesticated into national laws and regulations. Of particular relevance are the standards that require full disclosure of contracts and of information on beneficial ownerships, as well as transparency of payments and other commercial transactions throughout the decision chain and at every stage of the minerals value chain, from licensing to exploration, procurement, and marketing, a call already made at the 2007 Big Table on "Managing Africa's Natural Resources for Growth and Poverty Reduction" organized by UNECA in February 2007, in Addis Ababa, Ethiopia.

It is encouraging to see that several countries in Africa are already pursuing such a strategy. For example, Madagascar's EITI work plan for 2014 includes goals to: (i) improve transparency with regard to procedures for awarding-mining permits; (ii) ensure transparency of oil contracts; (iii) clarify regulations in the upstream oil sector; (iv) create transparency in mining and oil production; (v) verify the extractive industries' social contribution; (vi) improve the management and redistribution of income from the extractive industries; (vii) verify/improve management of public spending; (viii) improve and measure the economic and social impacts of mining projects on target populations; and (ix) improve the overall contribution of the extractive industry to sustainable development, to name a few.

Improving the level and quality of the resource potential data

Africa is one of the least explored continents. On average, the continent attracts about 15 percent of world annual global expenditure, far less than its 20 percent share of the Earth total land mass. Geological mapping and mineral inventory work has not covered the entire continent. In many African countries, investment in geological mapping and mineral inventory is not a government priority. Yet, on the one hand, without these investments the true geological potential of the continent would be masked. On the other hand, the less that is known about the potential value of a resource, the greater the share of the rents that a potential investor will understandably demand, due to the high risk of discovering or dimensioning the resource. Better knowledge of Africa's resource potential is therefore a priority action in the road towards the implementation of the AMV. It would strengthen the continent's bargaining power during contract negotiations. It would also help improve the continent's attractiveness as a mineral destination, increase the percentage share of global exploration expenditure it attracts and expand the number of Africa's mineral exploration projects advancing to the development stage. Moreover, geoscience data is needed to support spatial planning, reduce the impacts of natural disasters, manage climate change, and improve water resources management as well as other economic activities.

To achieve this there is need of a concerted effort (a geosciense data revolution) at national, continental and international levels to scale-up Africa's geological mapping and mineral inventory. In response and under the leadership of the African Union Commission and in close consultation with African geological surveys and other stakeholders, the World Bank put together the key elements of the African Minerals Geoscience Initiative (AMGI), an ambitious programme to improve the collection, consolidation, processing, interpretation and effective dissemination of national and regional geodata. The AMGI, also known as the "Billion Dollar Map" is a pan-Africa initiative being championed by the African Union Commission aimed at ensuring the collection, consolidation, interpretation and effective dissemination of national and regional data through a geo-portal. Ultimately, the initiative will contribute to increasing the availability and accessibility in the public domain of accurate and updated geoscientific data.

A first concept of the AMGI was presented at the 8th African Development Forum (ADF)[11] on "Governing and harnessing natural resources for Africa's development" held in Addis Ababa, Ethiopia, in October 2012. Thereafter, the African Union Commission organised a multi-stakeholders consultative meeting on 9–11 July 2014 to discuss a draft AMGI Technical Report prepared by the World Bank as well as clarify the initiative governance structure and roles and responsibilities of the different interested parties, review issues on ownership of the project and the data, and assess strategies to ensure the overall sustainability of the initiative, beyond donor funding. A Technical Working Group was constituted under the leadership of the African Union Commission to spearhead the implementation of the initiative. It comprises of representatives of Regional Economic Communities (RECs), the United Nations Development Programme (UNDP), the African Development Bank (AfDB), the United Nations Economic for Africa (UNECA) and the African Minerals and Geosciences Centre (AMGI), formerly known as the Southern and Eastern African Mineral Centre (SEAMIC).

When fully operational, the AMGI has the potential to address Africa's deep knowledge gaps in terms of geological coverage and mineral inventory. As articulated in the AMV, this is a key requirement to strengthen the continent's bargaining power and ability to use mineral resources for development.

Institutional strengthening and capacity building, particularly on contract negotiations

The AMV has recognized that there is a dearth of capacity (in quality and quantity) in Africa to support the Vision's objectives of resource-driven broad-based development. The continent's educational complex cannot meet the growing demands and complex needs of the extractive sector. Capacity deficits have been identified in the critical areas of mineral policy formulation, tax administration and accounting, overall administration of the sector, planning and implementing resource-based infrastructure, development of the resource-sector linkages into the domestic economy, and in contract negotiations.[12] The latter constitutes a serious challenge.

In general, African states negotiate with international mining companies on unequal terms. Negotiations are asymmetrical and in most cases, mining companies are better resourced and skilled. Typically, the government's team comprise a single lawyer, a representative of the country's geological survey, and a mining engineer, as well as representatives of the ministry of finance and of the central bank. Depending on the size of the contract being negotiated, an international firm might also be brought in to provide specialized support. Invariably, mining companies come with a much larger team and benefit from back-up support from several lead firms at their headquarters.

Several initiatives have been launched to correct this asymmetry. For example, in 2010, the AfDB established the African Legal Support Facility (ALSF) to provide legal advice and technical assistance to African countries in the areas of debt management and complex commercial credit litigation, the negotiation of complex commercial contracts, especially in the extractive sector, and capacity building.[13]

Of similar relevance is the African Mineral Skills Initiative (AMSI) launched in Addis Ababa, Ethiopia, in October 2012 by UNECA, Australian Aid (AusAid) and AngloGold Ashanti, during ADF-VIII. AMSI initial objective was to provide a platform to coordinate efforts to foster innovative approaches to human and institutional capacity building in the minerals industry, beyond the confines of technical disciplines and the narrow boundaries of the extractive sector.

Promoting linkages and diversification

Many countries in Africa have a high degree of concentration of exports in primary commodities. This level of concentration and specialization exposes the countries to the vagaries of commodity price fluctuations and highlights the vulnerability of commodity-dependent export-strategies-to-price shocks (OFSE 2015). Obviously, this has serious development and policy implications for these countries.

Commodity price variations affect export revenues and associated macroeconomic indicators, such as the balance of payments, public finances, inflation, and exchange rates. More fundamentally, it increases countries' vulnerability and accentuates the difficulties in managing their economies. The problem is compounded when the commodities are not beneficiated locally, value addition is insignificant, local content minimal, and, overall, the sector forms an enclave locked in global value chains and with limited linkages with the local economy. In such circumstances, potential multiplier effects with job-creation ramifications are not realized and the share of wealth that is retained locally is smaller.

Commodity price volatility subjects governments to boom–bust cycles (OFSE 2015). When prices are high, very few governments save the resulting windfalls. Most cannot resist the temptation of using the increased revenues to finance government spending. The inability to sterilize the windfalls through stabilization mechanisms, prudent investments, and smart saving can trigger inflationary pressures. On the other hand, when prices are low, countries can face a fiscal crisis because of their failure to finance expenditure commitments built up during the boom years.

It becomes imperative, therefore, for resource-rich countries to reduce their overall level of dependence on commodities and establish a reliable revenue base which can withstand commodity price volatility. It is argued that pursuing mineral linkages and commodity-based industrialization can partially achieve those objectives on the strength of the backward and forward linkages that are fomented and the better terms of trade that value-added and manufactured products can potentially secure.[14]

The linkages and diversification agenda is at the core of the AMV. It seeks to integrate and make Africa a global player in the international division of labor and use mineral resources to build internationally competitive and diversified resource-driven industrial economies (UNECA 2011: 101–114).

This agenda can be achieved by adopting and implementing a coherent industrial policy; fostering mineral cluster formation; optimizing the use of local content policy to encourage local sourcing of goods and services and promote local entrepreneurship development; raising lead-firm procurement, sourcing, and processing; running supply-chain development programs (the focus of the AMSI workstream on mining entrepreneurship development); boosting local skills and technologies; addressing infrastructure bottlenecks; coordinating ministries to improve policy implementation; establishing platforms for collaboration and hives of research and development, innovation, diversification, and technology diffusion; and promoting regional integration to facilitate factor flows, reduce transaction costs, realize economies of scale, accelerate the emergence of national and regional champions, and boost the competitiveness of local firms (UNECA and AUC, 2013; UNECA 2004c, Pedro 2006).

In the past, several countries have successfully used tariff protection, subsidies, export restrictions, local content provision, scorecards, and other performance requirements as instruments to foster economic transformation and the deepening of industrialization. However, this policy space is currently shrinking and the viability of processing and beneficiation industries in raw-material-exporting developing countries can be constrained by tariff and non-tariff barriers in potential markets, especially in the developed countries, as reflected in agreements and rules of the World Trade Organization (WTO), Regional-Bilateral Free Trade Agreements (FTAs), and Bilateral Investment Treaties (BITs) (UNECA 2011: 115–127).

There is a growing concern that the development and implementation of investment policies for sustainable development through local content provisions, employment and supplier training requirements, and the establishment of national lead firms, as prescribed by the AMV, can be in direct contradiction with the negotiation and signing of investment treaties that are essentially designed to extend protections for foreign investors against nationalization or expropriation, assurances for the free transfer of funds, and the provision of dispute-settlement mechanisms between investors and host countries. Extracting sustainable development advantages from foreign direct investment is not automatic. It will be incumbent upon African governments to remain vigilant and ensure that there is coherence between their industrial policy and their trade and investment policies. Institutional cohesiveness and acquisition of adequate capacity to understand the implications of international trade regimes and investment treaties on their aspirations for resource-based industrialization are fundamental prerequisites to realizing the AMV goals on resource-driven linkages, investment, and diversification.

Addressing Africa's infrastructure constraints

In many African states, a resource-based development strategy is severely constrained by the lack of the requisite infrastructure (especially transport and energy) to realize the natural resources potential. This is particularly true for land-locked countries. The Vision suggests that the NEPAD Spatial Development Programme (SDP) and the resource for infrastructure model have a great potential to redress the continent's infrastructure gaps.

The SDP aims to synchronize infrastructure provision with users to enhance investment potential and to provide economic rigor for infrastructure investments. It helps to vet projects using solid economic/business rationale, thus achieving an effective investment prioritization of infrastructure projects. The SDP approach is anchored in the exploitation of Africa's natural resource endowments, in particular minerals. Because of the high rents that these resources generate, the economic/business rationale for infrastructure projects is boosted and the development of infrastructure becomes more viable.

A word on implementation

The trajectories to achieving the Vision at country and sub-regional levels will be different and the Vision will be implemented in a phased manner. As earlier indicated, the policy responses and strategies to realize the Vision at country level will vary depending on the bargaining power of the country, its organizational set-up and political economy of the sector, capacity to manage and restructure the economy, its learning curve, and the stage of development of its mineral economy.

Despite these differences, it is argued that Africa will only achieve its ultimate goal of industrialization and development by acting collectively. The chief responsibility for coordinating this effort has been vested on the AMDC. As articulated in the AMDC Business Plan, the work of the Centre will be organized in seven result areas, namely (i) policy and licensing; (ii) geological and mining information systems; (iii) governance and participation; (iv) artisanal and small-scale mining; (v) linkages, investment, and diversification; (vi) building human and institutional capacities: and (vii) communication and advocacy.[15]

Table 1.2 summarizes the goals and expected outcomes of each of the seven AMDC result areas.

For all of the result areas, a major focus of the AMDC will be to document good practices from the continent and beyond, demonstrate their value, and help support their domestication at national and sub-regional levels, as well as their replication across the continent.

Table 1.2 The AMDC result areas

Result area	Result area goals	Expected outcomes
Policy and licensing	To create a sustainable and well-governed mining sector that effectively garners and deploys resource rents and contributes to broad-based development	Enhanced capacities for mineral policy design and understanding the mining value chain; The mining sector in Africa supports a broader share of social and economic development objectives; and African countries receive an enhanced share of mineral revenue
Geological and mining information systems	To improve geological information and its use in mining and broad-based development processes in Africa	Improved decision-making capabilities to manage the mining sector, as well as other sectors requiring geospatial information; and Improved national and sub-regional capacities to manage geological and geospatial information for broader development objectives
Governance and participation	To create a mining sector that is environmentally and socially responsible and appreciated by all stakeholders, including surrounding communities	Strengthened stakeholder capacities to participate fully in governance processes; Improved balance and equity in decision making in the mineral sector; Improved human rights in Africa's mineral sector; and Improved social and environmental management of the mineral sector in Africa
Artisanal and small-scale mining	To create a mining sector that harnesses the potential of artisanal and small-scale mining to advance integrated and sustainable rural socio-economic development	A viable and sustainable artisanal and small-scale mining sector; Strengthened capacities of ASM operators; and Reduced negative environmental, health and welfare impacts from ASM
Linkages, investment and diversification	To create and investment-friendly mining sector that is a key component of a diversified, vibrant, and globally competitive industrial African economy	Increased private-sector funding for R&D leading to greater knowledge generation; Strengthened government planning capacities for integrated development and mapping of economic linkages between the minerals sector and other sectors of the economy;

Table 1.2 (cont.)

Result area	Result area goals	Expected outcomes
		Greater domestic availability of investment finance leading to greater wealth creation and ownership by nationals; and Integrated mining infrastructure and spatial development in Africa providing for greater economic and social benefits
Building human and institutional capacities	To create a mining sector that is knowledge driven and is the engine of an internationally competitive African industrial economy	A mining sector with a greatly strengthened and competitive skill base; Strengthened capacities of stakeholders to make decisions affecting various aspects of the mineral value chain; Educational and training delivery in which learning outcomes are aligned to the economic and social development objectives of the AMV; and Liberal movement of skills across regions due to accessibility and accreditation of training facilities
Communication and advocacy	To improve social and economic development options through a free flow of information among all stakeholders around the AMV, AMDC, and mineral-based transformation	Enhanced awareness and understanding among stakeholders of the AMV and AMDC activities and the role of these activities in the economic and social transformation of African mining countries; Strengthened capacities of stakeholders to make informed decisions affecting various aspects of the mineral value chain; Strengthened acceptance and ownership of AMV and AMDC activities by all stakeholders in African mining countries; and Increased access to information and knowledge packaging, resulting in improved analysis and decision making

Source: Modified from AMDC Business Plan (www.au.int/ar/sites/default/files/AMDC%20Business%20Plan%20EDITED%20Final%2017%20Sep%202012.pdf, accessed October 17, 2013).

The inauguration of the Africa Mining Vision Day (AMV Day) on February 3, 2014 at Mining Indaba 2014 is particularly significant for AMDC workstreams on communication, advocacy, and partnership building. Mining Indaba is the world and Africa's largest mining investment event. It attracts in excess of 7,000 participants from all over the world representing a large spectrum of interest groups, including governments, mining companies, service providers, fund managers and other investment specialists and financiers, industry analysts, and mining experts. The annual conference is the gateway to accessing Africa's mineral potential.

The AMV Day will be a permanent feature of Mining Indaba. This will provide the AMDC and its four implementing partners (the AUC, UNECA, AfDB, and UNDP) with a unique platform for partnership building and dialogue on the AMV construct with the world's key movers and shakers in the mining sector. During the inaugural AMV Day, the Chairperson of the AUC, as the chief AMV Champion, engaged the world in a candid conversation on the pathways toward the implementation of the Vision. The setting of the AMV Day could not have been better. Unlike the previous Mining Indaba, in 2013, CEOs were confronted with a depressed market and were managing margins to keep their operations profitable. Thus, the AMV Day offered to all stakeholders a forum for a sober discussion and reality check on the merits of a blueprint (the AMV), which was designed during the upbeat tempo of the "super cycle" narrative. As such, the event tested the stress levels and confidence margins of the AMV project to identify where adjustments, if any, should be made.

It became evident that despite the testing times, there is no alternative to a discourse (the AMV) which essentially aims to promote sustainable development in the extractive industry based on principles of ownership, equity, partnerships, and value for all.

The AU Chairperson, among other things, called for a "skills revolution" in the extractive industry as a means to address capacity gaps in the sector. Of equal significance was the call for the formulation and signing of an "AMV Compact with Business Leaders in Africa," which will define the contours and goal posts for collaboration between the African Union and the captains of industry (through Chambers of Mines) operating in Africa to support the AMV. Partnership building is key to the success of the AMV. Having a global compact with a major stakeholder such as the private sector is essential to the AMV.

The next leg: country mining visions

As articulated earlier, the success of the AMV will largely depend on the level at which its key tenets will be mainstreamed in national vision statements, development plans, policies, laws, and regulations. This exercise can be enabled by the formulation of country mining visions (CMVs) or similar instruments. The CMVs, if well formulated, can become an organically grown process of multi-stakeholder consultations and systems thinking to domesticate the AMV agenda, manage expectations, and promote alignment and common understanding on mineral-related benefit streams toward a shared vision and a robust social compact for change.[16] As a long-term societal and integrated compact, it represents an embodiment of national aspirations on the developmental role of the extractive industry, which is linked with a country's overall vision and development plan. It can help promote public participation in the extractive sector, facilitate interdepartmental collaboration, and overcome short-termism arising from political and electoral cycles. This is absolutely vital, given the long-term gestation period of mining projects.

A typical CMV involves the following phases:

- initial engagement with top leadership to determine actual or latent demand for a CMV;
- applied political economy study: to map challenges and undertake an institutional analysis of the main agencies and actors in public policy (legitimacy, capability, and incentives to move a reform agenda);
- local scan and detailed analysis of national economic and social landscape;
- mapping geological potential;
- regional and international scans: review of regional and global mineral development trends and identification of key external drivers to the sector and their impact on a country mineral sector;
- policy review: assess quality and relevance of fiscal regime, legal/regulatory frameworks and their fit with the findings of the political economy study and alignment with other sectoral policies;
- costs and benefits analysis;
- transformation maps: to map the stakeholders' aspirations on the role of extractives in development and the plausible trajectories to achieve them;
- communication, outreach and advocacy strategy: this is critical to manage stakeholders' expectations;
- multi-stakeholder dialogues toward the formulation of a common vision and identification of priorities and focus areas;
- the formulation of the CMV and supporting action plan/business plan with baseline data, benchmarks and clear targets;
- implementation of the CMV;
- monitoring and evaluation frameworks; and
- regular reporting.

To date, the AMDC has conducted pilot CMV processes in Mozambique (November 2013) and Lesotho (mid-2013 to present). In Tanzania, the World Economic Forum (WEF) Minerals Value Management survey has been recently concluded as part of an effort to map stakeholders' perceptions on how the extractive industry in the country can promote broad-based development and structural economic and social transformation. CMV processes are equally planned for Ghana, Guinea, Kenya, and DRC.

To support the conduct of the CMVs, the AMDC has recently published a country mining vision guidebook,[17] which offers a step-by-step guide on how to domesticate the AMV at country level.

Staying the course when commodity prices are low: a daunting challenge

The implementation of developmental policies such as those in the AMV becomes difficult when commodity prices are low, as we are experiencing at the time of writing (2014). The current downturn has reversed the mood and appetite for development mining, which characterized the commodity *super cycle* period of 2000–2008. As stated in the Ernst & Young 2015 Report "Business Risks Facing Mining and Metals 2015–2016: Moving from the Back Seat to the Driver's Seat":

> A clear legacy of the super-cycle for mining and metals is a "super correction," with markets ultimately self-correcting via the price mechanism – the greater price stimulus both in scale and duration, the greater the correction and the greater the volatility as markets seek to correct.

The report indicates that there is a change in dynamics. It notes that we have moved from a "sellers' market" (with producing countries in control), which epitomized the 2000–2008 super cycle, to a "buyers' market" in which the bargaining power is swinging to mining companies. The report further states that the latter are now in the driver's seat. The same views are reflected in PricewaterhouseCoopers (PwC) report "Mine 2015: The Gloves Are Off," which notes that commodity prices were volatile during 2014, particularly iron ore, copper, and coal. PwC further noted that in such an environment, Chief Executive Officers (CEOs) were forced to adopt more flexible operating strategies and review mine plans, including phasing expansions and introducing partial curtailments in production. Essentially, companies refocused their core businesses, limiting the pursuit of growth opportunities. They are managing margins, with the objective of reducing costs and developing a healthier balance sheet through strict capital discipline. PwC argues that such measures would help to create more resilience in both up and down cycles in future.

The PwC report also notes that during the super cycle, governments pursued strategies aimed at "maximizing returns from their national resources sector by increasing taxes and royalties, demanding local processing or beneficiation prior to export, imposing export restrictions and increasing export levies on unrefined ores, and restricting foreign ownership," which they consider as *resource nationalism*. The report argues that "aggressive resource nationalism policies by governments often make those countries less attractive for mining investment." PwC indicates that in a buyer's market environment, mining companies would be better placed to resist resource nationalism. Consequently, they anticipate that "gloves will be off" and disputes between governments and companies will increase.

As reflected in the two reports discussed above, the end of the super cycle may trigger significant *policy revisionism*. In similar circumstances in the 1980–90s, when commodity prices were down, we witnessed a "race to the bottom" similar to a "beauty contest," where country after country changed mineral policies, laws, regulations, and fiscal regimes to be more attractive than their neighbors. The outcomes were mixed.

Formulating a future for the extractive sector beyond the commodity super cycle would certainly require a balancing act and trade-offs. Achieving a win–win outcome can be very challenging, especially when markets are depressed and the industry faces many risks. This can only be achieved through multi-stakeholder platforms for dialogue such as those provided by the CMV. It is important to avoid another "race to the bottom" and the reversal of the policy gains of the last fifteen years spent in advancing sustainable development in the extractive industry and in giving real expression to the notion "social license to operate." This is particularly vital with the adoption of the Sustainable Development Goals (SDGs) in September 2015, which has committed the world to tackling the deep challenges of economic prosperity for all countries, social inclusion, and environmental sustainability.

It is in downturn periods when it is important to pursue *countercyclical* measures and make the necessary foundational investments and establish the institutions for change with the view to ensuring that the extractive industry generates a fair deal for all. Sticking to "development mining" can yield dividends for all and would secure an everlasting "license to operate." The contrary would create continuous instability.

The AMV success factors

The Africa Mining Vision is ambitious. If fully implemented, it can improve the legacy of mining on the continent and change the path and destiny of Africa's industrialization and fight against poverty. The realization of the Vision hinges on developing a new integrated development approach to mineral resources exploitation. This requires strong political will and commitment, capable and visionary leadership, strong administration, a good understanding of Africa's advantages and the dynamics of mineral commodities, maximizing the potential of regional integration, and building partnerships for change.

Most African governments desire to create manufacturing value-added from their mineral products and change the role they play in international trade. This is reflected in their mineral policies and development strategies. However, value creation has eluded more or less the entire continent, and mineral endowments have not been used to build competitive advantages. The main lesson is that the inclusion of provisions in policy frameworks is not a sufficient condition for creating value-added to mineral products. Policy needs to be backed by legislation, and prioritization of the mineral sector must be backed by relevant budget statements and allocations, specific incentives, and, above all, institutional capacity to implement resource-based industrialization and structural transformation. As illustrated in the Nordic countries, the state has a critical role to play in spearheading this transformation. States should lead and facilitate efforts to improve the quality of the business environment, foment public–private partnerships, nurture human resources development and skills formation, build R&D and science and technology infrastructure platforms and knowledge networks involving academia, industry, and the government itself, as well as provide supporting infrastructure and establish the required enabling markets and common platforms for services and instruments to foster cluster formation, agglomeration, collaboration, and sharing of information. In addition, resources need to be identified and earmarked to broaden geo-knowledge through greater systematic mapping and mineral inventory to fully define Africa's mineral assets. This will strengthen the continent's bargaining power.

International trade and investment treaties and agreements have a direct bearing on the future of Africa's mineral sector. It is therefore important that the continent continues to fight for policy space to pursue its industrialization drive. Particular attention needs to be paid to the implications of WTO and EPAS negotiations and other multilateral and bilateral trade and investment agreements and treaties on Africa's capacity to extricate itself from dependence on the export of raw materials and the vagaries of commodity price fluctuations. To be heard, Africa needs to speak in one voice on this matter. The importance of policy coherence (within countries and in different international fora) and coordination among countries across international policy-making and negotiating fora cannot be overemphasized. South–South cooperation could be key in engendering better development outcomes.

Coupling mineral policy with industrial policy and investment, trade, and market access agendas is an imperative for the success of the Africa Mining Vision. To unleash mineral-driven structural economic transformation at national level, holistic and sector-wide approaches to development and a new institutional arrangement combining the minerals, industry, trade and science, technology and innovation complexes are needed to build synergy and break departmental silos and rivalry. The realization of the Vision implies therefore a cross- or multi-sectoral approach to mineral development policy.

The role of regional cooperation and integration in reducing transaction costs, establishing intra-regional synergies, enhancing competitiveness and realizing economies of scale that would catalyze mineral cluster development should not be underestimated. However, for goods, services, capital, and other factors to freely flow in regional spaces, there is need to expedite intra-regional harmonization of laws, regulations, and fiscal regimes, among other critical factors.

Finally, the realization of the AMV will certainly benefit from the adoption of the SDGs in September 2015, which as a global compact defines the boundaries for the sustainable exploitation of natural resources, including minerals, and the contours for partnership building and responsible engagement.

Notes

1 See http://minerals.usgs.gov/minerals/pubs/country/2011/myb3-sum-2011-africa.pdf, accessed on April 11, 2014.
2 See www.au.int/ar/sites/default/files/AMDC%20Business%20Plan%20EDITED%20Final%2017%20Sep%202012.pdf, accessed on October 16, 2013.
3 www.africaminingvision.org/, accessed on May 24, 2016.
4 Available at www3.weforum.org/docs/WEF_MM_RMDI_Overview_2012-13.pdf, accessed May 3, 2016). The MVM is a tool developed as part of the WEF's Responsible Mineral Development Initiative (RMDI) to help create a shared understanding of the costs and benefits of mining and how to maximize value for all through collaborative processes for multi-stakeholder engagement. With the understanding that, in most cases, stakeholders do not have the same understanding of what creates value for them, the tool helps to identify common starting points based on seven broad and holistic definitions of value or benefits. These are fiscal returns; employment and skills creation; protection of the environment and biodiversity; social cohesion, culture, and socio-economic development; enhanced local procurement and supply; beneficiation and downstream industry; and infrastructure development. Through thorough situation analysis and focused dialogue, the MVM helps to identify the needs and priorities of each stakeholder, create a common understanding of value and to map realistic options to realize them.
5 Depending on which side you represent, resource nationalism can mean different things. For governments under pressure from their domestic constituencies, it can be an effort to create greater value for all by refining regulatory instruments with the view to empowering local entrepreneurs, imposing performance requirements, legislating on value addition, or banning the export of unprocessed minerals. Other governments use it to restrict access to strategic minerals and sectors. For mining investors, it can mean expropriation, killing the goose that lays the golden eggs, intrusive interference, and nationalization. To powerful elites, it can mean an opportunity to consolidate their grip on and capture of mineral rents. Both developing and developed countries apply one form or another of resource nationalism.
6 www.uneca.org/media-centre/stories/launch-african-minerals-development-centre-new-dawn-africa#.U2PJk6WKAps, accessed on April 24, 2014.
7 www.uneca.org/publications/harnessing-african-peer-review-mechanism-potential-advance-mineral-resources-governance accessed on May 24, 2016.
8 The APRM – a key component of NEPAD – was adopted by African Heads of State and Government as a systematic peer-learning and self-assessment mechanism based on the NEPAD foundational document, the "Declaration on Democracy, Political, Economic and Corporate Governance" adopted in Durban, South Africa, in July 2002. It is a mutually agreed instrument voluntarily acceded to by AU member states as an African self-monitoring mechanism. The APRM is often described as "Africa's unique and innovative approach to governance" with the objective of improving governance dynamics at the local, national, continental, and international levels. Since its adoption, the APRM has become the most visible achievement of NEPAD in promoting good governance in Africa.

9 http://aprm-au.org/sites/default/files/17TH%20APR%20FORUM%20-%20 FINAL%20COMMUNIQUE_0.pdf, accessed on May 24, 2016.
10 http://aprm-au.org/sites/default/files/Revised%20APRM%20Eng%20 Questionnaire%206%20Aug%2012.pdf, accessed on May 24, 2016.
11 The ADF is a major biennial event of UNECA, convened since 1999 in collaboration with the AUC and the AfDB. If offers a multi-stakeholder platform to share results of current research on development issues of interest to Africa and to formulate common positions and shared goals with the view to accelerating the continent's development. The Forum attracts over a thousand participants, including Heads of State and Government, leading academics, captains of industry, and high-level representatives of development partners, international organizations, civil society, media, and other opinion makers.
12 www.africanmineralskills.org/wp-content/uploads/2013/06/AMSI_Business-Plan_ May24.pdf, accessed on October 15, 2013.
13 www.afdb.org/en/topics-and-sectors/initiatives-partnerships/african-legal-support-facility/, accessed on May 24, 2016.
14 For example, there is a significant price differential between a metric ton of iron ore (average of US$60.25/mt during Jan–Apr 2015) and the equivalent in weight of hot rolled steel coil, hot rolled steel plate, and steel wire rods (US$509.25.00/mt, US$604.25/mt, and US$541.25/mt, respectively, during the same period).
15 www.au.int/ar/sites/default/files/AMDC%20Business%20Plan%20EDITED%20 Final%2017%20Sep%202012.pdf, accessed on October 17, 2013.
16 www3.weforum.org/docs/WEF_MM_RMDI_Overview_2012-13.pdf, accessed on May 24, 2016.
17 www.uneca.org/media-centre/stories/minerals-centre-produces-guidebook-domestication-african-mining-vision#.VHSTvf1xmUk, accessed on November 24, 2014.

References

African Union (2009). *Africa Mining Vision*. www.africaminingvision.org/amv_resources/AMV/Africa_Mining_Vision_English.pdf.

Bastida, Elizabeth, Waelde, Thomas, and Warden-Fernández, Janeth (eds) (2005). *International and Comparative Mineral Law and Policy: Trends and Prospects*. The Netherlands: Kluwer Law International.

The Hague Centre for Strategic Studies (HCSS) and TNO (2010). *Rare Earth Elements and Strategic Mineral Policy*. www.hcss.nl/reports/rare-earth-elements-and-strategic-mineral-policy/5/.

Iimi, Atsushi (2006). *Did Botswana Escape from the Resource Curse?* IMF Working Paper WP/06/138. https://www.imf.org/external/pubs/ft/wp/2006/wp06138.pdf.

International Council on Mining & Metals (ICMM) (2011). *Mining: Partnerships for Development Toolkit*. www.icmm.com/mpdtoolkit.

Lang, M. and Mokrani, D. (2013). *Beyond Development: Alternative Visions from Latin America*. The Netherlands: Transnational Institute. https://www.tni.org/files/download/beyonddevelopment_complete.pdf.

Morris, Mike, Kaplinsky, Raphael, and Kaplan, David (2012). *One Thing Leads to Another: Promoting Industrialisation by Making the Most of the Commodity Boom in Sub-Saharan Africa*. Cape Town, South Africa. www.prism.uct.ac.za/Downloads/MMCP%20Book.pdf.

OFSE (2015). *Commodity Dependence and Price Volatility in Least Developed Countries: A Structuralist Computable General Equilibrium Model with Applications* to Burkina Faso, Ethiopia and Mozambique. www.oefse.at/fileadmin/content/Downloads/Publikationen/Workingpaper/WP52_commodity_dependence.pdf.

Pedro, Antonio M. A. (2006). Mainstreaming Mineral Wealth in Growth and Poverty Reduction Strategies. *Minerals and Energy*, Vol. 21 No. 1, pp. 2–16.

United Nations Economic Commission for Africa (UNECA) (2004a). Improving Public Participation in the Sustainable Development of Mineral Resources in Africa. In *Sustainable Development Report on Africa: Managing Land-Based Resources for Sustainable Development*, pp.135–172.

United Nations Economic Commission for Africa (UNECA) (2004b). *Managing Mineral Wealth: Training Materials on Management of Mineral Wealth and the Role of Mineral Wealth in Social-Economic Development.* http://repository.uneca.org/handle/10855/3729?locale-attribute=en.

United Nations Economic Commission for Africa (UNECA) (2004c). *Mineral Cluster Policy Study in Africa: Pilot Studies of South Africa and Mozambique.* www.uneca.org/publications/minerals-cluster-policy-study-africa.

United Nations Economic Commission for Africa (UNECA) (2011). *Minerals and Africa's Development*. The International Study Group Report on Africa's Mineral Regimes. www.uneca.org/sites/default/files/PublicationFiles/mineral_africa_development_report_eng.pdf.

United Nations Economic Commission for Africa, and Africa Union Commission (UNECA, AUC) (2013). *Economic Report on Africa 2013 – Making the Most of Africa's Commodities: Industrializing for Growth, Jobs and Economic Transformation.* www.uneca.org/publications/economic-report-africa-2013.

United Nations Economic Commission for Africa, Africa Union Commission (UNECA, AUC) (2014). *Economic Report on Africa 2014 – Dynamic Industrial Policy in Africa.* www.uneca.org/sites/default/files/PublicationFiles/final_era2014_march25_en.pdf.

2 Capacity development for natural resource management

Findings from the 2013 Africa Capacity Indicators Report

Kobena T. Hanson

Introduction

Across Africa, and more so in recent years, there has been an exponential growth of extractive industry investment and agro-industrial projects implemented by large multinational and national companies.[1] The communities most affected by the growth in the exploitation of Africa's natural resources – whether forests, land, or extractive minerals – are, however, often marginalized and vulnerable, as much of the natural resource wealth is located in rural areas (Karl 1997; Sachs and Warner 2001; Humphreys et al. 2007). These communities, often in places with no or little formal national state presence, have to deal with the political, economic, and social pressures that accompany the arrival of large-scale investment projects (ACBF 2013). Specifically, companies' desire to expedite project development and win over communities often results in poorly thought-out social investment initiatives that tend to undermine state functions in health, education, and infrastructure, and create a culture of dependency on the company. When resources are depleted, or market conditions no longer justify their exploitation, it is the surrounding communities that suffer. These processes tend to polarize communities among those in favor of projects and those against, further undermining the social cohesion required in times of crisis, leaving entire populations vulnerable to illicit economic actors and armed groups (Godnick et al. 2008; ACBF 2013). As a result, the exploitation of renewable and non-renewable natural resources and its role in national development has been subject to political, social, and environmental struggles, social strife, and armed conflicts. The terms "resource curse," and/or "paradox of plenty," are often used to describe particular manifestations of this negative relationship strife (Barma et al. 2012; Collier 2007; Humphreys et al. 2007).

Despite the evidence in the literature, some of the claims of the resource curse theorists have been challenged more recently (Obi 2010) because the resource–conflict link is probably more complex than is conceptualized in the literature (Basedau and Lay 2009). Contrary to the rentier state theory, which posits that resource-rich states are weak, corrupt, authoritarian, and therefore susceptible to conflict (Obi 2010), the argument is that "governments use revenue from abundant resources to buy off peace through patronage, large-scale distribution policies and effective repression" (Basedau and Lay 2009: 758).[2] The notion of resource curse has also been criticized from a methodological and econometric perspective (Arthur 2012). These criticisms particularly concern the trade-based proxies (such as the share of primary product export) traditionally used to measure natural resource abundance. Manzano and Rigobon (2001), for example, submit that the cross-sectional results of Sachs and Warner (1997) suffer from an omitted variable bias, suggesting that the curse arises from the fact that resource-intensive countries accumulated foreign debt during the 1970s, when commodity prices were high, leading to a debt overhang when, in the 1980s, prices fell, analogously with other price bubbles. From this perspective, the disappointing growth performance of resource-rich countries is related to macroeconomic policies rather than to natural resources. Similarly, Lederman and Maloney (2007), using the net natural resource export per worker in a panel system estimator, found a strong positive relationship between this variable and growth, concluding that there is no evidence of a resource curse.

Daniele (2011) thus argues that the resource curse phenomenon is due to econometric and measurement fallacies, while resource wealth may represent an important factor for economic development. Similarly, Humphreys et al. (2007) have questioned the resource curse argument because, for them, there is considerable room for human agency to rectify the risks posed by the "paradox of plenty." Such criticisms and challenges against the resource curse theory have led to a partial move away from the initial debates over the "greed versus grievance" causal binary. It is therefore not surprising that much of the emphasis has shifted to issues related to capacity, leadership, and good governance (Barma et al. 2012; Collier 2010).

The *2013 Africa Capacity Indicators Report* (ACBF 2013) interrogates the evidence in the extant literature, the claims of resource curse theorists, and alternative views that challenge them using political economy and capacity analyses along the complex resource–conflict links. In so doing, it not only presents arguments to debunk the resource curse from a methodological and econometric perspective (ACBF 2013; Arthur 2012), but also covers perspectives that call into question the resource curse argument because it appears to neglect the potential of human agency (Obi 2010; Humphreys et al. 2007).[3] The Report thus argues that the so-called curse is not inevitable. Many countries such as Botswana, Chile, Indonesia, and Vietnam have managed to effectively utilize their natural resources to spur development.[4] While there are no silver bullets that enable countries to make the best possible use of natural resources for development, there generally are steps nations can take (UNDP 2011).

In questioning the resource curse thesis and its arguments, prevailing evaluation methodologies, specification of models, and spurious correlations, it would at the same time be insincere to ignore the general ills, economic challenges, leadership malaise, and socio-political woes that many resource-rich African nations face in managing their extractive resources (Arthur 2014; Obi 2010).

The analysis in the Report offers a fresh lens through which the challenges, opportunities, and possibilities and their respective links to developing a new policy outlook can be viewed. Addressing the challenges and beating a new path necessitates a rethink with regard to: the legacy of old natural resource management problems; the emergence of new development and possibilities; and the understanding of the changing natural resource management landscape – at the local, national, continental, and global levels. This chapter is structured into five sections. Following this introduction, the second section highlights the need to assess capacity, particularly as it relates to the natural resource sector. Section 3 speaks to the new dispensation in Africa's natural resource management (NRM) as the continent moves away from the legacy of its old NRM landscape. In the fourth section, an analysis of the revised landscape and its corresponding new developments and possibilities is presented. Section 5 maps out the new normative and policy environment and presents a conclusion.

Why measure capacity

Capacity means having the aptitudes, resources, relationships, and facilitating conditions needed to act effectively to achieve specified mandates (ACBF 2011). It is conceptualized at three levels: individual, organizational, and enabling environment (interactions between individuals and organizations); and takes meaning in specific settings – capacity for what? Capacity, thus, refers to

> the ability of people, organizations, and society as a whole to manage their affairs successfully; and is the process by which people, organizations, and society as a whole unleash, strengthen, create, adapt, and maintain capacity over time. Capacity for individuals, organizations, and societies to set goals and achieve them; to budget resources and use them for agreed purposes; and to manage the complex processes and interactions that typify a working political and economic system. Capacity is most tangibly and effectively developed in the context of specific development objectives such as delivering services to poor people; instituting education, public service, and health care reform; improving the investment climate for small and medium enterprises; empowering local communities to better participate in public decision making processes; and promoting peace and resolving conflict.
>
> (ACBF 2011: 30–31; ACBF 2013)

Central to why to measure capacity is the need to: better plan, manage, implement, and account for results of policies and programs; effectively integrate capacity-development objectives in development strategies and agendas for service delivery; gauge achievements on key policies and programs; and grasp underlying factors driving change and to foster change in areas identified as priorities (ACBF 2011, 2012, 2013).

Viewed from the perspective of natural resource governance, Africa is rich in stocks of materials that exist in the natural environment. Natural resources, notably extractives, contribute to growth, jobs, and fiscal revenue, but need effective management. Failure to govern is what renders natural resources a "curse" (Barma et al. 2012; Collier 2007; Humphreys et al. 2007).

To highlight the urgency of capacity for natural resources management, take the example that although oil, gas, and metals are of strategic importance, they do not even account for 5 percent of total global production of goods and services, making the importance of Africa's raw materials relative (ACBF 2013). While there may be substantial natural resource reserves in Africa, in most cases, the heart of usage – especially in the extractive industries – lies outside Africa. Despite Africa being top in the production of diamonds, gold, cobalt, and platinum, it is obvious that most of these minerals are exported in their raw form to developed economies and to emerging economies.[5] And even though resource-rich African states try to generate revenues through exports, this effort is still insignificant (see Geda 2012; Collier and Goderis 2007). Foreign markets, be they the traditional Western nations or increasingly emerging economies such as the MINT countries (Mexico, Indonesia, Nigeria, and Turkey), BRICs (Brazil, Russia, India, and China), or Gulf Cooperation Council, still disproportionately determine the path of Africa's economic growth and development, irrespective of the natural resource endowments, due to the structural dependency of African economies on natural resources in their raw/unprocessed form – a development that needs to change.

Countries dependent on natural resources need particularly to be capable of securing political and social stability. This calls for leadership and the political will to develop strong policy instruments, including, but not limited to, clear and well-conceived regulations and mining codes to manage the inflows of foreign direct investment (FDI). Such capabilities also include how a country manages at different levels – whether local, country, or regional level – to aggregate and address citizen needs, include diverse societies in decision making (women and excluded groups), and enhance accountability of public officials to the citizenry. If countries are not capable of securing social and political stability and they are rich in natural resources they remain poor and mired in conflict. The conflicts in Sierra Leone and Liberia in the 1990s, the crises in Nigeria's Niger delta region, and the ongoing strife in the eastern parts of the Democratic Republic of Congo are reflective of this (Alao 2007; NATO 2012; Rustad and Binningsbø 2010). Another key capability is that of tapping benefits from trade and integration, which presupposes the capacity to put in place an enabling environment with property rights, rule-based governance, a sound business regulatory environment, a functioning financial sector, and effective trade policies (Rustad et al. 2012). But countries also need to have skills to negotiate, discuss, and secure the appropriate terms of trade and trade policies and to engage in fair contractual agreements (Rustad et al. 2012; Diamond and Mosbacher 2013). Efforts by Mozambique and post-civil-war Liberia in the timber industry, Sierra Leone in the minerals sector, and the African Development Bank's (AfDB) African Legal Support Facility (ALSF) supporting countries' negotiation of extractives contracts are all steps in the right direction (Hanlon 2011; Barma et al. 2012; ACBF 2013).[6] That said, there is also a high need for management capability to remove constraints that bottleneck the effective extraction of resources, including supply-chain bottlenecks (transport logistics, business climate).

Within the African context, capacity is crucial because it is estimated that of the continent's vast resource wealth, only 20 percent has been exploited (Collier 2010). This reality, coupled with Africa's demographic dividend (notably its youth bulge), deepening political and macroeconomic reforms, and growing interest in its extractives driven by demand from the BRICS – notably China and India – have added implications (Maconachie 2009; Le Billon and Levin 2009; ACBF 2013). Also noteworthy is the growing interest and investments from the Gulf in the hydrocarbon and mineral sector, and, to a lesser extent, the demand from the MINT nations.

New dispensation in NRM in Africa

A wave of new optimism is sweeping across Africa – GDP is rising, consumer spending is increasing, and returns on investments are higher than global averages (IMF 2011; McKinsey Global Institute 2010a). Africa's real GDP rose by 4.9 percent a year from 2000 through 2008, more than twice its pace in the 1980s and 90s. Africa's collective GDP, at 1.6 trillion in 2008, is now roughly equal to Brazil's or Russia's. Africa has also benefited from the surge in commodity prices over the past decade. Oil rose from less than $20 a barrel in 1990 to over $145 in 2008 (McKinsey Global Institute 2010a, 2010b). Recent publications such as the *2013 Africa Capacity Indicators Report* (ACBF 2013), the *Economic Report on Africa* (ECA/AUC 2013), the *Africa Progress Report 2013* (Africa Progress Panel 2013), and the *2013 Resource Governance Index* (RWI 2013) all highlight an evolving natural resource landscape in Africa. RWI (2013), for instance, notes that Ghana, Guinea, Liberia, South Sudan, and Zambia have all "recently reformed their oil or mining legislation to include some principles of open government," in essence by increasing access to, and availability of, information about governmental activities; encouraging and supporting civic participation in decision making and policy formulation; and upholding the standards of professional integrity and accountability.

Closely linked to the above is the growing exposure of the problem of "missing revenues," and the growth of corporate social responsibility programs,[7] extensive and participatory discussions of value chains and jobs, development of trust funds/sovereign wealth funds, and the increasing mobilization of community interests, and community-based NRM are all images of the revised landscape (African Globe 2013; ACBF 2013; Giugale 2013). Yet another manifestation of the changing landscape is the Africa Mining Vision (AMV), which was adopted by African Heads of State and Government in February 2009 (ECA/AU 2013). The AMV is perceived as a "driver for a fundamental and structural transformation of African economies, based on establishing and harnessing linkages between different economic sectors and regions" (Africa-Canada Forum 2013: 3). As a way of moving the AMV forward, at the 3rd Ordinary session of the African Union (AU) Conference of Ministers Responsible for Mineral Resources Development in Maputo, Mozambique, in December 2013, the Economic Commission on Africa (ECA), the African Union Commission (AUC), and attending partners/stakeholders launched the Africa Mining Development Centre (AMDC), which will provide strategic operational support to the AMV and its Action Plan. The AMDC is expected to advance the capacity of African mining countries to derive economic and social benefits from implementing the AMV, while significantly contributing to the development of Africa's extractive economies based on consistent development-oriented mineral policies and regulatory frameworks. To this end, the AMDC will provide a central and strategic coordinating capacity (i.e. expanding the policy space, up-scaling geological exploration activities, improving the viability of small-scale mining, and addressing weaknesses in natural resources governance) for implementing the AMV and its Action Plan (UNECA 2013; Hanson et al. 2014).

Initiatives such as the EITI (Extractive Industries Transparency Initiative), Publish What You Pay (PWYP), and the Kimberley Process Certification Scheme (KPCS) continue to monitor resource-extraction activities, even as the United Nations Environment Programme's International Resource Panel (IRP) is steadily building up an understanding of global resource flows and why economic growth needs to be decoupled from rates of resource extraction (Swilling 2012).[8] However, for the aforementioned initiatives, and others such as the Natural Resource Charter (NRC) (www.naturalresourcecharter.org) and AMV to really benefit Africans as a whole, there is a "need for greater ownership and buy-in by African citizens…and greater policy space for [countries] to regulate and monitor resource extraction for the benefit of their populations" (Africa-Canada Forum 2013: 10). The plethora of transitional initiatives (i.e. NRC, EITI, AMV, and PWYP), each with its own established principles, standards, or precepts, poses a dilemma for African countries confronting the choice of whether to join one, two, three, or all initiatives. That said, the general consensus is for African countries to join the AU-endorsed AMV to harmonize their legislation with a transnational framework in addition to any other of the transitional initiatives (Hanson et al. 2014).

The situation of resource-rich economies in Africa is not immutable (ACBF 2013; Arthur 2012; Obi 2010). Many agree that better governance, transparency, and accountability are central to good resource management (NRC 2010) and enhance the potential value of natural resource endowments

(Collier 2010). The ACBF (2012) shares this view, and concurs with others (Arthur 2012; Barma et al. 2012; Besada 2013) who suggest that a "new" and evolving landscape is replacing the legacy of the "old" NRM landscape, which was characterized by: asymmetries of weak states versus strong external actors (multinational corporations (MNCs), consumer countries); low and often erratic commodity prices; unfair terms of trade; low technological and managerial capacity; insufficient and ineffective legal frameworks and policies; weak bargaining capacity and systems of taxation; lack of transparency and accountability across the value chain; windfall rents, which when realized are of benefit only to the elite; lack of economic diversification and shared growth; unmitigated environmental damage caused by extraction processes; and the socio-cultural displacement of affected communities.

To this end, the entire portfolio of stakeholders is subject to a new normative environment, as evidenced by the strong natural resource management policy environment emerging across Africa (RWI 2013). Policies frame the sphere of potential constructive action; there are now new spaces for agency. The expected rise in global prices of extractives, the expansion of new discoveries, and a growing demand from emerging economies, in spite of the projected slowdown in the Chinese market, represents an unparalleled opportunity for Africa. Countries need to advance and entrench policies that acknowledge the realities of their national contexts, that bring about rapid results in a context of urgent need, and that allow for incremental improvements to their governance processes (Marcel 2013: 2). Doing so effectively calls for countries to advance and enhance their capacities, promote good governance, and improve the resource-knowledge infrastructure (AUC et al. 2011). This will ensure that resource-rich African countries know not only the actual level and quality of their natural resource potential, but also the optimal strategy for determining and collecting adequate rent. Creating capacity to sustain auditing, monitoring, regulating, and improving resource-exploitation regimes and developing resource-sector linkages into the domestic economy should be another goal. This can be achieved by ensuring that there is a skills-transfer dimension in all contracted consultancies during lease/license negotiations as well as a targeted policy around the development of such an ongoing resource-governance capacity (Hanson et al. 2014; AUC et al. 2011).

So, while ongoing developments are in the right direction, resource-rich African states need to embrace policies and initiatives that aim to sustain the current momentum. As Marcel (2013: 5) argues:

> [i]nstead of encouraging [African countries] to pursue "best practice" standards, it may be more helpful to advise them to aim for *more appropriate practice*, which acknowledges the realities of the national context; *more effective practice*, which seeks to bring about rapid results in the context or urgent needs, or *better practice*, which aims at incremental improvements of governance processes through aspirational, but achievable, milestones.

The New Partnership for Africa's Development (NEPAD) Capacity Development Strategic Framework (CDSF), the AMV, and the AMDC are all practical initiatives in this regard (Hanson et al. 2014).[9]

Emergence of a revised landscape and possibilities

The aforementioned developments have led to the emergence of new possibilities in the natural resource sector (Aghion et al. 2009; ACBF 2013). Internal and external pressures have triggered a growing state coherence with strong policy frameworks and increasing regional and sub-regional integration and linkages.

The evolving landscape is characterized by: a growing state coherence with strong NRM policy frameworks and increasing regional and sub-regional integration and linkages; high (even if erratic) commodity prices fueled by a strong demand from emerging economies, notably BRICS; improving technical skills – legislature, science, and management – and a strong recognition of, and appreciation for, training programs for stakeholders across the entire natural resource management value chain; improved and informed leadership resulting in strengthened state–civil society–private sector partnerships and cooperation; enhanced national and regional initiatives; region-level adaptation/adoption of emerging best practices in natural resource governance; and an integration of local perspectives and practices and civil society into official policy responses; renegotiation of old contracts, adoption of robust and transparent governance structures, and employment of civil society organizations (CSOs) (local and international) as pressure groups to hold MNCs accountable to their corporate social responsibilities; and increasing sophistication and will to bargain – drawing on a plethora of initiatives, such as the KPCS, PWYP, EITI, and the AfDB's ALSF to ensure improved accountability, transparency, negotiation, and management of natural resources and the revenue they generate (Hanson et al. 2014; ACBF 2013; RWI 2013). Similarly, discussions around value chains and jobs; development of trust funds/sovereign wealth funds; promotion of green growth / reducing emissions from deforestation and forest degradation (REDD+) (AfDB 2010; Kedir 2012); and new dialogue configurations (World Bank 2011; Gaille 2011; Obeng-Odoom 2012).

The revised landscape has resulted in the exposure of the problem of "missing revenue," particularly in the oil industry, as well as the growth of corporate social responsibility initiatives. Again, the proliferation of CSOs with enhanced capacities and international linkages is another manifestation of the revised landscape. In this regard, CSOs in various countries have played a vital role in fostering debate to improve transparency and accountability (de Renzio et al. 2005: 59). CSOs likewise play an effective role in engaging transnational investment through direct pressure, such as strikes at the site of investment projects. This approach was successfully put into practice in Zambia, where Chinese investors have been very active in recent times. The death of forty-six Zambian workers in the Chinese-operated Chambishi mine in 2005 raised the alarms of civil society. This pushed the Chinese mine to increase its social investment, but also ignited a democratic debate about Zambia's partnership with China (Gonzalez-Vicente, 2011: 73–74).

Aside from direct pressure as exemplified in Zambia, CSOs are also involved in efficient resource governance by tackling ownership (i.e. shareholders) in the corporation's country of origin. This has been a preferred way for transnational advocacy networks to internationalize local struggles (Arthur 2012). In Ghana, CSOs have been active in advocating the adoption of legislation in line with international best practices. Here, as part of a strategy to reclaim and open up the space for the democratic participation of civil society in the consultation process, a preparatory workshop sponsored by Revenue Watch Institute, Oxfam America, Catholic Relief Services, and other organizations was held to collate civil society views and concerns to feed into the forum (Gyampo 2011: 11). While the prime objective of the meeting was to educate civil society on oil production and oil development issues on the basis of international best practices and to formulate a set of civil society demands, the meeting served as the rallying point for the civil society groups invited to the national forum to carry the voices of many who had been denied the opportunity to participate in the national consultative process (Gyampo 2011: 53). Relatedly, the Oil and Gas Platform, a network of approximately 35 CSOs working on oil and gas issues in Ghana, has been very active in engaging in analytical capacity and advocacy (Prempeh and Kroon 2012). Set up in 2008 with the support of Oxfam and the World Bank, the Oil and Gas Platform conducts capability audits to determine what capacity exists in the oil and gas sector and where it is lacking. Further, given the strategic role civil society is expected to play in promoting accountability and community participation, a grant of US$2 million has been provided under the World Bank's Governance Partnership Facility to support a wide range of activities to be championed and implemented by civil society and community-based organizations (World Bank 2011).

These developments have also engendered new configurations of dialogue among public and private entities, CSOs, and local communities – sparking more widespread rejection, for example, of conflict-based or -ridden diamonds and timber, and abuses by MNCs in oil and gas extraction.

Across the continent, governments are embracing and advancing initiatives such as the African Peer Review Mechanism (APRM), the AMV, and NEPAD's CDSF, which, in tandem with multilateral efforts by the AfDB's ALSF, the World Bank (the Dodd-Frank Act[10]), and others, are changing the NRM landscape. Again, a number of industry self-policing initiatives (e.g. EITI, KCPS, PWYP) are combining to empower Africa to evolve a new, more complex, more evidence-based and participatory vision of NRM.[11] This vision of natural resource-based development has a much more diversified and empowered portfolio of stakeholders and actors; the implication being that the continent can achieve real growth and transformation based on natural resources – the so-called paradox of plenty is *not* inevitable.

Nowhere has a positive resource management strategy been more evident than in Botswana, where the establishment of strong and transparent governance structures and anti-corruption systems,[12] and improvement in the integrity of public institutions have contributed to economic success (Arthur 2012, 2014). In addition to establishing a well-functioning judicial system that respects property rights and the rule of law, it has adopted a decision-making process that involves consulting traditional authorities (Hillbon 2008; McFerson 2009; Taylor 2012).[13] Other countries have quietly made strides in this regard, as well: Nigeria in involving civil society in the oil sector and Liberia's approach to increased transparency in the logging industry.[14]

The entire portfolio of stakeholders is also subject to a new normative environment, as evidenced by the strong natural resource management policy environment that is gaining momentum across the continent. The revised policy landscape frames the sphere of potential constructive action, providing new spaces for agency. For African countries to move forward, capacity needs to be enhanced in four key sectors: (a) policy environment, (b) processes for implementation, (c) development results at the country level, and (d) capacity development outcomes (ACBF 2013).[15] The policy environment examines the conditions that must be in place to make transformational change and development possible, with particular emphasis on effective and development-oriented organizations and institutional frameworks. Processes for implementation assess the extent to which the countries are prepared to deliver results and outcomes. Development results are tangible outputs that permit development. Capacity development outcomes tend to measure the desired change in the human condition (ACBF 2011, 2012, 2013).

Africa, for the most part, has managed to enhance its policy environment and is making strides in terms of its implementation processes (ACBF 2013). However, countries appear to be struggling with achieving development results (18.2 percent of countries surveyed ranked "low" or "very low" in this category, with only 2.3 percent of surveyed countries (i.e. Morocco alone) in the "very high" category). That said, the real Achilles heel has to do with achieving capacity development outcomes – an issue globally recognized and deliberated in much detail in many capacity development forums, including the 2011 4th High Level Forum on Aid Effectiveness in Busan, Korea. Analysis of this cluster reveals that over two thirds (72.7 percent) of countries surveyed fell in the "very low" capacity zone (Table 2.1).

The above-mentioned findings suggest that while many African countries are taking the requisite steps to advance their capacities for managing natural resources, progress has so far been made primarily in Clusters 1 and 2 – policy environment and implementation processes. This finding concurs with the recent literature – the *2013 Africa Capacity Indicators Report* (ACBF 2013), the *Economic Report on Africa* (ECA/AU 2013), the *Africa Progress Report 2013* (Africa Progress Panel 2013), and the *2013 Resource Governance Index* (RWI 2013) – all of which suggest that, increasingly, African governments are embracing sound and sustainable policy management of their natural resource wealth. The policy environment, in particular, has been very

Table 2.1 ACI 2013 – country percentage by cluster and level of capacity

Level of capacity	Policy environment	Implementation processes	Devt. results at country level	Capacity devt. outcomes
Very low	0.0	0.0	2.3	72.7
Low	0.0	0.0	15.9	22.7
Medium	0.0	13.6	56.8	2.3
High	15.9	63.6	22.7	2.3
Very high	84.1	22.7	2.3	0.0
Total	**100**	**100**	**100**	**100**

Source: 2013 ACI database.

dynamic, with a spate of sovereign wealth funds being opened across the continent as resource-rich nations look to manage their resources – a powerful sign that African states are embracing fiscal prudence (Blas 2013; African Globe 2013; Giugale 2013).

Over the past two years, oil producers Nigeria, Ghana, and Angola have established sovereign funds, managing $1bn, $100m, and $5bn, respectively, opening a new chapter for Africa (Blas 2013). Other nations who have just discovered resources – Tanzania, Uganda, Mozambique, and Kenya – have also just established or are planning to establish such a fund (ACBF 2013). As Blas (2013) points out, while the sovereign wealth funds of Nigeria, Ghana, and Angola are among the smallest in the continent, behind the diamond-funded rainy-day pot of Botswana ($6.9bn) and the giant funds of north African oil producers Algeria ($77bn) and Libya ($65bn), they are on par with – or larger than – the funds set up by Gabon ($380m), Mauritania ($300m), and Equatorial Guinea ($80m).

Also reflective of the changing landscape, the top five performers in the field of capacity for NRM – Rwanda (83.2), Ghana (80.6), Namibia (77.6), Botswana (77.3), and Nigeria (73.8) – have all, in recent times, stepped up efforts to enhance governance in the natural resource sector. Table 2.2 provides a ranking of countries surveyed.

The table, which reflects the findings from the country level, clearly suggests that the African policy environment is very strong, with most (77 percent) of the countries surveyed combining to display high to very high capacity (Figure 2.1). From a legitimacy and incentives perspective, the African picture, while not as positive as the policy landscape, is still laudable. Here, almost 54 percent of the countries surveyed showed at the high to very high level (Figure 2.2). Relatedly, the observation of an improved dialogue space speaks to the evolving resource management landscape and its associated prospects for dialogue and inclusion (Figure 2.3). These findings also emphasize the need to better match the capabilities of the state to its dependency on the resources and to find solutions – such as buying capacity – to bridge the gaps while countries take time to build their internal capability. Botswana stands out as a country that has effectively followed this approach.

Table 2.2 ACI-NRM 2013 – resource-endowed countries

Country	Policy environment	Processes for implementation	Devt. results	Capacity devt. outcomes	Index NRM	Rank NRM	J_1[a]
Rwanda	100.0	87.8	71.1	79.2	83.2	1	2
Ghana	85.2	83.6	79.5	75.0	80.6	2	3
Namibia	87.0	70.8	75.3	79.2	77.6	3	2
Botswana	88.9	77.9	69.9	75.0	77.3	4	3
Nigeria	79.6	75.3	66.4	75.0	73.8	5	3
São Tomé and Príncipe	74.1	57.2	72.2	71.4	68.0	6	4
Gambia	87.0	63.2	67.7	52.4	65.4	7	4
Morocco	61.1	77.4	63.3	54.8	63.2	8	2
Zimbabwe	57.4	70.3	60.1	62.5	62.2	9	2
Mali	75.9	68.8	67.0	45.8	62.1	10	2
Tanzania	61.1	71.6	51.0	64.3	61.0	11	3
Liberia	55.6	66.4	52.1	66.7	59.5	12	2
CAR	64.8	68.0	47.5	54.2	57.4	13	2
Uganda	63.0	53.4	62.0	48.1	55.9	14	2
Sierra Leone	70.4	59.4	52.5	45.8	55.6	15	2
Burkina Faso	51.8	51.6	50.5	66.7	54.4	16	2
Madagascar	57.4	59.9	49.1	51.9	54.2	17	2
Gabon	55.5	62.0	66.1	40.7	54.2	18	3
Malawi	79.6	61.3	42.0	45.8	53.7	19	2
Niger	81.5	64.6	48.8	37.5	53.4	20	3
Congo, Rep	66.7	62.5	71.3	33.3	53.3	21	1
Zambia	70.4	70.4	64.6	29.6	51.5	22	3
Mauritania	38.9	61.3	58.5	51.8	51.0	23	3

Ethiopia	66.7	45.6	42.3	51.9	50.1	24	4
Burundi	64.8	39.2	38.0	55.6	46.9	25	2
Togo	70.4	46.8	44.6	35.4	46.4	26	2
Guinea	74.1	64.3	34.0	33.3	45.2	27	2
Cameroon	72.9	50.5	57.1	26.2	44.8	28	3
Kenya	50.0	53.2	33.9	40.7	43.1	29	2
Tunisia	31.5	39.7	66.5	45.8	42.6	30	3
Chad	79.6	72.9	40.3	22.2	41.6	31	1
Swaziland	75.0	55.0	21.4	52.4	41.1	32	3
Djibouti	75.0	54.4	62.5	20.0	40.9	33	4
Benin	37.0	53.2	43.0	29.2	38.7	34	2
Mozambique	29.6	54.4	23.5	59.3	35.9	35	3
Senegal	46.3	58.9	70.6	16.7	35.5	36	3
Côte d'Ivoire	37.5	50.0	39.3	20.8	33.3	37	3
DRC	22.2	56.4	48.5	18.8	29.3	38	3
Lesotho	31.5	54.8	25.6	11.1	22.3	39	2

Source: ACBF 2013 (Figure 1:10, p. 35). Note that Angola and South Africa are excluded due to missing data, and Cape Verde, Guinea-Bissau, and Mauritius are excluded because they are not hydrocarbon, mineral, or prospecting nations.

[a] J_1 = country's natural resource status: 1 = Hydrocarbon producer only; 2 = Mineral producer only; 3 = Hydrocarbon and mineral producer; and 4 = Prospective (there is reasonable expectation that the country will be producing significant hydrocarbons and/or minerals).

52 Hanson

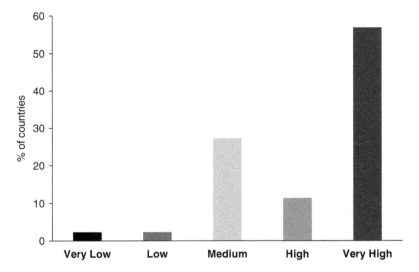

Figure 2.1 Policy environment/efficiency of instrument.
Source: Computed from ACIR 2013 database.

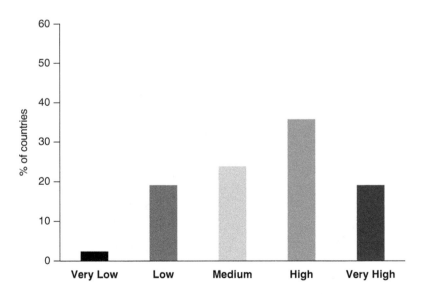

Figure 2.2 Legitimacy and incentives of NRM policy.
Source: Computed from ACIR 2013 database.

Capacity development for NRM 53

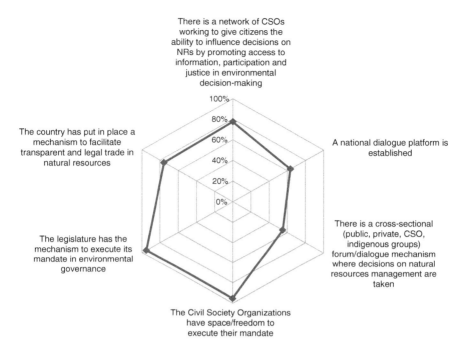

Figure 2.3 Dialogue and social inclusion on natural resource governance (percentage of countries).
Source: Computed from ACI 2013 database.

Botswana not only established a rainy-day fund to hedge against future unexpected economic shocks, but has also used its diamond resources to invest heavily in the health and education sectors – public health facilities, thousands of miles of paved and well-maintained roads, free public education for all up to age 13 (Arthur 2014). Again, the government finances almost the entire cost of the education of 12,000 students to study at the University of Botswana, established in 1982. Another 7,000 young people study overseas on full government scholarships (Arthur 2014). By collecting and efficiently managing the revenue, and investing for development, Botswana has demonstrated how good NRM and good governance can address social inequities and improve the lives of citizens (Hillbon 2008; McFerson 2009; Taylor 2012).

The revised landscape notwithstanding, many challenges still lie ahead. There is need for the advancement of: (a) transformational/development-oriented leadership; (b) independent, accountable, and transparent institutions; (c) effective natural resources regulation; (d) deepened capacity-building interventions; (e) conduits for learning from success stories; and (f) coordinating and integrating planning agencies, as key steps to ensure that the agency brought about by the revised landscape turns into realized potential (Hanson et al. 2014; ACBF 2013; Collier 2010; Barma et al. 2012).

Again, for countries – even those identified as doing well – to seize the day, they need to find ways to ensure meaningful policies are not beclouded with politics and implementation bottlenecks. This will, among other things, call for an enhancement in individual and institutional capacity not only to implement policies, programs, and projects (UNDP 2011) but to equip legislators to appreciate the intricate issues necessary to monitor natural resources activity. Equally, the capacity of the legislature in Africa to act as a countervailing force over the executive and understand the complexity of natural resource legislation needs to be bolstered (Ayee et al. 2011; Gboyega et al. 2011; Humphreys et al. 2007). Fiscal policy challenges still need addressing. Unfortunately, a discussion of Africa's policy-implementation challenges is beyond the scope of this chapter. The issue has been discussed elsewhere in the current literature (Hanson et al. 2014; Arthur 2014; ACBF 2013; Barma et al. 2012).

In acknowledgment of the aforementioned need to address implementation bottlenecks, ACBF (2013) cautions that the capacity of all actors and stakeholders involved in the natural resource value chain – extraction, processing, marketing, and management of revenue – is of fundamental importance in turning the sector into a benefit for broader society. Such capacity, however, ideally needs to be balanced among stakeholders (Rustad et al. 2012; Mehlum et al. 2006). There is a good deal of emerging evidence that "capacity imbalance" – wherein one set of stakeholders enjoys significant capacity while the other stakeholders experience inferior, and in some cases much lower, capacity – can result in corruption and exploitation due to a lack of effective checks and balances. The resulting animosity can then have profoundly negative outcomes as the lower-capacity stakeholders realize the imbalance and its repercussions. The experience of the Liberian timber/logging industry is a good case in point. Here, timber contracts after the war were for only three-year licenses for exploiting less than 5,000 hectares; and only after significant experience had been gained were larger awards put out for bid (Altman et al. 2012).

While African capacity development in the natural resource sector is usually thought of as being most needed by African stakeholders such as the government, civil society, and local communities, a great deal of capacity is lacking on the part of the international investor, who is in many cases unable to "read" local socio-political, ethno-cultural, and economic environments in Africa so as to be able to innovate and outline arrangements that work and are mutually beneficial. Thus, capacity development is needed not only for government stakeholders but also for stakeholders engaged in international and domestic processes in NRM (Rustad et al. 2012; Bruch et al. 2012; Carius and Maas 2012).

As highlighted in Figure 2.4, the linkages and sequencing of capacity development will vary from country to country, as well as between, say, a post-conflict and fragile state and a stable country on a reform path. Accordingly, it is critical to map out how to most effectively use a combination of approaches in the pursuit of development objectives. Deriving, regularizing, and formalizing the right mix of approaches to natural resource exploitation can support

Figure 2.4 Key linkages and sequencing of NRM in post-conflict/fragile vs. stable countries.
Source: ACBF 2013.

exploitation objectives and go a long way to optimizing sustainable and beneficial natural resource use across Africa (Bruch et al. 2012; Rustad et al. 2012).

The political will to engage in capacity development in a sustainable manner across diverse ethno-cultural, religious, geographic, socio-economic, linguistic, autochthonous, and migrant populations will require leadership to take the long view. And while political will at the topmost positions of government is important, such political will can be very effectively applied at many levels of government and civil society, in a wide variety of training and educational settings. Small expressions of political will can often have significant repercussions, both because those engaged directly in capacity building will have a number of stakeholders from different parts of society, and because examples set in capacity-development environments can have ongoing effects. For example, given that some stakeholders occupy positions of greater power than others (role in government, numerically advantaged, claim to resources, historical relationship to the colonial effort, etc.), providing capacity building in a balanced way can be difficult, while at the same time not doing so runs the risk of aggravating other problems, among them effective natural resource management.

While history has shown that broad capacity gains in a society do not always result in predictable outcomes (certain economic alliances or forms of government), they do facilitate the economic and political self-determination needed for countries to navigate their own way in a world where effective management and exploitation of natural resource endowments will become increasingly important.

Conclusion

Africa is at a crossroads in terms of growth, development, governance, and sustainability (Hanson et al. 2012): Can it seize its chances and transcend its somewhat lackluster first half-century? Evidence put forth suggests Africa is emerging with a new, more complex, evidence-based, more participatory, and coordinated vision of NRM, a vision of natural resource-based development motivated by an increasingly diversified and empowered portfolio of stakeholders and actors – indigenous groups/communities, civil society, media, governments, MNCs, and private investors. The implication is that real growth and transformation based on natural resources is possible. Numerous and important opportunities exist and their numbers are increasing. Africa can benefit from "new donors" and "innovative sources of finance" as it seeks to revise its natural resource sector: from sovereign wealth funds and new foundations to the Gulf States, Korea, Turkey, as well as the BRICS. New technologies already allow for the discovery of new sources of oil and gas from South Sudan to northern Mozambique, so new regions may arise around pipelines and other energy logistics/corridors (Lorenz-Carl and Rempe 2013). A number of such corridors exist across the continent, notable among them being the West African Gas Pipeline corridor, and the Maputo Development Corridor in Southern Africa. And in January 2014, energy ministers/delegates from nineteen countries committed to the creation of the Africa Clean Energy Corridor. This initiative will boost the deployment of renewable energy and help to meet Africa's rising energy needs with clean, indigenous, cost-effective power from sources including hydro, geothermal, biomass, wind, and solar. Also novel forms of "global" or "private" governance, from the KPCS and EITI to the "conflict minerals" component of the omnibus Dodd-Frank Act, present challenges of compliance and reporting (Hanson et al. 2012). There is a need, therefore, for Africans and global stakeholders in the natural resource sector to rethink and redouble efforts to advance leadership capacity, as well as individual and institutional capacity to tackle emerging issues and challenges, and more importantly to seek a "good fit" rather than a "best-practice" approach to the management and transformation of the continent's vast and diversified natural resource endowments.

Apart from good-fit policies at national and industry levels, the drive to ensure that Africa's natural resource endowments lead to development for all will entail fostering partnerships premised on trust, shared interests, and a mutual grasp of challenges and opportunities, in addition to fixing the imbalance between national and international regulatory frameworks for natural resource governance (Lisk et al. 2013).

Furthermore, as Owusu et al. (2014) suggest, African countries and stakeholders should enhance and advance efficient management and governance of natural resources by coordinating and integrating planning agencies operating across various sectors of the natural resources value chain. Equally important is the need to improve and maximize tax collection and utilize its proceeds to ensure sustainable development. Other steps include, but are not limited to, enhancing leadership capacity, deepening capacity-development interventions, advancing peer-learning and knowledge sharing, and strengthening existing institutions, while building accountable and transparent new ones, and adopting good-fit approaches and policies that can help African states manage the entire natural resource value chain – from exploration to negotiation, contracting, exploitation, and ultimately management and transformation of resource proceeds.

African countries generally have it within their grasp to build up the governance structures required for the management of their resource endowments from short-term political pressures. The key is ensuring that the institutions set up for the purpose of "immunizing from the vicissitudes of the political process…[are accompanied by requisite] fiscal, monetary, and exchange rate policies and institutions…to increase as far as possible the efficiency of revenue collection and to uproot the scourge of overvaluation" (Gylfason 2011: 29).

Notes

1 2013 saw almost US$3 billion worth of investment in Nigeria, Mozambique, South Africa, Democratic Republic of Congo, and Ghana alone. See also Geda (2012), Ramdoo and Bilal (2014), and Hanson et al. (2014) on the distinction between multinational corporations and national companies/modes of engagement/characterization of investments.
2 According to Basedau and Lay (2009), the main function of the state in rentier economies is to distribute rents. The rents provide ruling elites with vital revenue and other resources through which to address and offset any potential pressures for violence and instability.
3 Human agency refers to the capacity of each human being to make conscious choices, and contrasts the notion that humans are completely governed by either nature or environmental factors because we possess an innate capacity to think for ourselves. For more, see Forbes-Pitt (2011).
4 In spite of Botswana being flagged an African success story, there are some who point out that minority groups (Kalanga and Basarwa) and rural communities have not entirely benefited from resource rents.
5 See also Ramdoo and Bilal (2014) on beneficiation/upstream and downstream linkages/the "smile curve", etc.
6 Established in 2010, the African Legal Support Facility (ALSF) is hosted by the AfDB, and dedicated primarily to providing legal advice and technical assistance to African governments. Membership in the ALSF is open to all sovereign nations and international organizations. With a currently membership of 52 (47 countries and 5 international organizations), the ALSF also grants and advances funds to African countries for legal advice from top legal counsel in areas of debt management and litigation, natural resources/extractive industries management and contracting, etc. ALSF's goal is to ensure fair and balanced negotiations (www.afdb.org/en/topics-and-sectors/initiatives-partnerships/african-legal-support-facility/).
7 Surveys of CSR amongst businesses in Africa have found that the most common approach to CSR issues is through philanthropic support, in particular focusing on education, health, and environment (Forstater et al. 2010). For example, in Kenya, the causes receiving the highest proportion of corporate donations are health and medical provision, education and training; HIV/AIDS; agriculture and food security; and underprivileged children. In Zambia, on the other hand, supporting orphanages is the most common activity identified as CSR, followed by sponsorship of sporting events, cultural ceremonies, education and health provision, and donations to religious and arts organizations (Forstater et al. 2010: 15–16). Recently, Africa's regional institutions, CSOs, and others have begun to call for free, prior, and informed consent processes (FPIC) when natural resource projects

have the potential to impact local communities (Greenspan 2014). Relatedly, extractive industry companies and associations, lenders, and investors have also created policies requiring FPIC, which in turn further underscores its growing acceptance globally (Greenspan 2014).
8 UNEP's International Resource Panel (IRP) was established in 2007 to provide independent, coherent, and authoritative scientific assessments on the sustainable use of natural resources and the environmental impacts of resource use over the full lifecycle. The IRP's assessments aim to provide a better appreciation of how to decouple human development and economic growth from environmental degradation (for more, please see www.unep.org/resourcepanel/).
9 For more on the CDSF, see www.oecd.org/development/governance-development/43508787.pdf.
10 See www.gpo.gov/fdsys/pkg/PLAW-111publ203/pdf/PLAW-111publ203.pdf.
11 While these initiatives are great first step, they face some challenges, the most significant being their voluntary nature.
12 In 1994, the Government of Botswana created the Directorate on Corruption and Economic Crime (DCEC), responsible for combating corruption through investigation, prevention, and education. Other related laws include, but are not limited to: the Botswana Bank of Botswana (Amendment) Act 1999; Botswana Banking (Anti-money laundering) Regulations 2003; Botswana Companies Act 1959 (as amended 1984); Botswana Corruption and Economic Crime Act 1994. For more on the subject, see www.track.unodc.org/LegalLibrary/pages/LegalResources.aspx?country=Botswana.
13 For further insights on this important development, see Taylor (2012).
14 Liberia has emerged as a success story of post-conflict transition in Africa. Since the election of Ellen Johnson Sirleaf, Liberia's economy has grown by 4.6 percent and 5.6 percent in 2009 and 2010, respectively (World Bank 2011). The period has also witnessed reforms and improvement to the regulation of the timber industry. The pillar of reform was the establishment of the Private Use Permits (PUPs) under the 2006 National Forestry Reform Law (NFRL), which aims to regulate and govern the logging trade, especially the relations between private landowners and government-approved companies. Since its adoption, the government has awarded about 63 PUPs, totaling 2,582,501 hectares, approximately 23 percent of Liberia's total land area (Jallah et al. 2012). The PUPs have helped curb illegal trade in timber, minimized disputes between landowners and logging firms, and increased demand for Liberia's timber. Other benefits of the PUPs include generating revenue through the payment of rents by PUP operators to the government; enhancing oversight and regulation over the timber sector; attracting FDI; and improving economic benefits to landowners at the community level through fair trade by government-approved companies.
15 For more on the methodology around the *Africa Capacity Indicators* data survey, and the computation of the core ACI (Africa Capacity Index) and sub-indices, see, ACBF (2011) *Africa Capacity Indicators 2011: Capacity Development in Fragile States*, Harare, Zimbabwe (http://elibrary.acbfpact.org/acbf/collect/acbf/index/assoc/HASHe1dc.dir/doc.pdf).

References

ACBF (2011) *African Capacity Indicators Report 2011: Capacity Development in Fragile States*. Harare, Zimbabwe: African Capacity Building Foundation.

ACBF (2012) *Africa Capacity Indicators Report 2012: Capacity Development for Agricultural Transformation and Food Security*. Harare, Zimbabwe: African Capacity Building Foundation.

ACBF (2013) *Africa Capacity Indicators Report 2013: Capacity Development for Natural Resources Management*. Harare, Zimbabwe: African Capacity Building Foundation.

AfDB (African Development Bank) (2010) *Climate Finance Newsletter*, December 1 Issue. Tunis: AfDB.

Africa-Canada Forum (2013) *The African Mining Vision: A Transformative Agenda for Development*. Available at: www.ccic.ca/_files/en/working_groups/2013-04-02-AMV_backgrounder_EN.pdf (last accessed May 4, 2016).

Africa Progress Panel (2013) *Africa Progress Report 2013. Equity in Extractives: Stewarding Africa's Natural Resources for All*. Geneva: Africa Progress Panel.

African Globe (2013) "Africa: The Rise of the Sovereign Wealth Fund." Available at: www.africanglobe.net/business/africa-rise-sovereign-wealth-fund/ (last accessed May 4, 2016).

Aghion, P., Hemous, D. and Veugelers, R. (2009) *No Green Growth Without Innovation*. Bruege Policy Briefs No. 2009/07, November. Brussels: Bruegel.

Alao, A. (2007) *Natural Resources and Conflict in Africa: The Tragedy of Endowment*. Rochester, NY: University of Rochester Press.

Altman, S., Nichols, S. and Woods, J. (2012) "Leveraging High-Value Natural Resources to Restore the Rule of Law: The Role of the Liberia Forest Initiative in Liberia's Transition to Stability." In P. Lujala and S. A. Rustad (eds), *High-Value Natural Resources and Peacebuilding*. London: Earthscan, 337–365.

Arthur, P. (2012) "Averting the Resource Curse in Ghana: Assessing the Options." In L. Swatuk and M. Schnurr (eds), *Natural Resources and Social Conflict: Towards Critical Environmental Security*. London: Palgrave Macmillan, 108–127.

Arthur, P. (2014) "Governance of Natural Resource Management in Africa: Contemporary Perspectives." In K. T. Hanson, C. D'Alessandro and F. Owusu (eds), *Managing Africa's Natural Resources: Capacities for Development*. London: Palgrave Macmillan, 39–65.

AUC, AfDB and ECA (African Union Commission/African Development Bank/Economic Commission for Africa) (2011) "Building a Sustainable Future for Africa's Extractive Industry: From Vision to Plan: Action Plan for Implementing the AMV." Available at: www.africaminingvision.org/amv_resources/AMV/Action%20Plan%20Final%20Version%20Jan%202012.pdf (last accessed March 15 2014).

Ayee, J. R. A., Soreide, T., Shukla, G. P. and Minh Le, T. (2011) *Political Economy of the Mining Sector in Ghana*. World Bank Policy Research Working Paper, July WPS5730, 1–48). Washington, DC: World Bank.

Barma, N. H., Kaiser, K., Minh Le, T. and Viñuela L. (2012) *Rents to Riches: The Political Economy of Natural Resource-Led Development*. Washington, DC: World Bank.

Basedau, M. and Lay, J. (2009) "Resource Curse or Reenter Peace? The Ambiguous Effects of Oil Wealth and Oil Dependence on Violent Conflict." *Journal of Peace Research*, 46 (6): 757–776.

Besada, H. (2013) *Doing Business in Fragile States: The Private Sector, Natural Resources and Conflict in Africa*, Background Research Paper, Submitted to the High Level Panel on the Post-2015 Development Agenda (May).

Blas, J. (2013) "Sovereign Funds Expand in Africa." *The Financial Times* (December 15). Available at: www.ft.com/cms/s/0/515caa8e-5750-11e3-9624-00144feabdc0.html#axzz2sAB3iQxg (last accessed May 4, 2016).

Bruch, C., Jensen, D., Nakayama, M. and Unruh, J. (2012) *Post-Conflict Peacebuilding and Natural Resources: The Promise and the Peril*. New York: Cambridge University Press.

Carius, A. and Maas, A. (2012) "Thinking Back-End: Improving Post-Conflict Analysis Through Consulting, Adapting to Change, and Scenario Building." In D. Jensen and S. Lonergan (eds), *Assessing and Restoring Natural Resources in Post-Conflict Peacebuilding*. London: Earthscan.

Collier, P. (2007) *The Bottom Billion: Why the Poorest Countries Are Failing and What Can Be Done about It*. New York: Oxford University Press.

Collier, P. (2010) "The Political Economy of Natural Resources." *Social Research*, 77 (4): 1105–1132.

Collier, P. and Goderis, B. (2007) *Commodity Prices, Growth, and the Natural Resource Curse: Reconciling a Conundrum*. CSAE Working Paper Series/2007–15). Oxford: Oxford University Press.

Daniele, V. (2011) "Natural Resources and the "Quality" of Economic Development." *Journal of Development Studies*, 47 (4): 545–573.

de Renzio, P., Gomez, P. and Sheppard, J. (2005) "Budget Transparency and Development in Resource-Dependent Countries." *International Social Science Journal* (Supplement 1), 57: 57–69.

Diamond, L. and Mosbacher, J. (2013) "Petroleum to the People: Africa's Coming Resource Curse—and How to Avoid It." *Foreign Affairs*, September/October. Available at: www.foreignaffairs.com/articles/139647/larry-diamond-and-jack-mosbacher/petroleum-to-the-people (last accessed May 4, 2016).

ECA/AUC (Economic Commission on Africa/ African Union Commission) (2013) *Economic Report on Africa 2013: Making the Most of Africa's Commodities: Industrializing for Growth, Jobs and Economic Transformation*. Addis Ababa, Ethiopia: ECA/AU.

Forbes-Pitt, K. (2011) *The Assumption of Agency Theory*. Milton Park/New York: Routledge.

Forstater, M., Zadek, S., Guang, Y., Yu, K., Hong, C. X. and George, M. (2010) *Corporate Responsibility in African Development: Insights from an Emerging Dialogue*. Working Paper No. 60, Harvard University J.F. Kennedy School of Governance CSR Initiative (October). Available at: https://www.hks.harvard.edu/m-rcbg/CSRI/publications/workingpaper_60.pdf (last accessed May 4, 2016).

Gaille, S. (2011) "Mitigating the Resource Curse: A Proposal for Microfinance and Educational Lending Royalty Law." *Energy Law Journal*, 32: 81–96.

Geda, A. (2012) *Resource Flows from Booming Natural Resource/Primary Commodity Sectors in Africa and Their Macroeconomic Policy and Capacity Building Challenges*. ACIR 2013 Background Paper Number 2. Harare, Zimbabwe: ACBF.

Gboyega, A., Soreide, T., Minh Le, T. and Shukla, G. P. (2011) *The Political Economy of the Petroleum Sector in Nigeria*. World Bank Policy Research Working Paper, August, WPS5779: 1–48. Washington, DC: World Bank.

Giugale, M. (2013) "How to Tell When Your Country Is Managing Its Riches Well." The World Post (01/08/2013)." Available at: www.huffingtonpost.com/marcello-giugale/how-to-tell-when-your-cou_b_2435233.html (last accessed May 4, 2016).

Godnick, W., Klein, D., González-Posso, C., Mendoza, I. and Meneses, S. (2008) *Conflict, Economy, International Cooperation and Non-renewable Natural Resources*. Initiative for Peacebuilding. Available at: www.initiativeforpeacebuilding.eu/pdf/Conflict_Economy_International_Cooperation_and_Non_Renewable_Natural_Resources.pdf (last accessed March 29, 2014).

Gonzalez-Vicente, R. (2011) "China's Engagement in South America and Africa's Extractive Sectors: New Perspectives for Resource Curse Theories." *Pacific Review*, 24 (1): 65–87.

Greenspan, E. (2014) Free, Prior and Informed Consent in Africa: An Emerging Standard for Extractive Industry Projects. Oxfam America Research Backgrounder series. Available at: www.oxfamamerica.org/publications/fpic-in-africa (last accessed May 4, 2016).

Gyampo, R. E. V. (2011) "Saving Ghana from Its Oil: A Critical Assessment of Preparations So Far Made." *Africa Today*, 57 (4): 48–69.

Gylfason, T. (2011) *Natural Resource Endowments: A Mixed Blessing?* CESifo Working Paper 3353. Munich, Germany: CESifo.

Hanlon, J. (2011) *Understanding Land Investment Deals in Africa. Country Report: Mozambique*. Oakland, CA: Oakland Institute.

Hanson, K. T., Kararach, G. and Shaw, T. (eds) (2012) *Rethinking Development Challenges for Public Policy: Insights from Contemporary Africa*. London: Palgrave Macmillan for ACBF.

Hanson, K. T., D'Alessandro, C. and Owusu, F. (eds) (2014) *Managing Africa's Natural Resources: Capacities for Development*. London: Palgrave Macmillan.

Hillbon, E. (2008) "Diamonds or Development? A Structural Assessment of Botswana's Forty Years of Success." *Journal of Modern African Studies*, 46 (2): 191–214.

Humphreys, M., Sachs, J. D. and Stiglitz, J. E. (2007) *Escaping the Resource Curse*. New York: Columbia University Press.

IMF (2011) *Regional Economic Outlook: Sub-Saharan Africa*. Washington, DC: International Monetary Fund.

Jallah, J. D., Coleman, F., Sele, J., Nah, T. D., Bloe, D. and Dorliae, K. (2012) *Special Independent Investigation Body (SIIB) Report on the Issuance of Private Use Permits (PUPs)*. SIIB Report, 7, Monrovia, Liberia: Special Independent Investigation Board.

Karl, T. L. (1997) *The Paradox of Plenty: Oil Booms and Petro States*. Berkeley, CA: University of California Press.

Kedir, A. (2012) *Debating Critical Issues of Green Growth in Africa: Thinking Beyond Our Lifetimes*. ACIR 2013 Background Paper Number 18. Harare, Zimbabwe: ACBF.

Le Billon, P. and Levin, E. (2009) "Building Peace with Conflict Diamonds? Merging Security and Development in Sierra Leone's Diamond Sector." *Development and Change*, 40 (4): 693–715.

Lederman, D. and Maloney, W. F. (eds) (2007) *Natural Resources: Neither Curse nor Destiny*. Washington, DC: World Bank and Stanford University Press.

Lisk, F., Besada, H. and Martin, P. (2013) *Regulating Extraction in the Global South: Towards a Framework for Accountability*. Background Research Paper, submitted to the High Level Panel on the Post-2015 Development Agenda (May).

Lorenz-Carl, U. and Rempe, M. (eds) (2013) *Mapping Agency: Comparing Regionalisms in Africa*. Farnham: Ashgate for UNU-CRIS.

McFerson, H. (2009) "Governance and Hyper-Corruption in Resource-Rich African Countries." *Third World Quarterly*, 30 (8): 1529–1548.

McKinsey Global Institute (2010a) *Lions on the Move: The Progress and Potential of African Economies*. McKinsey Global Institute (www.mckinsey.com/mgi).

McKinsey Global Institute (2010b) *What's Driving Africa's Growth?* McKinsey Global Institute. Available at: www.mckinsey.com/insights/economic_studies/whats_driving_africas_growth (last accessed May 5, 2016).

Maconachie, R. (2009) "Diamonds, Governance and "Local" Development in Post-Conflict Sierra Leone: Lessons for Artisanal and Small-Scale Mining in Sub-Saharan Africa?" *Resources Policy*, 34 (1–2): 71–79.

Manzano, O. and Rigobon, R. (2001) *Resource Curse or Debt Overhang?* Available at: (http://web.mit.edu/rigobon/www/Robertos_Web_Page/Research_files/resourcecurse.pdf) (last accessed May 4, 2016).

Marcel, V. (2013) *Guidelines for Good Governance in Emerging Oil and Gas Producers* (September). London: Chatham House (The Royal Institute of International Affairs).

Mehlum, H., Moene, K. O. and Torvik, R. (2006) "Institutions and the Resource Curse." *Economic Journal*, 116 (5): 1–20.

NATO (2012) "Global Dynamics of National Security: Alliances and Resources – the Future of Resource Conflicts: the Africa Pattern." Available at: www.libraryindex.com/pages/1941/Global-Dynamics-National-Security-Alliances-Resources-FUTURE-RESOURCE-CONFLICTS-AFRICA-PATTERN.html (last accessed March 15, 2014).

NRC (Natural Resource Charter) (2010) *Natural Resource Charter* (November). Available at: www.naturalresourcecharter.org (last accessed May 4, 2016).

Obeng-Odoom, F. (2012) "Problematizing the Resource Curse Thesis." *Development and Society*, 42 (1): 1–29.

Obi, C. (2010) "Oil Extraction, Dispossession, Resistance, and Conflict in Nigeria's Oil-Rich Niger Delta." *Canadian Journal of Development Studies*, 30 (1–2): 219–236.

Owusu, F., D'Alessandro, C. and Hanson, K. T. (2014) "Moving Africa Beyond the Resource Curse: Defining the 'Good Fit' Approach Imperative in Natural Resource Management and Identifying the Capacity Needs." In K. T. Hanson et al. (eds), *Managing Africa's Natural Resources: Capacities for Development*. Houndmills, Basingstoke: Palgrave Macmillan, 206–225.

Prempeh, K. and Kroon, C. (2012) "The Political Economy Analysis of the Oil and Gas Sector in Ghana: Summary of Issues for Star-Ghana." Available at: www.starghana.org/assets/STAR%20Ghana%20Recommendations%20and%20Summary%20of%20Issues%20for%20Oil%20&%20Gas%20Call.pdf (last accessed 31August, 2012).

Ramdoo, I. and Bilal, S. (2014) *Extractive Resources for Development: Trade, Fiscal and Industrial Considerations*. ECDPM Discussion Paper No. 156), January, 2014. Available at: http://ecdpm.org/wp-content/uploads/DP-156-Extractive-Resources-for-Development-2014.pdf (last accessed May 4, 2016).

Rustad, S. A. and Binningsbø, H. M. (2010) *Rapid Recurrence: Natural Resources, Armed Conflict and Peace*, Working Paper, Center for the Study of Civil War. Oslo: Peace Research Institute Oslo.

Rustad, S. A., Lujala, P. and Le Billon, P. (2012) "Building or Spoiling Peace? Lessons from the Management of High-Value Natural Resources." In P. Lujala and S. A. Rustad (eds), *High-Value Natural Resources and Peacebuilding*. London: Earthscan, 570–621.

RWI (Revenue Watch Institute) (2013) *The 2013 Resource Governance Index*.

Sachs, J. D. and Warner, A. M. (1997) *Natural Resource Abundance and Economic Growth*. Working Paper Series WP 5398. Cambridge: NBER.

Sachs, J. D. and Warner, A. M. (2001) "Natural Resources and Economic Development: The Curse of Natural Resources." *European Economic Review*, 45: 827–838.

Swilling, M. (2012) *Beyond the Resource Curse: From Resource Wars to Sustainable Resource Management in Africa*. Paper presented at the Winelands Conference on Integrity and Governance, Stellenbosch, South Africa (April). Available at: www.sustainabilityinstitute.net/si-library/40-archive-categories/research-project-outputs/1651-beyond-the-resource-curse-from-resource-wars-to-sustainable-resource-management-in-africa (last accessed May 4, 2016).

Taylor, I. (2012) "Botswana as a Development-Oriented Gate-Keeping State: A Response." *African Affairs*, I444 (111): 466–476.

UNDP (United Nations Development Programme) (2011) *Managing Natural Resources for Human Development in Low Income Countries*. Working Paper 2011–002, December. New York: Palgrave Macmillan.

UNECA (United Nations Economic Commission for Africa) (2013) *Eighth African Development Forum (ADF-VIII): Governing and Harnessing Natural Resources for Africa's Development*, Addis Ababa, Ethiopia, 23–25 October 2012. Available at: www.uneca.org/sites/default/files/uploaded-documents/ADF/ADF8/ADFVIII-ConceptNote.pdf (last accessed May 4, 2016).

World Bank (2011) *Building Capacity to Manage Ghana's Oil- World Bank Assists with US$38 Million*. Press Release No: 2011/272/AFR. Available at: http://web.worldbank.org/WBSITE/EXTERNAL/COUNTRIES/AFRICAEXT/GHANAEXTN/0,,contentMDK:22794423~menuPK:351972~pagePK:2865066~piPK:2865079~theSitePK:351952,00.html (last accessed May 4, 2016).

3 The other resource curse
Extractives as development panacea

Chris W. J. Roberts

Introduction

Despite millennia of metallurgy and decades of industrial mining and oil production, most sub-Saharan African (SSA) jurisdictions are still emerging players within globalized extractive industry (EI) markets and value chains.[1] Over the last twenty years, myriad regulatory and fiscal changes have characterized liberalized EI governance. Strong and sustained economic growth rates across many African economies over the last decade and into the foreseeable future have been driven in large part by (mostly foreign) investments in and exports of extractives (United Nations Economic Commission for Africa (UNECA) and African Union (AU) 2012, 2013; United Nations (UN) Department of Economic and Social Affairs (DESA) 2013, 2014). Despite these advances, Africa's geological affluence is still vastly underexplored and under-exploited: African mineral production is roughly 10 percent of world output and accounts for 15 percent of total investment.[2] Oil and gas output is set to grow rapidly as Ghana, Mozambique, Tanzania, Uganda and others ramp up production, but overall levels of exploration are still comparatively limited and have slowed recently. Over the last decade, new international players, particularly from China and India, but also elsewhere, including African firms, have challenged traditional Western dominance in extractive sectors. Additionally, pre-colonial and colonial "enclave" inheritances, new prospects and projects, and global competition are shaping what has become a new era of EI growth across most African jurisdictions.

African governments and stakeholders everywhere, however, continue to wrestle with the decades-old conundrum of how extractives best fit into the pursuit of broad-based economic growth, structural transformation and poverty alleviation, especially as climate change and social responsibility concerns add considerable constraints on and costs to EI development. Since 2009, a pendulum shift back towards the pole of greater state involvement, activist industrialization policy making, and resource nationalism has reflected a growing assertiveness and willingness of African governments to challenge the liberalization orthodoxies that took root in EI sectors from the early 1990s onwards. Some now view the possibility of mining "no longer being seen as an extractive industry, but as a development industry" (O'Keefe 2013). Recent UN and AU affiliated reports stress the need to leverage EIs for deeper economic transformation. The annual *World Economic Situation and Prospects 2014* report is typical in this regard:

> Africa's recent relatively robust growth is heavily driven by commodity production and exports; it remains far below the continent's potential, however. Growth is still failing to translate into meaningful job creation and the broad-based economic and social development needed to reduce the high poverty and rising inequality rates seen in many countries. It is therefore essential that African countries embark on strategies to transform their economies through increased value addition in the primary commodity sector and diversification into higher productivity sectors, especially manufacturing and modern services.
>
> (UN DESA 2014, 120)

Even the World Bank now speaks the language of "extractives for development." Since 2010, many African governments have taken this message to heart and proposed or revised EI regulatory frameworks in material ways, changing tax and ownership obligations or value-added stipulations (see Appendix).

This backlash is problematic given that twenty years is not a long time in the extractives economic life-cycle. In fact, the probable outcome of less foreign and domestic investment attuned to global market signals combined with more direct state intervention harkens back to an earlier era when the same expected combination of extensive reliance on extractives exploitation for broad-based socio-economic uplift and sustained industrialization did *not* occur across much of SSA. The idea that natural resource inheritances should fuel faster and more equitable economic development is hardly new and continues to generate scholarly attention (see, for example, Runge and Shikwati (2011) as well as the Making the Most of Commodities Project[3]). A similar assumption drove the impetus for post-colonial nationalization efforts and state-owned enterprise (SOE) creation that began in the 1960s. A 1980 industrial strategy for oil producer Nigeria stressed "an urgent need ... for a comprehensive review of our industrial strategy ... [T]oo little attention has been given in the past to the need to maximise the benefits that would accrue to the national economy from a fuller exploitation of the resources with which the nation is abundantly endowed" (Ciroma 1980, 7–8). The report went on to discuss the maximization of local value-added, utilization of local raw materials, linkages and backward integration, as well as manpower and technological development, including and beyond the crude oil sector. The Organization of African Unity (OAU)-sponsored *Lagos Plan of Action, 1980–2000* (referenced in UNECA and AU 2011, 101) echoed these sentiments with an additional emphasis on regional coordination. Similarities between the aforementioned

Nigerian industrial policy document and the Lagos Plan are hardly coincidental: Nigerian President Shagari hosted the OAU Summit that produced the Lagos Plan, and Ciroma was one of his ministers.

Today, a complex mix of domestic and transnational laws and regulations, normative guidelines and impulses, incomplete institutional (including constitutional) transformations, political pressures, varied governance orientations, missing transportation and energy infrastructure, and commodity market volatility generate the dense and uncertain setting in which EI decision making operates across SSA.

The "other resource curse" – the prevailing assumption that natural resources can easily be monetized to generate public goods and leveraged for industrial transformation – lies behind recurring policy disappointments since the independence era. More problematically, the "other resource curse" creates the conditions for the traditional resource curse or paradox of plenty. This chapter claims that stakeholders and scholars require a more comprehensive understanding and set of analytical tools to gauge the prospects and limits of extractives for development as the "other resource curse" regains prominence.

First, the chapter outlines interrelated analytical frameworks and conceptual tools that aid analysis of EI regulatory change and contradictory impulses across SSA, out of which four distinct though interrelated levels of analysis emerge. Second, the extractives value pyramid is delineated. This additional frame of reference helps to explain why certain geological resources are developed as opposed to others, especially in "frontier" mineral jurisdictions, and makes clear that not all extractives have the same potential for economic linkage. Third, the chapter provides a synopsis of key EI governance and regulatory eras leading up to the current period, one marked by assertiveness and a reawakened resource nationalism. Lastly, it concludes with a discussion of the implications of the "other resource curse" in terms of the policy-making and analytical strategies for EI stakeholders. Governments, companies, non-governmental organizations (NGOs), academics and citizens need to be aware of the interplay of governance orientations and regulatory objectives inspired by laudable goals that may nonetheless produce unpredictable, unintended and unwelcome consequences.

Natural resource abundance alone is neither a panacea nor intrinsically beneficial or harmful to socio-economic transformation. Rather, "natural resources put the institutional arrangements to a test" (Mehlum et al. 2006, 3). The "other resource curse" is precisely the overriding assumption that links, linearly, geological abundance with economic development. This assumption skips over the critical assessment of whether appropriate governance and institutional frameworks beyond EIs are or can be put in place that can convert geological abundance into long-term economic opportunity, an assumption that – if ignored – may unfortunately feed traditional forms of the resource curse (for example, see Stoddard 2012).

Extractives levels of analysis and conceptual tools

Regulatory and institutional frameworks are not exogenous to the mining and hydrocarbon sectors: they shape how the industry and the players within it evolve. Regulatory variability in SSA is driven by a complex push and pull of domestic elite-driven governance orientations (including post-conflict and constitutional transitions); populist and local community political pressures, especially as electoral competition becomes a political reality (Chikwanha 2012); transnational influences, networks and impositions; and competing discourses about the role and objectives of extractives in development. Thus, governance orientations, politics, international interventions, and ideas generate the institutional framework for EIs as well as the economy as a whole. Additionally, regulatory variability reflects ongoing debates over the efficacy of command-and-control regulatory modes versus voluntary, private-sector self-regulation, or some hybrid position (Ayres and Braithwaite 1992). Incremental or responsive regulatory changes are expected as learning and experience induce necessary adjustments. Major shifts, however, signal new governance orientations or regulatory objectives, and may profoundly affect future EI directions. Since 2010, many SSA jurisdictions have introduced or hinted at such major shifts just as commodity prices have drifted lower and global EI investment appetite has waned.

Governance and regulatory levels of analysis

Regulatory objectives and approaches take shape under over-arching *governance orientations* and *institutional competencies* (see Figure 3.1). Governance does not simply entail a technical, instrumental tinkering to enhance developmental and operational outcomes. Governance is never politically or policy neutral. It "concerns primarily the manner in which power is exercised" (McFeron 2010, 338). After 1989, the "good governance" turn emerged as a core corrective concept and discourse within the donor community with regard to the problem of African underdevelopment (Abrahamsen 2000). As a natural extension of liberalization and structural adjustment policies that emerged in the 1980s, the focus on good governance sought to restructure and entrench a new relationship between the state and the economy. This entailed a significant shift from state-led to private-sector-led economic development: the state as regulator and enabler rather than owner, employer and operator.

Challenges to that discourse were always present, but financial crisis and policy conditionality compelled government after government to adopt liberalization and privatization measures during the 1980s and 1990s, thereby restricting their policy options. EIs flourished – especially in terms of exploration – in many countries after the liberalization of the mining and hydrocarbon sectors, two sectors that received targeted nurturing from international financial institutions (IFIs) and bilateral partners, including Australia and Canada. But

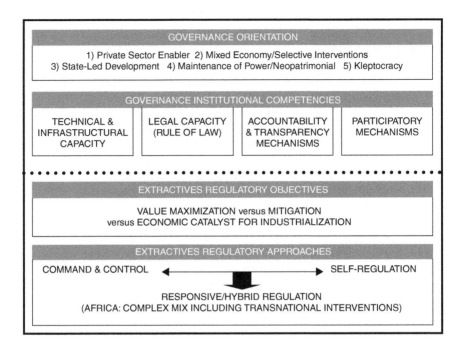

Figure 3.1 Four governance and regulatory levels of analysis.

broad-based socio-economic benefits did not automatically and quickly materialize, whereas environmental and local community impacts inevitably did, generally due to weak institutional competencies related to the imposed governance orientation. Too often overlooked or simplified, this critical interplay of governance orientations, institutional competencies, regulatory objectives and regulatory approaches provides a complicated web to unravel for policy makers and stakeholders who aspire to leverage resource riches for sustainable economic benefit and structural transformation. In the absence of institutional competencies, there is no way for extractives to carry the load of economic structural transformation: the traditional resource curse beckons.

Regulatory objectives: value maximization, mitigation, and economic catalyst objectives

African jurisdictions have been caught between the commonsense notion that rich geological inheritances should be easily leveraged as a development catalyst and the unfortunate dilemma that extractives can also trigger negative economic, environmental, social and political effects.

The purpose of this chapter, however is not to review the "paradox of plenty" or "resource curse" literature.[4] From a political economy perspective,

Extractives as development panacea 69

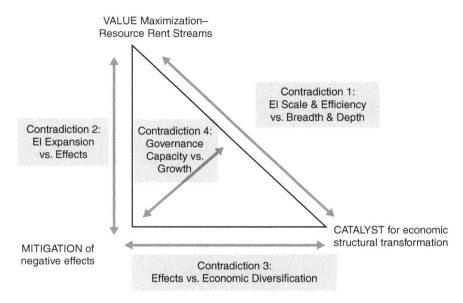

Figure 3.2 Conflicting objectives of extractive industry regulations.

the ongoing competition among EI *value maximization*, *mitigation of effects* and *catalysts for structural transformation* objectives provides the context and potential trade-off consideration for every regulatory impulse. These three competing objectives produce four contradiction dyads (see Figure 3.2). While certainly relevant for extractives within emerging jurisdictions, these three competing objectives are present in any resource-rich jurisdiction (for an example of soul searching in Canada, see Drohan 2012).

The first objective, value maximization, refers to realizing and maximizing the *monetary* value of mineral and hydrocarbon resources. Cultivating maximal value streams for resources via extensive exploration and production increases the fiscal pie from which profits and resource rents can be allocated among industry actors, host governments and communities. Resources in the ground that are not part of active exploitation or reserve calculations have no effective (or net present) value. Value maximization requires an active exploration pipeline that drives continuous EI project and production expansion: it can take evaluations of 10,000 mineral showings or occurrences to produce a single mine (Natural Resources Canada [NRCAN] 2013, 2).

Geology is just one component of a larger risk equation that determines whether specific mineral occurrences are economically feasible to develop. Otto (2006) suggests that geological prospectivity is the first of *nine* risk criteria categories (or modifying factors) used within the industry to gauge potential opportunities: (1) geological; (2) political; (3) marketing; (4) regulatory; (5) fiscal; (6) monetary; (7) environmental and social; (8) operational and infrastructural; (9) profit. Geology or mineral prospectivity alone thus cannot determine mineral resource potential, although highly prospective geology can overcome some (but not all) perceived risk hurdles.

Delineating geological potential or assets is not simply a scientific or technical undertaking; determination is complicated by variable and often uncertain market forces, taxation and royalty frameworks, existing infrastructure, available technology and processes, mitigation expectations, political stability, etc. But if any jurisdiction seeks to maximize the long-term value of its extractive potential, regulatory frameworks that promote wide-scale exploration and production *over time* are required. Otto (2009) describes this as the "grow the herd approach": a reasonable and predicable regulatory and tax burden encourages exploration and project development, thus attracting newer entrants and increasing the size of the sector as well as the tax base. The opposite "cash cow" approach will keep the sector small by "milking" every viable operation and dissuading others from investing.

The second objective for any EI jurisdiction is mitigation of adverse effects. Mining and hydrocarbon sectors are naturally involved in transforming geological assets into economic assets. There is no escaping negative environmental effects and human impacts during this process. Conscious mitigation of the negative effects of mining represents a relatively recent and still incomplete phenomenon. Environmental impact assessments (EIAs) were only integrated into mine development proposals after 1969 in the United States and for hydrocarbons in 1973 in Canada. The first major project to incorporate a mine closure and remediation plan at the feasibility stage did not occur until 1979, and this measure took time to become a standard practice in global mining (Thomson and Joyce 2006). South Africa only included legislated EIA requirements for mining projects in 1991, written into the Minerals Act and supervised by the Department of Minerals and Energy, not even an independent, arms-length department. Prior to the legislation, the Ministry only provided environmental guidelines (Hoffman 2007). Nigeria, the continent's largest oil exporter, introduced strict environmental reporting standards for the petroleum industry only in 1991. Even following this development, officials lamented that EIA reports became pro forma exercises with no industry follow-through and weak departmental oversight and monitoring (Agha et al. 2002). The execution of the Ogoni Nine activists by the Abacha military dictatorship in 1995 illustrates only the most egregious, and in some cases ongoing, failings of Nigeria's putative environmental regulatory regime (Bassey 2013, 134–137). African jurisdictions also face the ongoing struggle between industrial-scale and artisanal operations. Mature EI jurisdictions have gradually accumulated experience on mitigation issues over decades. Most SSA jurisdictions, however, experienced extreme, swift EI governance reorientations concurrent with rapid EI growth and concern with mitigation issues. It is no surprise, then, that a long history of transnational policy and development interventionism in SSA extended rapidly into the mitigation arena.

The third competing regulatory objective faced by EI jurisdictions is that which privileges EI as a catalyst for structural economic transformation (in short, industrialization). The focus here is to increase the breadth and depth of mineral and hydrocarbon integration within the host economy. Value-added processing, beneficiation, and employment creation via regulatory encouragement of downstream linkages are the most obvious manifestations of this orientation. But additional regulatory intervention to stimulate upstream linkages (that is, local content, ownership and contracting requirements) and sidestream linkages (for example, infrastructure, corporate social responsibility (CSR) and local financial-listing requirements) are part of a wholesale strategy of broad-based economic leverage (see Figure 3.3). As delineated below, leveraging EI as economic catalyst entails a different, often contrary, set of regulatory imperatives than value maximization, and can also challenge stakeholder objectives around mitigation as the state takes on roles as both regulator *and* proponent of or operator in specific economic sectors.

Four contradictions: tensions between mitigation and growth

Value maximization, mitigation and catalyst objectives for EI produce at least four core contradictions that create tension within any regulatory jurisdiction (as per Figure 3.2). The first contradiction, between value maximization and catalyst objectives, is the tension between increasing the scale and efficiency of the EI sector itself to find, develop and monetize natural resources, on the one hand, and the desire to leverage those resources across the breadth and depth of the economy (in other words, horizontal and vertical integration). At first glance, it seems these are not competing objectives. However, regulatory intervention that promotes catalyst objectives – economic diversification or industrialization – around mineral development, including higher royalty obligations or non-pecuniary mandates, increases the marginal risk and investment threshold for economic feasibility assessments of any specific project. As in many other sectors of the economy, there are trade-offs between value- and catalyst-oriented objectives with regard to EI which policy makers and publics must understand.

The second contradiction, between EI expansion and its adverse effects, presents the most obvious tension. Promotion of geological assets to attract investment drives exploration and development activity and enlarges the footprint of EI, increasing its environmental and human impact. Many African jurisdictions in the 1990s, with the assistance of the Foreign Investment Advisory Services (FIAS) of the Multilateral Investment Guarantee Agency (MIGA) and the International Finance Corporation (IFC), rushed prematurely to compete for EI investment before developing the institutional capacity to manage the growing environmental and human impacts (irrespective of the regulatory framework implemented). The ensuing accumulation of mitigation crises – from the development of oil reserves in (then) southern Sudan and conflict-prone Chad to the displacement of artisanal miners in Ghana

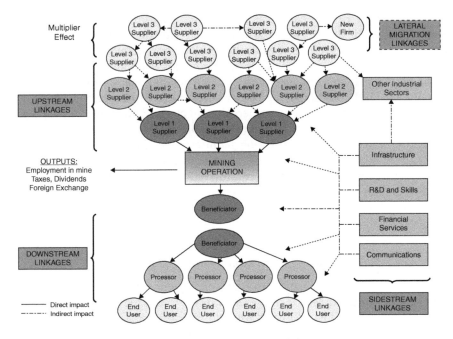

Figure 3.3 EI upstream, downstream and sidestream linkages.
Source: UNECA and AU 2011, 103.

and Tanzania and the "blood diamonds" that prolonged violent conflict in Liberia, Sierra Leone, and Angola (Grant 2012) – provoked various local and international responses.

The third contradiction pits mitigation of effects against catalyzed industrial expansion, not just EI sectoral expansion. In other words, initiatives to leverage EI as a catalyst for economic transformation stimulate various industrial sectors, including power generation and transportation fuels. Uganda, for instance, plans to build a large-scale refinery so that fuel products can be produced locally and not just crude is exported (Kasita 2012; Naresh 2013), but this entails a whole range of legislative, resettlement, environmental and market considerations that have slowed overall sector progress. Downstream advanced processing and beneficiation of extractives often involves greater adverse environmental, and other, consequences than do basic production and processing operations.

A commitment to value-added strategies, therefore, can drastically increase the range of environmental and other mitigation issues compared with a value-oriented emphasis. And as policy makers become invested in the catalyst objective there can be significant pressure to minimize mitigation measures and stakeholder concerns that may slow down catalytic processes. The conundrums are many and real: in October 2012, Tanzania's

Minister of Energy and Minerals, Professor Sospeter Muhongo, told a business and diaspora audience in Canada that Tanzania must develop its vast coal resources in large part to generate power. "We are not responsible for greenhouse emissions," he said, arguing that climate change and industrial pollution caused by centuries of Western industrialization should not now hold back the aspirations of developing countries that intend to use their own geological inheritance.

The fourth contradiction is the tension between overall economic growth (via EI sector expansion and/or catalytic transformation) and the governance orientation and capacity to keep pace across various institutional dimensions (including technical, legal, accountability). Even with high-level political and international commitment to mitigation, capacity constraints – whether of a purely technical nature or caused by a more broadly interpreted "retreat of the state" in the post-structural adjustment era (Campbell 2010) – often undermine effective EI governance and regulation. In some jurisdictions, problems of political (un)accountability and (non-)transparency work directly against regulatory enforcement. In others, the governance orientation of the host jurisdiction is dominated by concerns over the maintenance of power, or even more perverse motivations.

The governance orientation contradiction can lead to a spiraling negative feedback loop with debilitating effects on EIs. As local and international efforts are made to address mitigation shortcomings, overlapping yet incomplete regulatory oversight can drive up uncertainty and costs for EIs and promote forum shopping by aggrieved stakeholders. Firms and investors will address uncertainty by modifying their investment thresholds, leaving altogether or changing the rules of the game (for example, leveraging high-level political or international contacts, hard-nosed negotiation or threats to obtain tax exemptions or higher rates of return). Public consternation can in turn be directed at EI firms, for advancing projects either too quickly or too slowly, and towards governments that do not seem responsive or capable of regulating effectively. Governments may turn to new regulatory measures or approaches to address populist concerns, continuing the cycle of regulatory uncertainty, ineffective enforcement and policy incongruity. The quality of international partners will decline as only the cowboys and adventurers, or strategic state-sponsored investors, will remain. In sum, policy makers, publics and scholars need to be aware of these inherent contradictions that result from different regulatory objectives, and how these contradictions can reveal and often deepen institutional competency gaps and weaknesses.

The extractives value pyramid: what gets produced where, when and why?

The extractives value pyramid (see Figure 3.4) provides some context as to where, when and why certain extractive sectors evolve versus others. Geology alone cannot answer these questions. The extractives value pyramid highlights

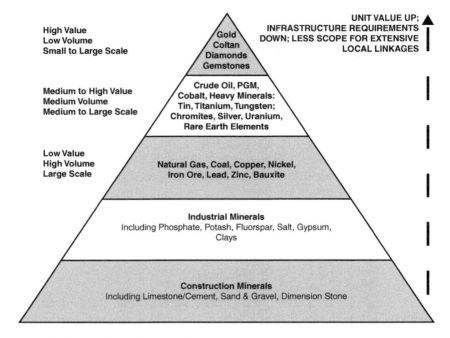

Figure 3.4 Extractives value pyramid.

the characteristics of over sixty economically valuable minerals plus oil and gas. Regulatory objectives and frameworks need to take these differences between extractives into account. For instance, while most fiscal frameworks accept that the royalties on high-value gold and low-value iron ore should not be the same, not all do so. Towards the top of the value pyramid the unit value is higher, but the potential for extensive economic linkages is lower. Gold and gemstones only have so many processing and beneficiation possibilities, and "coltan"[5] requires highly specialized proprietary processing for eventual use in electronics. Production and export of these higher-value, low-volume commodities require more limited infrastructure compared with most medium- and low-value, high-volume extractives.

Within the second tier – medium value but across a range of production scales – oil is qualitatively different in terms of production, markets and the higher proportion of resource rent that may accrue to host governments, but the general characteristics are similar to the other minerals here. The middle-tier commodities, which include natural gas, coal, copper and iron ore, need the largest infrastructural support to be viable but also have the greatest potential for employment creation and economic linkages. West Africa's iron ore boom – in Liberia and Sierra Leone so far but with massive Guinea resources on the horizon (see *The Economist* 2014) – is fueled by rehabilitated rail links from high-quality ore reserves situated relatively close to export terminals (Marais 2012), and backed by a long-term focus on power generation. Monetizing growing natural gas reserves that remain stranded or flared in places such as Angola, Ghana, Mozambique, Nigeria and Tanzania still requires billions of dollars of investment in pipelines, liquefied natural gas (LNG) trains and export terminals, as well as local power plants and petrochemical facilities. In these countries, natural gas exploitation is underway, but it can take many years to get a critical mass of infrastructure, regulations and policies in place to leverage natural gas for structural economic transformation.

The extractive values pyramid is a useful starting point to think about the wide varieties of extractives and the implications for exploitation, economic linkages and mitigation of adverse effects. It also suggests the reasons why many "new" mining jurisdictions see gold exploration and production emerge first: limited infrastructure required for export, readily available technologies for mining and processing, and usually higher margins over relatively short mine lives mean that long-term commercial and political risks are limited. Gold is often the bridgehead sector in frontier mining jurisdictions, and success there can establish confidence to expand interest into other, more capital-intensive and infrastructure-sensitive sectors.

If the rules change too radically and too early, as may have been the case in Tanzania in its mining policy revisions over 2009–2010 (Rodin 2013), both the vanguard sector (usually gold but not always) and other potential sectors can see their investment attractiveness dissipate. Milking the "cash cow" may be possible once a certain industrial critical mass is established, but future possibilities for either expanding the resource base or growing organic linkages deeper into the economy will be significantly curtailed. Since 2010, many African jurisdictions have moved in this more regulated direction although with considerable variation: compare Zimbabwe's draconian domestic majority ownership requirements with Mali's comparatively gentle tax and regulatory revisions and promise to review existing mining contracts. Despite Mali's political and military crisis that lasted most of 2012–2013, a critical mass of gold-mining operations and ongoing exploration provided a catalyst for the development of a world-class gold refinery in the country. Construction on the Kankou Moussa Gold Refinery began in March 2013, a joint venture between Swiss and Malian companies.[6] There are hints that the government may eventually ban the export of any unrefined gold (by industrial and artisanal miners alike),[7] but with a world-class gold refinery – officially inaugurated in November 2015 and based on market conditions and not government fiat – such a policy decision may not dissuade current and future investors and negatively impact the future growth of EIs overall.

Evolution of EI regulatory complexity across SSA

Leaving aside South Africa until the 1990s, since independence, five relatively discrete eras of EI evolution can be identified. Context is critically important in order to understand how EI governance, institutional competencies and regulatory approaches have changed and thus produced the current era of assertiveness that is fundamentally rooted in the "other resource curse." Table 3.1 chronologically lists major milestones over the most recent four eras.

Post-colonial resource nationalism (1950s–1980s)

The first era of EI evolution runs from the independence wave of the late 1950s and 1960s through to the "lost decade of the 1980s" and the Brundtland Commission report of 1987. It can be characterized as mostly state-led in orientation with weak governance competencies inherited from the colonial state. Governments pursued a catalyst regulatory objective via command-and-control approaches, including nationalization and/or creation of SOEs.

Post-colonial African states started at a distinct disadvantage. They inherited EIs designed expressly for the needs of imperial powers, enclave projects where benefits accrued abroad with limited integration into local economies (UNECA and AU 2011, 12–15). Mineral SOEs became policy instruments (including employment, local ownership and patronage) and revenue generators for central coffers and not standalone enterprises designed to reinvest in exploration and productivity. Cyclical commodities markets often produced soft extractives prices that exacerbated overall declining terms of trade between developing and industrial economies. To attempt to correct for this, SOEs and mandated joint ventures became the norm in SSA mining and hydrocarbon sectors by the 1970s and 1980s (Prichard 2009, 241–242). Major examples include Gecamines, formed as Belgian mining interests in Katanga were taken over by the Mobutu regime in 1966, and Zambia's efforts to take a majority interest in copper-mining operations from 1968. Nigeria incrementally nationalized its upstream oil sector in the 1970s, combining regulatory and operator responsibilities into the Nigerian National Petroleum Corporation (NNPC) in 1977. Botswana's joint venture with De Beers in 1968, Debswana, may seem to epitomize these trends. However, Botswana's governance orientation can be more accurately described as a mixed economy, with careful attention to strengthening institutional pillars, promoting value maximization through incremental intervention, and ensuring regulatory stability.

Foreign direct investment (FDI) remained selective during this period, as new states did not have sufficient financial or technical capacity to support it, but state-led governance orientations, often supported by both Western and Eastern donors during the Cold War, gradually closed off many African jurisdictions to most foreign EI investment. In a 1979 resource map published in the *Hammond world atlas*, neither Mali nor Tanzania – now top five gold producers in Africa – contained any significant gold occurrences.

Table 3.1 Contemporary extractives milestones for SSA

1986	Ghana's new Mineral and Mining Law, first significantly liberalized EI sector
1987	Brundtland Commission: sustainable development/generational equity go mainstream
1988	MIGA created; FIAS and Investment Promotion Centers launched
1990	Nelson Mandela released from prison; South African firms expand into Africa
1991	EIAs first legislated in South African mining and Nigerian oil and gas
1991	Pan African Energy secures Songo Songo natural gas lease in Tanzania
1992	World Bank/IFC Mining Strategy; Rio Earth Summit on Sustainable Development (mining excluded)
1993	Transparency International launched
1994	World Bank Governance Strategy; all MIGA technical assistance focused on investment promotion; first annual MIGA African Mining Conference
1995	Junior mining exploration boom, largely caused by BRE-X success in Indonesia
1995	Ogoni 9 trial and executions in Nigeria
1996	First gold poured at Sadiola, the first new large-scale gold mine in Mali
1997	Global Reporting Initiative
1997	Junior mining exploration bust, caused by BRE-X and smaller scandals
1997–2001	Many juniors in East and West Africa bought out by larger players
1998	Golden Pride gold mine commissioned in Tanzania, first of five new gold mines in next few years
1998–1999	First major oil exports from Sudan; conflict in south escalates; Talisman CSR crisis
1998–2002	Conflict escalation across SSA; dot.com bubble
1999	Global Mining Initiative (GMI) and MIGA/IFC Environmental Assessment & Disclosure Policy
1999	MiningWatch Canada created
2000	Mining, Minerals and Sustainable Development (MMSD) launched 2000; first discussions in Kimberley, South Africa, about diamond certification
2000	Chad–Cameroon Petroleum Development and Pipeline Project approved by World Bank
2000–2001	Canadian Nl 43–101 standards released to regulate reporting of mineral resources and reserves
2001	NEPAD (extractives not a big focus, but governance is)
2001	International Council on Mining and Metals (ICMM) established
2002	World Summit on Sustainable Development Johannesburg; Global Dialogue on mining and metals sponsored by Canada and South Africa

Table 3.1 (*cont.*)

2002	EITI and Revenue Watch Institute created; Publish What You Pay coalition founded
2003	Kimberley Diamond Process and Equator Principles launched; Canadian Nl 51–101 standards for oil and gas reporting standards released
2004	World Bank Extractives Industry Review; first use of natural gas for power in Tanzania
2004	First meeting of Intergovernmental Forum on Mining, Minerals, Metals & Sustainable Development (IGF); African Mining Partnership launched
2006	China's resurgence in Africa recognized in West
2006–2008	EI mergers and acquisitions at top of market
2007	First gold poured at new gold mine in Burkina Faso
2008	Oil hits US$147/barrel in July, drops to nearly US$30 by end of year; various metal prices follow similar pattern
2008	Oxfam America works with Economic Community of West African States (ECOWAS) on standardization of mining codes, including public participation
2008–2009	Global economic crisis; commodity prices and stocks plummet
2009	Africa Mining Vision initiative; transnational Natural Resource Charter launched; Canada releases CSR Strategy
2009	MIGA adds coverage for "non-honoring of sovereign financial obligations"
2010	Ghana launches significant oil production; first Natural Resource Charter conference
2010	ECOWAS Directive on the Harmonization of Guiding Principles and Policies in the Mining Sector
2010	Dodd-Frank Act passed in United States: securities reform includes certification for conflict minerals and payments to host governments
2010–2012	Additional round of EI mergers and acquisitions at high market premiums
2010–2013	Many SSA EI jurisdictions make significant amendments to EI regulatory frameworks
2011	UN endorses Prof. Ruggie's Guiding Principles for Business and Human Rights; Mining Policy Framework-IGF
2011	Sierra Leone's first major iron ore shipment in over thirty years
2011	South African beneficiation strategy released; UNECA Report on Mining
2011	Organisation for Economic Co-operation and Development (OECD) Due Diligence Guidance for Responsible Supply Chains of Minerals from Conflict-Affected and High-Risk Areas adopted; Canadian International Development Agency (CIDA) announces Official Development Assistance (ODA) pilot projects with NGOs and mining firms in Africa and Latin America

Table 3.1 (cont.)

2012	World Bank Extractives For Development initiative: E4D = Discovery, Development, Depletion, Distribution; IFC releases updated Sustainability Framework/Performance Standards
2012	Marikana Massacre in South Africa: police fire on striking platinum mine workers, killing 34
2012–2013	Major mining firms take huge write-downs given reduced valuations of acquired assets
2013	Both Nigeria and South Africa propose significant regulatory changes to hydrocarbon sector
2013	Canada strengthens anti-bribery legislation; commits to support African Mineral Development Centre
2014–2015	Most precious metal, non-precious metals and minerals, and crude oil prices drop to levels last seen in 2009–2010, negatively affecting production, exports, revenue, and investment in EI-reliant jurisdictions

Liberalization and early sustainable development (1986–1997)

During the 1970s and 1980s, debt levels rose precipitously across the region, including in oil-rich states that borrowed heavily against expected future revenues. Many large mineral SOEs, including Gecamines in Zaire, Zambia Consolidated Copper Mines Ltd. (ZCCM) in Zambia and the State Gold Mining Company and Ashanti Goldfields (then 40 percent government owned) in Ghana began to exhibit signs of decline, with too little capital investment, lower prices, growing debts and too many workers on the payroll. In the 1980s, structural adjustment, policy conditionality and debt relief became favored solutions during Africa's lost decade. Concurrently, sustainable development went mainstream after the 1987 Brundtland Commission, changing the regulatory landscape forever.

The two transitional pillars of liberalization and sustainable development influenced the new trajectory of SSA EIs. The demise of the Cold War also reduced the authority of state-led development orientations. The World Bank used its leverage over African states in economic crisis and political transition to push for aggressive liberalization policies within various economies, though this liberalization was often half-hearted in practice. Ghana's early FDI and mining reforms began in 1986 and led to a revitalized Ghana mining sector. Liberalization in extractives promoted a private-sector-led governance orientation, attention to some governance pillars (technical, legal), value maximization through increased exploration and a hybrid regulatory approach away from command-and-control inclinations.

Simultaneously, gaps-generated transnational efforts promoted the earliest forms of mitigation, including EIAs and social impact best practices of the period. Transparency International was launched in 1993 to support the good governance agenda. The Global Reporting Initiative,[8] launched in 1997, is illustrative of a rapid increase in non-governmental and transnational mobilization to integrate sustainable development and ethical considerations more fully into global economic practices. MIGA's creation in 1988 was designed to foster a stronger framework for political risk mitigation to attract global EI firms to invest in liberalizing jurisdictions. MIGA also spearheaded investment promotion centers across SSA and an annual "Investing in African Mining" conference beginning in 1994. The World Bank released its Strategy for African Mining technical paper in August 1992, outlining the steps necessary for African governments to attract mining risk capital and thus grow mineral exploration and production. It did not describe mining as a panacea for development or poverty reduction; rather, it outlined the "important benefits in terms of exports, foreign exchange earnings and tax receipts to support economic recovery and growth in Africa" (World Bank 1992, x), that is, a focus on macroeconomic and balance-of-payments benefits.

A liberalizing trend accompanied this active exhortation for FDI into African EI jurisdictions. Between 1990 and 2000, 30 states introduced revised mining and FDI legislation that reduced royalties and corporate taxes, provided exemptions for imports of capital equipment, loosened labor and local content requirements and allowed repatriation of profits (Besada and Martin 2012, 2, 6–9). Many states privatized SOEs and revitalized or established regulatory institutions, including geological surveys and environmental agencies. Changes in FDI regulations, the ending of monopolies for local SOEs and other regulatory changes opened up the hydrocarbons sector, particularly in countries without established oil and gas industries. Even Nigeria, after 1992, reduced NNPC's stake in new petroleum sharing contracts and liberalized the downstream sector to stimulate local and FDI. Earliest successes from this process included new and/or revitalized gold mines in Ghana, Mali and Tanzania before the end of the 1990s, natural gas development in Tanzania and a huge jump in exploration and capital investment across the region.

Crisis, consolidation and transition (1997–2002)

A third, short interregnum era had both economic and political causes and consequences. After the euphoric "unlocking" of Africa's mineral wealth during an initial rapid liberalization and investment boom, two obstacles slowed EI growth. The first was economic; scandals, lower commodity prices and the emergence of the dot.com investment bubble drew capital away and curtailed investment interest in extractives.

The infamous BRE-X Minerals Ltd. gold-mining scandal of March 1997 resulted in requirements for more sophisticated and standardized reporting by publicly traded mining companies in Canada and had large spillover effects. Investors had poured money into junior EIs, particularly gold firms, looking for the next BRE-X. An independent assessment ultimately revealed an enormous fraud: drill samples had been spiked with alluvial gold. BRE-X itself quickly lost its US$5 billion market capitalization, but investors also lost confidence in the entire EI sector. Many junior mining and energy firms active in Africa found they could no longer generate investment for exploration and development. Some quietly dissolved or were acquired by large firms such as Placer Dome, Barrick Gold, Talisman and the China National Petroleum Corporation. From this debacle the Canadian NI43-101 "Standards of disclosure for mineral projects" emerged for publicly listed firms, designed to rebuild investor confidence. A few years later, the energy sector had its own standards, NI 51–101. Both standards influence developments outside their listing jurisdictions, and the National Instrument (NI) 43–101 approach has been widely influential because of the number of mining companies listed or cross-listed on Canadian exchanges (Australia's Joint Ore Reporting Committee [JORC] standard is similarly influential).[9] These stricter reporting standards mitigate risks for investors but raise the costs of compliance. They also force companies to report data and developments, verified by an independent third party, information that can be used by host governments to track current project resource and reserve calculations, etc.

Much more disheartening than scandal, however, was the upsurge and continuance of interstate and civil conflict in Africa during this period, with minerals or oil often interwoven into the conflict. The Great Lakes region degenerated throughout the entire decade, the Rwandan genocide and Burundi's civil war spilling over into Zaire. Kleptocratic President Mobutu was overthrown in 1997 but the "new" Democratic Republic of the Congo (DRC) played host to a wider African war between 1998 and 2003 that drew in Namibia, Rwanda, Uganda and Zimbabwe. Sierra Leone and Liberia only emerged from conflict in 2002 and 2003, respectively. Civil war broke out in oil producer Congo-Brazzaville between 1997 and 1999. Ethiopia and Eritrea fought to a bloody standstill between 1998 and 2000. Sudan's drive for oil development exacerbated the long-running civil war with the south. Côte d'Ivoire experienced its first ever coup in 1999, and by 2002 had slid into civil war, leading to a decade of political instability and conflict. Burundi remained in perpetual crisis until 2003. Nigeria only emerged from two decades of military rule in 1999 and Angola's civil war only ended in 2002. Mining powerhouse Zimbabwe saw its positive growth track derailed by political machinations from 1998. The link between protracted conflict and minerals emerged as a global concern, fueled in part by the communications revolution that increased the demand for coltan and other heavy minerals. Africa appeared to be, as *The Economist* captured in its May 13, 2000 cover story, "The hopeless continent."

Despite the chaos across the continent, EI development did continue in those areas free of conflict – including Botswana, Burkina Faso, Gabon, Ghana, Mali, Mozambique (where the giant Mozal aluminum smelter was commissioned in 2000 to process imported bauxite), Namibia, South Africa and Tanzania – but exploration expenditure dropped across Africa from its peak in 1997. After considerable IFI pressure, Zambia's belated privatization of ZCCM took place during 1999–2000, although the government retained a significant minority shareholding stake in the unbundled firms. Zambian copper production subsequently rose in 2001 for the first time since 1973 (Toovey 2011). Madagascar was also a late mover towards mining liberalization in 1999. The World Bank approved its controversial participation in the Chad–Cameroon Pipeline Project in 2000. Environmental, CSR (including HIV/AIDS), conflict diamonds, resettlement, post-privatization retrenchments and transparency and accountability concerns that rapidly emerged in the late 1990s stimulated growing transnational attention and initiatives towards mitigation. Initial discussions about how to deal with conflict diamonds occurred in Kimberley, South Africa, in 2000 (Grant 2012).

The extractives commodities "super cycle" (2002–2008)

As wars and political instability shifted towards post-conflict reconstruction and a refocus on governance and investment attraction, many of the countries that missed the 1990s EI investment boom were able to attract attention, particularly but not solely from China. African leaders adopted and global partners subsequently endorsed the New Partnership for Africa's Development (NEPAD) in 2001. Central to NEPAD was a good governance agenda. While NEPAD did not directly target EIs, its underlying assumption – that good governance and better infrastructure facilitated investment and poverty reduction – supported governance orientations and competencies appropriate for a value maximization regulatory objective to continue. To enhance revenue transparency and accountability in this key sector, the Extractives Industry Transparency Initiative (EITI) was launched in 2002. By July 2014, 24 SSA jurisdictions were compliant, candidate, temporarily suspended or otherwise EITI affiliated, and by November 2015, that number had risen to 26 (see Appendix, which does not yet include Seychelles, which was accepted as an EITI candidate country in August 2014).

From 2001 until the global economic crisis of 2008–2009, the renaissance of African EI development drove economic growth, investment and trade in the region. Concurrently, across the continent, mitigation efforts expanded on all fronts: CSR became a mainstream practice driven by corporations and NGOs (Dashwood 2012). IFIs, EI multinationals, and NGOs mobilized, and often clashed, as they tried to instill environmental and social best practices earlier into project development cycles. In some countries undergoing political transitions, newly elected governments reassessed previous EI agreements and were able to get more favorable terms (for example, Liberia) without scaring away investors. However, domestic institutional capacity for environmental monitoring and enforcement, tax auditing and other complex regulatory functions remained weak in many jurisdictions. The DRC's emergence from all-out warfare in 2003 attracted considerable interest, both in the Katangan copper belt in the south and the rich gold, diamond, cobalt and coltan areas in the east. But neither regulatory stability in Kinshasa nor security in the east took hold, placing risk-taking mining firms in uncomfortable commercial, security and human rights dilemmas.

Extractives as development panacea 83

As commodity prices and EI investment shot up during a commodity "super cycle," African governments and publics became increasingly aware that windfall returns were accruing mostly to foreign firms, with a limited upside for state coffers and local economies. The short boom instigated regional reconsideration of the role of EIs in development, which led to the widespread governance and regulatory reorientations after 2010.

Back to the future? Assertive Africa rising (2009 to present)

Since the global economic crisis of 2008–2009, many African leaders, their electorates, civil servants, scholars, NGOs and international organizations have found policy space to push against the liberalization orientations and value maximization objectives prevalent since the late 1980s.

Six main factors account for this more recent assertiveness. First, the economic boom prior to the collapse in 2008 drove up commodity prices to such a degree that investment in and appetite for exploration and projects appeared limitless. Second, and concurrently, windfall resource rents were not accruing to host governments, a condition noted by elites and voting publics alike. Third, Western economies weakened during the crisis along with their economic credentials. Fourth, the resurgence of China and other EI actors changed the landscape of inward investment: strategic agreements beyond EIs, non-market-based calculations of investment thresholds, and ready access to cheap equity and debt financing via government-backed banks and export credit agencies reduced dependence on Western capital markets (see Morris et al. 2012; on the Angolan case, see Corkin 2013). Exposure to China's style of development, including its own vast SOE EI sectors tied into rapid industrialization, also provided ideological alternatives to Western models. Fifth, resource nationalism policies in Latin America and Asia also presented intriguing policy alternatives. And, sixth, some measure of experience with globalized EI sectors gave African governments more confidence in challenging prevailing orthodoxies and external impositions, alone and in concert. Expected broad-based economic benefits from EI, particularly industrial linkages and corporate tax receipts, had not materialized by the late 2000s. Responding to public pressure, or mobilizing it, elites could make a case for EI regulatory reform to fund Millennium Development Goals and integrated national development "visions."

If value maximization and, increasingly, mitigation objectives were the focus of the last twenty years, a rapid swing back to the economic catalyst objective characterizes the contemporary EI era in SSA. In the mining sector, the Africa Mining Vision (AMV) initiative, launched in 2009, crystallized a comprehensive approach to mining and development that promotes catalyst objectives as well as mitigation.[10] But the key question is whether governance orientations, institutional competencies and regulatory approaches have been sufficiently assessed to determine whether each African jurisdiction can manage such an abrupt policy change without scaring away investment and suffering political and economic (read "resource curse") ramifications.

Conclusion: from panacea to cultivation of institutions and processes

As listed in the Appendix, from 2010 to 2013 many African jurisdictions amended their mining and/or hydrocarbon legislation or regulations in significant ways, generally away from value maximization toward catalyst objectives. This may comprise any one or more of the following: increasing the share of revenue accruing to the state through taxes, fees and royalty adjustments; increasing direct government ownership stakes via free carried interest or SOE participation; promoting increased local private ownership via various incentives or mandates; increasing local contracting requirements (upstream linkages); mandating greater environmental protection and CSR provisions; and, most controversially, setting requirements for downstream processing and/or beneficiation.

At the same time, political crises, from coups and violent conflict (for example, in Central African Republic, DRC, Guinea, Mali, Mauritania, Niger, Sudan/South Sudan) to internal or external political shocks (for example, in Burkina Faso, Eritrea, Kenya, Mozambique, South Africa, Zimbabwe), further raise political risk calculations. Global EI firms have been hit by fast-rising operational costs, lower or at least more volatile prices (Dobbs et al. 2013), diminished investor interest and huge write-downs on assets purchased at top-of-market prices. Rio Tinto's US$3 billion write-down against its Mozambique coal assets, acquired when it bought Riversdale in 2011 (Ferreria-Marques and Holton 2013), turned into a fire sale in 2014 when Rio Tinto sold out to an Indian joint venture for just US$50 million (Antonioli and Regan 2014). The concurrent tide of resource nationalism, however defined (see Bello 2013), and a refocus on catalyst objectives come at a time of crisis within an always cyclical industry. For example, Zambia's significant fiscal reforms announced in late 2014 will increase royalties on copper production to 20 percent, and this comes on the heels of massive changes in the fiscal regime just two years previously. Unsurprisingly, amid a globally soft copper market, mines are closing or reducing production, miners are being laid off and investments are being canceled. The "other resource curse" captures this impulse, which may be driving SSA towards abrupt policy changes at precisely the wrong time.

There were signals from many jurisdictions that liberalization, value maximization and domestic and transnational capacity building around mitigation objectives were cultivating both managed EI expansion and desired economic linkages. Mali now boasts a world-class gold refinery, opened in late 2015. In Zambia, the Zambia Environmental Management Agency is celebrated for its growing efficiency by the private sector. Tanzania and Uganda have both launched online cadastre systems to increase information and transparency around mining licenses and related information, with Rwanda following suit. A Ugandan firm recently constructed East Africa's first small-scale iron ore smelter to utilize local ore. Both Kenya and Tanzania have attracted considerable interest in their expansive iron ore and coal deposits. Nigeria's Dangote

Cement recently announced a massive investment in southern Tanzania to take advantage of plentiful natural gas and industrial development around Mtwara. Nigerian oil and gas firm Oando was recently listed in Canada to expand its access to equity capital. In Mozambique, Midal of Bahrain announced that it will set up an aluminum cable plant near the Mozal smelter, the first domestic use of Mozal's aluminum ingots.

The contemporaneous focus on increased transparency and accountability, from local civil society and NGO pressures to Transparency International, Publish What You Pay (PWYP), EITI, the Dodd-Frank Act (Section 1504), and other transnational initiatives has indeed prompted better institutional mechanisms. A decade of voluntary corporate and transnational practices and reporting standards relating to the human and social impacts of international business have been built into Professor John Ruggie's *Guiding Principles for Business and Human Rights*, endorsed by the UN Human Rights Council in 2011. International partners have lined up to support the AMV-inspired African Mineral Development Centre, including Australia and Canada. There is perhaps an over-abundance of regulatory influences and they do not form a consensus. But overall, local, national and transnational efforts have done much in the last twenty years to improve mitigation and initiate processes that can enable the economic linkages so badly desired by policy makers and stakeholders.

It is thus a unique era of EI governance: an SSA paradox of both too much governance (that is, a resurgence of state-led development orientations and command-and-control regulatory approaches, overlaid by an international web of overlapping initiatives particularly around mitigation issues) and too little governance (that is, significant gaps in practical local expertise, agency budgets, infrastructure and appropriate legal, technical, accountability, transparency and participatory mechanisms). In many cases, the pendulum has swung too far back towards economic catalyst objectives and increased state intervention at the precise time when twenty years of difficult liberalization and mitigation efforts were starting to gain traction.

Additionally, EIs are an easy target for other policy failures: from Kenya, Nigeria, and Tanzania to South Africa and Zimbabwe, directives try to counteract long-term policy failures (for instance, the lack of reliable and affordable power or skills gaps in the civil service). In some countries, EI wealth masks political practices (that is, governance orientations) that negate the possibility of economic transformation, employment creation and poverty alleviation (for instance, Equatorial Guinea and Gabon could be more like Norway and Botswana). Angola's tremendous oil wealth benefits a tiny domestic elite and drives some infrastructure development, leveraging a decade-long financial relationship with China (Corkin 2013). But the tight grip of the ruling family on a competent and globalized SOE, Sonangol, as well as on the means of coercion is designed "to ensure the viability of incumbents" (de Oliveria 2007, 596; see also Laximidas 2014) and not the socio-economic upliftment of the majority.

This chapter has outlined the recent historical evolution and important theoretical and practical considerations necessary to understand the critical juncture facing SSA today concerning extractives. There are no silver-bullet policy choices that either host governments or outsiders can implement to turn mineral and hydrocarbon riches into broad-based economic growth, structural transformation and poverty alleviation. Institutional strengthening remains key, but it is a multifaceted process that takes both time and governing elites that desire institutional strengthening. But in SSA, domestic political uncertainty (sometimes conflict), institutional and infrastructural fragility, skills shortages and international interventions limit host governance and regulatory capacity and blur lines of accountability.

Leaders and policy makers thus have to be committed to institutional strengthening *within* and *outside* EI sectors. They have to make their governance orientation clear and determine what regulatory objectives can realistically be pursued. This can help to normalize EI sectors through regulatory stability and reduce African risk premiums that are again on the upswing. Publics need to be consulted as well as educated about the potential for EIs, their rights in the process, and the benefits to be expected. Politicians too need better briefings on how EIs operate in a twenty-first-century global market. Countries have to avoid the mistakes of the recent past; many extractive SOEs became a revenue drain on governments rather than a revenue generator. SOEs, if created or maintained, need to operate as standalone companies with minimal sovereign backing to reduce moral hazard risks to central government accounts, and, conversely, cannot operate only at the behest of incumbent elites. Policy makers should amend and revise regulatory frameworks based on experience and learning. Incremental experimentation, not wholesale policy shifts, reduces uncertainty and costly missteps that negatively impact future projects. Critical evaluation of the role of taxation and royalties in development can reduce unrealistic expectations.

There is no guarantee that revenue streams accruing to government are easily convertible into "development" or public goods. As the resource curse literature warns, increased revenue flowing to central state coffers may instigate processes that work precisely against broad-based socio-economic uplift and political stability. To reiterate, extractives are a test of all institutions, both within and outside EIs.

In summary, the late 1980s and early 1990s marked a critical transition from state-led to private-sector-led development across most of SSA, with EIs positioned as a leading sector and mostly Western firms serving as investors, prospectors, developers and operators. Governance and regulatory frameworks underwent wholesale changes in response to global EI evolution as well as evident capacity and governance gaps to manage rapid EI expansion across the continent. Over the last few years, however, a substantially new EI paradigm has taken shape. Chinese, Indian and other firms are challenging Western company dominance. Assertive African governments are changing the rules of the game, demanding a larger share of resource rents as well as greater local economic integration and linkages.

Extractives as development panacea 87

These regulatory changes – coming on-stream just as the benefits of the difficult liberalization era begin to materialize in terms of a critical mass of exploration, development, production and linkage projects – have significantly affected the risk calculations of many EI investors and will continue to do so. Cost structures for firms continue to escalate while investment appetite for extractives has diminished. The content of the new regulations and the uncertainty generated by a substantive change in the rules of the game will keep the risk-averse away and attract only the strategic players and high-risk speculators. The "other resource curse" may be taking hold in African capitals, which may lead to traditional forms of it, that is, a revived view that extractives are indeed a panacea to development when in fact their positive or negative impact remains firmly tied to their wider institutional milieu.

Appendix

Table 3.2 SSA regulatory revisions in mining/oil and gas 2010–2013

EITI status Nov 2015	Country	Mining[a]	Oil & Gas[b]	Regulatory risks[c]	Political risks[d]
	Angola	m	H	*	
	Benin	m	h		*
	Botswana	M	h	*	
Compliant	Burkina Faso	M		*	*
	Burundi	m		*	*
Compliant	Cameroon	m	H	*	*
Suspended	Central African Republic	m			*
Compliant	Chad	m	H		
Compliant	Congo-Brazzaville	m	H		
Compliant	DRC	M	h	*	*
Compliant	Côte d'Ivoire	m	H	*	*
	Equatorial Guinea		H		
	Eritrea	M	h		*
Candidate	Ethiopia	M	h	*	
Lost status	Gabon	m	H	*	
Compliant	Ghana	M	H	*	
Compliant	Guinea	M		*	*
	Guinea-Bissau				*
	Kenya	m	h	*	
Compliant	Liberia	M	h		
Candidate	Madagascar	M	h		*
Candidate	Malawi	m	h	*	
Compliant	Mali	M	h	*	*
Compliant	Mauritania	M	h	*	*
Compliant	Mozambique	M	H	*	*
	Namibia	M	h	*	
Compliant	Niger	M	h		*
Compliant	Nigeria	m	H	*	*
	Rwanda	M	h		

Table 3.2 (cont.)

EITI status Nov 2015	Country	Mining[a]	Oil & Gas[b]	Regulatory risks[c]	Political risks[d]
Candidate	São Tomé and Príncipe		H		
Candidate	Senegal	m	h	*	
Compliant	Sierra Leone	M	h		
	Somalia		h		*
	South Africa	M	h	*	*
	South Sudan		H		*
	Sudan	m	H		*
Suspended	Tanzania	M	h	*	
Compliant	Togo	m			
	Uganda	M	H	*	
Compliant	Zambia	M	h	*	
	Zimbabwe	M	h	*	*

EITI status: http://eiti.org/countries.

a major (M) or minor/emerging (m) mining sector in that country.
b major (H) or minor/emerging (h) hydrocarbons sector in that country.
c * indicates significant or proposed regulatory changes.
d * indicates heightened political uncertainty or actual crisis.

Notes

1 This chapter represents a slightly revised and updated version of an article originally published in the *Cambridge Review of International Affairs*, Vol. 28, Issue 2 (June 2015), pp. 283–307, http://dx.doi.org/lQ.lQ8Q/Q9557571.2Q15.1023259. Copyright © 2015.
2 See, for example, Africa Report, www.theafricareport.com/north-africa/ africa-versus-global-mining-activities.html, www.africanmining.com/africa_ by_numbers.php; and the 2013 report of the Africa Progress Panel, www.africaprogresspanel.org/publications/policy-papers/africa-progress-report-2013.
3 See http://commodities.open.ac.uk/mmcp.
4 For recent re-examinations of the resource curse, see Diamond and Mosbacher (2013), Hujo (2012), Stoddard (2012) and Morris et al. (2011). The "other resource curse" I refer to here does not assume instrumental elite rent-seeking from extractives but rather captures the belief that geology alone can be harnessed to drive economic development via structural industrial transformation. In some cases, that assumption is highjacked by elites for private and/or political purposes, but the more fundamental belief – amongst politicians, policy-makers, voters, and scholars – widely persists.
5 Coltan (more properly, columbite-tantalite ore) is now a widely recognized shorthand for one of the "conflict minerals" from the Great Lakes region. Tantalum is critical for the electronic, computer and mobile phone industries.
6 See March 5, 2013 corporate press release, www.prweb.com/releases/ swissbullioncompany/kmr/prweb10491925.htm.
7 See Africa Mining Intelligence, December 17, 2013: www.africaintelligence. com/AMA/exploration-production/2013/12/17/shake-up-in-unrefined-gold-exports-in-2015,107999693-EVE.
8 www.globalreporting.org.

9 For more information about the Canadian National Instrument 43–101 mineral reporting standards, see http://turl.ca/cbukyn or www.bcsc.bc.ca/For_Companies/Mining. For 51–101 oil and gas reporting standards, see http://turl.ca/jrvztos. For JORC standards, see www.jorc.org.
10 www.africaminingvision.org.

References

Abrahamsen, Rita (2000) *Disciplining democracy: development discourse and good governance in Africa* (New York: Zed Books).
Agha, G. U., D. O. Irrechukwu and M. M. Zagi (2002) "Environmental impact assessment and the Nigerian oil industry: a review of experiences and learnings," *SPE International Conference on Health, Safety and Environment in Oil and Gas Exploration and Production* (Kuala Lumpur: Society of Petroleum Engineers).
Antonioli, Silvia and Jim Regan (2014) "Rio Tinto set to sell ill-fated Mozambique coal venture," *Africa Report*, July 30.
Ayres, Ian and John Braithwaite (1992) *Responsive regulation: transcending the deregulation debate* (New York: Oxford University Press).
Bassey, Nnimmo (2013) *To cook a continent: destructive extraction and climate crisis in Africa* (Ibadan: Kraft Books).
Bello, Oladiran (2013) *Resource nationalism threatens Africa's mining boom*, South African Institute of International Affairs, February 3, www.saiia.org.za/opinion-analysis/resource-nationalism-threatens-africas-mining-boom, accessed November 1, 2015.
Besada, Hany and Philip Martin (2012) "Mining codes in Africa: emergence of a "fourth" generation?", *NSI research report, Governance of Natural Resources Program* (Ottawa: North-South Institute), www.nsi-ins.ca/publications/mining-codes-in-africa-emergence-of-a-fourth-generation-2, accessed November 1, 2015.
Campbell, Bonnie (2010) "Revisiting the reform process of African mining regimes," *Canadian Journal of Development Studies*, 30: 1–2, 197–217.
Chikwanha, Annie (2012) "The many shades of resource nationalism," *South African Institute of International Affairs*, November 27, www.saiia.org.za/opinion-analysis/the-many-shades-of-resource-nationalism, accessed November 1, 2015.
Ciroma, Mallam Adamu (1980) *Nigerian industrial policy & strategy: guidelines to investors* (Lagos: Ministry of Industries/Federal Government of Nigeria Press).
Corkin, Lucy (2013) *Uncovering African agency: Angola's management of China's credit lines* (Farnham, UK: Ashgate).
Dashwood, Hevina S. (2012) *The rise of global corporate social responsibility: mining and the spread of global norms* (New York: Cambridge University Press).
De Oliveria, Ricardo Soares (2007) "Business success, Angola-style: postcolonial politics and the rise and rise of Sonangol," *Journal of Modern African Studies*, 45: 4, 595–619.
Diamond, Larry and Robert A. Mosbacher (2013) "Petroleum to the people," *Foreign Affairs* 92: 5 (September/October), 86–98.
Dobbs, Richard, Jeremy Oppenheim, Fraser Thompson, Sigurd Mareels, Scott Nyquist and Sunil Sanghvi (2013) *Resource revolution: tracking global commodity markets: trends survey 2013* (London: McKinsey Global Institute), www.mckinsey.com/,/media/McKinsey/dotcom/Insights/Energy%20Resources%20Materials/Resource%20revolution%20Tracking%20global%20commodity%20markets/MGI_Resources_ survey_Full_report_Sep2013.ashx, accessed November 1, 2015.

Drohan, Madelaine (2012) *The 9 habits of highly effective resource economies: lessons for Canada* (Toronto: Canadian International Council), a summary can be found here: www.republicofmining.com/2012/10/09/the-9-habits-of-highly-effective-resource-economies-lessons-for-canada-by-madelaine-drohan-canadian-international-council-policy-report-october-5-2012, accessed November 1, 2015.

The Economist (2014) "Let the people benefit, for once," 7 June, www.economist.com/news/middle-east-and-africa/21603507-guineas-government-may-last-be- dealing-sensibly-its-mineral-riches-let, accessed November 1, 2015.

Ferreria-Marques, Clara and Kate Holton (2013) "Rio Tinto CEO Tom Albanese quits," *Business Day*, January 17, www.bdlive.co.za/world/asia/2013/01/17/ rio-tinto-ceo-tom-albanese-quits?utm_source=African + News+ Clipping+ Service+ -+January+ 17%2C+ 2013+-, accessed November 1, 2015.

Grant, J. Andrew (2012) "The Kimberly Process at ten: Reflections on a decade of efforts to end the trade in conflict diamonds," in Päivi Lujala and Siri Aas Rustad, (eds) *High-value natural resources and peacebuilding* (London: Earthscan) www.environmentalpeacebuilding.org/assets/Documents/LibraryItem_000_Doc_092.pdf, accessed November 1, 2015.

Hoffman, Armand Rousseau (2007) *An appraisal of the quality of mining EIA reports*, Master's thesis, North-West University, Potchefstroom, http://dspace.nwu.ac.za/ bitstream/handle/10394/56/hoffmann_armandr.pdf?sequence=1, accessed November 1, 2015.

Hujo, Katja (ed.) (2012) *Mineral rents and the financing of social policy: opportunities and challenges, social policy in a development context* (New York: Palgrave Macmillan/UNRISD).

Kasita, Ibrahim (2012) "Delaying oil laws is expensive for Uganda," *New Vision*, November, www.newvision.co.ug/news/179-blog-delaying-oil-laws-is-expensive-for-uganda.aspx, accessed November 1, 2015.

Laximidas, Shrikesh (2014) "Big rewards beckon in Angola, but little transparency," *Thomson Reuters Foundation*, August 2, www.trust.org/item/20130802122314-uktr6/?source=dpagerel, accessed November 1, 2015.

McFeron, Hazel M. (2010) "Extractive industries and African democracy: can the "resource curse" be exorcised?" *International Studies Perspectives*, 11, 335–353.

Marais, Jana (2012) "West Africa rails rebuilt with iron ore boom's proceeds: freight," *Bloomberg.com*, February 21, www.bloomberg.com/news/2012-02-22/west-africa-rails-rebuilt-with-iron-ore-boom-s-proceeds-freight.html, accessed November 1, 2015.

Mehlum, Halvor, Karl Moene and Ragnar Torvik (2006) "Institutions and the resource curse," *Economic Journal*, 116, 1–20.

Morris, Mike, Raphael Kaplinsky and David Kaplan (2011) *A conceptual overview to understand commodities, linkages and industrial development in Africa*, Africa Export Import Bank, http://oro.open.ac.uk/30534/2, accessed November 1, 2015.

Morris, Mike, Raphael Kaplinsky and David Kaplan (2012) "One thing leads to another: promoting industrialisation by making the most of commodities in Sub-Saharan Africa," http://tinyurl.com/CommoditiesBook, accessed November 1, 2015.

Naresh, Amrit (2013) "What's at stake in Uganda's oil bills?" *OpenOil*, January 24, http:// openoil.net/2013/01/24/will-uganda-ever-let-its-oil-flow/, accessed November 1, 2015.

NRCAN (2013) *Exploration and mining guide for Aboriginal communities* (Ottawa: Natural Resources Canada), https://www.nrcan.gc.ca/sites/www.nrcan.gc.ca/files/mineralsmetals/files/pdf/abor-auto/mining-guide-eng.pdf, accessed November 1, 2015.

O'Keefe, ed. (2013) "African mining changes the tune, but will actions follow?" *FT. Com*, February 12, http://blogs.ft.com/beyond-brics/2013/02/12/guest-post-african-mining-changes-the-tune-but-will-actions-follow/#axzz2L3Cn1u00, accessed November 1, 2015.

Otto, James M. (2006) "The competitive position of countries seeking exploration and development investment," in M. D. Dogget and J. R. Parry (Eds) *Wealth creation in the minerals industry: integrating science, business, and education* (Littleton, CO: Society of Economic Geologists), 109–126.

Otto, James M. (2009) "Mining policies, laws and fiscal systems for the 21st century," www.ibram.org.br/sites/1300/1382/00000513.pdf, accessed November 1, 2015.

Prichard, Wilson (2009) "The mining boom in Sub-Saharan Africa: continuity, change and policy implications," in R. Southall and H. Melber (eds) *A new scramble for Africa? Imperialism, investment and development* (Scottsville, South Africa: University of KwaZulu-Natal Press), 240–273.

Rodin, Jonathan (2013) "Long-term potential of Tanzanian mining industry impressive," *Creamer Media's MiningWeekly.com* (October 11, 2013), www.miningweekly.com/article/despite-challenges-the-long-term-potential-of-the-tanzanian-mining-industry-remains-impressive-2013-09-30, accessed November 1, 2015.

Runge, Jurgen and James Shikwati (eds) (2011) *Geological resources and good governance in Sub-Saharan Africa* (London: CRC Press/Taylor & Francis).

Stoddard, E. (2012) "The resource curse-resource nationalism nexus: implications for foreign markets," *Journal of Energy Security*, November, http://ensec.org/index.php?option=com_content&view=article&id=389:the-resource-curse-resource-nationalism-nexus-implications-for-foreign-markets&catid=130:issue-content&Itemid=405, accessed November 1, 2015.

Thomson, Ian and Susan Joyce (2006) "Changing mineral exploration industry approaches to sustainability," in M. D. Dogget and J. R. Parry (eds) *Wealth creation in the minerals industry: integrating science, business, and education* (Littleton, CO: Society of Economic Geologists), 149–169.

Toovey, Leia Michele (2011) "Copper mining in Zambia," *Copper Investing News*, March 14, http://copperinvestingnews.com/5595-copper-mining-in-zambia.html, accessed November 1, 2015.

UN DESA (2013) *World economic situation and prospects 2013* (New York), www.un.rg/en/development/desa/policy/wesp/archive.shtml, accessed November 1, 2015.

UN DESA (2014) *World economic situation and prospects 2014* (New York), www.un.org/en/development/desa/policy/wesp/index.shtml, accessed November 1, 2015.

UNECA and AU (2011) *Minerals and Africa's development: the International Study Group report on Africa's mineral regimes* (Addis Ababa), www.africaminingvision.org/amv_ resources/AMV/ISG%20Report_eng.pdf, accessed November 1, 2015.

UNECA and AU (2012) *Economic report on Africa 2012: unleashing Africa's potential as a pole of global growth* (Addis Ababa), www.uneca.org/publications/economic-report-africa-2012, accessed November 1, 2015.

UNECA and AU (2013) *Economic report on Africa 2012: making the most of Africa's commodities: industrializing for growth, jobs and economic transformation* (Addis Ababa), www.uneca.org/publications/economic-report-africa-2013, accessed November 1, 2015.

World Bank (1992) *Strategy for African mining* (Washington: World Bank), www-wds.worldbank.org/servlet/WDSContentServer/WDSP/IB/1999/10/21/000178830_98101904142281/Rendered/PDF/multi_page.pdf, accessed November 1, 2015.

Part II
Governance aspects

4 Natural resources, global economic volatility, and Africa's growth prospects

George Kararach and Walter Odhiambo

Introduction

In recent years, Africa's economies have posted high growth figures of 5 percent per annum and above. At the same time, the continent has also continued to report discoveries of vast natural resources – renewable (such as water, forestry, and fisheries) and non-renewable (minerals, coal, gas, and oil). Natural resources are increasingly becoming critical to the performance of many of these economies and are central to the systems of livelihoods therein. The resources form the basis of income and subsistence for populations and are a principal source of public revenue and national wealth. Given the right conditions, a natural resource boom can be an important catalyst for growth, transition, and broader socio-economic development. Unfortunately, in many African countries, natural resource booms have only to a limited extent set off a dynamic growth process and enhanced human development. This is largely due to the failure to implement inclusive growth policies that can deal with global economic volatility and to ensure that strong institutions are in place – thus making it very difficult to have a big push towards diversification and sustainable development. There is also another concern that much of Africa is not industrialized and exists in a staple trap, dependent on exports of a few natural resources. More importantly, commodity booms are transitory and prices tend to show some degree of mean reversion over time. Consequently, countries that experience one or more commodity export price booms typically also face high volatility of export prices. In many cases, natural resource booms encourage less prudent fiscal policies with limited control and inflation, further hampering growth, equity, and the alleviation of poverty. Historically, the majority of resource-rich countries tended to have limited transparency in the management of natural resource revenues, leading to the creation of parallel budgets as well as rent-seeking behaviors among the political and business elites.

So why is it important to revisit the discussions around the natural resources, global volatility, and growth prospects of the continent? The answer to this question can be wide ranging and include how natural resources can become sources of opportunities as well as originators of economic/governance challenges. Indeed, there has been a huge debate on the notion of the natural resource curse – ideas around the negative effects of oil, natural gas, and mineral production that go beyond authoritarianism and have economic, military, and societal consequences. Recently, some important publications have challenged the "resource curse" argument, creating doubts about these negative effects. Many studies respond to these critiques but also provide a consistent set of explanations about oil and minerals as well as other natural resources and their effects on authoritarianism, patriarchy, interstate and civil wars, and economic underdevelopment. These dynamics merit us revisiting the discussions to outline a transformation agenda for Africa. We argue that the continent needs to address itself to two important policy questions: (a) how does the volatility in the global economy contribute to volatility of growth in GDP per capita and to growth and development in general? and (b) what are the natural resource governance policies and frameworks that need to be put in place in order to enhance the development prospects of African economies?

Africa's recent growth experiences: commodity booms and the desire for transformation

Africa has experienced unparalleled growth in the past decade (see Figure 4.1). Real GDP rose by 4.9 percent a year from 2000 through 2010, more than twice the pace in the 1980s and 90s. Over this period, more than six of the world's fastest-growing economies were in Africa. In 2012–2013, it is estimated that Africa achieved an average growth rate of about 5 percent, and forecasts indicated that it would remain at 5.3 percent in 2014 (African Development Bank Group et al., 2013 and African Development Bank Group, 2012). Africa's increased growth momentum in the last decade has changed the narrative on the continent's development prospects. Long viewed as an economic basket case, the continent is now regarded as the "next frontier" in terms of foreign investment. What is intriguing, however, is that poverty has not been declining in comparable measure with the growth performance achieved in many African countries. This has raised serious questions on the inclusivity of Africa's recent growth performance.

Africa's increased economic momentum has been attributed to a number of factors. Analysts agree that the continent has benefited from the surge in world commodity prices. Soaring prices for oil, minerals, and other commodities have helped in lifting Africa's GDP. Close to a third of the continent's growth momentum has been attributed to natural resource windfalls (McKinsey Global Institute, 2010). Indeed, the recent fall in commodity prices and the lower demand from countries such as China has seen a slight dip in Africa's growth prospects. Other factors accounting for the remaining growth include the internal structural changes that most African countries have been implementing. More efficient use of resources has boosted domestic productivity, which has in turn boosted domestic demand for goods and services. Statistical analysis by the McKinsey Global Institute (2010) and Beny and Cook (2009) has confirmed that Africa's recent growth can be attributed

Natural resources and Africa's growth prospects 97

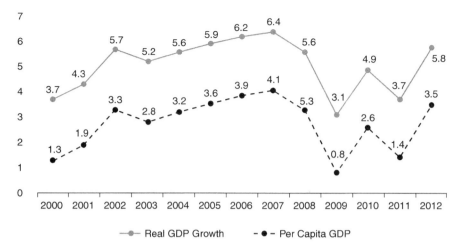

Figure 4.1 Real GDP and per capita growth of African countries.
Source: AfDB,OECD Development Center, UNDP and UNECA (2011) African Economic Outlook, www.africaneconomicoutlook.org

to favorable commodity prices and the effect of economic reforms. Indeed, countries such as Ethiopia, Rwanda, and Uganda, which up to now have not been considered as resource-rich, have been among the best performers.

The other question that remains, or needs, to be answered is whether the growth performance is sustainable. As we noted above, the growth may be driven by a combination of external factors (aid, debt relief, or commodity windfalls) and the removal of some of the worst policy distortions of the past, including political instability and civil strife. Domestic productivity has been given a boost by an increase in demand for domestic goods and services as a middle class emerges (AfDB, 2013; Ncube and Shimeles, 2012) and more efficient use of resources (UNCTAD, 2015). However, it is not clear where future productivity gains will come from (Rodrik, 2014). Part of the problem is the weakness of these economies' "incomplete" structural transformation. African economies have remained dominantly agrarian, undiversified and exporting a limited range of commodities. Researchers at the African Center for Economic Transformation (ACET) in Accra, Ghana, recently described the continent as growing rapidly yet transforming slowly (ACET, 2013).

Like in other developing countries, farmers in Africa are migrating to the cities. However, as a study from the Groningen Growth and Development Centre shows, rural migrants do not end up in modern manufacturing industries, as was the case in East Asia, but in the service sectors such as retail trade and distribution (de Vries et al., 2015). Despite having higher productivity than much of agriculture, these services are not that technologically dynamic in Africa and have been falling behind the world frontier (Rodrik,

2014). Equally noticeable is the fact that the African economic landscape's dominant feature – an informal sector comprising microenterprises, household production, and unofficial activities – is absorbing the growing urban labor force and acting as a social safety net. But the evidence suggests that it cannot provide the productive dynamism necessary to absorb the youth bulge (AfDB, 2014). Studies show that few microenterprises become formalized to be a major source of the required dynamism (La Porta and Shleifer, 2008).

Table 4.1 lists African countries that are highly dependent on commodities exports while Table 4.2 provides a simplified commodity current account for Africa in 2008 and 2009 at the height of the recent global economic/financial crisis. With the exception of a few commodities like cocoa, sugar, and gold, most commodities experienced a steep price increase in 2008 that was followed by a sharp decrease in 2009 due to the global downturn. The higher commodity prices in 2008 affected the African current account positively as key commodities exports exceeded key commodities imports by USD 319 billion, compared to USD 192 billion in 2008. Nevertheless, the impact is highly dependent on the type of commodity (Triki and Affes, 2011).

Commodity imports

Historically, state-controlled institutions have had a monopoly on imports of key agricultural commodities in most African countries, with significant implications for stabilization programs. These institutions mainly deal on the cash market and manage price risk only by timing their tenders and

Table 4.1 Classification of commodities

Commodity category	Commodity sub-categories	Country with a share of experts from commodity superior to 20%(2009 data)
Agricultural	Grains and oilseeds: corn, wheat, soybeans, soymeal, soyoil, oat, and rice Soft commodities: sugar, cocoa, coffee, and cotton	Benin, Burundi, Burkina Faso, Cameroun, Côte d'Ivoire, Ethlipia, Ghana, Mall, Rwanda, São Tomé and Príncipe, Swaziland, Togo, Uganda.
Energy	Crude oil Ethanol Natural gas Coal	Equatorial Guinea, Angola, Nigeria, Chad, Libiya, DRC, Sudan, Algeria, Gabon, Cameroon, Egypt, Somalia,
Minerals and metals	Precious: cold, silver, platinum, palladium Base: copper Ferrous: steel Other: uranium	Zambia, Burkina Faso, Namibia, Mali, DRC.

Source: Authors' calculation, data is from AfDB statistics department; COMTRADE Database and UN division.

Table 4.2 Africa's simplified commodity current account (2008–2009)

Billion USD	Year 2008		Year 2009	
	Import	Export	Import	Export
Grains and oilseeds				
Corn	2.65	0.41	2.27	0.53
Wheat	10.60	0.11	7.06	0.14
Soybeans	0.76	0.02	0.08	0.01
Soybean oil/byproducts	3.06	0.13	2.22	0.12
Palm oil	2.83	0.22	2.13	0.18
Rice	13.30	0.86	10.58	0.88
Total grains and oilseeds	**33.20**	**1.76**	**25.08**	**1.87**
Soft commodities				
Sugar, prep, honey	3.27	1.44	3.67	1.38
Cocoa	0.16	7.75	0.21	7.75
Coffee and substitute	0.66	1.90	0.45	1.72
Cotton	0.38	1.59	0.25	0.97
Total soft commodities	**4.48**	**12.68**	**4.59**	**11.83**
Metals and minerals				
Copper	2.32	4.94	1.71	3.72
Gold, non-monetary	5.17	7.31	1.30	7.65
Ores and concentrate of uranium	0.00	0.25	0.00	0.28
Platinum and related metals	0.01	14.27	0.06	8.78
Silver, unwrought, unworked	0.02	0.08	0.01	0.03
Total metals	**7.53**	**26.84**	**3.08**	**20.45**
Energy				
Gas, natural and manufactured	3.02	38.99	2.15	33.45
Petroleum and crude oil	8.36	295.04	8.86	167.77
Total energy	**11.38**	**334.03**	**11.02**	**201.13**
Total commodities	**56.59**	**375.30**	**43.76**	**235.27**
Total trade	**437.53**	**585.14**	**368.46**	**382.52**

Source: Authors' estimates, data is from AfDB statistics department; COMTRADE Database and UN division.

managing their inventories to smooth the effects of global volatility on commodities. Being relatively passive in managing price risk, state-owned enterprises have tended to face increasing deficits, thus creating a burden for government budgets. Since the 1980s many African countries liberalized trade on selected commodities, including agricultural ones. For instance, the Office des Céréales in Tunisia privatized trade of corn and soybean. Now private players are increasingly trying to lock in prices by buying derivatives. However, important variations in risk management exist across Africa. While animal-feed producers in Algeria and Tunisia are actively covering their price exposure, the cotton company of Zimbabwe does not seem to use derivatives to manage commodity price risk.

Equally, the procurement of energy inputs is often controlled by government agencies as well, on national security grounds. Unfortunately and in the absence of hedging, any new purchases are exposed to higher prices on the spot market. With notable exceptions such as Ghana, which put in place a commodity price risk-management policy in 2010, most African countries do not actively manage price risk. Arguably, the concept of risk management is not known or well understood (AFRAA, 2006). Importers of metal and mineral commodities, for example, do not seem to be actively involved in managing price risk. For instance, metal importers in Tunisia, including the state-owned Fouledh, which controls 50 percent of the market, do not hedge. The conclusion one can draw is that volatility of commodity imports will continue to strain the macroeconomic stances of many African countries.

Commodity exports

Another important feature on the engagement of African countries in global trade has been how state marketing boards act as monopolies in the export of agricultural and other commodities. These agencies have a long tradition of paying producers fixed prices but on-selling at international prices. The marketing boards thus bear the upside and downside risk. However, the downside risk tends to be small since the fixed price paid to producers is often significantly low compared to international prices (Triki and Affes, 2011). Due to the privatization of the 1980s, few African exporting countries are still using marketing boards. However, some of these boards, notably Ghana's Cocoa Board (Cocobod), were successful in hedging their exposure. Since the abolition of marketing boards, some cooperatives, such as the Kilimanjaro Native Co-operative Union (KNCU) in Tanzania have become increasingly engaged in export markets (Afeikhena and Olawale, 2000). Cooperatives can guarantee minimum price to farmers, exposing them to downside risk. Most cooperatives are now not actively hedging their price risk despite successful experiences, because of legal reforms defining their roles in the context of market liberalization (Rutten and Youssef, 2007).

For Africa's energy commodities, especially oil, export activities are largely and jointly overseen by the national oil companies (NOCs) and private oil companies. The degree of NOCs' exposure depends on the contract signed with their private partners and production levels at a given point in time. For example, Algeria has been operating a production-sharing agreement where the government retains a 51 percent share, while the government of Cameroon, on the other hand, retains only 20 percent participation through its NOC. Whether private companies who partner with NOCs should hedge or not is an ongoing debate that needs to be settled to give a clearer picture on how African economies should behave in the face of global volatility. For example, while a company like Exxon Mobil does not hedge, Shell reportedly hedges its entire production (Triki and Affes, 2011). Risk-management practices also vary across African NOCs. The bigger firms such as Sonatrach (Algeria),

Sasol (till recently owned by the South African government), and Sonangol (Angola) have been actively managing oil price risk through options, swaps and structured oil-backed financing. However, the smaller NOCs are less active in hedging price risk. The market for minerals and metal commodities seems to be less dominated by governments. Of note also is the fact that many "junior" mining companies often do not hedge, as one of their key selling points is that investors hold their shares to gain exposure to commodity price fluctuations. The larger players reportedly do limited or full hedging (ibid.).

The shifts in Africa's global connection and the role of commodities in recent growth performance

Although Africa's growth story might be about more than just resources, the continent will continue to be impacted by rising global demand for oil, natural gas, minerals, food, arable land, and the like. McKinsey Global Institute forecasts that over the next decade, the world's liquid-fuel consumption will increase by 25 percent – twice the pace of the 1990s. Projections of demand for many hard minerals show similar growth and more, including those linked to new discoveries (Melina and Xiong, 2013).

Evidence suggests that the demand for commodities is growing fastest in the world's emerging markets, particularly in Asia, Latin America, and the Middle East. In spite of longstanding commercial and historical ties with Europe, Africa now conducts half its trade with developing economic regions ("South–South" exchanges). From 1990 through 2008, Asia's share of African trade doubled, to 28 percent, while Western Europe's portion shrank, to 28 percent, from 51 percent (ibid.).

This geographic shift in trade concentration provides new grounds for economic relationships whereby African governments are increasingly able to strike multiple long-term deals at once. For example, the Chinese have been granted access to ten million tons of copper and two million tons of cobalt in the Democratic Republic of the Congo in exchange for a $9 billion package of infrastructure investments amid controversy over mining rights. As of 2010, $6 billion was finalized and $3 billion in funding is under further discussion, including mine improvements, roads, rail, hospitals, and schools. India, Brazil, the and Middle East economies are also building new broad-based investment partnerships in Africa (Alden and Schoeman, 2013).

The other side of the growth story is that Africa is gaining increased access to international capital. The annual flow of foreign direct investment (FDI) into Africa increased from $9 billion in 2000 to $62 billion in 2008 – relative to GDP, almost as large as the flow into China. Africa's resource sectors have also attracted the most new foreign capital. FDI also rose in tourism, textiles, construction, banking, and telecommunications, as well as in a broad range of countries (ibid.). Remittances became a major source of development finance and since 2011 have surpassed official development assistance (ODA), opening new doors of resources for the continent (AfDB, 2014)

Understanding the natural resources, global volatility, and growth nexus: what the literature suggests

There has been a great deal of work to establish the linkages between natural resources, volatility, and growth. Much of this work has concentrated on the relationship between resource abundance and economic performance. Observers, including economists and political scientists, believe that reliance on natural resources has adverse consequences for economic growth. A large number of studies have provided evidence that seems to support this so-called "resource curse" hypothesis, including those by Auty (1986, 1993, 2001a), Lal and Myint (1996), and Sachs and Warner (1997). More recent evidence on this relationship are studies by Rosser (2006 and Haber and Menaldo (2011). Using a sample of ninety-five countries, covering the period 1970–90, Sachs and Warner (1997) find a clear relationship between natural resource-based exports and economic growth. This they confirm in their subsequent studies (Sachs and Warner, 1999a, 1999b). Similarly, Auty (2001a) finds that resource-poor countries grow almost three times faster than those that are resource abundant. Many other studies have generated similar evidence, making the "resource curse" hypothesis almost a given in the development discourse.

Substantial work has also gone into explaining the mechanisms through which large resource revenues affect economic performance. Several economic processes, from the Dutch disease to market volatility to issues of sustainability, have been identified and discussed. More recently, focus has turned to policy failure, rent-seeking, and other institutional issues. We examine some of these economic processes.

The Dutch disease

The Dutch disease, in its broadest sense, has to do with the negative macroeconomic effects associated with the "resource curse." It is seen as the economic phenomenon in which the discovery and exploitation of natural resources leads to the deindustrialization of a nation's economy. This happens when, because of the resource–revenue inflows, the country's currency rises and domestic-spending patterns and other internal resource-allocation effects make tradable manufactured goods and other tradable sectors, including parts of agriculture, less competitive. The contraction of manufacturing and the tradable sector in general leads to slow growth, implying that the natural resource sector lacks positive externalities (Sachs and Warner, 1997). The argument is that the expansion of the natural resource sector is not enough to offset the negative effects of deindustrialization on economic growth.

The role of industrialization or manufacturing in explaining the presence of the Dutch disease has, of course, been challenged in the literature. A number of studies, including those by Auty (1994) and Stijns (2005), have argued that there is lack of evidence showing that a decline in manufacturing has a negative effect on growth. There has also been controversy over whether empirical evidence supports the existence of the Dutch disease (Leite and Weidmann, 2002; Mikesell, 1997; Wright and Czelusta, 2003).

Revenue volatility

The revenue patterns in the natural resource sector are intricately linked to global demand and supply trends. Revenue from oil, gas, and mineral resources is very volatile and is driven by fluctuations in prices, sometimes over very short periods of time. This creates problems to countries, ranging from increased uncertainty of investors to governments adopting "stop go" policies. This negatively affects growth. There is plenty of empirical support for the volatility of resource revenues. Ploeg and Poelhekke (2008) show in their work that resource curse syndrome is foremost a problem of volatility. According to these authors, "the high volatility of world prices of natural resources causes severe volatility of output per capita growth in countries that depend heavily on then" (p. 19). This volatility, if sustained, can have long-term negative effects that can be viewed as a curse.

Competition over rents

Rent-seeking behavior concerns how people compete for transfers, some of which are artificial. Most studies pursuing this explanation of the resource curse examine the behavior of interest groups seeking to capture transfers created by the government. Torvik (2002) presents a model with rent-seeking where a greater amount of natural resources increases the number of entrepreneurs engaged in rent-seeking and reduces the number of entrepreneurs running productive firms. The result is that the expenditure by government creates no social value but instead distorts the market and the way the economy operates. There is general consensus that rent-seeking behavior can produce undesirable results on the economy, although this concern is not specific to natural resources only but could apply to other sources of rent such as foreign aid (Lederman and Maloney, 2008). The existence of large oil, gas, or mineral revenue creates an environment for rent-seeking to thrive. The ultimate effect of rent-seeking will, however, depend on how and where the proceeds are invested.

Quality of institutions and policies

Yet another explanation of the resource curse hinges on the quality of institutions and policies. The lack of strong institutions has been identified as one of the key reasons explaining the existence of resource curse. Mehlum et al. (2006) and Torres et al. (2013) contend that better institutions can avoid the resource curse, but they stress the fact that natural resources can affect institutional quality. In another study, Isham et al. (2005), while confirming that natural resource abundance had no direct impact on growth, found that abundance penalizes growth through institutional quality, but only when resources are geographically concentrated, such as with oil.

The nature of the policies pursued by countries that have large windfall resource revenues also has a bearing on economic progress. Where governments make bad decisions, partly to meet high population expectation or because they find themselves with large reserves that weaken their prudence and control, windfalls do not lead to any social value (Stevens, 2003). Further, windfalls may prompt governments to adopt inappropriate policies that fail to develop the productive base of the economy. These could, for example, be in industry where, because of natural resource windfalls, countries may resort to policies that stifle rather than promote industrial development. According to Krause (1995) and Mikesell (1997), many resource countries failed to convert the oil booms of the early 1970s and 1980s into meaningful industrial development. Similarly, booms in resource revenues may prompt countries to introduce protectionism or subsidy programs which turn out to be unsustainable in the long run (Auty, 1994). Sachs and Warner (1995) found a positive correlation between dependency on primary products and closed trade regimes.

Commodities, global volatility, and economic growth: a review of the evidence

There have been a number of attempts to establish the relationships among commodities, global volatility, and economic growth. We review what researchers have put forth for policy makers to the national stances on natural resource development activities. The general discussions are clustered around seven broad "evidence" areas.

Evidence 1: The Dutch disease

As noted earlier, the discussions here are linked to the macroeconomics of the business cycle and its association with natural resource booms. This phenomenon arises when a strong, yet likely to be temporary, upward swing in the world price of the export commodity causes some or all of the following side effects (Frankel, 2012a):

- a large real appreciation in the currency (taking the form of nominal currency appreciation if the country has a floating exchange rate or the form of money inflows and inflation if the country has a fixed exchange rate, see Edwards,1986; Chen and Rogoff, 2003);
- an increase in spending (especially by the government, which increases spending in response to the increased availability of tax receipts or royalties);
- an increase in the price of non-traded goods (goods and services such as housing that are not internationally traded) relative to traded goods (manufactures and other internationally traded goods other than the export commodity);

- a resultant shift of labor and land out of non-export-commodity traded goods (pulled by the more attractive returns in the export commodity and in non-traded goods and services); and
- a current account deficit (despite the enhanced revenue from commodity exports), thereby incurring international debt that may be difficult to service when the commodity boom ends (Manzano and Rigobon, 2008; Arezki and Brückner, 2010a, 2010b).

Why are these adjustments problematic for economic development? First, in the event that the complete cycle is not adequately foreseen, any decline in the world price of the export commodity can cause difficult and painful reversals or adjustments towards initial conditions. In that case, the phenomenon is an example of the costs of volatility in commodity prices. Second, even if the perceived longevity of the increase in world price is validated, the crowding out of non-commodity exports is undesirable, perhaps because the manufacturing sector has greater externalities for long-run growth ("deindustrialization") (Van Wijnbergen, 1984; Matsuyama, 1992; Gylfason et al., 1999). In this case, an example of the costs of crowding out manufacturing, the problem is the resulting high level of commodity prices and not cyclical fluctuations per se.

Arguably, the reallocation of resources across tradable sectors, say from manufactures to oil, may be the inevitable adjustment of the fundamentals of the global economy, regardless of national macroeconomics. But the shift to non-traded goods is macroeconomic-related and requires a thoughtful strategy from the monetary authorities. In which case, the neoliberal orthodoxy of "letting the markets work" is not a fully adequate guide to policy and platform for intervention.

Adjustments in the non-traded goods sector with the possible overheating of the economy (inflation and asset bubbles) are not solely a result of real appreciation of the currency. Fiscal policy and adjustments also play a large role. Many authors have shown that fiscal policy tends to be procyclical in developing countries, especially in comparison with industrialized countries (Cuddington, 1989; Gavin and Perotti, 1997; Tornell and Lane, 1999; Kaminsky et al., 2004; Talvi and Végh, 2005; Alesina et al., 2008; Mendoza and Oviedo, 2006; Ilzetski and Végh, 2008; Medas and Zakharova, 2009). A critical driver of procyclical spending is precisely that government receipts from taxes or royalties rise in booms, and the government fails to resist the temptation or political pressure to increase spending significantly in the euphoria of a natural resource find. Procyclicality is especially pronounced in countries that possess natural resources and where income from those resources tends to dominate the business cycle (Cuddington, 1989; Arezki et al., 2011). Two large budget items that account for much of the increased spending from oil booms are investment projects and the government wage bill (Gelb, 1986; Medas and Zakharova, 2009). Essentially, the Dutch disease hypothesis seeks to provide an understanding of the "general equilibrium effects of a minerals boom," including the spending effects of the mineral rents (Stijns, 2003).

Corden and Nearly (1982), in their seminal paper attempting to test the Dutch disease model, assumed three sectors: the booming sector, the lagging sector, and the non-tradable sector. It is assumed that the prices of tradable products from the first two sectors are determined at world markets, with capital and labor being the two factors utilized in each of the three sectors. Capital is modeled as being sector specific, while labor is mobile across these sectors, with the ability of equalizing wages across the sectors.

The extant literature generally assumes that natural resource booms tend to harm the countries in which they occur. For example, Sachs and Warner (1995) argue that economies with a high ratio of natural resource exports to GDP in 1971 tended to have low growth rates during the subsequent period 1971–1989. This negative relationship holds true after controlling for other determinants of economic growth, such as initial per capita income, trade policy, government efficiency, and investment rates.

Sachs and Warner (1995) conclude that "one of the surprising features of modern economic growth is that economies abundant in natural resources have tended to grow slower than economies without substantial natural resources." However, this conclusion needs careful re-examination, because of its implications for both development policy in Africa and macroeconomic policy in industrialized countries. At the same time, there is a growing debate among academics, development- and environment-related lobbyists and policy makers regarding whether or not resource-abundant countries should be encouraged to exploit their resource bases, as such exploitations may have implications for environmental assets.

The other issue of note is that the empirical studies of the Dutch disease are mostly a collection of country – sometimes comparative – case studies among countries. Spatafora and Warner (1999) is the only exception. Their dataset is composed of eighteen oil-exporting developing countries covering a period running from the mid-1960s to the 1980s. They find that Dutch disease effects are "strikingly absent" from their data. However, there exists limited cross-country econometric tests of the consequences of resource booms on real manufacturing trade (see Forysth, 1985; McMahon, 1997; Larsen, 2006). Many of the studies that provide cross-country econometric estimates of the Dutch disease focus on positive income shocks that arise either from remittances (Amuedo-Dorantes and Pozo, 2004; Lartey et al., 2008) or aid transfers (Adenauer and Vagassky, 1998; Rajan and Subramanian, 2009), rather than resource income. Furthermore, empirical analyses (e.g. see Harding and Venables, 2010) often confine themselves to researching the correlation between resource abundance and the share of tradable sectors in the overall economy, without empirically exploring either the intermediate mechanisms that lead to the Dutch disease (i.e. resource movement effects and spending effects) or the spatial aspects studied by Papyrakis and Raveh (2013).

Most authors conclude that there are some symptoms of the negative effects of a commodity boom on an economy but that it is very difficult to disentangle Dutch disease effects from the domestic and international macroeconomic conditions prevailing at the time of the shock on long-term growth prospects. For example, price-led energy booms tend to be followed by global recessions. Hamilton (1983) demonstrated this pattern for the United States and provides evidence that this pattern should be always anticipated. Rotemberg and Woodford (1996) explained the surprisingly strong elasticity of output to oil prices – a 10 percent oil price innovation is associated, five or six quarters later, with a 2.5 percent decline in output – based on imperfect competition in product markets. The Dutch disease models suggest that volatility in commodity prices tends to harm growth prospects unless proactive strategic policy stances are adopted (see Makochekanwa's (2007) work on Botswana).

Evidence 2: Resource curse

It is now readily acknowledged by economists that oil, minerals, and agricultural resources can bring great riches to those who possess them – especially in the event of booms (Frankel, 2012a). Paradoxically, countries that are abundantly endowed with such natural resources have tended to deliver disappointing economic performance (Easterly and Levine, 1997; Sachs and Warner, 1995, Auty, 2001b; AfDB et al., 2013; EPRC et al., 2013). This phenomenon can be cyclical, with the effects reversed when commodity boom turns to commodity bust. But it can also be permanent: countries endowed with natural resources more often develop social structures in which autocratic or corrupt political elites finance themselves through physical control of the natural resources (Frankel, 2012a). Generally, governments that lack these endowments have no choice but to develop decentralized, democratic, and diversified economies with market incentives that are more conducive to the development of manufacturing and non-natural resource sectors (Ben Hammouda et al., 2006).

Auty (1993, 2001a) coined the phrase "natural resource curse" to describe the puzzling phenomenon whereby countries endowed with oil, minerals, or other natural resources tend to have experienced much less satisfactory economic performance. Sachs and Warner (1995) pioneered the econometric literature by showing that economic dependence on oil and minerals is correlated with slow economic growth. Sachs and Warner (2001) extended their previous model and showed that countries with great natural resource wealth tend to grow more slowly than resource-poor countries. The authors controlled for a wide range of variables such as geography, climate, ethnicity, as well as alternative ways of measuring resource abundance, but reportedly found the same evidence of a natural resource curse. Their paper also claims that there is little direct evidence of a bias in their estimates resulting from some other unobserved growth deterrent. Other studies confirming a negative effect of oil, in particular, on economic performance, include Kaldor et al. (2007), Sala-i-Martin and Subramanian (2003), and Smith (2004).[1]

What is the theoretical explanation of this phenomenon? Developing countries tend to be smaller economies and more likely to specialize in the exports of basic commodities like oil and raw agro-products. As a result, they are more likely to be price-takers in world markets, not just for their import goods but for their export goods as well. As Frankel (2012a) noted, the price-taking assumption requires three general conditions: low monopoly power, low trade barriers, and intrinsic perfect substitutability in the commodity as between domestic and foreign producers – a condition usually met by primary products, and usually not met by manufactured goods and services. Kalecki (1976) argues that developing economies such as those of Africa producing primary commodities are flex-price economies due to limited monopolistic structures in their productive sectors and are thus vulnerable to volatility in prices and demand in the world market.

So is there evidence for a resource curse in Africa and what has been the role of commodity prices? Recent analysis by Lundgren et al. (2013) provides a number of interesting pieces of evidence. First, and as we have shown elsewhere in this chapter, the real GDP per capita of resource-rich economies has grown more than that of other non-resource-rich African countries, although this growth has not translated into higher living standards. Second, and related to the first, is that oil exporters spend considerably less as a share of their GDP on public education and health than other African countries. This poor show has been worsened by weaknesses in natural resources and macroeconomic management, all of which have created the conditions for a resource curse. Lastly, the authors note that the role of the natural resource sector in driving growth in most African countries is grossly understated "by looking only at production-side measures of sectoral contribution." This, they argue, leaves out other causes, including the effects of commodity prices on non-resource activities.

Evidence 3: The Prebisch-Singer hypothesis

Another attempt to search for the effects of volatility on commodities and their subsequent effects on growth prospects has been associated with the Prebisch-Singer hypothesis (associated with Raul Prebisch (1950) and Hans Singer (1950)). The idea is that the prices of mineral and agricultural products follow a downward trajectory in the long run relative to the prices of manufactures and other products. Essentially, the world demand for primary products is perceived to be inelastic with respect to world income. An alternate proposition is Engel's Law: that households spend a lower fraction of their income on food and other basic necessities as they get richer. An increase in income does not translate into a proportionate rise in the demand for raw materials.

This hypothesis tended to support the conclusion that specializing in natural resources was a bad deal and therefore growth prospects of resource-based economies are depressed due to long-term price trends. To relieve the constraints of the tendency for the terms of trade for developing countries to deteriorate, Prebisch and Singer urged developing countries to have limited engagement in international trade with tariff and non-tariff barriers, to allow their domestic manufacturing sector to develop behind protective walls, rather than exploit their traditional comparative advantage in natural resources as the classic theories of free trade implored. This partly informed the import-substitution industrialization policy that was adopted in much of the developing world in the 1950s, 60s, and 70s – including in Africa. The fashion reverted in subsequent decades, however.

However, upon reflection and taking into account developments in environmental economics, there also exist persuasive theoretical arguments that prices of oil and other minerals do experience *upward* trends in the long run. These arguments begin with the assumption that these are non-perishable non-renewable resources and are not exploited under conditions of legal uncertainty over ownership. If the fixed deposits of oil or any other minerals in the earth's crust are all sufficiently accessible, the costs of exploration, development, and extraction are small compared to the value of the oil one arrives at. The important theoretical principle is that the price of oil in the long run should rise at a rate equal to the "world" interest rate (Hotelling, 1931).

The current reality is that supply of these commodities is not fixed. It is true that at any point in time there is a certain stock of mineral reserves that have been discovered. However, the historical pattern has long been that, as the stock is depleted, new reserves are found, as the example from Africa today seems to confirm (Melina and Xiong, 2013). When the price goes up, it makes exploration and development profitable for deposits that are farther underground or are underwater or in other hard-to-reach locations. This is especially true as new technologies are developed for exploration and extraction. The converse is also largely true.

With strong theoretical arguments on both sides of the Prebisch-Singer hypothesis, either for an upward trend in commodity prices or for a downward trend, one must say that it remains an empirical question. Although specifics will vary depending on individual measures, it is possible to generalize somewhat across commodity prices (Pindyck and Rotemberg, 1990). Frankel (2012a) argued that the terms of trade for commodity producers had a slight upward trend from 1870 to World War I, a downward trend in the inter-war period, upward in the 1970s, downward in the 1980s and 1990s, and upward in the first decade of the twenty-first century. Simple extrapolation of medium-term trends is foolish. One must take a longer-term perspective.

So what is the overall statistical trend in the long run? The jury seems to be out. Some studies find a slight upward trend, some a slight downward one (Cuddington, 1992; Cuddington et al., 2007; Cuddington and Urzua, 1989; Grilli and Yang, 1988; Pindyck, 1999; Hadass and Williamson, 2003; Reinhart and Wickham, 1994; Kellard and Wohar, 2006; Balagtas and Holt, 2009; Harvey et al., 2010). The econometric evidence seems to depend on the end date of the sample period. Studies written after the commodity price increases of the 1970s found an upward trend, but those written after the

1980s found a downward trend, even when both kinds of studies went back to the early twentieth century. For authors such as Deaton and Miller (1996), this phenomenon is less surprising than it sounds. Real commodity prices seem to undergo large cycles around a trend, each lasting twenty years or more (Cuddington and Jerrett, 2008). As a consequence of the cyclical fluctuations, estimates of the long-term trend are very sensitive to the precise time period studied and the judgment to be imbued on the future growth prospect of the economy, making policy decision more an issue of strategic judgment.

So what does that mean for a policy planner in Africa? One should seek to avoid falling prey to *either* of two reductionist arguments framed around the extremes of the Prebisch-Singer thesis. Good planning would require actions guided by caution around the structuralist theses of the 1950s, focusing on the decline in the terms of exchange between primary and manufactured products (Prebisch, 1950), the volatility of primary product prices, or the limited linkages between the natural resource sector and the rest of the economy (Hirschman, 1958). It may well be that country-specific studies are required as none of the structural explanations was unequivocally confirmed by empirical tests (e.g. Moran, 1983; Behrman, 1987; Cuddington, 1992; Lutz, 1994; Dawe, 1996; Fosu, 1996). One must seek a broad perspective in which all relevant reasoning and evidence are brought to bear in the balance.

Evidence 4: The imminent stillbirth or death of industrialization

The other trend in the literature is the alarm bells sounded to those developing African economies with a huge thirst to industrialize. The idea is that natural resource booms hinder the industrial sector, assumed as the main driving force of the economy, either through real exchange-rate appreciation or the absorption of production factors (Neary and van Wijnbergen, 1986). The argument goes thus: the expansion of the natural resource sector is not enough to offset the negative effect of deindustrialization on economic growth. Additionally, there is a change in the composition of exports in favor of raw materials, or even a drop in total exports, thus reducing economic growth (Torres et al., 2013; Gylfason, 2001a). However, the empirical evidence does not provide great support for the Dutch disease as an explanation of the resource curse (e.g. Leite and Weidmann, 2002; Sala-i-Martin and Subramanian, 2003). The case study by Auty (2001a) also dismisses this thesis by showing the complexity and diversity of cases among natural resource-abundant countries, including several exceptions to the curse, such as Norway, which has seized its oil abundance to become a rich country.

The current urge for African countries to increase value addition and gear up for "manufacturing" as part of their transformation agenda (AfDB, 2013) comes from a long tradition in economics beyond Prebisch-Singer to Nicholas Kaldor to Adam Smith. Outside of classical economics, diversification out of primary commodities into manufacturing is considered self-evidently desirable for reasons of sustained dynamism in the economy and being caught in a low productivity frontier (Rodrik, 2011). Yet, is industrialization the sine qua non of economic development? Is encouragement of manufacturing necessary to achieve high income? Classical economic theory rejects that proposition and instead suggests that the current production practice of relying on commodities is the right one for African economies. In the grand scheme of things, countries are better off producing whatever is their comparative advantage, whether that is natural resources or manufacturing or agro-commodities. In this classical view, attempts by Brazil to industrialize were as foolish as it would have been for Great Britain to try to grow coffee and oranges in hothouses (Frankel, 2012a).

However, some authors such as Nicholas Kaldor (1972) and Dani Rodrik (2007) have argued that countries only get sustainably rich if they industrialize (oil-rich sheikdoms notwithstanding) and that industrialization in turn requires an extra push from the government through a proactive industrial policy. The manufacturing sector is assumed to be characterized by learning by doing, while the primary sector is not (for the formalization of this view, see Matsuyama (1992)). The implication is that deliberate policy-induced diversification (Ben Hammouda et al., 2006) out of primary products into manufacturing is justified, and that a permanent commodity boom that crowds out manufacturing can indeed be harmful (van Wijnbergen, 1984; Sachs and Warner, 1995).

However, Frankel (2012a) points out that there is no reason why learning by doing should be the exclusive preserve of the manufacturing sector. He notes that some countries have experienced tremendous productivity growth in the oil, mineral, and agricultural sectors. For example, American productivity gains were driven by American public investment in such institutions of knowledge infrastructure as the US Geological Survey, the Columbia School of Mines, the Agricultural Extension Program, and Land-Grant Colleges (Wright and Czelusta, 2003).

Even though governments can play a useful role in supplying public goods for the natural resource sector to positively contribute to long-term growth, this is different from mandating government ownership of the resources themselves. Attempts by governments to force linkages between the mineral sector and processing industries do not always work, as the experience of countries like Zambia has shown. Other explanations for the resource curse, include the disincentive for entrepreneurship (Sachs and Warner, 2001), the decrease in savings and physical investment (Gylfason, 2001a; Papyrakis and Gerlagh, 2007), and lower investment in education and human capital (Gylfason, 2001b; Birdsall et al., 2001; Bravo-Ortega and Gregorio, 2007), all of which have long-term effects on a economy's growth prospects. Makochekanwa (2007) shows how Botswana managed to beat the Dutch disease effects of diamonds by taking deliberate policy actions, including majority control of value-chain enhancement.

Evidence 5: Quality institutions for growth in the face of a commodity boom or bane

At the heart of the growth-diagnostic according to Rodrik-Hausmann-Valesco is the thinking regarding economic development that the quality of institutions is a major determinant of growth performance, and it is therefore futile to recommend good macroeconomic or microeconomic policies if the institutional structure is not there to support them. Weak institutions arguably lead to inequality, intermittent dictatorship, and lack of constraints to prevent elites and politicians from plundering the country (see Barro, 1991; Acemoglu et al., 2003; Easterly and Levine, 2002; Hall and Jones, 1999; Rodrik et al., 2003; Acemoglu and Robinson, 2012).

The notion that natural resources have a positive effect on long-run development is premised on the assumption that the quality of institutions and governance is conducive. Some studies focus on outright corruption (Hodler, 2006; Caselli, 2006; Leite and Weidmann, 1999; Gylfason, 2000; Papyrakis and Gerlach, 2004; Arezki and Brückner, 2009) or rent-seeking. The thesis stresses the negative impact on growth of rent-seeking activities rampant with natural resource abundance (Torvik, 2002; Robinson et al., 2006; Sandbu, 2006). As mentioned above, Torvik (2002) showed that where there is an abundance of natural resources, the number of entrepreneurs engaged in rent-seeking increases while the number of those running productive firms decreases. With a demand externality, it is shown that the resulting drop in income is higher than the increase in income from the natural resource extraction. Therefore, more natural resources lead to lower welfare. On the other hand, the "rent-cycling theory" of Auty (1990, 2001a, 2007) differs slightly by holding that economic growth requires recycling rents via markets rather than via patronage. In high-rent countries (which many African nations have tended to be over the years), the natural resource provokes a political contest to capture ownership, with the possibility of protracted conflict like that in the Niger Delta of Nigeria and Eastern DRC, whereas in low-rent countries, the government must motivate people to create wealth, for example by pursuing comparative advantage, promoting equality, and fostering civil society.

The theory is extended to explain the possibility that natural resource booms undermine democratic institutions as governments' access to rents, in the form of windfall revenue, may free them from the need to tax their peoples, and that this in turn frees them from the need for democracy (see Mahdavy, 1970; Luciani, 1987; Vandewalle, 1998). The need for tax revenue is believed to require democracy under the theory "no taxation without representation" (see Huntington, 1991 for a generalization). A number of studies also find that economic dependence on oil or minerals is indeed correlated with authoritarian governments (Barro, 2000; Ross, 2001; Wantchekon, 2002; Jenson and Wantchekon, 2004; Ross, 2006; Ulfelder, 2007).[2]

The possibility that natural abundance may affect institutional quality is associated with explanations based on endogenous institutions, where the type of natural resource affects the institutional context, in which the form of government and the quality of policies are the main aspects (e.g. Auty, 2001a, 2001b; Ross, 2001; Atkinson and Hamilton, 2003; Torres et al., 2013). Leite and Weidmann (2002), for example, found no direct impact of natural resource abundance on economic growth from 1970 to 1990, but showed an important indirect effect through the impact of those resources on corruption, which, in turn, negatively affects growth (e.g. Mauro, 1995).

Isham et al. (2005) and Sala-i-Martin and Subramanian (2003), confirm Mauro's results by examining the influence of natural resources on broader indicators of institutional quality and policies. These studies showed that, for a given level of institutional quality, natural resource abundance has no direct impact on growth. Natural resource abundance undermines growth indirectly, through institutional quality, but only when resources are geographically concentrated (these agglomerations of resources are also known as "resource points"). These recent studies therefore explain the resource curse through the negative effect of geographically concentrated resources on the quality of institutions.

But it is critical to distinguish between policies and institutions and how they may reinforce each other in a chicken-and-egg manner. The distinction between policies and institutions is also important because the way each evolves or emerges may be different, with differentiated demands to "succeed." Brunnschweiler and Bulte (2009) outline two approaches to assessing institutions: one that conceptualizes institutions as "deep and durable" features of societies, traditionally used in resource curse studies, and another that looks at institutions as reflecting a flux of policy-implementation outcomes (see Torres et al., 2013 for further discussions). Humphreys et al. (2007) discuss how policies may constrain the choices of public and private actors bent on otherwise undermining social-welfare goals in oil-producing states, especially where institutions are not strong.

A number of studies have sought to outline the challenges of policy – especially fiscal policy – in dealing with the high volatility of natural resources (e.g. Davis, 2001, 2003; Atkinson and Hamilton, 2003; Bleaney and Halland, 2009) and the ramifications for long-term growth prospects. For example, Atkinson and Hamilton (2003) argue that the curse may be a manifestation of the inability of governments to manage large resource revenues sustainably. They emphasized cases where the combination of natural resources, macroeconomic and public expenditure policies has led to a low rate of genuine saving. Davis (2001) demonstrates the importance of stabilization funds for non-renewable resources in dealing with the challenges of high volatility and uncertainty of revenue streams. Botswana, an example of good public management of natural resource revenues, saves part of those proceeds and distributes them between generations through a public fund – the Pula Fund.

In a slightly different vein, Papyrakis and Gerlagh (2007) provide evidence of a resource curse within regions of the United States. They show that, even in a developed economy, resource abundance (as measured by the primary sector share in gross state product) fosters corruption (correlated to poor institutions), reduces investment, schooling, and R&D.

Also of note are the studies by Sala-i-Martin and Subramanian (2003) and Bulte et al. (2005) showing that the resources that undermine institutional quality and thereby growth include oil and some particular minerals, but not agricultural resources (for whatever reasons). Isham et al. (2005) show that the commodities that are damaging to institutional development (or "point source" resources) are, in addition to oil: minerals, plantation crops, and coffee and cocoa. Essentially, institutional quality is critical for long-term growth under either a commodity boom or bane.

Evidence 6: Unsustainability of long-term growth by means of commodities

Another argument pointing to the problems of dependence on commodities is linked to the sustainability of "good times" even if prices were to remain stable. The growth prospect of the economy is undermined by unsustainably rapid depletion of resources – especially in the cases on non-renewable items.

How should society react when a depletable natural resource is indeed depleted? What does this mean for the long-term growth prospects of a continent such as Africa with a large part of its many economies being nature-dependent? This question is of concern not only to environmentalists but to everyone in light of current debates around climate change and the need to manage environmental assets sustainably. The possibility of depletion is one motivation for the strategy of diversifying the economy beyond natural resources into other sectors (Frankel, 2012a; Ben Hammouda et al., 2006). Depletion is also a reason to make significant savings of the rents from exhaustible natural resources to stabilize inter-generational income or flow of consumption after an exhaustion of total wealth (Hartwick, 1977; Solow, 1986).

The issue of natural resource governance has gained greater currency in recent years with a number of initiatives such as the Extractive Industries Transparency Initiative (EITI) and the Africa Mining Vision to tackle excesses that undermine beneficiation as well as conservation and sustainable usage. Sometimes it is the government that has control of the natural resource, and excessive depletion shows failure in governance (Frankel, 2012a). The political elite are known to extract at a rate in excess of the efficient path because they over-discount the future (Robinson et al., 2006) and are more intent on surviving the next election or coup attempt. In this regard, privatization and other private-sector involvement provides a possible answer to the problem of excessive depletion, if a full assignment of property rights were possible to allow for adequate incentive to conserve the resource in question. Unfortunately, it is often not possible, either physically or politically, to guarantee these rights. The difficulty in enforcing property rights over some non-renewable resources constitutes a category of natural resource curse of its own and has been one of the many reasons undermining private-sector engagement in schemes such as public–private partnerships and other development contracts (Farlam, 2005).

Because of the desire to extract rents, a government's physical possession of mineral wealth may undermine the motivation to establish a broad-based regime of property rights for the rest of the economy, on the one hand, and on the other, some natural resources do not lend themselves to property rights whether the government wants to apply them or not. The latter is relevant if these are "open access" resources due to the "tragedy of the commons." The difficulty in imposing property rights to control depletion is particularly extreme when the resource is dispersed over a wide area, as timberland and other biodiversity assets. Unenforceability means that the resource will be depleted more rapidly than predicted by optimal calculations (Dasgupta and Heal, 1985). By extension, free trade might become undesirable: a society or country might be better off without the ability to sell/export the resource, if doing so exacerbates the excess rate of exploitation (Brander and Taylor, 1997).

Frankel (2012a) defines common pool resources as those that are at the same time (i) subtractable (as are private goods) and (ii) costly to exclude users from consuming (as are public goods), while yet (iii) not impossible to exclude users from (Ostrom and Ostrom, 1977). Enforcement of property rights is all the more difficult in a frontier situation (Barbier, 2005a, 2005b, 2007; Findlay and Lundahl, 1994, 2001) in which there is a mad rush, such as the uncontrolled logging in the equatorial forests of the Congo.

Resource depletion creates the possibility for conflict. Conflict, especially when violent, is deleterious to economic development. Where extraction of a valuable resource such as oil or diamonds is not regulated and production does not require substantial inputs of labor and capital investment, factions are more likely to fight over it, with significant opportunity for criminality, such as the case has been in DRC and recently in Angola, Sierra Leone, and Liberia. Some studies have shown that economic dependence on oil and mineral wealth is correlated with civil war (De Soysa, 2000; Fearon and Laitin, 2003; Collier and Hoeffler, 2004; Humphreys, 2005; Collier, 2007).

Evidence 7: Estimating volatility in commodity prices on economic growth

Commodity prices are known to be highly volatile. The world market prices for oil and natural gas are the most volatile of all, but aluminum, bananas, coffee, copper, sugar, and others are close behind (Frankel, 2012a).

Although intuitive conclusions could be drawn, some studies have made attempts to show precisely that volatility of natural resource prices is bad for long-term economic growth (Blattman et al., 2007; Hausmann and Rigobon, 2003; Poelhekke and van der Ploeg, 2008). Cyclical adjustments of the factors of production (labor, land, and capital) back and forth across sectors – mineral, agricultural, manufacturing, services – may impose needless transaction costs on the economy. Frictional unemployment, underutilization of the capital stock, and incomplete occupancy of housing are deadweight costs that the economy could do without.

So what is the fundamental reason for the volatility? Frankel (2012a) explained it in terms of low short-run elasticities. Any given increase in price does not cause demand to fall much in the short run nor supply to rise. Demand elasticities are low in the short run mostly because the capital stock at any point in time is designed physically to operate within a particular input–output ratio. Supply elasticities tend to be low in the short run because output adjusts with significant time lags. Whenever there is a shock, such as a bad harvest (reducing the supply of agricultural products) or a cold winter (raising demand for energy products), the corresponding price has to rise hugely to clear the market.

It is to be noted that positing that a country endowed with commodities suffers more volatility than others is not to suggest that it would benefit from barriers to trade. The classical gains from international trade can apply also in the case of commodity volatility, as international integration offers opportunities to diversify shocks (Jacks et al., 2011). Indeed, experiences of regional blocs such as the Common Market of East and Southern Africa (COMESA) and the East African Community (ECA) show the importance of regional integration in the "battle" against commodity price and supply volatility within a global context. These blocs have allowed members to diversify their market bases in the face of volatility away from traditional importers.

The existing literature on commodity prices has tended to study three issues: (i) characteristics and determinants of commodity price volatility, (ii) its macroeconomic effects, and (iii) the optimal policy responses to volatility. The first stream of the literature (i) use stylized facts about real commodity prices (Cashin et al., 2004; Deaton, 1999): a strong asymmetry of price cycles (a long-lasting downward trend is followed by a sharp upward) (Deaton and Laroque, 1992), a high persistence of shocks (Cashin et al., 2004), and a strong correlation between theoretically unrelated commodity prices (Pindyck and Rotemberg, 1990). Secondly, supply and demand constraints as well as commodity-market mechanisms are then used to explain these characteristics (Deaton and Miller, 1996; Akiyama et al., 2003). The third stream of literature (iii) outlines the appropriate policy responses to commodity price instability, highlighting the difficulty of either tackling the causes of volatility or offsetting its impact: buffer stocks, buffer funds, international commodity agreements to stabilize prices, government intervention in commodity markets, use of commodity derivative instruments for hedging against volatility and associated risks (Guillaumont, 1987; Larson et al., 1998; Varangis and Larson, 1996).

Many authors have also studied the importance of commodity volatility on growth. For example, Ramey and Ramey (1995) seek to identify the consequences of excess volatility for long-run growth. Blattman et al. (2007) test for the impact of terms-of-trade volatility on the growth performance of a panel of thirty-five commodity-dependent countries between 1870 and

1939. Their results show the adverse effects of volatility on foreign investment and economic growth in what they call "periphery" nations. Aghion et al. (2009), using a system generalized method of moments (GMM) dynamic panel data method for eighty-three countries over 1960–2000, show that higher levels of exchange-rate volatility can stunt growth, especially in countries with relatively underdeveloped capital markets. Bleaney and Greenaway (2001) estimate a panel data model for a sample of fourteen sub-Saharan African countries over the period 1980 to 1995 and show that growth is negatively affected by terms-of-trade volatility, and investment is affected by real exchange-rate instability. Van der Ploeg and Poelhekke (2009) find that the volatility of unanticipated GDP per capita growth has a significant negative impact on economic growth.

Collier and Goderis (2007), using panel cointegration methodology, find that commodity booms have positive short-term effects on output but adverse long-term effects. The long-term effects are confined to "high-rent," non-agricultural commodities. Within this group, we find that the resource curse is avoided by countries with sufficiently good institutions. The study sought to investigate possible transmission channels and found that real exchange-rate appreciation, public and private consumption, and, to a lesser extent, external debt, manufacturing, and services, explain the resource curse. This lends support to the large literature that stresses the importance of Dutch disease in resource-rich economies. It also supports the theory that points to inefficient redistribution in return for political support as the root of the negative effects of natural resource abundance on long-term growth. Their findings have important implications for non-agricultural commodity exporters with weak institutions, many of which are located in sub-Saharan Africa.

Cavalcanti et al. (2014) study the impact of the growth and volatility of commodity terms of trade (CToT) on economic growth, total factor productivity, physical capital accumulation, and human capital acquisition. They use the standard system GMM approach as well as the dynamic common correlated effects pooled mean group (CCEPMG) methodology for estimation to account for cross-country heterogeneity, cross-sectional dependence, and feedback effects. Using both annual data for 1970–2007 and five-year non-overlapping observations, their study finds that while CToT growth enhances real output per capita, CToT volatility exerts a negative impact on economic growth, operating mainly through lower accumulation of physical and human capital. Productivity, however, is not affected by either the growth or the volatility of CToT. The results suggest that the negative growth effects of CToT volatility offset the positive impact of commodity booms. Therefore, the general conclusion is that volatility, rather than abundance per se, drives the "resource curse" paradox – the negative effects of natural resource abundance on Africa's long-term growth prospects.

However, there are a number of skeptics that question whether there really is a natural resource curse and whether volatility as a given economic phenomenon is the problem. They point to examples of commodity-exporting countries that have done well, persuasively arguing that natural resource endowments do not necessarily doom a country to slow growth. Everyone recognizes that Norway is conspicuous as an oil producer at the top of the international league tables for governance and economic performance (Røed Larsen, 2004). Botswana and the DRC are both abundant in diamonds; yet Botswana is one of the best performers in terms of democracy, stability, and rapid growth of income (Engelbert, 2000; Sarraf and Jimanji, 2001; Acemoglu et al., 2003; Iimi, 2006), while the DRC is among the very worst on the continent (Beny and Cook, 2009).

The skeptics question the negative relationship even as a statistical generalization that holds on average. Delacroix (1977), Davis (1995), Herb (2005), and Alexeev and Conrad (2009) all find no statistical evidence of the natural resource curse.

Why do different studies come to opposite conclusions? In some cases, the explanation for different results may be that resource wealth may raise the *level* of per capita income, while reducing or failing to raise the *growth rate* of income (or the end-of-sample level of income, if the equation conditions on initial income) (Rodriguez and Sachs, 1999; Alexeev and Conrad, 2009). This is especially likely to make a difference if the data do not go back to a time before oil or minerals were discovered. Many authors argue that the important question is whether the country already has good institutions at the time that oil or other minerals are discovered. In which case, it is more likely to be put to use for the national welfare instead of the welfare of an elite (Mehlum et al., 2006; Robinson et al., 2006; McSherry, 2006; Smith, 2007; Collier and Goderis, 2007; Boschini et al., 2007).[3] Arezki and Van der Ploeg (2010) use instrumental variables to control for the endogenous component of institutional quality and trade; they confirm that the adverse effect of natural resources on growth is associated with exogenously poor institutions and, especially, if it is associated with exogenously low levels of trade.

The skeptics argue that "resource dependence" and commodity booms are not exogenous. In some cases, the crucial difference is whether "natural resource intensity" is measured by true endowments ("natural resource wealth") or rather by exports ("natural resource dependence"). The skeptics argue that commodity exports are highly endogenous (Maloney, 2002; Wright and Czelusta, 2003, 2004).[4] In other words, oil wealth is not necessarily the cause and institutions the effect; it could be the other way around.

The endogeneity can arise in several different ways. Industrialization may determine commodity exports rather than the other way around. The reverse causality could explain the negative correlation: those countries that fail at manufacturing have a comparative advantage at commodity exports, by default. Or the reverse causality might have a positive sign: good institutions and technological progress are just as useful for developing natural resources as they are for the other sectors of the economy, as the United States, Canada, Australia, and Chile have shown.[5]

We estimate a function to see the effects of volatility on growth in the tradition of Colliers and Goderis (2007). The general regression for testing the effects of volatility on growth needs to take into account the short-run and long-run effects of commodity export prices/rents on GDP. The specified model is given thus:

$$\Delta GDP_{it} = \alpha_0 + \alpha_1 PerCapitaGDP_{it} + \alpha_2 HumanCapital_{it} \\ + \alpha_3 FinancialDepth_{it} + \alpha_4 TradeOpenness_{it} + \alpha_5 FDI_{it} \\ + \alpha_6 CaptialFormation_{it} + \alpha_7 NaturalResources_{it} \\ + \alpha_8 Inflation_{it} + \alpha_9 Remittances_{it} + \alpha_{10} PoliticalStability_{it} \\ + \alpha_{11} Infrastructure_{it} + \varepsilon_{it} \tag{1}$$

The descriptions of the variables are given in Table 4.3 (see Annex). Three issues need to be raised with respect to the variables and model: (a) we proxy the quality of institutions through the political instability variable. Many of the measures of the quality of institutions and governance on the continent are not long series – for example: the Mo Ibrahim Index on Governance is less than a decade old; (b) the issue of diversification needed better capturing – herewith trade openness "proxy" is used – by using commodities share in GDP or some Herfindahl–Hirschman-type indicator; and (c) commodity volatility – where we include the share of natural resource rents in GDP as opposed to the commodity price index, given the unavailability of this data. We also use the inflation variable to test for the commodity terms of trade by including the US rate of inflation, but the results did not change significantly.

Our results are reported in Tables 4.4–4.8 in the Annex. We experimented with pooled ordinary least squares (OLS) and instrumental variable regressions. We also explored the use of country and year dummies to show how the equations behaved with respect to country- and time-specific effects. In the three estimation techniques, every variable used showed up as significant at least once, with the exceptions of political stability and infrastructure. Natural resources (rents) showed positive effects on growth within the context of a pooled regression with country and year dummies, thus not confirming a resource curse. Table 4.5 presents the correlation coefficients among the variables. Most are shown to be significant. GDP per capita is highly correlated with infrastructure and human capital, suggesting over-correction in the equations through its inclusion.

Our results could be read in line with those of a few other studies suggesting the resource curse may derive from weaker growth in the resource sector, given the persistence of other variables such as initial conditions, financial depth, FDI, human capital, trade openness and capital formation in the equations. For example, Davis's (2011) empirical study finds that the relatively slower growth in mineral and energy economies may simply reflect a resource drag whereby optimally managed per capita resource production does not grow substantially over time and hence introduces a drag on the measured growth of per capita economic output, which would have implications for trade and industrial policies implemented on the assumption that there are growth-reducing market failures associated with mineral and energy production (Torres et al., 2013).

A number of previous studies had raised the possibility of a resource drag, but Davis (2011) made the initial attempt to test the hypothesis. Sachs and Warner (1995) only mention the resource drag hypothesis without much focus on it. Alexeev and Conrad (2009) argued that while resource-based economies do not appear to have grown more slowly in the long run, they may well grow more slowly in the short run due to static or declining mineral production.

While the above argument of a resource drag is plausible, it does not explain why resource-rich countries such as Botswana have not been held back in their development, implying that other factors must also be at work. Indeed, other studies have shown that different resource proxies and statistical issues may also play a part in explaining the resource curse result (Torres et al., 2013).

With respect to the econometric "problems," Alexeev and Conrad (2009) point to the possible endogeneity of the initial income term included in cross-section resource curse regressions, an issue also highlighted by Herb (2005). Alexeev and Conrad (2009) and Herb (2005) argue that natural resource exports depend on domestic consumption, and both consumption and income may be correlated with democracy (in our case, political stability). Thus, the inclusion of the initial level of income introduces endogeneity if it is measured after oil discovery. The authors remove the oil component from the initial income level, and find that the oil curse disappears. On the other hand, Tsui (2011) stresses that fuel is a noisy measure of natural resources and, as a flow variable, it also understates the oil wealth of the swing producers who produce below their full capacity. Our own take is that the econometric question remains a work in progress that researchers in Africa's policy think-tanks and academic departments need to explore further as countries continue to refine their natural resource management tools.

Conclusion

We have noted that both natural resources and global volatility will continue to influence the debates around Africa's development agenda for decades to come. To date, theoretical propositions and associated statistical evidence imply that the existence of natural resources, be they renewable or non-renewable, can confer both negative and positive effects on a country, depending of the natural resource management and governance frameworks. We considered a number of channels whereby natural resources have been hypothesized to affect economic performance and outlined some specific actions that need to be taken to tame the effects of global commodity volatility on Africa's long-term growth prospects. Of note is that the Prebisch-Singer hypothesis of a negative long-term trend in commodity prices needs to be treated with caution because of empirical findings that there is no consistent trend either way. The call for managing volatility is based on a commonsense approach because it imposes risk and transaction costs on economies and thus must be avoided as much as possible. Second is the concern that specialization in natural resources can be detrimental to growth if it crowds out the manufacturing sector and the latter is the locus of positive externalities. In some instances, natural resource endowments lead to institutional decays, characterized by corruption, inequality, class structure, and absence of rule of law as well as human insecurity. Countries that are endowed with natural resources, such as the DRC and Nigeria, have over the years been affected by pockets of insecurity and armed conflict linked to resources. The absence of and difficulties of enforcing property rights can also exacerbate the incentive to deplete natural resource endowments too rapidly, leaving the country with few assets, including environmental ones. In concrete terms, African countries need to invest in building institutions that enhance beneficiation and natural resource governance, strengthen investments as well as savings from commodity booms using tools such as sovereign wealth funds, enhance regional integration to diversify markets, strengthen product diversification and develop the necessary skills base through professional and vocational training to absorb the shocks associated with declining sectors.

Notes

1 See also Ross (2001). But Mitchell (2012) refutes him. Ross (2012) is a humbled response to the skeptics with a hypothesis that the negative effect of oil began only after the oil price increases of the 1970s.
2 But other studies reject the implied causal link from resources to lack of democracy: see Karl (1997), Noland (2008), Dunning (2008), Wacziarg (2012), and Haber and Menaldo (2011), amongst others.
3 Bhattacharyya and Hodler (2009) provide evidence that natural resource rents lead to corruption, but only in the absence of high-quality democratic institutions.
4 The most common measure of endowments are endogenous by reflecting discoveries, which in turn respond to both world prices and the productivity of the exploration industry both globally and locally.
5 Norman (2009) suggests that the discovery and development of oil is not purely exogenous, but rather is endogenous with respect to, among other things, the efficiency of the economy.

References

Acemoglu, Daron, and J. Robinson (2012) *Why Nations Fail: The Origins of Power, Prosperity, and Poverty* (New York: Random House).
Acemoglu, Daron, Simon Johnson, and James Robinson (2003) "An African success: Botswana." In Dani Rodrik (ed.) *In Search of Prosperity: Analytic Narratives in Economic Growth* (Princeton, NJ: Princeton University Press).
Adenauer I., and L. Vagassky (1998) "Aid and the real exchange rate: Dutch disease effects in African countries." *Intereconomics* 33(4): 177–185.
Afeikhena, J., and O. Olawale (2000) *Characteristics and Behavior of African Commodity/Product Markets and Market Institutions and Their Consequences for Economic Growth*. Working Paper No. 35. New York: Center for International Development, Harvard University.

African Airlines Association (AFRAA) (2006) *Strategy for the Development of the Air Transport Industry in Africa*. Available at: http://christianfolly kossi.com/docs/FundingRequirementsSummary-TunisMay06.pdf (accessed May 6, 2016).

ACET (2013) *African Transformation Report: Growth with Depth*. Accra: ACET.

African Development Bank Group (AfDB) (2012) *African Development Report 2012: Towards Green Growth in Africa* (Tunis: AfDB).

African Development Bank Group, African Development Bank, Development Centre of the Organisation for Economic Co-operation and Development, United Nations Development Programme, and Economic Commission for Africa (2013) *African Economic Outlook 2013, Structural Transformation and Natural Resources* (Tunis: AfDB).

AfDB (2014) *Ending Conflict and Building Peace in Africa: A Call to Action – Report of the High Level Panel on Fragile States*. Tunis: African Development Bank.

Aghion, P., P. Bacchetta, R. Rancière, and K. Rogoff (2009) "Exchange rate volatility and productivity growth: The role of financial development." *Journal of Monetary Economics* 56: 494–513.

Akiyama, T., J. Baffes, D. F. Larson, and P. Varangis (2003) *Commodity Market Reform in Africa*. World Bank Policy Research Working Paper 2995.

Alden, C., and M. Schoeman, M. (2013) "South Africa in the company of giants: The search for leadership in a transforming global order." *International Affairs* 89(1): 111–129.

Alesina, Alberto, Filipe Campante, and Guido Tabellini (2008) "Why is fiscal policy often procyclical?" *Journal of the European Economic Association* 6(5): 1006–1036.

Alexeev, Michael, and Robert Conrad (2009) "The elusive curse of oil." *Review of Economics and Statistics* 91(3): 586–598.

Amuedo-Dorantes, C, and S. Pozo (2004) "Workers' remittances and the real exchange rate: A paradox of gifts." *World Development* 32(8): 1407–1417.

Arezki, Rabah, and Markus Brückner (2009) *Oil Rents, Corruption, and State Stability: Evidence From Panel Data Regressions*. IMF Working Papers 09/267, International Monetary Fund. University of Adelaide, School of Economics WP no. 2011-07.

Arezki, Rabah, and Markus Brückner (2010a) *International Commodity Price Shocks, Democracy, and External Debt*. IMF Working Paper 10/53 (Washington, DC: International Monetary Fund).

Arezki, Rabah, and Markus Brückner (2010b) *Resource Windfalls and Emerging Market Sovereign Bond Spreads: The Role of Political Institutions* (Washington, DC: International Monetary Fund).

Arezki, Rabah, and Frederick van der Ploeg (2010) "Trade policies, institutions and the natural resource curse." *Applied Economics Letters* 17(15): 1443–1451.

Arezki, Rabah, Kirk Hamilton and Kazim Kazimov (2011) *Resource Windfalls, Macroeconomic Stability and Growth: The Role of Political Institutions* (International Monetary Fund: Washington DC).

Atkinson, Giles and Kirk Hamilton (2003) "Savings, growth and the resource curse hypothesis." *World Development* 31(11): 1793–1807.

Auty, Richard M. (1986) "Resource-based industrialization and country-size: Venezuela and Trinidad and Tobago." *Geoforum* 17(3–4): 325–410.

Auty, Richard (1990) *Resource-Based Industrialization: Sowing the Oil in Eight Developing Countries* (Oxford: Clarendon Press).

Auty, Richard M. (1993) *Sustaining Development in Mineral Economies: The Resource Curse Thesis* (New York: Oxford University Press).

Auty, Richard M. (1994) "Industrial policy reform in six large newly industrialized countries: The resource curse thesis." *World Development* 12(1): 11–26.

Auty, Richard M. (2001a) "Introduction and overview." In Richard M. Auty (ed.) *Resource Abundance and Economic Development* (Oxford: Oxford University Press), 3–16.

Auty, Richard M. (2001b) "Conclusions: Resource abundance, growth collapses, and policy." In Richard M. Auty (ed.) *Resource Abundance and Economic Development* (Oxford: Oxford University Press), 315–328.

Auty, Richard (2007) "Patterns of rent-extraction and deployment in developing countries: Implications for governance, economic policy and performance." In G. Mavrotas and A. Shorrocks (eds) *Advancing Development: Core Themes in Global Economics* (London: Palgrave), 555–577.

Balagtas, Joseph, and Matthew Holt (2009) "The commodity terms of trade, unit roots and nonlinear alternatives: A smooth transition approach." *American Journal of Agricultural Economics* 91(1): 87–105.

Barbier, Edward (2005a) "Frontier expansion and economic development." *Contemporary Economic Policy* 23(2): 286–303.

Barbier, Edward (2005b) *Natural Resources and Economic Development* (Cambridge, UK: Cambridge University Press).

Barbier, Edward (2007) "Frontiers and sustainable economic development." *Environmental and Resource Economics* 37: 271–295.

Barro, Robert (1991) "Economic growth in a cross-section of countries." *Quarterly Journal of Economics*, CVI: 407–444.

Barro, Robert (2000) "Inequality and growth in a panel of countries." *Journal of Economic Growth* 5: 5–28.

Behrman, J. (1987) "Commodity price instability and economic goal attainment in developing countries." *World Development* 15(5): 559–573.

Beny, Laura, and Lisa Cook (2009) "Metals or Management? Explaining Africa's Recent Economic Growth Performance." *American Economic Review* 99(2): 268–274.

Bhattacharyya, Sambit, and Roland Hodler (2009) "Natural Resources, Democracy and Corruption." *European Economic Review* 53: 293–308.

Birdsall, N., T. Pinckney, and R. Sabot (2001) "Natural resources, human capital, and growth." In Richard M. Auty (ed.) *Resource Abundance and Economic Development* (Oxford: Oxford University Press).

Blattman, Christopher, Jason Hwang, and Jeffrey Williamson (2007) "Winners and losers in the commodity lottery: The impact of terms of trade growth and volatility in the Periphery 1870–1939." *Journal of Development Economics* 82(1): 156–179.

Bleaney, M., and D. Greenaway (2001) "The impact of terms of trade and real exchange rate volatility on investment and growth in sub-Saharan Africa." *Journal of Development Economics* 65(2): 491–500.

Bleaney, M., and H. Halland (2009) *The Resource Curse And Fiscal Policy Volatility.* CREDIT Research Paper No. 9.

Boschini, Anne, Jan Pettersson, and Jesper Roine (2007) "Resource curse or not: A question of appropriability." *Scandinavian Journal of Economics* 109(3): 593–617.

Brander, James, and M. Scott Taylor (1997) "International trade and open-access renewable resources: The small economy." *Canadian Journal of Economics* 30(3): 526–552.

Bravo-Ortega, C., and J. Gregorio (2007) "The relative richness of the poor? Natural resources, human capital and economic growth." In D. Lederman and W. Maloney (eds) *Resources: Neither Curse nor Destiny* (Washington, DC: Stanford University Press), 71–99.

Brunnschweiler, Christa, and Erwin Bulte (2009) "Natural resources and violent conflict: resource abundance, dependence, and the onset of civil wars." *Oxford Economic Papers* 61(4): 651–674.

Bulte, Erwin, Richard Damania, and Robert Deacon (2005) "Resource intensity, institutions and development." *World Development* 33(7): 1029–1044.

Caselli, Francesco (2006) *Power Struggles and the Natural Resource Curse*. LSE Research Paper, London School of Economics.

Cashin, P., C. McDermott, C. John, and C. Pattillo (2004) "Terms of trade shocks in Africa: Are they short-lived or long-lived?" *Journal of Development Economics* 73(2): 727–744.

Cavalcanti, T. V. De V., K. Mohaddes, and M. Raissi (2014) "Commodity price volatility and the sources of growth." *Journal of Applied Econometrics* 30(6): 857–873.

Chen, Yu-Chin, and Kenneth Rogoff (2003) "Commodity currencies." *Journal of International Economics* 60(1): 133–160.

Collier, Paul (2007) *The Bottom Billion: Why the Poorest Countries Are Falling Behind and What Can Be Done About It* (Oxford: Oxford University Press).

Collier, Paul, and Benedikt Goderis (2007) *Commodity Prices, Growth, and the Natural Resource Curse: Reconciling a Conundrum*. Centre for the Study of African Economies Working Paper Series, 274.

Collier, Paul, and Anke Hoeffler (2004) "Greed and grievance in civil war." *Oxford Economic Papers* 56(4): 563–595.

Corden, W. Max and J. Peter Neary (1982) "Booming sector and de-industrialisation in a small open economy." *The Economic Journal* 92(368): 825–848.

Cuddington, John (1989) "Commodity export booms in developing countries." *World Bank Research Observer* 4: 143–165.

Cuddington, John (1992) "Long-run trends in 26 primary commodity prices." *Journal of Development Economics* 39, 207–227.

Cuddington, John, and Daniel Jerrett (2008) "Super cycles in real metals prices?" *IMF Staff Papers*, 55, December, 541–565.

Cuddington, John, and Carlos M. Urzua (1989) "Trends and cycles in the net barter terms of trade: A new approach." *Economic Journal* 99: 426–442.

Cuddington, John, Rodney Ludema, and Shamila Jayasuriya (2007) "Prebisch-Singer redux." In D. Lederman and W. F. Maloney (eds) *Natural Resources: Neither Curse Nor Destiny* (Washington, DC: Stanford University Press), 103–140.

Dasgupta, Partha, and Geoffrey Heal (1985) *Economic Theory and Exhaustible Resources* (Cambridge, UK: Cambridge University Press).

Davis, Graham (1995) "Learning to love the Dutch disease: Evidence from the mineral economies." *World Development* 23: 1765–1779.

Davis, G. A. (2011) "The resource drag." *International Economics and Economic Policy* 8: 155–176.

Davis, J. (2001) *Stabilization and Savings Funds for Non-Renewable Resources: Experience and Fiscal Policy Implications* (Washington, DC: International Monetary Fund).

Davis, J. (2003) *Fiscal Policy Formulation and Implementation in Oil-Producing Countries* (Washington, DC: International Monetary Fund).

Dawe, D. (1996) "A new look at the growth in developing countries." *World Development* 24(12): 1905–1914.

Deaton, A. (1999) "Commodity prices and growth in Africa." *Journal of Economic Perspectives* 13(3): 23–40.

Deaton, A., and R. Miller (1996) "International commodity prices, macroeconomic performance and politics in Sub-Saharan Africa." *Journal of African Economies* 5(3): 99–191.

Deaton, A., and G. Laroque (1992) "On the behavior of commodity prices." *Review of Economic Studies* 59: 1–24.

Delacroix, Jacques (1977) "The export of raw materials and economic growth: A cross-national study." *American Sociological Review* 42: 795–808.

De Soysa, Indra (2000) "The resource curse: Are civil wars driven by rapacity or paucity?" In M. Berdal and D. Malone (eds) *Greed and Grievance: Economic Agendas in Civil War* (Boulder, CO: Lynne Rienner), 113–135.

de Vries, G., M. Timmer, and K. de Vries (2015) "Structural transformation in Africa: Static gains, dynamic losses." *The Journal of Development Studies* 51(6): 674–688.

Dunning, Thad (2008) *Crude Democracy: Natural Resource Wealth and Political Regimes* (New York: Cambridge University Press).

Easterly, Willliam, and Ross Levine (1997): "Africa's growth tragedy: Policies and ethnic divisions." *Quarterly Journal of Economics* 112(4): 1203–1250.

Easterly, William, and Ross Levine (2002) *Tropics, Germs, and Endowments.* NBER WP No. 9106; Carnegie-Rochester Conference Series on Public Policy.

Edwards, Sebastian (1986) "A commodity export boom and the real exchange rate: The money-inflation link." In J. P. Neary and S. van Wijnbergen (eds) *Natural Resources and the Macroeconomy* (Cambridge: MIT Press).

Englebert, Pierre (2000) *State Legitimacy and Development in Africa* (Boulder, CO: Lynne Rienner).

EPRC, KIPPRA, and Brookings Institution (2013) *Oil and Gas Management for Inclusive and Sustainable Development: an East African Regional Forum.* " Proceedings Report Available at: www.brookings.edu/~/media/Research/Files/Papers/2013/3/07-oil-gas-management-africa/0307--nrm-conference.pdf?la=en (accessed May 6, 2016).

Farlam, P. (2005) "Working together: Assessing public–private partnerships in Africa." SAIIA NEPAD Policy Focus Series Report 2. Available at: http://saiia.org.za/images/upload/PPP-NepadReport-Final9Feb05.pdf (accessed May 7, 2016).

Fearon, James, and David Laitin (2003) "Ethnicity, insurgence and civil war." *American Political Science Review* 97(2): 75–90.

Findlay, Ronald, and Mats Lundahl (1994) "Natural resources 'vent for surplus' and the staple theory." In Gerald Meier (ed.) *From Classical Economics to Development Economics: Essays in Honor of Hla Myint* (New York: St. Martin's Press).

Findlay, Ronald, and Mats Lundahl (2001) "Natural resources and economic development: The 1870–1914 experience." In Richard Auty (ed.) *Resource Abundance and Economic Development* (World Institute for Development Economics Research).

Forsyth, P. (1985) "Booming sectors and structural change in Australia and Britain: A comparison." In Neary, P., and Van Wijnbergen, S. (eds) *Natural Resources and the Macroeconomy* (Oxford: Blackwell).

Fosu, A. (1996) "Primary exports and economic growth in developing countries." *World Economy*, 19(4), 465–475.

Frankel, Jeffrey (2012a) *The Natural Resource Curse: A Survey of Diagnoses and Some Prescriptions.* HKS Faculty Research Working Paper Series RWP12-014. John F. Kennedy School of Government, Harvard University.

Frankel, Jeffrey (2012b) "A solution to fiscal procyclicality: The structural budget institutions pioneered by Chile." Paper in *Fiscal Policy and Macroeconomic Performance*, Fourteenth Annual Conference of the Central Bank of Chile. NBER WP No. 16945.

Gavin, Michael and Roberto Perotti (1997) "Fiscal policy in Latin America." *NBER Macroeconomics Annual* 12: 11–61.

Gelb, A. (1986) "Adjustment to windfall gains: A comparative analysis of oil-exporting countries." In J. Peter Neary and Sweder van Wijnbergen (eds) *Natural Resources and the Macroeconomy: A Theoretical Framework* (Cambridge, MA: MIT Press), 54–93.

Grilli, Enzo, and Maw Cheng Yang (1988) "Primary commodity prices, manufactured goods prices, and the terms of trade of developing countries: What the long run shows." *World Bank Economic Review* 2(1): 1–47.

Guillaumont, P. (1987) "From export instability effects to international stabilization policies." *World Development* 15(5): 633–643.

Gylfason, Thorvaldur (2000) "Resources, agriculture and economic growth in economies in transition." *Kyklos* 53(4): 545–579.

Gylfason, Thorvaldur (2001a) *Natural Resources and Economic Growth: What Is the Connection?* CESifo Working Paper No. 50.

Gylfason, Thorvaldur (2001b) "Natural resources, education and economic development." *European Economic Review* 45(4): 847–859.

Gylfason, Thorvaldur, Tryggvi Thor Herbertsson, and Gylfi Zoega (1999) "A mixed blessing." *Macroeconomic Dynamics* 3: 204–225.

Haber, Stephen, and Victor Menaldo (2011) "Do natural resources fuel authoritarianism? a reappraisal of the resource curse." *American Political Science Review* 105(1): 1–26.

Hadass, Yael, and Jeffrey Williamson (2003) "Terms of trade shocks and economic performance 1870–1940: Prebisch and Singer revisited." *Economic Development and Cultural Change* 51(3): 629–566.

Hall, Robert, and Chad Jones (1999) "Why do some countries produce so much more output per worker than others?" *Quarterly Journal of Economics* 114(1): 83–116.

Hamilton, J. D. (1983) "Oil and the macroeconomy since World War II." *Journal of Political Economy* 91: 228–248.

Hammouda B., Hakim, Stephen Karingi, Angelica Njuguna, and Mustapha Sadni Jallab (2006) *Diversification: Towards A New Paradigm For Africa's Development*. MPRA Paper No. 13359. Available at: https://ideas.repec.org/p/pra/mprapa/13359.html (accessed May 6, 2016).

Harding, T., and A. J. Venables (2010) *Foreign Exchange Windfalls, Imports and Exports*. Mimeo, University of Oxford, UK.

Hartwick, John (1977) "Intergenerational equity and the investing of rents from exhaustible resources." *American Economic Review* 67(5): 972–974.

Harvey, David, Neil Kellard, Jakob Madsen, and Mark Wohar (2010) "The Prebisch-Singer Hypothesis: Four centuries of evidence." *Review of Economics and Statistics* 92(2): 367–377.

Hausmann, Ricardo, and Roberto Rigobon (2003) "An alternative interpretation of the "resource curse": Theory and policy implications." In Jeffrey Davis (ed.) *Fiscal Policy Formulation and Implementation in Oil-Producing Countries* (Washington, DC: International Monetary Fund), 12–44.

Herb, Michael (2005) "No representation without taxation? Rents, development and democracy." *Comparative Politics* 37(3): 297–317.

Hirschman, A. (1958) *The Strategy of Economic Development*. New Haven, CT: Yale University Press.

Hodler, Roland (2006) "The curse of natural resources in fractionalized countries." *European Economic Review* 50(6): 1367–1386.

Hotelling, Harold (1931) "The economics of exhaustible resources." *Journal of Political Economy* 39(2): 137–175.

Humphreys, Macartan (2005) "Natural resources, conflicts, and conflict resolution: Uncovering the mechanisms." *Journal of Conflict Resolution* 49: 508–537.

Humphreys, Macartan, Jeffrey Sachs, and Joseph Stiglitz (2007) *Escaping the Resource Curse* (New York: Columbia University Press).

Huntington, Samuel (1991) *The Third Wave: Democratization in the Late Twentieth Century* (Norman, OK: University of Oklahoma Press).

Iimi, Atsushi (2006) *Did Botswana Escape from the Resource Curse?* IMF Working Paper No. 06/138, June.

Ilzetski, Ethan, and Carlos Végh (2008) *Procyclical Fiscal Policy in Developing Countries: Truth or Fiction?* NBER WP no. 14191.

Isham, Jonathan, Michael Woolcock, Lant Pritchett, and Gwen Busby (2005) "The varieties of resource experience: Natural resource export structures and the political economy of economic growth." *The World Bank Economic Review* 19(2): 141–174.

Jacks, David, Kevin O'Rourke, and Jeffrey Williamson (2011) "Commodity price volatility and world market integration." *Review of Economics and Statistics* 93(3): 800–813.

Jensen, Nathan, and Leonard Wantchekon (2004) "Resource wealth and political regimes in Africa." *Comparative Political Studies* 37: 816–841.

Kaldor, M., T. L. Karl, and Y. Said (eds) (2007) *Oil Wars* (London: Pluto Press).

Kaldor, N. (1972) "The irrelevance of equilibrium economics." *Economic Journal* 92(328): 1237–1255.

Kalecki, M. (1976) *Essays on Developing Economies*. Hassocks, UK, Harvester Press.

Kaminsky, Graciela, Carmen Reinhart, and Carlos Végh (2004) "When it rains, it pours: Procyclical capital flows and macroeconomic policies." *NBER Macroeconomics Annual 2004* 19: 11–82.

Karl, Terry Lynn (1997) *The Paradox of Plenty: Oil Booms and Petro-States* (Berkeley, CA: University of California Press).

Kellard, Neil, and Mark Wohar (2006) "On the prevalence of trends in primary commodity prices." *Journal of Development Economics* 79(1): 146–167.

Krause, L. B. (1995) "Social capability and long-term economic growth." In B. H. Koo and D. H. Perkins, (eds) *Social Capability and Long-term Economic Growth* (New York: Macmillan).

La Porta, R., and Andrei Shleifer (2008) "The unofficial economy and economic development." *Brookings Papers on Economic Activity, Economic Studies Program, The Brookings Institution* 39(2): 275–363.

Lal, D., and H. Myint (1996) *The Political Economy of Poverty, Equity and Growth* (Oxford: Clarendon Press).

Larsen, E. R. (2006) "Escaping the resource curse and the Dutch disease?" *American Journal of Economic Sociology* 65(3): 605–640.

Larson, D. F., P. Varangis, and N. Yabuki (1998) *Commodity Risk Management and Development*. World Bank Policy Research Paper No. 1963.

Lartey, E., F. Mandelman, and P. Acosta (2008) *Remittances, Exchange Rate Regimes and the Dutch Disease: A Panel Data Analysis.* Federal Reserve Bank of Atlanta Working Paper 2008–12.

Lederman, Daniel, and William Maloney (2008) "In search of the missing resource curse." *Economia* 9(1): 1–56.

Leite, Carlos, and Jens Weidmann (1999) *Does Mother Nature Corrupt?* IMF Working Paper 99/85, July.

Leite, Carlos, and Jens Weidmann (2002) "Does Mother Nature corrupt? Natural resources, corruption, and economic growth." In George T. Abed and Sanjeev Gupta (eds) *Governance, Corruption, and Economic Performance* (Washington, DC: IMF), 159–196.

Luciani, Giacomo (1987) "Allocation versus production states: A theoretical framework." In Hazem Beblawi and Giacomo Luciani (eds) *The Rentier State* (New York: Croom Helm), 63–82.

Lundgren, Charlotte J., Alun H. Thomas, and Robert C. York (2013) *Boom, Bust, or Prosperity? Managing Sub-Saharan Africa's Natural Resource Wealth.* IMF Departmental Paper No. 13/2.

Lutz, M. (1994) "The effects of volatility in the terms of trade on output growth: New evidence." *World Development* 22(12): 1959–1975.

McKinsey Global Institute (2010) *Lion on the Move: The Progress and Potential of African Economies.* Washington, DC: McKinsey Global Institute. Available at: www.mckinsey.com/global-themes/middle-east-and-africa/lions-on-the-move.

McMahon, G. (1997) *The Natural Resource Curse: Myth or Reality?* Mimeo, World Bank Institute.

McSherry, Brendan (2006) "The political economy of oil in Equatorial Guinea." *African Studies Quarterly* 8: 23–45.

Mahdavi, H. (1970) "The patterns and problems of economic development in rentier states: The case of Iran." In M. Cook (ed.) *Studies in the Economic History of the Middle East* (Oxford: Oxford University Press).

Makochekanwa, A. (2007) *An empirical test of the Dutch Disease hypothesis on Botswana's main exports.* Mimeo, University of Pretoria. Available at: https://www.gtap.agecon.purdue.edu/resources/download/4244.pdf.

Maloney, William (2002) "Missed opportunities: Innovation, natural resources and growth in Latin America." *Economia* 3(1): 111–169.

Manzano, Osmel, and Roberto Rigobon (2008) "Resource curse or debt overhang?" *Economia* 9(1).

Matsuyama, Kiminori (1992) "Agricultural productivity, comparative advantage, and economic growth." *Journal of Economic Theory* 58: 317–334.

Mauro, P. (1995) "Corruption and growth." *Quarterly Journal of Economics* 110(3): 681–712.

Medas, Paolo, and Daria Zakharova (2009) *Primer on Fiscal Analysis in Oil-Producing Countries.* IMF Working Paper 56 (Washington, DC, IMF).

Mehlum, Halvor, Karl Moene, and Ragnar Torvik (2006) "Institutions and the resource curse." *Economic Journal* 116(508): 1–20.

Melina, G., and Y. Xiong (2013) *Natural Gas, Public Investment and Debt Sustainability in Mozambique.* IMF Working Paper, WP/13/261, November. Available at www.imf.org/external/pubs/ft/wp/2013/wp13261.pdf (accessed June14, 2014).

Mendoza, Enrique, and P. Marcelo Oviedo (2006) *Fiscal Policy and Macroeconomic Uncertainty in Developing Countries: The Tale of the Tormented Insurer.* NBER Working Paper No. 12586, October 2006.

Mikesell, Raymond (1997) "Explaining the resource curse, with special reference to mineral-exporting countries." *Resources Policy* 23(4): 191–199.

Mitchell, Timothy (2012) *Carbon Democracy: Political Power in the Age of Oil* (London: Verso).

Moran, C. (1983) "Export fluctuations and economic growth." *Journal of Development Economics* 12(1): 195–218.

Ncube, M., and A. Shimeles (2012) *The Making of the Middle Class in Africa*. African Development Bank. Available at: www.afdb.org/fileadmin/uploads/afdb/Documents/Knowledge/AEC%202012%20-%20%20The%20Making%20of%20the%20Middle%20Class%20in%20Africa.pdf (accessed May 6, 2016).

Neary, J. Peter, and Sweder van Wijnbergen (1986) "Natural resources and the macroeconomy: A theoretical framework." In P. J. Neary and S. van Wijnbergen (eds) *Natural Resources and the Macroeconomy* (Cambridge, MA: MIT Press), 13–45.

Noland, Marcus (2008) "Explaining Middle Eastern political authoritarianism I: The level of democracy." *Review of Middle East Economics and Finance* 4(1): 1–30.

Norman, Catherine (2009) "Rule of law and the resource curse: Abundance versus intensity." *Environmental Resource Economics* 43(2): 183–207.

Ostrom, Elinor, and Vincent Ostrom (1977) "Public goods and public choices." In Emanuel Savas (ed.) *Alternatives for Delivering Public Services: Toward Improved Performance* (Boulder, CO: Westview Press), 7–49.

Papyrakis, E., and R. Gerlagh (2004) "The resource curse hypothesis and its transmission channels." *Journal of Comparative Economics* 32(1): 181–193.

Papyrakis, E., and R. Gerlagh (2007) "Resource abundance and economic growth in the US." *European Economic Review* 51(4): 1011–1039.

Papyrakis, E., and O. Raveh (2013) *An Empirical Analysis of a Regional Dutch Disease: The Case of Canada*. OxCarre Research Paper 106. Available at: www.oxcarre.ox.ac.uk/files/OxCarreRP2013106%281%29.pdf (accessed May 6, 2016).

Pindyck, Robert (1999) "The long-run evolution of energy prices." *The Energy Journal* 20(2): 1–27.

Pindyck, Robert, and Julio Rotemberg (1990) "The excess co-movement of commodity prices." *The Economic Journal* 100(403): 1173–1189.

Poelhekke, Steven, and Frederick van der Ploeg (2008) *Volatility, Financial Development and the Natural Resource Curse*. Report CEPR DP6513.

Prebisch, Raul (1950) *The Economic Development of Latin America and Its Principal Problems* (New York: United Nations).

Rajan, R., and A. Subramanian (2009) "Aid, Dutch Disease and manufacturing growth." *Journal of Development Economics* 94(1): 106–118.

Ramey, G., and V. A. Ramey (1995) "Cross-country evidence on the link between volatility and growth." *American Economic Review* 85(5): 1138–1151.

Reinhart, Carmen, and Peter Wickham (1994) "Commodity prices: Cyclical weakness or secular decline?" *IMF Staff Papers* 41, June.

Robinson, James, Ragnar Torvik, and Thierry Verdier (2006) "Political foundations of the resource curse." *Journal of Development Economics* 79(2): 446–468.

Rodriguez, Francisco, and Jeffrey Sachs (1999) "Why do resource-abundant economies grow more slowly?" *Journal of Economic Growth* 4(3): 277–303.

Rodrik, Dani (2007) "Industrial development: Some stylized facts and policy directions." In United Nations, *Industrial Development for the 21st Century* (New York: United Nations), 7–28.

Rodrik, Dani (2011) "The future of economic convergence." NBER Working Paper 17400, Available at: www.nber.org/papers/w17400 (accessed May 7, 2016).

Rodrik, Dani (2014) *An African Growth Miracle?* Paper Written for the Centre for Global Development, Richard H. Sabot Lecture. Available at: http://drodrik.scholar.harvard.edu/files/dani-rodrik/files/an_african_growth_miracle.pdf?m=1435002878 (accessed May 6, 2016).

Rodrik, Dani, Arvind Subramanian, and Francesco Trebbi (2003) "Institutions rule: The primacy of institutions over geography and integration in economic development." *Journal of Economic Growth* 9(2): 131–165.

Røed Larsen, Erling (2004) *Escaping the Resource Curse and the Dutch Disease? When and Why Norway Caught up with and Forged ahead of Its Neighbors.* Discussion Papers No. 377, May, Statistics Norway, Research Department.

Ross, Michael (2001) "Does oil hinder democracy?" *World Politics* 53(3): 325–361.

Ross, Michael (2006) "A closer look at oil, diamonds, and civil war." *Annual Review of Political Science* 9: 265–300.

Ross, Michael (2012) *The Oil Curse: How Petroleum Wealth Shapes the Development of Nations* (Princeton, NJ: Princeton University Press).

Rosser, Andrew (2006) *The Political Economy of the Resource Curse: A Literature Survey.* IDS Working Paper 268. Brighton: Institute of Development Studies at the University of Sussex.

Rotemberg, J., and M. Woodford (1996) "Imperfect competition and the effects of energy price increases on economic activity." *Journal of Money, Credit, and Banking* 28(4), Part 1: 550–577.

Rutten, L., and F. Youssef (2007) *Market-Based Price Risk Management: an Exploration of Commodity Income Stabilization Options for Coffee Farmers.* Winnipeg: International Institute for Sustainable Development.

Sachs, Jeffrey, and Andrew Warner (1995) "Natural resource abundance and economic growth." In G. Meier and J. Rauch (eds) *Leading Issues in Economic Development* (New York: Oxford University Press).

Sachs, Jeffrey, and Andrew Warner (1997) *Natural Resource Abundance and Economic Growth* (Cambridge MA: Center for International Development and Harvard Institute for International Development, Harvard University).

Sachs, Jeffrey, and Andrew Warner (1999a) "The big push, natural resource booms and growth." *Journal of Development Economics* 59(1): 43–76.

Sachs, Jeffrey, and Andrew Warner (1999b) "Natural resource intensity and economic growth." In B. Chambers, A. Farooq, and J. Mayer (eds) *Development Policies in Natural Resource Economies* (Cheltenham: Edward Elgar), 13–38.

Sachs, Jeffrey, and Andrew Warner (2001) "The curse of natural resources." *European Economic Review* 45(4–6): 827–838.

Sala-i-Martin, Xavier, and Arvind Subramanian (2003) *Addressing the Natural Resource Curse: An Illustration from Nigeria.* IMF Working Paper WP/03/139.

Sandbu, Martin E. (2006) "Natural wealth accounts: A proposal for alleviating the natural resource curse." *World Development* 34(7): 1153–1170.

Sarraf, Maria, and Moortaza Jiwanji (2001) *Beating the Resource Curse: The Case of Botswana.* Environmental Economics Series Paper No. 83.

Singer, Hans W. (1950) "US foreign investment in underdeveloped areas: The distribution of gains between investing and borrowing countries." *American Economic Review, Papers and Proceedings* 40: 473–485.

Smith, Benjamin (2004) "Oil wealth and regime survival in the developing world, 1960–1999." *American Journal of Political Science* 48(2): 232–246.

Smith, Benjamin (2007) *Hard Times in the Land of Plenty: Oil Politics in Iran and Indonesia* (Ithaca, NY: Cornell University Press).

Solow, Robert (1986) "On the intergenerational allocation of natural resources." *The Scandinavian Journal of Economics* 88(1): 141–149.
Spatafora, N., and A. M. Warner (1999) *Macroeconomic and Sectoral Effects of Terms-of-Trade Shocks: The Experience of the Oil-Exporting Developing Countries.* IMF Working Papers 99/134.
Stevens, Paul (2003) "Resource impact: Curse or blessing? A literature survey." *Journal of Energy Literature* 9(1): 1–42.
Stijns, J. (2003) "An Empirical Test of the Dutch Disease Hypothesis Using a Gravity Model." Paper presented at the Congress of EEA, Stockholm, August 20–24.
Stijns, J. C. (2005) *"Natural Resource Abundance and Economic Growth Revisited." Resources Policy* 30: 107–130.
Talvi, Ernesto, and Carlos Végh (2005) "Tax base variability and procyclicality of fiscal policy." *Journal of Development Economics* 78(1): 156–190.
Tornell, Aaron, and Philip Lane (1999) "The voracity effect." *American Economic Review* 89(1): 22–46.
Torres, N., Ó. Afonso, and I. Soares (2013) *A Survey of Literature on the Resource Curse: Critical Analysis of the Main Explanations, Empirical Tests and Resource Proxies.* CEF.UP Working Paper 2013–02, Faculty of Economics, University of Porto.
Torvik, Ragner (2002) "Natural resources, rent seeking and welfare." *Journal of Development Economics* 67: 455–470.
Triki, T. and Y. Affes (2011) "Managing commodity price volatility in Africa." *AfDB Africa Economic Brief* 2(12).
Tsui, K. (2011) "More oil, less democracy: Evidence from worldwide crude oil discoveries." *Economic Journal* 121(551): 89–115.
Ulfelder, Jamy (2007) "Natural resource wealth and the survival of autocracies." *Comparative Political Studies* 40(8): 995–1018.
UNCTAD (2015) *Progress in the Development of African Commodity Exchanges.* 2nd Extraordinary Session of the Conference of Ministers of Trade, 21–24 November, 2005, Arusha, United Republic of Tanzania.
Van der Ploeg, F., and S. Poelhekke (2009) "Volatility and the natural resource curse." *Oxford Economic Papers* 61: 727–760.
Van der Ploeg, F., and S. Poelhekke (2010) "The pungent smell of "red herrings": Subsoil assets, rents, volatility and the resource curse." *Journal of Environmental Economics and Management* 60(1): 44–55.
Vandewalle, Dirk (1998) *Libya since Independence: Oil and State-Building* (Ithaca, NY: Cornell University Press).
van Wijnbergen, Sweder (1984) "The "Dutch Disease": A disease after all?" *Economic Journal* 94: 41–55.
Varangis, P., and D. F. Larson (1996) *Dealing with Commodity Price Uncertainty.* World Bank Policy Research Working Paper No. 1667.
Wacziarg, Romain (2012) "The First Law of Petropolitics." *Economica* 79: 641–657.
Wantchekon, Leonard (2002) "Why do resource-dependent countries have authoritarian governments?" *Journal of African Finance and Economic Development* 2: 57–77.
Wright, Gavin, and Jesse Czelusta (2003) "Mineral Resources and Economic Development." Paper presented at Conference on Sector Reform in Latin America, Stanford Center for International Development, Nov. 13–15.
Wright, Gavin, and Jesse Czelusta (2004) "The myth of the resource curse." *Challenge* 47(2): 6–38.

Annex

Table 4.3 Definitions of variables

Variable	Definition	Source
ΔGDP	Annual growth rate of real gross domestic product (constant local currency)	WDI
Per capita GDP	Logarithm of real GDP per capita (constant 2005 international dollar)	WDI
Human capital	Total primary completion rate (percentage of relevant age group)	WDI
Financial depth	Money and quasi money (M2) as percentage of GDP	WDI
Trade openness	Total trade as percentage of GDP	WDI
FDI	Foreign direct investment as percentage of GDP	WDI
Capital formation	Gross fixed capital formation as percentage of GDP	WDI
Natural resources	Total natural resources rents as percentage of GDP	WDI
Inflation	Annual growth rate of GDP deflator	WDI
Remittances	Personal remittances received as percentage of GDP	WDI
Political stability	Political stability index from the World Governance Indicators	AfDB
Infrastructure	Logarithm of Africa infrastructure development index	AfDB

Source: Authors' calculation based on data provided by the World Bank WDI database and the African Development Bank data portal.

Table 4.4 Descriptive statistics (1990–2012)

Variable	Mean	Median	Max	Min	Std. Dev.	Skewness	Kurtosis	Obs.
ΔGDP	0.04	0.04	1.06	−0.56	0.08	1.90	48.17	1172
Per capita GDP	7.44	7.19	10.22	4.62	1.02	0.67	2.88	1148
Human capital	0.59	0.58	1.33	0.14	0.25	0.33	2.39	694
Financial depth	0.35	0.25	1.52	0.01	0.25	1.73	6.14	1127
Trade openness	0.74	0.66	2.75	0.11	0.36	1.21	4.88	1130
FDI	0.04	0.02	1.45	−0.83	0.10	5.39	69.86	1120
Capital formation	0.20	0.19	1.14	−0.02	0.11	2.51	15.18	1065
Natural resources	0.12	0.05	2.19	0.00	0.19	3.68	25.99	1129
Inflation	0.57	0.07	267.62	−0.33	8.23	29.70	952.11	1172
Remittances	0.04	0.01	0.79	0.00	0.08	5.27	35.63	873
Political stability	−0.54	−0.34	1.19	−3.30	0.95	−0.47	2.51	636
Infrastructure	2.57	2.59	4.44	−0.99	0.82	−0.26	3.63	583

Table 4.5 Correlation coefficients

Variable	1	2	3	4	5	6	7	8	9	10	11	12
1. ΔGDP	1.00											
2. Per capita GDP	0.08 (0.01)	1.00										
3. Human capital	0.07 (0.06)	0.68 (0.00)	1.00									
4. Financial depth	−0.09 (0.00)	0.37 (0.00)	0.40 (0.00)	1.00								
5. Trade openness	0.16 (0.00)	0.43 (0.00)	0.35 (0.00)	0.12 (0.00)	1.00							
6. FDI	0.23 (0.00)	0.02 (0.47)	0.15 (0.00)	−0.04 (0.16)	0.39 (0.00)	1.00						
7. Capital formation	0.30 (0.00)	0.29 (0.00)	0.28 (0.00)	0.14 (0.00)	0.52 (0.00)	0.51 (0.00)	1.00					
8. Natural resources	0.12 (0.00)	0.23 (0.00)	0.00 (1.00)	−0.21 (0.00)	0.35 (0.00)	0.20 (0.00)	0.19 (0.00)	1.00				
9. Inflation	−0.03 (0.27)	−0.06 (0.04)	−0.03 (0.48)	−0.04 (0.13)	−0.02 (0.55)	0.01 (0.83)	−0.04 (0.18)	0.04 (0.19)	1.0			
10. Remittances	0.04 (0.29)	−0.08 (0.02)	0.08 (0.06)	0.12 (0.00)	0.43 (0.00)	0.14 (0.00)	0.49 (0.00)	−0.14 (0.00)	−0.02 (0.51)	1.00		
11. Political stability	0.03 (0.53)	0.46 (0.00)	0.36 (0.00)	0.27 (0.00)	0.26 (0.00)	0.02 (0.66)	0.26 (0.00)	−0.24 (0.00)	−0.12 (0.00)	0.09 (0.05)	1.00	
12. Infrastructure	−0.08 (0.05)	0.74 (0.00)	0.73 (0.00)	0.48 (0.00)	0.21 (0.00)	−0.05 (0.24)	0.08 (0.06)	−0.02 (0.57)	−0.11 (0.01)	0.02 (0.72)	0.48 (0.00)	1.00

Notes: The levels of significance for correlation coefficients are reported in parentheses.

Table 4.6 Pooled OLS regression

Variable	1	2	3	4	5	6
Per capita GDP	−0.0014	−0.0010	−0.0024	−0.0076***	−0.0082***	−0.0102**
	(−0.51)	(−0.34)	(−0.86)	(−2.66)	(−2.72)	(−2.43)
Inflation	−0.0004***	−0.0004***	−0.0004***	0.0037	0.0008	0.0022
	(−2.79)	(−2.63)	(−2.67)	(0.18)	(0.03)	(0.08)
Financial depth	−0.0185**	−0.0190**	−0.0153**	−0.0142	−0.0041	−0.0046
	(−2.47)	(−2.55)	(−2.02)	(−1.64)	(−0.33)	(−0.31)
Trade openness	0.0035	−0.0046	−0.0053	−0.0097*	−0.0125**	−0.0126**
	(0.73)	(−0.91)	(−1.10)	(−1.95)	(−2.34)	(−2.15)
FDI	0.0984***	0.0867***	0.0760***	0.0577**	0.0019	0.0453
	(3.73)	(3.08)	(2.67)	(2.29)	(0.04)	(0.66)
Human capital	0.0202**	0.0210**	0.0236**	0.0454***	0.0292**	0.0227*
	(2.00)	(2.04)	(2.43)	(4.70)	(2.39)	(1.79)
Capital formation		0.0699***	0.0689***	0.0412	0.0550	0.0552
		(3.13)	(3.07)	(1.54)	(1.35)	(1.10)
Natural resources			0.0260	−0.0023	0.0216	0.0249
			(1.32)	(−0.13)	(0.93)	(0.95)
Remittances				−0.0049	−0.0082	−0.0040
				(−0.24)	(−0.35)	(−0.18)
Political stability					0.0039	0.0040
					(1.31)	(1.18)
Infrastructure						0.0037
						(0.58)
Constant	0.0385**	0.0272	0.0342*	0.0726***	0.0884***	0.0950***
	(2.31)	(1.51)	(1.90)	(4.04)	(4.24)	(3.75)
Observation	649	611	611	518	307	272
R-squared	0.0588	0.0828	0.0879	0.0741	0.0606	0.0729
F-statistic	6.28***	6.65***	6.27***	5.29***	4.44***	4.89***
	($p = 0.0000$)	($p = 0.0000$)	($p = 0.0000$)	($p = 0.0000$)	($p = 0.0000$)	($p = 0.0000$)

Table 4.7 Pooled OLS regressions with country and year dummies

Variable	1	2	3	4	5	6
Per capita GDP	0.0190	0.0239*	0.0165	0.0577***	0.1023***	0.1161**
	(1.40)	(1.65)	(1.11)	(2.75)	(3.08)	(2.51)
Inflation	−0.0002	−0.0002	−0.0002	−0.0101	−0.0648**	−0.0760
	(−1.59)	(−1.59)	(−1.48)	(−0.39)	(−2.45)	(−2.43)
Financial depth	−0.0944***	−0.1104***	−0.0990***	−0.0706**	−0.0998***	−0.0560
	(−3.99)	(−3.97)	(−3.61)	(−2.25)	(−2.86)	(−1.58)
Trade openness	0.0205	0.0157	−0.0044	−0.0314*	−0.0203	−0.0167
	(1.38)	(0.97)	(−0.30)	(−1.91)	(−1.04)	(−0.67)
FDI	0.0479	0.0219	0.0190	−0.0374	−0.0725	−0.0769
	(1.36)	(0.54)	(0.46)	(−1.19)	(−1.32)	(−1.09)
Human capital	−0.0132	−0.0157	−0.0174	−0.0117	0.0259	0.0104
	(−0.6)	(−0.66)	(−0.74)	(−0.45)	(1.00)	(0.36)
Capital formation		0.0628*	0.0789**	0.0529*	0.0594	0.0192
		(1.91)	(2.51)	(1.72)	(1.20)	(0.28)
Natural resources			0.1486**	0.1246**	0.0947	0.1128
			(2.34)	(2.31)	(1.42)	(1.44)
Remittances				0.0837**	0.0083	0.0035
				(2.08)	(0.14)	(0.05)
Political stability					−0.0024	−0.0001
					(−0.39)	(−0.01)
Infrastructure						0.0169
						(1.15)
Constant	−0.0725	−0.0183	0.0248	−0.3864**	−0.5115	−1.1700***
	(−0.76)	(−0.20)	(0.26)	(−2.25)	(−2.71)	(−2.75)
Observation	649	611	611	518	307	272
R-squared	0.3004	0.3160	0.3408	0.3434	0.4135	0.3111
F-statistic	3.23***	3.35***	3.69***	3.04***	2.83***	3.07***
	($p = 0.0000$)	($p = 0.0000$)	($p = 0.0000$)	($p = 0.0000$)	($p = 0.0000$)	($p = 0.0000$)

Table 4.8 Instrumental-variables regressions

Variable	1	2	3	4	5	6
Per capita GDP	-0.0086***	-0.0069**	-0.0062*	-0.0128***	-0.0105	-0.0044
	(-2.81)	(-1.97)	(-1.68)	(-2.95)	(-1.40)	(-0.47)
Inflation	-0.0020	-0.0018	-0.0018	0.0091	0.1104	0.1357
	(-1.23)	(-1.21)	(-1.20)	(0.25)	(0.84)	(0.95)
Financial depth	-0.0092	-0.0110	-0.0127	-0.0019	0.0305	0.0401**
	(-1.13)	(-1.35)	(-1.52)	(-0.17)	(2.01)	(2.10)
Trade openness	-0.0038	-0.0149**	-0.0149**	-0.0002**	-0.0169	-0.0222
	(-0.67)	(-2.02)	(-2.00)	(-0.03)	(-1.15)	(-1.34)
FDI	0.2463**	0.2720**	0.2900**	-0.0309	0.0072	0.0291
	(2.30)	(2.23)	(2.11)	(-0.26)	(0.05)	(0.22)
Human capital	0.0300**	0.0283**	0.0272*	0.0446***	0.0119	0.0243
	(2.22)	(1.97)	(1.83)	(3.18)	(0.53)	(1.11)
Capital formation		0.1004***	0.0997***	0.1012***	-0.0030	-0.0257
		(2.64)	(2.63)	(2.60)	(-0.04)	(-0.36)
Natural resources			-0.0157	-0.0065	0.0123	0.0042
			(-0.64)	(-0.35)	(0.39)	(0.14)
Remittances				-0.0465	0.0205	0.0420
				(-1.41)	(0.32)	(0.59)
Political stability					0.0086	0.0092
					(1.20)	(1.24)
Infrastructure						0.0130
						(-1.30)
Constant	0.0841***	0.0604**	0.0574**	0.0916***	0.1128**	0.0967**
	(4.43)	(2.59)	(2.39)	(3.53)	(2.57)	(2.00)
Observation	541	509	509	432	191	191
Wald Chi²-statistic	31.23***	41.41***	42.51***	48.24***	85.00***	54.50***
	($p = 0.0000$)	($p = 0.0000$)	($p = 0.0000$)	($p = 0.0000$)	($p = 0.0000$)	($p = 0.0000$)

5 Natural resources, volatility, and African development policy
Some agenda for action

George Kararach and Walter Odhiambo

Introduction

Given the importance of economic volatility on any development trajectory, the single most important policy challenge is to stabilize or negate the effects of any variations on African economies. Government policy responses to volatility create an unavoidable dynamic between the private and public sector as each anticipates how the other will respond to their actions in the local market and world economy. If this interaction is positive and based on credibility and predictability, then governments could potentially achieve their development policy objectives in a less costly way as they could depend on the private sector to undertake certain functions (e.g. intra-year grain storage of a sufficient quantity to moderate seasonal price rises), and traders would have strong incentives to perform lest the public sector be compelled to enter the market if pre-established trigger conditions were met. In contrast, if the government's actions are unpredictable, then the private sector will be less likely to perform functions like seasonal storage for agro-products, thereby raising the magnitude of any price rises, causing the government to undertake more storage itself, with a greater associated burden on the treasury. Issues of "credible commitment" thus arise, whereby the willingness of governments to adhere to "rules-based" targets for entering the market would determine the extent to which they could rely on the private sector to perform socially useful functions at no cost to the treasury. To the extent that governments can induce the private sector to perform these roles within clearly specified bounds, this would free up the budget to invest in productivity-enhancing public goods and services that have the greatest impacts on development and poverty reduction. This chapter seeks to chart a number of policy actions for African governments to manage their natural resources in the face of volatility to ensure a "stabilized" development path.

The following section discusses briefly the history of "stabilization" policies in Africa – highlighting some of the salient features and challenges countries have faced in the past. The third section discusses in detail a number of policy options that countries can adopt, drawing on the discussions from the previous chapter. The final part forms our conclusion.

A short history of stabilization policies in Africa

African governments often adopt policies in the name of dealing with commodity price volatility that do not work or are actually harmful, as the history of stabilization programs has tended to show. Many of these programs have involved setting up commodity marketing boards, controls on exports, price controls, cartels, and bans on derivative markets, to name but a few.

From the existing literature, stabilization policy can be defined broadly as a collection of measures with the aim of dampening fluctuations in total economic output and other macroeconomic aggregates associated with the business cycle or other sources of shocks. The presumed ability to implement stabilization policy successfully in the post-war era contributed significantly to the expanded role of the state in a number of both developed and developing economies (Tanzi, 1997, 2005b). This expanded role for the state was manifested, inter alia, in active monetary policy by politically controlled central banks and vastly expanded powers of expenditure and taxation, as well as unprecedented accumulation of peacetime debt by (quasi)fiscal authorities, as the example from the Reserve Bank of Zimbabwe up to 2009 showed (Kararach, 2014).

For more than fifty years, stabilization policies in market economies have been dominated by monetary and fiscal policies as preferred instruments (Friedman, 1968; Modigliani, 1977; Mundell, 2000). It would be misleading to suggest these efforts have not been without success in the developed world, as stabilization policies were partly responsible for the improved stability of these economies since the Second World War (Lucas, 2003). However, with the rise of neo-liberalism, the role of discretionary stabilization policy in this favorable outcome has become controversial. The general enthusiasm for active discretionary interventions has largely been replaced by a consensus on a rule-based framework whereby a monetary policy rule shoulders much of the stabilizing burden (Taylor, 1997, 2000). In our view, this consensus is ideologically driven (Kararach, 2011).

Many governments in the African region have pursued stabilization policies throughout their histories, even during their periods of ostensible market liberalization (Jayne, 2012). A lot of the documented stabilization interventions have been related to the agricultural sector, although countries like Nigeria, Gabon, Algeria, Angola, and Libya have been active members of the Organization of the Petroleum Exporting Countries.[1] For example, white maize has tended to be considered the strategic political crop in most of eastern and southern Africa, and food price stabilization focused mainly on this crop. According to Jayne (ibid.), contemporary maize price stabilization in the region has been driven by two main factors. First, the countries that made heavy use of marketing boards to offer above-market floor prices to farmers tended to have colonial legacies with bi-modal farm structures and powerful farm lobbies. Historically, farm lobbies were strongest in the countries with European settler agriculture, such as Zimbabwe, Zambia, and

Kenya (Keyter, 1975; Mosley, 1983). These political dynamics ensured large commercialized farmers benefited greatly from price supports, and the farm lobbies in these countries primarily represented their interests in the political process with the use of lobbies. After independence, the agricultural sector and land in particular became the cornerstone of an implicit and sometimes explicit "social contract" that the post-independence governments made with the African majority to redress the neglect of smallholder agriculture during the colonial period (Jayne and Jones, 1997). This political commitment has been maintained and strengthened with the rise of a privileged class of African farmers, many of whom have acquired land with the help of political connections, as the experience of Zimbabwe over the last decade suggests (Deininger and Byerlee, 2011; Sitko and Jayne, 2013). Because these farmers tend to be relatively large-surplus producers, their interests are closely associated with the more traditional large-scale commercial farmers. The "indigenization" of the formerly white farm lobbies has provided new impetus for price stabilization – and protection of the agricultural sector – through strong marketing board operations. In contrast, countries with less powerful farm lobbies, such as those in West Africa, have largely abandoned the use of marketing boards (Anderson and Masters, 2009; Masters and García, 2010). And second, government use of stabilization policies has to do with longstanding concern for the effects of price instability on poor rural and urban consumers with affiliate political consequences. From fear of political backlash, there is much less regional difference; most governments throughout Africa are strongly committed to keeping food prices from rising beyond tolerable levels, as demonstrated by government responses to the 2007/2008 world food price crisis (Jayne, 2012). Despite their efforts, most governments in the region were unable to prevent domestic food prices from rising up to, or exceeding, import parity levels during the 2008/2009 crisis (Minot, 2011), arguably because of a number of constraints such as fiscal space and differentiated agro-product markets.

Although the social contract and associated political commitment succeeded unevenly in promoting smallholder incomes and raising consumer welfare, a common result was an unsustainable drain on the treasury and the burgeoning of inefficient agro-parastatals. Arguably, the cost of supporting smallholder production – through input subsidies, credit programs with low repayment rates, commodity pricing policies that subsidized transport costs for farmers in remote areas, and the export of surplus production at a loss – contributed to fiscal deficits in the 1980s and early 1990s and, in some cases, macroeconomic instability (Jayne, 2012). Under increasing budget pressure, international lenders gained leverage over domestic agricultural policy starting in the 1980s, partly allowing them to push through structural adjustment programs in many African countries (Mosley et al., 1991). While structural adjustment is generally misunderstood as a policy regime imposed on African governments by international lenders, some form of adjustment was clearly unavoidable due to the fiscal crises that the social contract policies were causing (Jayne and Jones, 1997).[2] Indeed, the status quo was hardly an option in many African countries, and in some of these, the controlled marketing systems had already broken down even prior to liberalization, as parallel markets and hoarding as well as smuggling became the only viable channels for most farmers and consumers. The erratic and poor performance of the state-led systems for stabilization, reflected by frequent shortages of basic commodities and late or partial payments to producers, created support for reform among some domestic constituencies (Jayne and Jones, 1997). Most of the marketing boards and mechanisms to control prices and quotas became sources of rent-seeking (Bates, 1981).

The liberalization and privatization initiatives associated with the structural adjustment programs had repercussions beyond the reconfiguration of ownership of the economy, including redefinition of political practice. The rise of multi-party electoral processes in the early 1990s made it even more difficult for governments in many African countries to withdraw from "social contract" policies. Elections can be won or lost through policy tools that reward some producers with higher prices and consumers with lower prices or other means to redistribute productive assets such as land, mines, and/or disinvested state-owned enterprises (Bates, 1981; Bratton and Mattes, 2003; Sahley et al., 2005; Masters and García, 2010). Because stabilization programs provide demonstrable support for millions of politically linked producers and consumers, a retreat from the social contract policies exposes leaders to attack from opposition candidates. For this reason, it remains difficult for leaders to publicly embrace market liberalization, even as they accepted structural adjustment loans under conditionality agreements from international donors to reform their internal and external markets (Jayne, 2012). Since the early 2000s, commodity marketing boards have once again become the dominant players in the market in Kenya, Malawi, Zambia, and Zimbabwe. These countries have reportedly highly unpredictable and discretionary approaches to agro-trade policy, commonly imposing sudden and unanticipated export and import bans or changes in import tariff rates, or issuing government tenders with opaque selection criteria for private firms to import grain at highly subsidized prices (ibid.). Uncertainty over import duties, import intentions, and the prices at which the government releases buffer stocks onto domestic markets leads to problems of credible commitment and strategic interactions between the public and private sectors (Jayne et al., 2006; Tschirley and Jayne, 2010; Ellis and Manda, 2012). The asymmetry and uncertainty arising from poorly managed stabilization programs has tended to produce situations of acute shortages and price spikes far above the cost of import (Tschirley and Jayne, 2010; Abbink et al., 2011).

As noted earlier above, many stabilization programs have included setting up commodity marketing boards, controls on exports, price controls, cartels, and bans on derivative markets. These "situations" are arguably applicable beyond the agricultural sector, including in the mineral and other extractive sectors. What is required is institutional innovation that can help avoid the negative consequences of engaging in natural resource extraction and achieve sustainable long-term growth and socio-economic transformation for the continent and its people.

Managing Africa's natural resources and responding to volatility

From the huge literature that we reviewed, one is tempted to conclude that natural resource wealth need not necessarily lead to inferior economic or political development. As Frankel (2012a) noted, it is better to view commodity abundance as a double-edged sword, with both benefits and dangers depending on the policies and institutional contexts surrounding extraction and usage of proceeds. The policy and programmatic priority for any country should be on identifying ways to sidestep the pitfalls that have afflicted other commodity producers, and to identify the holy grail for success. We turn to explore some of the policy and programmatic responses to ensure such long-term growth.

Indexation of delivery contracts to world prices

It would be generally helpful to "insure" both producers and buyers against uncertainty associated with futures and price variability. Development contracts between producing countries and foreign investors are often plagued by "time inconsistency": A price is set by contract, but later the world price goes up, and the government wants to renege as it seeks to optimize resource rents. The risk that the locals will default makes foreign companies reluctant to do business in such an uncertain environment in the first instance. This limits the availability of necessary capital to the country. Renegotiating development contracts can have large transactions costs, including interruptions in the export flow and diplomatic fall-outs. The reverse may also occur. In the event of price fall, foreign firms may be tempted to renege. Frankel (2012a) suggests that the logical solution is indexation of the contracts to eliminate uncertainties associated with futures markets. Indexation shares the risks of gains and losses without the costs of renegotiation or damage to a country's or firm's reputation from defaulting.

Hedging of export proceeds on futures markets

Dealers in commodities on international spot markets are generally exposed to the risk that the "dollar" price rises or falls at the time of delivery. The producer can hedge by selling the quantity on a forward or futures market. In this regard, hedging provides efficient risk sharing and automatic adjustment to changes in world prices. Futures markets have one serious bureaucratic or political drawback. If a government hedges on the futures market, the political leadership gets no credit for saving the country from disaster when the world price falls but is lambasted when the price rises. By using options, a country can eliminate the risk of a *fall* in price in the commodity (Duclaud and García, 2011). Mexico has used this strategy since the early 1990s and in the more recent past with an option to sell oil at $70 a barrel, which was exercised in mid-2008 when the price fell to $40 a barrel. Unfortunately, this tool does not eliminate the upside risk and can be politically costly.

Denominating debt in terms of the export commodity's world price

This is a debt-management strategy for those countries that borrow in global financial markets despite their commodity wealth. For example, a copper-producing country can index its debt to the world copper price. The debt-service commitments adjust automatically with any fluctuation in the value of commodity exports (Chen and Rogoff, 2003). Debt crises hit Mexico in 1982 and Indonesia, Russia, and Ecuador in 1998, when the dollar prices of their oil exports fell and their debt-service ratios therefore worsened abruptly. This would not have happened if their debts had been indexed to the oil price. Although the idea has been around for a long time, it has never been put into practice because of concern that there is not enough demand for such bonds (Frankel, 2012a). What might be required is some form of "advanced market creation" by financial institutions such as the African Development Bank: It could, for example, lend to interested oil-producing countries in terms of oil in place of lending to them in dollars, and then offset its collective exposure to oil-market conditions by selling to investors a bond denominated in a common oil price index. Such lending activities would create the necessary and viable market for the debt instrument.

Countercyclical fiscal rules

Roughly one third of developing countries in the decade 2000–09 managed to shift from the historic pattern of procyclical fiscal policy to countercyclical fiscal policy. The countercyclical approach was particularly instrumental in the case of Chile: It ran large surpluses during the copper boom of 2003–2008 and was able to ease its fiscal policy substantially in the recession of 2009. This achievement was partly facilitated by an institutional framework put into place in 2000, and one that can offer useful lessons in managing windfalls for other countries (Frankel, 2012b; Frankel et al., 2011; Ilzetski and Végh, 2008).

Chile's fiscal institutions consist essentially of three rules. First, every government must set a budget target. Second, the target is phrased in structural terms: Deficits are allowed only to the extent that (i) output falls short of trend, in a recession, or (ii) the price of copper is below its trend thus creating potential for budget surplus in the event of copper price rise and commodity boom. Third, ten-year trends are projected by two panels of independent experts, outside the political process, to ensure forecasts in booms are not biased toward over-optimism.

Strategic exchange-rate policy for reserves accumulation and currency appreciation

Countries need to choose appropriate and strategic exchange-rate regimes depending on their contexts (Eichengreen and Hausmann, 1999). For a country pursuing exchange-rate targeting, a natural resource export boom may require some intervention in the foreign exchange markets to dampen the upward pressure on the currency in the early stages of the booms, while seeking to prevent the explosion of money supply (e.g. by raising reserve requirements on banks). In short, some form of sterilization is required. The aim would be to contain inflation, maintain the credibility of the existing exchange-rate anchor and accumulate some foreign exchange reserves for use in case of future disaster but also for inter-generational investment smoothing.

In the event of a persistent commodity boom or domestic inflation that is difficult to contain, the authorities can allow a gradual appreciation to accommodate the terms-of-trade shock rather than artificially suppressing it. However, giving up the existing exchange rate as the nominal anchor for monetary policy purposes means a country will need to devise a new one (Frankel, 2012a). Sub-Saharan African countries have experienced mixed successes in insulating their real exchange rates from resource pressures. Generally, oil and copper exporters have encountered the greatest difficulty in keeping the real exchange rate stable, while gold and "other" (precious stones) have had the least effects in the face of rapidly increasing prices (Lundgren et al., 2013).

Nominal GDP targeting strategy for the Central Bank

In recent times, inflation targeting has been the most popular alternative to exchange-rate targeting as a monetary policy framework. But for countries with terms-of-trade volatility, it might be more useful pursue product price targeting (PPT) (Frankel, 2003, 2005, 2011, 2012b; Frankel et al., 2011). The idea is that the price index that is computed and tracked is output-oriented rather than consumption-oriented. The important point is that the index gives a heavy weight to commodities that are produced for export and little weight to commodities that are imported, as opposed to the consumer price index (CPI), which does it the other way around (Frankel, 2012a).

This is a big departure from the inflation-targeting approach. Because the export commodity is in the index, monetary policy automatically accommodates fluctuations in the export price: The currency appreciates when the world market for the export commodity is strong and depreciates when it is weak (Frankel, 2012b). However, if the import commodity is in the index, as in CPI-targeting, then monetary policy reacts perversely to fluctuations in the import price. The domestic currency appreciates when import prices are high and depreciates when they are low. This worsening of the terms-of-trade fluctuations is an undesirable property that the PPT approach fortunately lacks. The PPT accommodates terms-of-trade fluctuation just like a floating exchange-rate regime is supposed to do (Broda, 2004; Edwards and Levy Yeyati, 2005), and yet at the same time it provides a nominal anchor, as exchange-rate targeting and inflation targeting do (Frankel, 2012a).

Professionally managing commodity funds

Making inter-generational savings and investments is another critical area for consideration (Humphreys and Sandhu, 2007; Humphreys et al., 2007; see also Davis et al., 2001a, 2001b). The windfalls of a commodity boom must be used to establish transparent sovereign wealth funds in order to ensure that future generations share the proceeds, while investing in assets that earn a higher rate of return to smooth inter-generational income streams (Holmøy, 2010; Røed Larsen, 2004; see also Truman, 2010). Botswana's "Pula Fund," built on earnings from the sale of diamonds, is one of the best continental practices worth emulating (Iimi, 2006; Sarraf and Jiwanji, 2001; Acemoglu et al., 2003). The fund is made up of securities denominated in other currencies, thus acting as a sink fund to offset the depletion of diamonds and a buffer to smooth global fluctuations. The daily management of the Pula Fund is under the care of independent asset management professionals without much political interference. Nigeria also established an oil stabilization fund, the Excess Crude Account (ECA) in 2004. The account was very successful during the 2004–2008 period but has faced serious challenges with the recent fall in oil prices.

Equitable per capita distribution of commodity revenues

The other approach is to invest in a fund and later allow the distribution of the investment earnings on an equal per capita basis, as is the case of the Alaska Permanent Fund. The vast literature in public choice as well as neoclassical economics suggests that citizens know how to spend their money better than their government does (Ross, 2007; Jensen and Wantchekon, 2004; Herb, 2005). Sharing windfalls on this basis enhances beneficiation and the sense in citizens that they are full stakeholders in the Fund in ways that enhance state building and democratic practice (Ross, 1999, 2012; Vandewalle, 1998. See also Wacziarg, 2009; Wantchekon, 2002; Ulfelder, 2007). Sala-i-Martin and Subramanian (2003) and Shaw (1984) implore Nigeria to distribute its oil earnings on an equal per capita basis. Gelb and Majerowicz (2011) and Ross (2007) make the same proposal for Uganda.

Diversification as a hedging strategy

As we noted already, Africa suffers from trade shocks and global commodity volatility due to the domination of traditional integration arrangements in its external trade. First, there have been heated debates about the effects of global volatility and many studies have sought to confirm the tendency of structural decline of real prices of primary commodities over time (Deaton and Miller, 1995; see also Findlay and Lundahl, 2001).

The second issue concerns the commodity concentration of traded goods (Hadass and Williamson, 2003), where Africa is caught in the revenue trap with agricultural and mine products representing about 70 percent of total exports. In addition, manufactured exports are concentrated geographically in a few countries, among which are North African countries, South Africa, and Mauritius. And more than 70 percent of the total imports constitute manufactured goods. This structure of African foreign trade signifies the failure of the attempts to diversify and modernize African economic structures that began in the 1960s and 1970s, thus perpetuating the traditional North–South divide.

Third and finally, even with the aggressive entry of countries such as China and India, African external trade is still geographically concentrated in Western Europe. This geographical composition is a reproduction of the traditional integration scheme with Africa exporting raw materials to Europe and in return importing manufactured goods. The post-independent import-substitution strategies failed to enhance structural transformation of African economies and exacerbated the colonial legacy of enclave configurations with limited diversification.

In the economic literature, the importance of diversification as a mechanism to hedge from global volatility and trade shocks is not new (Dasgupta and Heal, 1985). As far back as the 1930s, MacLaughlin (1930) explained the economic cycles in American cities by the degree of concentration of economic activities. He demonstrated that cities with a higher level of concentration suffered the most from the resultant crisis of the inter-war period. The debate later extended to the study of the fall in prices of raw materials like coffee for Latin American countries and what that meant for the structural-transformation strategies of those economies and their desire to escape from commodity price integration based on raw materials (Cuddington et al., 2007). These conversations later gave birth to structuralist appreciation of underdevelopment as expounded by the Economic Commission for Latin America and the Caribbean (ECLAC). From the 1940s up to the 1970s, commentators and researchers developed several themes exploring this new paradigm and defining new development issues including import-substitution industrialization as a development strategy (Prebisch, 1950; Singer, 1950). For example, Rosenstein-Rodan and Leontief put emphasis on the concept of the effects of cumulative drive and the density of inter-sectoral matrices.

Recently, the debate on diversification and its role in growth dynamics has been renewed (Ben Hammouda et al., 2006). The resurgent literature explains the fragility of African economies and the continent's marginalization in the global economy by the poor diversification of African economic structures. A number of authors use Romer-type models to highlight the beneficial effect of diversification expressed through the availability of inputs within an economy and potentially contributing to increasing labor productivity and human capital. Diversification may also contribute to growth by increasing the number of sectors and, accordingly, investment opportunities and reducing investors' risks, especially in a volatile global economy. Indeed, to some of the authors, diversification has a major role in economic growth through the stabilization of export revenues, as specialization in only one product was always considered a source of volatility and great instability. A number of studies have shown the correlation between diversification and stability of export revenues and accordingly the sustainability of growth dynamics.

Regional integration and regional approaches

Regional integration is an important strategy for adjusting and hedging against global volatility as it can transform the way African countries trade and participate in the world economy. First, countries adopt spatial development initiatives (SDIs) or spatial development programs (SDPs), which are usually trans-frontier in format and have transport corridors as their main component. By definition, spatial initiatives promote growth by increasing the diversification of the various national economies (Rodrik, 2006) in which the SDPs are located, stimulating cross-border economic activity, and shielding local businesses from global shocks. Regional integration thus becomes an important aspect of any economic growth and diversification strategy. A number of countries such as Tanzania and DRC have overlapping memberships in regional associations, thus increasing their access to multiple regional economic spheres which can serve as markets for their products.

Second, enhancing regional integration among African economies includes harmonizing various technological standards and regulations and reforming customs and border controls. These measures are critical for strengthening the business climate in Africa in the face of an inherently volatile global environment (Bulte et al., 2005). Regional integration is especially important as a platform for pooling resources for things such as R&D and trade negotiations given the small size of most African states and their economies. Regional economic communities (RECs) can be foundations for effective economic global competition by creating common markets, pooling resources, and providing a framework to coordinate the regional management of infrastructure such as transportation corridors, energy, and natural resources in particular. RECs are critical in the building and strengthening of capacities related to regional human resources, health, security, and the environment for sustainable transformation. Badiane and Odjo (2015) have demonstrated that policy actions aimed at promoting cross-border trade can reduce volatility in regional markets and help lower the vulnerability of domestic food markets to shocks. Of the three main regional trading blocs in Africa, the Southern African Development Community (SADC) has the highest level of aggregate volatility with a coefficient variation of 18.66, which is more than twice and three times that of the Economic Community of West African States (ECOWAS), and the Common Market for Eastern and Southern Africa (COMESA), respectively (Badiane and Odjo, 2015, 20–15). The fact that intra-African and intra-regional trade, though still small, is increasing, especially for agricultural products, suggests that cross-border trade flow will be a major factor in the level and stability of domestic food supplies.

Finally, a regional approach to risk management, as shown by the work of the Africa Trade Insurance Agency (ATIA) and Afreximbank, is critical. It is relatively well known that most agricultural commodities in Africa are produced by small-scale farmers who have limited financial resources to access exchanges and even less to manage price risk. This contrasts with experiences of developed countries like the US. For example, 90 percent of farmers in the US sell their products on the Chicago Board of Trade. As we noted earlier, size affects the extent of derivative market development and the market-size-problem can be resolved by regional integration. We know that the existence of a thriving spot market is necessary for the success of a derivatives exchange. Outside of Nigeria, South Africa, Ethiopia, and a few North African countries, commodity markets in Africa are small and highly informal (UNCTAD, 2005), turning them into impediments to the development of liquid spot markets and consequently derivatives markets.

Building necessary capacity

Equally, countries need to invest in the capacities or technical capabilities necessary for managing risks in a volatile global environment (Sachs, 2007; Smith, 2004). Given the complex nature of commodity risk management and related instruments, countries and traders need a certain level of financial literacy. The volatility and unpredictable nature of natural resource prices, and hence resource revenues, complicates macroeconomic management and budget planning. There is therefore need for capacity building for the institutions concerned. It is also important for traders to select risk-management instruments and design a strategy appropriately. This can be daunting, especially for small producers and buyers. More often than not, African producers and dealers do not understand how commodity markets work, the advantages of managing risk, and how risk can be effectively mitigated. Capacity building is thus needed to help African producers and buyers understand the full range of instruments available to manage commodity price risk. Capacity building also has to cover financial institutions and intermediaries which are likely to sell these products as well as supervisory authorities that will oversee risk-management activities at the national as well as regional levels (Kararach, 2014). For example, the Africa Mining Development Center, housed at the UN Economic Commission for Africa, has started providing training to countries on mining contract negotiations to enhance value addition and beneficiation. The African Legal Facility housed at the African Development Bank has been doing the same.

Developing appropriate market structures

Another important programmatic response to manage global volatility for African countries is to develop appropriate market structures (Rodrik et al., 2003; Ostrom and Ostrom, 1977; Jacks et al., 2011). African commodity markets often lack both physical and soft infrastructure. Soft infrastructure includes transaction facilitators, information analyzers, credibility enhancers, and regulators to mention just a few (Ostrom, 1990; Rodrik et al., 2003). Given a lack of market research, commodity producers and buyers face difficulties in setting prices (both spot and future), defining the quantity they should buy or sell, and identifying which markets offer the best options for trading at any given time. Additionally, as the experience of some of the African commodity exchanges show, traded commodities on African markets are not easily traceable and thus not "graded." This restricts African producers' access to international markets where there are significant worries about quality and environmental practices at the sites of production. Furthermore, physical infrastructure is key to the success of a commodity exchange, especially warehouses where physical transactions take place and goods are stored. Transportation and distribution are essential so that delivery location and terms can be credibly specified in the contract. To remove mismatch in the market, physical and communication networks are crucial to provide traders with spot market information critical to estimating the basis. The efficiency of the physical infrastructure and moving products around different geographical positions in different time frames influences the basis and thus the competitiveness of any exchange.

Instituting the right regulatory barriers

African countries need to develop the right regulatory frameworks to preserve macroeconomic and social stability as well as sustainable use of natural resources (Engerman and Sokoloff, 1997, 2000, 2012). For example, foreign exchange control may make it difficult for domestic buyers and sellers to hedge on international markets (Edwards, 1986). Since the 1990s, many African countries have liberalized their capital account yet some do not authorize foreign investments for hedging purposes. In order to overcome such restrictions, importers in countries like Tunisia hedge their price risk through their commodity suppliers. While such practice reduces their exposure to price risk, it prevents them from adjusting their hedging positions to price movements or using options in anticipation of shocks. International providers of risk-mitigation instruments such as the ATIA and Afreximbank are facing increasing pressure to fulfill the Know Your Client requirements. This has led to an increasing reluctance by many of these financing agencies to deal with African clients because of providers' excessive risk aversion (AFRAA, 2006).

Derivatives and broader financial sector development

Derivatives are another set of hedging instruments that African countries could use in the face of global volatility in the prices of their commodities. Commodity derivatives can significantly reduce the losses from adverse movements in world commodity prices through market-based instruments. There are two types of derivative securities: futures/forward and call/put options. Futures and forwards options lead to predefined payments while call and put derivatives give the holder flexibility to buy or sell, thus translating into flexible flows that depend on market movements. Producers and buyers can hedge by being directly active on derivatives exchanges, through intermediaries like trading houses or brokers, or through over-the-counter (OTC) markets to hedge their price risk.

Generally, African markets offering commodity derivatives, with the exception of the South Africa-based SAFEX, have so far failed to attract significant trading volumes and largely remained as providers of price information and standardized regulation. The number of contracts traded on the JSE since 2010 increased year on year by 12 percent to stand at 2.1 million in 2013 (AfDB et al., 2013). Additional markets offering commodity derivatives are available in Kenya (African Mercantile Exchange) and Mauritius (the Global Board of Trade Ltd. (GBOT)). Bourse Africa in Botswana has opened with a vision to help buyers and sellers of African commodities achieve better price discovery. Essentially, there is need for greater financial sector development for instruments such as derivatives to be useful hedging tools for African economies in the face of global volatility of their commodity prices.

Conclusion

We have noted that both natural resources and global volatility will continue to influence the debates around Africa's development agenda for decades to come. To date, much of the theoretical propositions and associated statistical evidence imply that the existence of natural resources, be they renewable or non-renewable, can confer both negative and positive effects on a country, depending on the natural resource management (NRM) and governance frameworks. However, with well-thought-out NRM policies and strategies, the Dutch disease can be relegated to history, as the experience of Botswana has shown. On the other hand, countries such as Nigeria, the Sudan, and the DRC have done rather poorly in harnessing the power of their resources for inclusive growth and transformative development. In this regard, the natural resource curse or how volatility hits countries should not be interpreted as a rule that says that resource-rich-countries have no long-term growth prospects and are doomed to failure.

We have in this chapter explored a range of policies to adopt to increase the chances of prospering. We note that a commonsense or "good fit" approach has to be adopted by countries as policies and institutions have to be tailored to local circumstances, country by country, in order to build the necessary capacity and capability for effective NRM in Africa. This approach is important because specific institutions that could be usefully applied elsewhere may not be easily translated or transplanted to another national context. Thus the best framework for a country to manage its natural resources in the face of global volatility depends on country-specific economic and institutional circumstances, including the level of resource dependency, resource wealth and reserves, the revenue horizon, and the country's development needs. In this regard, many African countries may not be able to handle the still-large government sectors of the Nordic countries or the success of Botswana, for example, without corruption or mismanagement. Land redistribution worked well in Japan, Korea, and Taiwan after the collapse of the Japanese colonial empire in 1945, but in most other contexts, such interference with property rights would inflict lasting damage, as the example of Zimbabwe has shown. Understanding the political-economy terrain will always remain a major tool in the armory to tackle the voracity that tends to come with natural resource finds and the related volatility for any country, including those in Africa.

Notes

1 Gabon left the group in 1994.
2 Indeed, countries such as Zimbabwe, Tanzania, and Uganda experimented with their own structural adjustment programs in the 1980s before the World Bank and IMF got truly involved in the 1990s.

References

Abbink, K., Jayne, T. S., and Moller, L. (2011) "The relevance of a rules-based maize marketing policy: an experimental case study of Zambia." *Journal of Development Studies* 47(2): 207–230.
Acemoglu, Daron, Johnson, Simon, and Robinson, James (2003) "An African success: Botswana." In Rodrik, D. (ed.) *In Search of Prosperity: Analytic Narratives in Economic Growth* (Princeton, NJ: Princeton University Press).
African Airlines Association (AFRAA) (2006) *Strategy for the development of the air transport industry in Africa* Available at http://christianfolly kossi.com/docs/FundingRequirementsSummary-TunisMay06.pdf.
African Development Bank, Organisation for Economic Co-operation and Development, United Nations Development Programme, Economic Commission for Africa (2013) *African Economic Outlook 2013, Structural Transformation and Natural Resources* (Tunis: AfDB).
Anderson, K., and Masters, W. (2009) "Introduction and summary." In Anderson, K., and Masters, W. (eds) *Distortions to Agricultural Incentives in Africa* (Washington, DC: The World Bank), pp. 3–67.
Badiane, Ousmane, and Odjo, Sunday (2015) *Regional Trade and Volatility in Staple Food Markets in Africa*. Discussion Papers No. 207696, University of Bonn, Center for Development Research (ZEF). Available at: http://EconPapers.repec.org.

Bates, R. (1981) *Markets and States in Tropical Africa: The Political Basis of Agricultural Policies.* (Berkeley, CA: University of California Press).

Ben Hammouda, Hakim and Karingi, Stephen and Njuguna, Angelica, and Sadni Jallab, Mustapha (2006) *Diversification: Towards a New Paradigm for Africa's Development.* MPRA Paper No. 13359.

Bratton, M., and Mattes, R. (2003) "Support for economic reform? Popular attitudes in Southern Africa." *World Development* 31(2): 303–323.

Broda, Christian (2004) "Terms of trade and exchange rate regimes in developing countries." *Journal of International Economics* 63(1), pp. 31–58.

Bulte, Erwin, Damania, Richard, and Deacon, Robert (2005) "Resource intensity, institutions and development." *World Development* 33(7): 1029–1044.

Chen, Yu-Chin, and Rogoff, Kenneth (2003) "Commodity currencies." *Journal of International Economics* 60(1): 133–160.

Cuddington, John, Ludema, Rodney, and Jayasuriya, Shamila (2007) "Prebisch-Singer redux." In D. Lederman and W. F. Maloney (eds) *Natural Resources: Neither Curse Nor Destiny* (Washington, DC: Stanford University Press), pp. 103–140.

Dasgupta, Partha, and Heal, Geoffrey (1985) *Economic Theory and Exhaustible Resources* (Cambridge, UK: Cambridge University Press).

Davis, Jeffrey, Ossowski, Rolando, Daniel, James, and Barnett, Steven (2001a) "Oil funds: Problems posing as solutions?" *Finance and Development* 38(4).

Davis, Jeffrey, Ossowski, Rolando, Daniel, James, and Barnett, Steven (2001b) "Stabilization and savings funds for nonrenewable resources: Experience and fiscal policy implications." In Davis, J., Ossowski, R., and Fedelino, A. (eds) *Fiscal Policy Formulation and Implementation in Oil-Producing Countries* (Washington, DC: International Monetary Fund), pp. 273–315.

Davis, Jeffrey, Ossowski, Rolando, and Fedelino, Annalisa (eds) (2003) *Fiscal Policy Formulation and Implementation in Oil-Producing Countries* (Washington, DC: IMF).

Deaton, A., and Miller, R. (1995) *International Commodity Prices, Macroeconomic Performance and Politics in Sub-Saharan Africa.* Princeton Studies in International Finance, No.79.

Deininger, K., and Byerlee, D., with Lindsay, J., Norton, A., Selod, H., and Stickler, M. (2011) *Rising Global Interest in Farmland: Can It Yield Sustainable and Equitable Benefits?* (Washington, DC: World Bank).

Duclaud, Javier, and García, Gerardo (2011) *Mexico's Oil Price Hedging Program* (Washington, DC: International Monetary Fund).

Edwards, Sebastian (1986) "A commodity export boom and the real exchange rate: The money-inflation link." in Neary, J. and van Wijnbergen, S. (eds) *Natural Resources and the Macroeconomy* (Cambridge, MA: MIT Press).

Edwards, S., and Levy Yeyati, E. (2005) "Flexible exchange rates as shock absorbers." *European Economic Review* 49: 2079–2105.

Eichengreen, Barry, and Hausmann, Ricardo (1999) "Exchange Rates and Financial Fragility." Proceedings of *New Challenges for Monetary Policy* (Kansas City: Federal Reserve Bank of Kansas City), pp. 329–368.

Ellis, F., and Manda, E. (2012) "Seasonal food crises and policy responses: a narrative account of three food security crises in Malawi." *World Development* 40(7): 1407–1417.

Engerman, Stanley, and Sokoloff, Kenneth (1997) "Factor endowments, institutions, and differential paths of growth among new world economies: A view from economic historians of the United States." In Haber, S. (ed.) *How Latin America Fell Behind*, (Palo Alto, CA: Stanford University Press), pp. 260–304.

Engerman, Stanley, and Sokoloff, Kenneth (2000) "Institutions, factor endowments, and paths of development in the New World." *Journal of Economic Perspectives* XIV: 217–32.

Engerman, Stanley, and Sokoloff, Kenneth (2012) *Economic Development in the Americas Since 1500: Endowments and Institutions* (New York: Cambridge University Press).

Findlay, Ronald, and Lundahl, Mats (2001) "Natural Resources and Economic Development: The 1870–1914 Experience." In Auty, R. (ed.) *Resource Abundance and Economic Development* (World Institute for Development Economics Research).

Frankel, Jeffrey (2003) "A proposed monetary regime for small commodity-exporters: Peg the Export Price ("PEP")." *International Finance* 6(1): 61–88.

Frankel, Jeffrey (2005) "Peg the Export Price Index: A proposed monetary regime for small countries." *Journal of Policy Modeling* 27(4): 495–508.

Frankel, Jeffrey (2007) "On the Rand: Determinants of the South African exchange rate." *South African Journal of Economics* 75(3): 425–441.

Frankel, Jeffrey (2011) "A comparison of product price targeting and other monetary anchor options, for commodity-exporters in Latin America." *Economia* 12(11): 1–57.

Frankel, Jeffrey (2012a) *The Natural Resource Curse: A Survey of Diagnoses and Some Prescriptions*. HKS Faculty Research Working Paper Series RWP12-014 (Cambridge, MA: John F. Kennedy School of Government, Harvard University).

Frankel, Jeffrey (2012b) "A solution to fiscal procyclicality: The structural budget institutions pioneered by Chile." *Fiscal Policy and Macroeconomic Performance*, Fourteenth Annual Conference of the Central Bank of Chile. NBER WP No. 16945.

Frankel, Jeffrey, Végh, Carlos, and Guillermo, Vuletin (2011) *On Graduation from Procyclicality*. NBER Working Paper 17619.

Friedman, M. (1968) "The role of monetary policy." *American Economic Review* 58(1): 1–17.

Gelb, A., and Majerowicz, S. (2011) "Oil for Uganda – or Ugandans? Can cash transfers prevent the resource curse?" Center for Global Development Working Paper 261, July. Available at: www.cgdev.org/files/1425327_file_Oil_Uganda_Transfers_Gelb_FINAL_.pdf.

Hadass, Yael, and Williamson, Jeffrey (2003) "Terms of trade shocks and economic performance 1870–1940: Prebisch and Singer revisited." *Economic Development and Cultural Change* 51(3): 629–656.

Herb, Michael (2005) "No representation without taxation? Rents, development and democracy." *Comparative Politics* 37(3): 297–317.

Holmøy, Erling (2010) "Mineral rents and social policy: The case of the Norwegian Government Oil Fund." In Hujo, Katja and McClanahan, Shea (eds) *Financing Social Policy: Mobilizing Resources for Social Development* (London: UNRISD/Palgrave MacMillan).

Humphreys, Macartan, and Sandhu, Martin (2007) "The political economy of natural resource funds." In Humphreys, Macartan, Sachs, Jeffrey, and Stiglitz, Joseph (eds) *Escaping the Resource Curse* (New York: Columbia University Press).

Humphreys, Macartan, Sachs, Jeffrey, and Stiglitz, Joseph (2007) "Future directions for the management of natural resources." In Humphreys, M., Sachs, J., and Stiglitz, J. (eds) *Escaping the Resource Curse* (New York: Columbia University Press), pp. 322–336.

Iimi, Atsushi (2006) *Did Botswana Escape from the Resource Curse?* IMF Working Paper No. 06/138, June.

Ilzetski, Ethan, and Végh, Carlos (2008) *Procyclical Fiscal Policy in Developing Countries: Truth or Fiction?* NBER WP No. 14191.

Jacks, David, O'Rourke, Kevin, and Williamson, Jeffrey (2011) "Commodity price volatility and world market integration." *Review of Economics and Statistics* 93(3): 800–813.

Jayne, T. S. (2012) "Managing food price instability in East and Southern Africa." *Global Food Security* 1(2): 143–149.

Jayne, T. S., and Jones, S. (1997) "Food marketing and pricing policy in eastern and Southern Africa: A survey." *World Development* 25(9): 1505–1527.

Jayne, T. S., Zulu, B., and Nijhoff, J. (2006) "Stabilizing food markets in eastern and southern Africa." *Food Policy* 31(4): 328–341.

Jensen, Nathan, and Wantchekon, Leonard (2004) "Resource wealth and political regimes in Africa." *Comparative Political Studies* 37: 816–41.

Kararach, G. (2011) *Macroeconomic Policy and the Political Limits of Reforms in Developing Countries*. Nairobi: African Research and Resource Forum.

Kararach, G. (2014) "Capacity, innovative financing and private sector development in Africa's transformation." *Capacity Focus* 4(1).

Keyter, C. (1975) *Maize Control in Southern Rhodesia: 1931–1941: The African Contribution Toward White Survival*, Local Series 34. (Harare, Zimbabwe: Central African Historical Association).

Lucas, R. J. (2003) "Macroeconomic priorities." *American Economic Review* 93(1): 1–14.

Lundgren, J. C., Thomas, A. H., and York, R. C. (2013) *Boom, Bust or Prosperity? Managing Sub-Saharan Africa's Natural Resource Wealth, African Department* (Washington, DC: International Monetary Fund).

MacLaughlin, G. (1930) "Industrial diversification in American cities." *Quarterly Journal of Economics*, 44: 131–149.

Masters, W. A., and García, A. (2010) "Agricultural price distortions and stabilization." In Anderson, Kym (ed.) *Political Economy of Distortions to Agricultural Incentives* (New York: Cambridge University Press), pp. 215–240.

Minot, N. (2011) *Transmission of World Food Price Changes to Markets in Sub-Saharan Africa*. IFPRI Discussion Paper 1059 (Washington, DC: International Food Policy Research Institute).

Modigliani, F. (1977) "The monetarist controversy or, Should we forsake stabilisation policies?" *American Economic Review* 67(2): 1–19.

Mosley, P. (1983) *The Settler Economies: Studies in the Economic History of Kenya and Southern Rhodesia 1900–63* (Cambridge: Cambridge University Press).

Mosley, P., Harrigan, J., and Toye, J. (1991) *Aid and Power: The World Bank and Policy-Based Lending* Vol. 1 (London: Routledge).

Mundell, R. A. (2000) "A Reconsideration of the Twentieth Century." *American Economic Review* 90(3): 327–340.

Ostrom, Elinor (1990) *Governing the Commons: The Evolution of Institutions for Collective Action* (Cambridge, UK :Cambridge University Press).

Ostrom, Elinor, and Ostrom, Vincent (1977) "Public goods and public choices." In Savas, Emanuel (ed.) *Alternatives for Delivering Public Services: Toward Improved Performance* (Boulder, CO: Westview Press), pp. 7–49.

Prebisch, Raul (1950) *The Economic Development of Latin America and Its Principal Problems* (New York: United Nations).

Rodrik, Dani (2006) "Industrial development: stylized facts and policies." In United Nations, *Industrial Development for the 21st Century* (New York: United Nations), pp. 7–28.

Rodrik, Dani, Subramanian, Arvind, and Trebbi, Francesco (2003) "Institutions rule: The primacy of institutions over geography and integration in economic development." *Journal of Economic Growth* 9(2): 131–165.

Røed Larsen, Erling (2004) *Escaping the Resource Curse and the Dutch Disease? When and Why Norway Caught up with and Forged ahead of Its Neighbors*. Discussion Papers No. 377, May, Statistics Norway, Research Department.

Ross, Michael (1999) "The political economy of the resource curse." *World Politics* 51: 297–322.

Ross, Michael (2007) "How mineral-rich states can reduce inequality." In Humphreys, M., Sachs, J., and Stiglitz, J. (eds) *Escaping the Resource Curse* (New York: Columbia University Press), pp. 236–255.

Ross, Michael (2012) *The Oil Curse: How Petroleum Wealth Shapes the Development of Nations* (Princeton, NJ: Princeton University Press).

Sachs, Jeffrey (2007) "How to handle the macroeconomics of oil wealth." In Humphreys, M., Sachs, J., and Stiglitz, J. (eds) *Escaping the Resource Curse* (New York: Columbia University Press), pp.173–193.

Sahley, C., Groelsema, B., Marchione, T., and Nelson, D. (2005) *The Governance Dimensions of Food Security in Malawi: USAID Bureau of Democracy, Conflict, and Humanitarian Assistance* (Washington, DC: USAID).

Sala-i-Martin, Xavier, and Subramanian, Arvind (2003) *Addressing the Natural Resource Curse: An Illustration from Nigeria*. IMF Working Paper WP/03/139.

Sarraf, Maria, and Jiwanji, Moortaza (2001) *Beating the Resource Curse: The Case of Botswana*. Environmental Economics Series Paper No. 83.

Shaw, Timothy M. (1984) "The state of Nigeria: Oil crises, power bases and foreign policy" *Canadian Journal of African Studies* 18(2): 393–405.

Singer, Hans W. (1950) "US Foreign Investment in Underdeveloped Areas: The Distribution of Gains between Investing and Borrowing Countries." *American Economic Review, Papers and Proceedings* 40: 473–485.

Sitko, N., and Jayne, T. S. (2013) "Pathways for becoming an emergent farmer." In *Zambia: Can Current Land and Agricultural Policies Encourage Smallholder Extensification?* Working Paper 67 (Lusaka, Zambia: Indaba Agricultural Policy Research Institute).

Smith, Benjamin (2004) "Oil wealth and regime survival in the developing world, 1960–1999." *American Journal of Political Science* 48(2): 232–246.

Tanzi, V. (1997) *The Changing Role of the State in the Economy*. Washington, IMF Working Paper, WP/97/114.

Tanzi, V. (2005a) "Fiscal policy and fiscal rules in the European Union." *CESifo Forum* 3: 57–64.

Tanzi, V. (2005b) "The economic role of the state in the 21st century." *Cato Journal* 25(3): 617–638.

Taylor, J. B. (1997) "A core of practical macroeconomics." *American Economic Review* 87(2): 233–235.

Taylor, J. B. (2000) "Reassessing Discretionary Fiscal Policy." *Journal of Economic Perspectives* 14(3): 21–36.

Truman, Edwin (2010) *Sovereign Wealth Funds: Threat or Salvation?* (Washington, DC: Peterson Institute for International Economics).

Tschirley, D., and Jayne, T. S. (2010) "Exploring the logic of Southern Africa's food crises." *World Development* 38(1): 76–87.

Ulfelder, Jamy (2007) "Natural resource wealth and the survival of autocracies." *Comparative Political Studies* 40(8): 995–1018.

UNCTAD (2005) *Progress in the Development of African Commodity Exchanges*. 2nd Extraordinary Session of the Conference of Ministers of Trade, 21–24 November, 2005, Arusha, United Republic of Tanzania.

Vandewalle, Dirk (1998) *Libya since Independence: Oil and State-Building* (Ithaca, NY: Cornell University Press).

Wacziarg, Romain (2009) "The First Law of Petropolitics." *Economica* 79: 641–657.

Wantchekon, Leonard (2002) "Why do resource-dependent countries have authoritarian governments?" *Journal of African Finance and Economic Development* 2: 57–77.

6 Local content policies, natural resource governance, and development in the Global South

Jesse Salah Ovadia

Introduction

Natural resource governance is part of a larger emphasis that the World Bank and other Bretton Woods institutions have placed on the good governance agenda. While many important critiques have been made of this agenda, natural resource governance must be seen in the light of the history of the resource curse. The "resource curse" is a catch-all term used to explain low levels of economic growth, a lack of industrial development, authoritarian and repressive regimes, violence, corruption, and civil war. While the existence of the curse is hotly debated, the proposition that different economic policies produce different development outcomes can be made without reservation. Consequent to this postulate, resource governance is important precisely because of the role of state policy in fostering both positive and negative developmental outcomes.

Natural resource governance in the Global South has traditionally focused on strengthening institutions to fight corruption and rent-seeking while promoting transparency and accountability to encourage better usage of the revenues generated from resource extraction. These policies are put forward to address the need for economic and social development. In the first instance, good governance was put forward as an antidote to "bad governance," which was the implicit explanation for the failure of neoliberal structural adjustment (Abrahamsen, 2000). However, the flip side of this agenda is the recognition that the state can and must play a role in development – an admission that was finally made with the World Bank's 1997 report *The State in a Changing World*.

The role of the state in nurturing economic development must go well beyond avoiding doing harm or getting out of the way of the free market. The experience of the newly industrializing "Asian tigers" suggests that the state must actively promote the manufacturing sector in situations of late industrialization and protect infant industries (Chang, 2003, 2006). As I argue in *The Petro-Developmental State in Africa* (Ovadia, 2016a), resource-rich developing countries have a unique opportunity in the current moment to follow in the footsteps of the East Asian developmental states. They can do this be embracing local content policies in their petroleum industries. While this chapter discusses local content mostly in the context of the oil and gas industry, local content is also being embraced in many developing countries with minerals and other natural resources.

This chapter argues that local content policies (LCPs), which promote local and national participation in extractive industry, are essential for the sustainability of resource-led economic development. LCPs offer not only the potential for diversified growth, but also the potential to capture large amounts of foreign capital investment in the national economy. With reference to the oil and gas industries of Ghana and Nigeria, I argue that LCPs, properly defined, measured and implemented, are a valuable tool for nurturing economic development in the region's current and future oil exporters and in a wider range of countries with significant natural resource wealth. Their successful implementation should therefore be a concern in the promotion of resource governance in sub-Saharan Africa and across the Global South.[1]

Africa rising

Toward the end of a decade of an unprecedented commodity boom, business periodicals began to change their tune about investing in Africa. *The Economist* (2011, 2013), *The Wall Street Journal* (2012), *New York Times* (Kristoff, 2012), *Forbes* (Van Rensburg, 2012), and the *Financial Times* (Wallis, 2010) shifted discourse from Africa as a "hopeless continent" to a rising land of opportunity. A new discourse around "Africa rising" and "emerging Africa" began to displace older discourses of poverty and state failure. Natural resources and extractive industry were very much tied into this shift.

In May 2014, the International Monetary Fund even held a conference on the theme of "Africa Rising – Building to the Future" in Mozambique. At the event, Christine Lagarde praised the continent's impressive growth over nearly two decades while raising concerns about poverty, the distribution of wealth, and countries being "left behind." Her speech hit all the right notes – talking about "Africa's takeoff," its status as a growing investment destination, and the emergence of "frontier economies... roaring loud as *Africa's lions*" (Lagarde, 2014, emphasis in original). By this point, however, the commodity boom was over and an oil price shock was about to hit, which would see the price of crude oil cut in half.

In the new popular discourse of Africa rising, the continent was finally back on track and ready to catch up with the rest of the globe. It is also, as portrayed in Vijay Mahajan's *Africa Rising* (2009), filled with hundreds of millions of consumers and a rising middle class (which he calls "Africa Two"). Although the end of the commodities boom and slowdown in the Chinese economy have halted Africa's rapid growth, a period of pessimism and hopelessness would seem to have passed. In its place, there is a new determination to nurture structural transformation. The end of the boom has actually encouraged oil-exporting African countries such as Angola, Ghana, and

Nigeria to pay more attention to economic diversification. While their currencies have been weakened by the fall in commodity prices, the opportunity may be even greater to achieve significant industrial growth. While "Africa rising" and new forms of developmentalism in the Global South reflect a changed political and economic reality for many African countries, a modernizationist approach[2] to understanding these events can only be avoided by adding depth to an otherwise superficial analysis. This depth can be provided by looking more closely at LCPs in Africa.

Natural resource governance and local content

Late industrialization requires countries to find a niche in which they can rapidly develop a comparative advantage. As industrialization progresses, comparative advantage can be sought in activities that involve greater value-added activities. Given that there are few ways to add value to extractive industries, it is important to seek ways to link these industries into the national economy thereby allowing local industries to move up the value chain for these raw materials as well as back along the supply chain for goods and services related to extraction.

In oil and gas, LCPs increase the utilization of national human and material resources in the petroleum sector and domicile in-country oil- and gas-related economic activity that was previously located abroad. Unfortunately, local content is fascinating because it has a dual nature – it is both a mechanism for promoting large-scale economic development and also at the same time a mechanism for the elite to capture oil rent. This second aspect to LCPs occurs because these policies allow state institutions to play favorites and privilege particular local capitalists by providing various incentives and even requiring international oil companies (IOCs) to use their goods and services (Ovadia, 2012).

Local content is also a useful entry point for discussing many of the most important issues in countries such as Nigeria. It can be used in topics ranging from changing methods of elite accumulation and the growing gap between rich and poor to new economic growth and development through private-sector initiative, and even to conflict in the Niger Delta, which is often related to conflicts among local elite over local content.[3]

Local content encourages the employment of locals by the oil companies, but also recognizes that oil and gas is an enclave industry that will never be a significant employer in its own right without linkages to the service sector and beyond. Therefore, the policies force international companies involved in extractive industry to use local companies to supply goods and services and force them to invest in facilities for local manufacturing and service provision. Due to the strategic nature of many natural resources and the fact that they cannot simply be moved out of a particular jurisdiction to a more favorable fiscal or regulatory regime, countries with natural resource wealth can insist on these policies and have significant leverage to ensure their implementation.

The benefit in terms of capital retained in the local economy from LCPs has the potential to be larger than the royalties and taxes from extraction of a particular resource. For this reason, local content may be the single most significant innovation in energy policy in the Global South in recent decades.

The importance of LCPs can also be explained with reference to what Mkandawire (2010) calls the "investment-trade nexus." This concept stresses that it is not trade but the accumulation of physical and human capital that is fundamental for economic growth. According to Bourgain and Nem Singh (2013), policy debates at the international and domestic levels have placed a great deal of emphasis on minimizing rent-seeking. They suggest a need to link an international political economy approach to natural resources to "the developmental roles of states, democratization and, most importantly, a political approach to resource management as embedded in global governance discourses." This, they suggest, goes hand in hand with thinking about pathways upon which natural resource extraction can lead to inclusive and sustained development (Bourgain and Nem Singh, 2013: x).

After a slow start, the international community is starting to realize the need to promote LCPs and devote resources to ensure their proper implementation. A host of recent reports on local content have been prepared by a variety of institutions such as the World Bank (Tordo et al., 2013), USAID (Kaplan, 2013), African Development Bank (Kayizzi-Mugerwa and Annaywu, 2015), International Finance Corporation (IFC, 2015), OECD (2015), UNECA (2013), and others. Even consulting firms like Ernst & Young (2014) have prepared reports on the topic. Not all of these reports are positive about local content. For example, a recent UNU-WIDER report (Kolstad and Kinyondo, 2015) recommends only a more minimal local content approach. Nevertheless, attention on these policies suggests a shift away from neoliberal approaches to trade and development.

There is great potential for national content policies to foster economic development and to develop the oil services sector as an anchor for growth in manufacturing and other linked areas of economic activity. This state-led approach to development was crucial to the success of the "Asian tigers" (Taiwan, South Korea, Singapore, and Hong Kong, see Chang, 2003). Undoubtedly, the experience of East Asia is highly relevant to contemporary policies to promote industrialization and manufacturing in Africa. Chang (2003) emphasizes South Korea's coordinating of investments within and across sectors to promote complementary activity and also its prescription of excessive entry and competition within sectors to promote economies of scale. Already there is some evidence of the growth of industry and entrepreneurship in two of sub-Saharan Africa's largest oil producers, Angola and Nigeria, and use of regimes of incentives to encourage local capitalists.[4]

State intervention in the market is required in the case of local content even though these policies are in the long-term interest of the private sector – particularly international oil companies. Strong state governance is required because the promotion of LCPs may involve short-term loss in order to achieve long-term gain. Even in the case of oil and gas, where investment decisions must anticipate long-term commitment, the higher costs associated with local procurement and the time and money spent on training and skills development may seem too burdensome for international companies involved in mineral extraction. However, the long-term benefits include lower transportation costs, lower costs associated with expatriate staffing, smoother-flowing supplies of goods and services, greater skills and experience for workers and managers, a strengthened relationship with the host government, and a strengthened social license to operate. Additionally, over time, local procurement costs are likely to decline. Despite the long-term gain, in Nigeria, the local content managers of two international oil companies admitted privately that it was a long struggle to embrace LCPs and it might not have been successful without regulation.[5]

Natural resource governance and the Resource Governance Index

In 2013, Revenue Watch Institute (since renamed the Natural Resource Governance Institute after merging with the Natural Resource Charter) launched the Resource Governance Index (RGI), a quantitative measure of various indicators of resource governance covering four categories: (1) institutional and legal setting, (2) reporting practices, (3) safeguards and quality control, and (4) enabling environment. Taken together, these categories provide a measure of transparency and accountability in the oil, gas, and mining sectors of fifty-eight countries.[6]

The findings of the RGI are that, in terms of transparency and accountability, "80 percent of countries fail to achieve good governance in their extractive sectors." In response, the RGI report (Revenue Watch Institute, 2013) calls for greater contract disclosure, more comprehensive reporting, better governance in national oil companies, a more concerted fight against corruption and implementation of the rule of law, and better reporting by international companies. The implication of this approach is that putting in place better governance through the ideals of transparency and accountability will lead to more effective use of revenues from resource extraction, which will in turn lead to better developmental outcomes. This approach to resource governance, as the institute has also begun to acknowledge, can be complemented by promoting development through local content.

Local content fits into multiple areas of the Natural Resource Charter, which is an important tool for understanding natural resource-based development. In particular, Precept 5 of the charter recommends taking opportunities to develop local benefits from extraction while Precept 10 suggests that local content can be a part of private-sector development.[7] In a briefing on local content, NRGI stops short of recommending LCPs, however. Instead, they write:

> Generally, countries face a question about the benefit or sustainability of investing in local content. Because extractive resources are finite, it can

be detrimental to create more economic focus on the extractive industries. Proponents of economic diversification suggest using local content provisions to develop a workforce with transferable skills.

(NRGI, 2015: 4)

How local content policies work and how they fit into resource governance

Before moving on, it is worth pausing to fully understand how LCPs promote complementary activity and the extent to which this insight is now coming to the attention of the international community, which is an important stakeholder in natural resource governance. Despite the small numbers of jobs available in oil and gas, the large number of goods and services needed for oil exploration and production offer numerous possibilities for employment. The potential of LCPs is in linking the oil and gas industry to other sectors of the economy. As the idea of a dual nature to local content suggests, the benefit of LCPs will accrue disproportionately to the domestic elite. However, through specific policy interventions, more of the benefit can be directed to small and medium enterprises (SMEs) and to communities affected by oil extraction. In this way, SMEs in sectors indirectly linked to oil and gas can still benefit from the enormous annual investment in resource extraction while expanding outside of the limits of the oil industry.

The extension of the benefit outside of the oil sector through linkage programs is the result of spin-off effects. In economics, a spin-off effect is the positive effect of new investment. Spin-off effects include the secondary benefits from job creation and, in the case of local content in oil and gas, the opportunities created for infant industries in the non-oil economy to grow on the basis of oil sector investment. Infant industries in the non-oil economy can benefit from local content if they supply some goods to the oil and gas sector. For example, companies providing cleaning, maintenance, security, and catering can build off their oil sector contracts to find non-oil opportunities and contracts. Companies supplying concrete, industrial paints, line pipes, information technology, and more can also have activities in both the oil and non-oil sectors.

Local content is also important because it addresses two of the most pressing concerns for sustainable economic and social development in sub-Saharan Africa. These are economic diversification and youth unemployment. While mineral resources were primarily understood as a benefit in terms of increased government revenue from mineral rents, the positive impact from local content on economic growth, job creation, diversification, and other pressing concerns adds to the value from increased retention of capital. It is therefore not surprising that slowly the World Bank, African Development Bank (AfDB) and other international institutions are beginning to promote LCPs as part of natural resource governance. The World Bank's Oil, Gas & Mining Unit released a report in January 2012 detailing efforts to support

162 *Ovadia*

local procurement in mining in West Africa as part of their support for the Africa Union's Africa Mining Vision 2050, which outlines a new resource-based industrialization and development strategy for Africa, based on downstream, upstream and sidestream linkages. In making recommendations to regional organizations, national governments, civil society, and communities and mining companies, the report's authors write: "This focus on local procurement represents a shift in policy approach: rather than concentrating on the contribution by mining companies through taxes, governments are increasingly exploring ways in which mines can become more closely integrated with local economies" (World Bank, 2012a: vii).

Additionally, in a note released on local content reporting in the context of the Extractive Industries Transparency Initiative (EITI), the World Bank (2012b) discusses the potential benefits and challenges of increasing local content transparency through robust monitoring and evaluation and recommends multi-stakeholder discussions, reporting, disclosure, verification, and dissemination of developed policy and reports. The note was to be considered by EITI's strategy working group in April 2012, but in the end was not included explicitly in the revisions to the EITI standard because, according to one person close to the strategy review, of concerns related to implementation and enforcement of a standard for measuring local content across member countries.[8] Nevertheless, LCPs remain an area of concern for governance and transparency advocates and a new focus in the World Bank, which, according to a senior manager, plans to continue advocating for local content in oil and gas mining.[9]

In September 2013, the World Bank followed through on this plan by holding a major conference on local content in Vienna, Austria, to share and discuss recent research on LCPs and how to make them more effective for the benefit of governments, industry, and communities.[10] At the same time, they released two very comprehensive reports on LCPs (Tordo et al., 2013) and case studies of local content in various countries (Tordo and Anouti 2013). In research and also in funded projects, the World Bank has shown itself to be serious about promoting LCPs. Another international conference on local content was held by the World Bank in Mexico City in January 2016.

Local content has also become a priority of the African Union (AU) Heads of State and Government, through the Africa Mining Vision (AMV), which is a partnership of the AU, AfDB, and UNECA. These organizations have established the African Minerals Development Centre (AMDC) to provide strategic operational support for the AMV and its Action Plan. The AfDB has also established the African Natural Resources Center (ANRC) to provide support on natural resources policy design and policy dialogue; in essence, to support better natural resource governance. In the ANRC strategy for 2015–2020, local content is one of the three "pillars" for "good governance of natural resources" (AfDB, 2015: 8). The strategy notes that local content

> presents an opportunity for governments to use natural resources for economic development in many sectors of the economy beyond the mere

procurement of goods and services. The Center will work with governments to design policies that broaden the policy scope and to enable them to capitalize upon project life cycles supply chains, project finance and employment opportunities to boost local economies. This can increase trade competitiveness and serve as an effective flywheel for employment creation, research and development, growth of the financial sector, manufacturing industries and service sectors.

(AfDB, 2015: 10)

Local content policies: the case of Nigeria

In April 2010, Nigeria passed the Nigerian Oil and Gas Industry Content Development Act[11] (henceforth referred to as the Nigerian Content Act or NCA). The NCA created the Nigerian Content Development and Monitoring Board (NCDMB) to monitor and enforce local content and ensure successful implementation of the local content objectives that the country began pursuing in 2001.[12] Nigeria was already building on almost a decade of promoting LCPs through the Nigerian National Petroleum Corporation (NNPC). Therefore, the case is useful for looking at the implementation of LCPs and how they may operate in practice.

The Nigerian Content Act defines Nigerian content as:

> The quantum of composite value added to or created in the Nigerian economy by a systematic development of capacity and capabilities through the deliberate utilization of Nigerian human, material resources and services in the Nigerian oil and gas industry.

It goes on to set minimum targets for Nigerian participation in 280 categories of oil services. Despite some resistance from the international oil companies and some problems with implementation because capacity simply does not exist to accomplish some of the targets, there has been a marked improvement in local content. Improvement is hard to quantify because there is still some difficulty in understanding how to measure local content (see Ovadia, 2013b). However, in numerous presentations and publications, the NCDMB estimates local capture of oil industry spend has gone from 5 percent to roughly 40 percent in the last decade. The 40 percent figure is generally accepted by industry experts. With average annual investment in the range of US$15 billion, local content is retaining over US$5 billion in the Nigerian economy annually.

There is a danger that local content will ultimately be more about reinforcing the power of the Nigerian elite and giving them new opportunities for rent-seeking. Therefore, this section will begin by analyzing some of the latest changes and newest initiatives put in place by the NCDMB and by the IOCs before proceeding to track some important implementation challenges, such as dealing with a lack of capacity to meet the local content targets set out in the NCA and developing a system to measure local content and a standard metric to be used by the government and all the oil companies. Once targets have been set, as they have been in Nigeria, the task remains of determining how to evaluate compliance with those targets.

The Board began reviewing and approving tenders for contracts within six months of being set up and also began a program of monitoring and evaluation. However, enforcement of Nigerian content is still quite informal. The NCDMB has yet to issue any fines or cancel any projects. Instead, when the Directorate of Monitoring and Evaluation has found violations, it has chosen to begin a dialogue with the company involved on how best to remedy the situation. This approach, according to an NCDMB official in the Directorate of Monitoring and Evaluation, may result in a new training program, hiring of new Nigerian staff, or other actions to satisfy the Board.[13] While the approach is useful for building local capacity and probably significantly more effective than issuing fines (which a company may calculate to be less burdensome than complying with the law), it does add a level of discretion in enforcement which could be abused.

Another area of concern for LCPs in Nigeria is that the NCA's approach of providing targets for Nigerian content that simply cannot be met in some cases has resulted in a system of granting ministerial waivers that is vulnerable to abuse. The waiver system became even more flawed when the formal system for granting waivers expired in April 2012, three years after the NCA came into force. At the "Stimulating Local Capacity" workshop in December 2012, organized by the Local Content Committee of the National Assembly to gather opinions about the waiver issue, there was widespread agreement that the system as it stands now is discretionary. There are few guidelines for the acceptance of waiver applications and a need for greater transparency, publication of waiver applications and approvals, and explicit penalties for not following waiver commitments.

The targets in the NCA are expressed as percentages in terms of overall spend, hours of labor, tonnage, or other defined measures. However, that is only the beginning of addressing the crucial question of how to measure local content. The real question is how to calculate the percentage of local content in any given activity to determine what the existing level is compared to the target in the Act. In the absence of concrete definitions and guidelines for how to measure Nigerian content, the NCDMB has fallen back on simplistic or surface measures for monitoring and evaluation – concentrating mostly on Nigerian ownership (whether or not a company is 51 percent Nigerian-owned).

The NCA requires full compliance with all targets in order to operate in Nigeria. The inability of Nigerian companies to supply the goods and services required by the NCA is not in dispute. Ernest Nwapa, Pioneer Executive Secretary of the NCDMB, has directly stated: "if you read the Schedule of the Act, you will know that there is hardly any part of that Schedule that you can comply with a hundred percent."[14] Robust metrics for measuring and reporting on local content are required to ensure effective implementation of the NCA. For these to be developed, the NCDMB will have to work together with the operating companies, industry groups, and labor and other civil society organizations to develop a strong measurement system with independent evaluation capacity.

Local content policies: the case of Ghana

LCPs are new in Ghana, as is the discovery and production of oil itself. The government of Ghana released a policy framework for LCPs in 2010, which laid out goals, objectives, and directions.[15] Ghana's new Local Content Law (GLCL) was passed in November 2013, which put in place regulations for local content and local participation in the petroleum sector.[16] The GLCL defines local content similarly to Nigeria as "the quantum or percentage of locally produced materials, personnel, financing, goods and services rendered in the petroleum industry value chain and which can be measured in monetary terms." The law seems to be modeled on Nigeria's NCA in that it sets up a new regulatory body for monitoring the implementation of LCPs and enforcing the new regulations. In this case, that body is a Local Content Committee, which operates as part of the Petroleum Commission. The Ghanaian law contains a very similar First Schedule to the Schedule of the NCA, setting minimum levels of local content in virtually the same categories of oil service activities. The GLCL replicates some of the problems with Nigeria's NCA in defining and measuring local content. While a strong definition is provided, the difficulty is in the lack of distinction between the goals of increasing participation of Ghanaian businesses and giving first consideration to goods manufactured in Ghana.

Clause 9 of the GLCL says that local content plans will be submitted to ensure that "first consideration is given to services provided within the country and goods manufactured in the country where the goods meet the specifications of the petroleum industry as established by the Standards Authority by other internationally acceptable standards." However, Clauses 11 and 12 are used to set the criteria for evaluating bids. In these clauses, preference is given only to Ghanaian companies. Furthermore, Clause 10 specifies that the minimum levels of local content are found in the First Schedule. That schedule provides targets only in terms of a percentage target for either Ghanaian labor or for a measurement (such as volume, tonnage, spend). For those measurements, it is not clear what constitutes local content. If the local content target is simply understood to mean the percentage supplied by an indigenous Ghanaian company, any good or service would be considered local content if the contract is with a Ghanaian company.

Unlike the NCA, the GLCL does not set further regulations about local content to avoid the practice of "fronting" (see Ovadia, 2013a). Additionally, in Ghana, there do not seem to be any provisions about companies sub-contracting foreign service companies or importing goods manufactured abroad. Although the GLCL makes it an offense for a Ghanaian to act as a "front," it defines front as "to deceive or behave in a particular manner to conceal the fact that a company is not an indigenous Ghanaian company," a definition which may be very hard to use to prevent the activities in practice. Finally, the GLCL does not tie winning a bid to local content by any measure other than ownership, and it is not clear that the minimum levels of local content required and reported in local content plans are measured in any way other than ownership.

There are many ways a foreign company can get around ownership laws.[17] For example, it can set up a joint venture that is 51 percent owned by a Ghanaian. There could be a side agreement on ownership, decision making, and/or profits. This could technically be a violation of the GLCL. Alternatively, if that joint venture company does not own its own machinery or carry out the work with its own employees, but instead sub-contracts from the multinational firm, there may be almost no profit for the joint venture company. Instead, all of the spend ends up abroad. It is unclear as of now that such an arrangement would be a violation of the law. In any case, it seems doubtful that Ghana would have the capacity to investigate and pursue these cases.

In Nigeria, there is a long history of failed "indigenization" (see Ovadia, 2013a). Therefore, the NCA promotes "domiciliation" over indigenization, particularly with respect to more technologically advanced or capital-intensive goods and services. Domiciliation means the focus is on requiring multinational oil service companies to set up facilities in-country to manufacture or fabricate goods or deliver services. Angola similarly divides services into categories based on complexity and has different local content requirements for different categories.

Without clear guidelines on how to measure local content in a more nuanced way in the local content reports submitted to the Petroleum Commission's Local Content Committee, there is no way to promote services provided within the country and goods manufactured in the country over goods and services provided by companies that are 51 percent owned by Ghanaians. Given the flaw in the law that allows any multinational to form a joint venture that is 51 percent Ghanaian and still keep the vast majority of the profits from the contracts it wins, and given that local content seems to be measured solely in terms of participation of Ghanaian companies, it is possible for companies to meet the local content targets of the GLCL without contributing significantly local content as defined in the GLCL.

Conclusion

LCPs have already contributed to oil sector transformation in Nigeria and across sub-Saharan Africa (Ovadia, 2016b). Capturing more of the annual investment in extractive industries through productive economic activity could have a dramatic impact on African economies. Elsewhere, from Brazil to Oman to Malaysia, LCPs have been making a positive impact on development and economic diversification.

In Nigeria, the NCDMB has the potential to succeed where previous attempts by the government and NNPC failed. What remains to be seen, however, is whether the NCDMB is enabled to conduct itself competently and professionally – particularly after the transition to a new Executive Secretary in 2015. The effectiveness of the NCDMB bureaucracy as well as the new Local Content Committee of the Petroleum Commission in Ghana will be major factors in determining the outcome of any development project. Those bodies will need high-level support to successfully implement LCPs; however, effective oversight can only be guaranteed if civil society is given a role in LCP and, importantly, in ensuring that the benefits of local content specifically, and oil extraction more generally, reach the majority of people.

Robust metrics for measuring and reporting on local content are required to ensure effective implementation of LCPs. For these to be developed, state institutions will have to work together with the operating companies, industry groups, labor, civil society organizations, research institutions, and other stakeholders to develop a strong measurement system with independent evaluation capacity. At the same time, they will have to expand their outreach to communities and to the public more generally to communicate the successes, challenges, and opportunities presented by local content. This outreach must go hand in hand with a standard for measuring local content in order for a clear picture to emerge about where the sector started from and what has been accomplished in terms of national development.

The schedules to the NCA and GLCL are controversial with the international oil industry. While in Nigeria IOCs are calling for significant reductions in the categories of services covered by the NCA, a more important priority is to set achievable targets that can be revised upwards as capacity develops. However, there is nothing wrong with the government communicating their priorities for building indigenous capacity. In fact, Ohno and Ohno note that goal orientation is key to successful state-led development. In many East Asian cases, the top government leader proclaimed a long-term national vision and direction without specifying details, and the appropriate government organizations were then created or designated to draft ambitious but feasible strategies and execute concrete action plans to realize this (Ohno and Ohno, 2012: 229–230). This is the model that the NCDMB and Local Content Committee must seek to emulate.

Local content has attracted surprisingly little attention from civil society groups. State agencies have made few efforts to engage civil society, and for their part, many organizations simply have not paid sufficient attention. Outside the international oil industry, international institutions are only now waking to the potential and significance of LCPs. For that reason, there is a lot that can be accomplished through applied research and encouraging public participation in the creation, implementation, and enforcement of these important policies and in ensuring an enabling governance environment for local content to operate and make good on Africa's development through natural resources.

Notes

1 This chapter is based upon an earlier article, Ovadia (2014) and draws heavily upon that material in several sections.
2 For a good summary of some of the flaws of modernization theory, see Valenzuela and Valenzuela (1978).
3 For a more in-depth exploration of the connection between LCPs and conflict in the Niger Delta, see Ovadia (2013d).
4 On Nigeria, see Ovadia (2013c); on Angola, Ovadia (2013e). For a complete picture of my arguments on local content and state-led development, see my recently published book (Ovadia, 2015a).
5 Interviews, December 2012.
6 See www.revenuewatch.org/rgi.
7 See http://naturalresourcecharter.org/.
8 Personal communication, July 2013. One area of local content that did make it into the revised EITI standard is provision 3.4(d), which requires that EITI reports include the number of jobs involved in the extractive sector as a total number and as a percentage of total employment. See http://eiti.org/document/standard.
9 Personal communication, May 2013.
10 See www.worldbank.org/en/events/2013/10/01/local-content-policies-in-oil-gas-mining-sector.
11 Available online at www.ncdmb.gov.ng/images/DOWNLOADS/NC-ACT/NC_ACT.pdf.
12 For a more in-depth history of local content in Nigeria and overview of the legal and regulatory framework, see Ovadia (2013a).
13 Interview, November 2012.
14 Presentation at "Operationalizing a Development Agenda for Local Content," June 25–26, 2012, Port Harcourt.
15 Available at http://ghanaoilwatch.org/images/laws/local_content_policy.pdf.
16 Available at www.energymin.gov.gh/wp-content/upLoads/Local-Content-LI-21.pdf.
17 I have discussed this problem in Ovadia (2012).

References

Abrahamsen, R. (2000) *Disciplining democracy: Development discourse and good governance in Africa*, London: Zed Books.

AfDB (2015) *African Natural Resources Center (ANRC) Strategy (2015–2020)*. Available: www.afdb.org/fileadmin/uploads/afdb/Documents/Boards-Documents/ANRC_Strategy_2015-2020_Rev_.pdf [May 21, 2016].

AMV (2011) *Building a sustainable future for Africa's extractive industry: From vision to action*, African Union Commission, African Development Bank & United Nations Economic Commission for Africa, December.

Bourgain, F. and Nem Singh, J. (eds) (2013) *Resource governance and developmental states in the Global South: Critical international political economy perspectives*, Basingstoke: Palgrave Macmillan.

Chang, H. (2003) "The East Asian development experience," in Chang, H. (ed.) *Rethinking development economics*, London: Anthem Press.

Chang, H. (2006) *The East Asian development experience: The miracle, the crisis and the future*, London: Zed Books.

Economist (2011) "Africa rising" *The Economist*, 3 December. Available: www.economist.com/node/21541015 [May 11, 2016].

Economist (2013) *Special report: Emerging Africa: A hopeful continent*, 2 March. Available: www.economist.com/sites/default/files/20130203_emerging_africa.pdf [May 11, 2016].

Ernst & Young (2014) *Creating shared value in Africa: Local content in the oil and gas industry*. Available: www.ey.com/Publication/vwLUAssets/EY-creating-shared-value-in-africa/$FILE/EY-creating-shared-value-in-africa.pdf [May 11, 2016].

IFC (2015) *The art and science of benefit sharing in the natural resource sector*. Washington, DC: International Finance Corporation.

Kaplan, Z. (2013) *Policy options for strengthening local content in Mozambique. Mozambique Support Program for Economic and Enterprise Development (SPEED)*, Maputo: USAID.

Kayizzi-Mugerwa, S. and Annaywu, J. C. (2015) *Creating local content for human development in Africa's new natural resource-rich countries*. Flagship Report No. 6, Abidjan: African Development Bank and Bill & Melinda Gates Foundation.

Kolstad, I. and Kinyondo, A. (2015) *Alternatives to local content*. WIDER Working Paper 2015/106, Helsinki: UNU-WIDER.

Kristoff, N. D. (2012) "Africa on the rise," *The New York Times*, July 1, SR11.

Lagarde, C. (2014) *Africa rising – Building to the future*, Keynote Address, Maputo, May 29. Available: www.imf.org/external/np/speeches/2014/052914.htm [May 11, 2016].

Mahajan, V. (2009) *Africa rising: How 900 million African consumers offer more than you think*, Upper Saddle River, NJ: Wharton School Publishing.

Mkandawire, T. (2010) "From maladjusted states to democratic developmental states in Africa," in Edigheji, O. (ed.) *Constructing a democratic developmental state in South Africa: Potentials and challenges*, Cape Town: Human Sciences Research Council.

NRGI (2015) *Local content: Strengthening the local economy and workforce*. NRGI Reader, March 2015, New York: Natural Resource Governance Institute.

OECD (2015) *Operational framework on public–private collaboration for shared resource-based value creation* (advanced draft), Paris: OECD Development Centre.

Ohno, I. and Ohno, K. (2012) "Dynamic capacity development: What Africa can learn from industrial policy formulation in East Asia," in Norman, A., Botchway, K., Stein, H. and Stiglitz, J. E. (eds) *Good growth and governance in Africa: Rethinking development strategies*, Oxford: Oxford University Press.

Ovadia, J. S. (2012) "The dual nature of local content in Angola's oil and gas industry: Development vs. elite accumulation," *Journal of Contemporary African Studies*, vol. 30, no. 3, pp. 395–417.

Ovadia, J. S. (2013a) "Indigenization vs. domiciliation: A historical approach to national content in Nigeria's oil and gas industry," in Falola, T. and Achberger, J. (eds) *The political economy of development and underdevelopment in Africa*, London: Routledge.

Ovadia J. S. (2013b) *Measurement and implementation of local content in Nigeria*, Lagos: Centre for Public Policy Alternatives. Available: http://cpparesearch.org/ [6 May 2013].

Ovadia, J. S. (2013c) "The making of oil-backed indigenous capitalism in Nigeria," *New Political Economy*, vol. 18, no. 2, pp. 258–283.

Ovadia, J. S. (2013d) "The Nigerian 'one percent' and the management of national oil wealth through Nigerian content," *Science & Society*, vol. 77, no. 3, pp. 315–341.

Ovadia, J. S. (2013e) "The reinvention of elite accumulation in Angola: Emergent capitalism in a rentier economy," *Cadernos de Estudos Africanos*, vol. 25, pp. 33–63.

Ovadia, J. S. (2014) "Local content and natural resource governance: The cases of Angola and Nigeria," *The Extractive Industries and Society*, vol. 1, no. 2, pp. 137–146.

Ovadia, J. S. (2016a) *The petro-developmental state in Africa: Making oil work in Angola, Nigeria and the Gulf of Guinea*, London: Hurst Publishers.

Ovadia, J. S. (2016b) "Local content policies and petro-development in Sub-Saharan Africa: A comparative analysis," *Resources Policy* [online]. Available: www.sciencedirect.com/science/article/pii/S0301420716300502 [April 13, 2016].

Revenue Watch Institute (2013) *The resource governance index: A measure of transparency and accountability in the oil, gas and mining sector*, New York. Available: www.revenuewatch.org/rgi [May 11, 2016].

Tordo, S. and Anouti, Y. (2013) *Local content in the oil and gas sector: Case studies*, Washington, DC: The World Bank.

Tordo, S., Warner, M., Manzano, O. E., and Anouti, Y. (2013) *Local content policies in the oil and gas sector*, Washington, DC: The World Bank.

UNECA (2013) *Making the most of Africa's commodities: Industrializing for growth, jobs and economic transformation, Economic Report on Africa 2013*, Addis Ababa: United National Economic Commission for Africa.

Valenzuela, J. Samuel and Valenzuela, Arturo (1978) "Modernization and dependency: Alternative perspectives in the study of Latin American underdevelopment," *Comparative Politics*, vol. 10, no. 4, pp. 535–557.

Van Rensburg, H. (2012) "Africa is rising fast," *Forbes*, September 11. Available: www.forbes.com/sites/techonomy/2012/11/09/africa-is-rising-fast/ [May 11, 2016].

Wall Street Journal (2012) "Hidden sub-Saharan boom is African growth 'miracle'," *The Wall Street Journal*, November 5.

Wallis, W. (2010) "Africa's frontier market ready to score," *Financial Times*, June 2.

World Bank (1997) *World development report: The state in a changing world*, Washington, DC: World Bank.

World Bank (2012a) *Increasing local procurement by the mining industry in West Africa, Report No. 66585-AFR*, January, Washington, DC: World Bank.

World Bank (2012b) *Note: Reporting on local content in the context of EITI*, April [Online], Available: http://eiti.org/ [8 July 2013].

7 When nature becomes a resource

Spaces of environmental protection, land management, and development issues in francophone Africa

Cristina D'Alessandro

Introduction

Environmental protection, conservation of nature, and sustainable development are political processes in which a number of social actors are involved in different ways as stakeholders. They are also geographical dynamics concerning first and foremost territories that are submitted to regulations and restrictions governing the way resources can be used when the environment is protected. As key issues in contemporary human geography, they greatly influence the relations between societies, as well as those between social groups and individuals, and the territories they live in or to which they are related for some reasons (tourism, migration, etc.) and they can engender conflicts between stakeholders with conflicting goals and points of view on resource use.

When environmental protection strategies are implemented in developing contexts, peculiar situations arise in which environmental protection is supposed to facilitate economic development. A long-term and sustainable development plan, however, also has to take into account the environment and its preservation. Today, this is a fundamental component of the sustainable development paradigm as it links to globalization. The situation is therefore paradoxical as the environment emerges as both a resource and a constraint, with stakeholders struggling to reconcile these two dimensions through ordinary procedures. If the synergy between development and environment does not happen, often because of incompatible and divergent interests, conflicts or problems may arise.

Francophone sub-Saharan Africa has a common history of environmental protection rooted in French colonization and common patterns that emerged from this legacy. This chapter looks at environmental protection in the context of francophone sub-Saharan Africa from a human geography perspective and, more precisely, in an approach inspired by a French political geography trend. Using this branch of human geography, it is possible to analyze transboundary environmental protection: the creation of a transboundary protected area that spans boundaries of more than one country, wherein political borders are abolished. These transboundary areas may be contiguous or a network of separated parks/reserves. New protected areas may be created and added to already existing parks and reserves. The developmental goal and the peacebuilding mission are emphasized in recent experiences.[1] When the ambition to create large transboundary protected areas becomes a reality in Africa, aiming to defy the political structure of the state and its preponderance, concerns and problems are very likely to arise. Successes are much more common at the local level, although limitations still exist even at this level. This text outlines some lessons that can be drawn from this statement on territorial governance and on related capacities. As this chapter cannot be exhaustive given the large number and heterogeneity of environmental protected areas, the text aims only to detail some lessons learned using select case studies, focusing on land issues and land-management concerns.

In line with what has previously been said, the chapter is divided into eight sections. After a short presentation of environmental protection from a geographical point of view, the differences between conservation and environmental protection, as well as their links with development, will follow with an overview on environmental protection in francophone Africa. National parks and transboundary protected areas will then be presented, focusing on the limits of these types of spaces, as they are often more conservationist than integrated and participative realities. This chapter will continue with a focus on the possibilities to reconcile environmental protection and socio-economic development, as evidenced through local environmental protection case studies. These case studies will permit insight into how approaches to land governance inspired by theoretical views on environmental governance can promote a better understanding of environmental protection contexts as well as better coordination of action and positioning of the different stakeholders involved. Environmental protection in francophone Africa, according to this analysis, will have greater opportunity to work in local contexts where land governance is related to smaller territories. Their reduced size more easily creates and promotes a sense of identity among local populations, which in turn helps to reduce or avoid conflicts that may arise from natural resource management and exploitation.

Environmental protection: a geographical perspective

Conservation of nature is the most extreme manifestation of environmental concerns: These nature-based approaches are mostly interested in preserving ecosystems and their components (fauna and flora) from any possible attack or threat caused by social activities or natural phenomena, such as climate change. However, environmental protection cannot be considered only as the management of natural resources. Rather, this crucial social domain is also an important sector of political action and activism, to which natural protected territories and land are central. Independent of size and typology (transboundary protected area, national park, regional park or reserve, local community reserve, etc.), these territories are submitted by competent park authorities to the spatial monitoring of human activities and of ecosystems' functioning and evolution (Chartier and Rodary 2007).

"Nature" is in fact a social (meaning a political) construction: Wilderness is an ideal, normally understood as a variety of spaces considered natural, according to their connotation as socially positive and esthetically enjoyable spaces. Nature is the set of phenomena, knowledge, discourses, and practices that result from a selective process of incorporation of physical and biological dynamics in a given society (Lévy and Lussault 2003). Interacting with the physical milieu of a territory at a precise time in history, a given society builds its own peculiar regime of legitimate relationships between human beings and physical spaces accepted by the majority. If, for instance, hunting was allowed in a given area, it may be prohibited when the same territory becomes a protected area. Even within the same society, the definition of nature is not ubiquitous as it varies according to the stakeholders considered: The nature of a park does not have the same meaning for park authorities, environmentalist NGOs, and tourism operators. The representation of nature and the relations between social groups and what they call nature are then crucial and often problematic.

Conservation of nature, born in the Western world with modernity and the nature/culture dualism, comes from the industrial revolution and the progressive destruction of environments engendered by industrialization (Rodary 2011). With this damage, particularly acute in urban areas at the beginning of the industrial era, the consciousness of these adverse effects and the will to avoid, protect, and restructure grew. This paradigm was consequently exported, becoming a global pattern during the era of colonization.

Environmental protection is a less extreme view in comparison with the conservationist positions that became common in the 1970s. The United Nations Conference on the Human Environment held in Stockholm, Sweden, encouraged the establishment of environmental protected areas around the world (Australia and China, for example). The United States Environmental Protection Agency, created in 1970, contributed to encourage environmental protection in the country. Since then, these activities have tried to reconcile global environmental concerns with social preoccupations and, more precisely, with economic development in the developing world (Rist 1996). These strategies also promote the participation of local communities in the management of their environmental resources. This chapter is in fact concerned with the different types and degrees of environmental protection in francophone Africa, as well as with the related land-management issues.

In fact, in Africa, as elsewhere, the territorial functioning of environmental protected areas can vary greatly (a game reserve in Botswana and a *forêt classée* in Senegal do not have the same goal and regulations), according to cultural conceptions, the distinct political conditions within which they are managed, their age, and their evolution (Depraz 2008). A double tendency has developed nowadays, explaining the predominance of two diametrically opposed scales of environmental protection. On one hand, global strategies are encouraged, through worldwide concerns such as global warming, animating calls for unified responses, networks of parks, and large-scale transborder protected areas, considered by the International Union for the Conservation of Nature (IUCN[2]) as the future of environmental protection. Peace Parks in Southern Africa are an example, which explicitly show that they are intended to contribute to peacebuilding. On the other hand, the micro-level is also widely privileged in some discourses eager to push and sustain local appropriation of national policies by communities and involve them in this reinterpretation and in their application to different realities. In Benin, for example, Law 93–009 (July 2, 1993) stipulating that the state owns the land of every protected forest has in practice encouraged collective use of forest land by local communities, given the impossibility for the state to centrally manage the land. Land and resource management has been locally agreed in the Kouffé Mountains, for instance, to allow the different stakeholders (women, fishermen, farmers, cattle breeders, loggers, etc.) to be part of this collective management system (Akouehou 2004).

Environmental protection and land management in francophone Africa: an overview

Environmental protection was introduced in Africa during colonial times and was continued after independence by African states and international organizations as a set of rules and policies for territorial planning and management. Among the contemporary stakeholders involved in these processes, the European Economic Community, which later became the European Union, and the IUCN have played a central role, both in funding or promoting scientific research and encouraging the creation of new environmental protected areas. During colonization, and less systematically afterwards, these processes have been imposed on African societies by force at first and, progressively after independence, by encouraging African governments and stakeholders through development discourses and a mirage of potential economic benefits from international funding mechanisms and ecotourism. These environmental protection strategies could have inspired popular movements of contestation but they have instead been "nipped in the bud" (Rodary 2011, 25) by the development industry of aid and its inspiring philosophy. In fact, African societies that have not previously had written environmental protection policies and laws but rather social traditional rules for the use of resources (Hannah 1992) have been considered as unaware and incapable of managing their natural environments. The introduction of restricted access to environmental resources and the regulation of human activities such as hunting, fishing, and traditional food gathering, caused conflicts to arise during colonial times in African societies that refused to acknowledge imposed rules and colonial authorities. French colonial archives report numerous stories of partially or totally protected forests in Côte d'Ivoire during the colonial time where the local population kept using the land for agricultural purposes: Colonial administrators were then forced to cancel these environmental protected areas. After independence, conflicts have still been common between societies or local communities struggling to see the anticipated economic benefits linked to environmental protection and the states or international organization that have led these processes. For this reason, for example, from 1990 to today, the Anguédédou forest near Abidjan has been protected and then partially given back to local stakeholders twice for concerted land management!

The first environmental protected areas on the African continent were created in Southern Africa around 1890 as game reserves, limiting and then prohibiting hunting activities in these areas and encouraging the practice of photographic tourism. The first park created on the continent was, in fact, the Kruger National Park, established in 1898 (www.sanparks.org/parks/kruger/). On this part of the continent, most of the subsequent reserves and parks were created between 1950 and 1970.

The history of environmental protected areas in francophone Africa is different, however, as hunting for sport is less common. Here environmental protection has been oriented from its beginning in the 1930s towards the creation of *forêts classées* (protected forests), most of which maintained their status of national protected areas after independence (Ribot 2001), even increasing in number after the 1960s (Mengue-Medou 2002). The surface of environmental protected areas in francophone Africa is very relevant: the Aïr and Ténéré reserve, in Niger, is the largest environmental protected area in Africa, covering 7.7 million hectares (http://whc.unesco.org/fr/list/573/), more than the surface of a country like Ireland. In Cameroun, environmental protected areas cover more than 20,504 km^2, or an estimated 4.3 percent of the country (Sournia 1998).

In francophone Africa, three generations of environmental protected areas can be identified: the colonial phase (1930–1950), the post-independence period (1960–1990) and the post-1990 period after the 1992 United Nations Conference on Environment and Development held in Rio de Janeiro, Brazil (Mengue-Medou 2002). Independent of their age and origin, in the former French colonies, the management of these territories is not autonomous but jointly executed with the competent central state structure, such as the Ministry of Tourism and Environment (in Burkina Faso, Cameroun, Gabon, Togo, etc.) or the Ministry of Rural Development and Agriculture (Chad, Mauritania, Mali, Niger, etc.) (Mengue-Medou 2002). In practice, the control exerted by central ministries is limited and park management can be considered as mainly autonomous in most former French colonies, such as in Senegal and Burkina Faso. Nevertheless, numerous challenges are reported to affect these territories, among which the lack of individual and institutional capacities affecting park management seems particularly dramatic over the long term.

From national parks to transboundary protected areas: the legacy used to envision the future

National parks: territories as resources for different stakeholders

The 1994 worldwide IUCN definition of a national park as "an area of land and/or sea especially dedicated to the protection and maintenance of biological diversity, and of natural and associated cultural resources, and managed through legal or other effective means" (Dudley and Stolton 2008,159), which underlines the recreational purpose of these territories as well as their final goal of ecosystem protection, raises various concerns and has been criticized for its limited criteria (Locke and Dearden 2005). In francophone Africa, especially in West Africa, ecotourism in national parks, for example, is a very limited phenomenon (Giraut et al. 2004) with marginal economic impacts, especially when compared to Southern Africa. The fact that the International Ecotourism Society (TIES) consists of twenty-four professional members in South Africa, compared to five in Benin (one of the francophone countries where ecotourism is more developed), four in Chad, and one in Niger speaks for itself.

Despite the heterogeneity of regulations, management and status, national parks in francophone Africa have in common certain legacies from the colonial period and the direct involvement of the state in the regulation and control of such spaces. Often these parks are created by including and extending the perimeter of a colonial *forêt classée* (several examples can be quoted, such as the Samba Dia forest in Senegal, the Ndama in Guinea, the Bassila in Benin, and others in Côte d'Ivoire, Gabon) or of a park that has existed since the colonial era (as in DRC with the Virunga, the Garamba and the Upemba national parks created during Belgian colonization). The state supervises these territories: in Senegal, for instance, national parks are the responsibility of the Direction des Parcs Nationaux (DPN), a service created in 1969 and housed by the Ministry of Environment, Conservation of Nature, Withholding Basins, and Artificial Lakes. Through environmental protection, states can then control these territories, which are often peripheral, and consequently can integrate them into continental or global processes, decreasing the capacity for action of local populations (Héritier 2007). Despite common discourses of integrated management and local participation, it has been demonstrated that in Southern Africa local populations are normally excluded from the dynamics related to national parks (Rodary et al. 2003). Even in francophone Africa, such difficulties and conflicts still exist because access to vital resources (forestry and land) can be restricted by environmental protection. The Anguédédou protected forest in Côte d'Ivoire, already mentioned above, is an appropriate example as the numerous subsequent conflicts were linked to the pressure on land for agricultural purposes driven by the urban growth of Abidjan. The increasing need of land by local stakeholders was limited by environmental protection restrictions.

In response, communities tend to find circumvention strategies commensurate with these restrictions. This is what happened, for instance, in

Madagascar, in the Ranomafana and Andringitra national parks. The former was created in 1921 during the colonial period, while the latter, born in 1991, is a more recent entity; they are both part of the forest corridor of Fianarantsoa (Toillier and Serpantié 2007). Between centralized decision making and local strategies of adaptation as well as transversal corridors of activity, a spatial perspective at the regional scale is needed. Confronted by these restrictions, local communities have developed different strategies with the commonality of an increased pressure on arable land. As most traditional farming activities are regulated or forbidden, local farmers have shifted to the production of local rum, converting their fields to grow sugar cane. Thus, traditional land management based on social rules has been replaced by an economic practice whereby land is exploited as a mining resource.

A park is a territory that includes a set of resources: Different stakeholders may be interested in different resources, resources to which they ascribe different meanings. If local communities are principally concerned by forest and land resources, NGOs and conservationists may consider biodiversity as the primary resource (with the goal of protecting the fauna and the flora from any possible threat), while the central state may understand the park as an administrative decentralized territory, possibly including other resources. This is the case in the Virunga national park in DRC, where international stakeholders (WWF, IUCN, UNESCO, and the private sector) have been involved after the government granted two oil companies, Total and Soco, concessions inside the perimeter of the park to explore underground oil reserves. The WWF initiated complaint proceedings against Soco for violation of social responsibility (Caramel 2013). In June 2014, Soco abandoned drilling in the Virunga Park (www.theguardian.com/environment/2014/jun/11/soco-oil-virunga-national-park-congo-wwf). As demonstrated in this case, environmental protection and economic development are difficult to reconcile because they represent different visions of resources in the territories concerned. Stakeholders may not have the same vision of such territorial resources and of the means by which to manage and protect them, but, as this example demonstrates, the territory is always considered as a resource for the resources that it contains, independent of the type of stakeholder and of the precise history associated with it. The complexity of these dynamics and the likelihood of conflict, directly proportional to the number of stakeholders and to the resources available, both increase with the size of these areas. Already high for national parks, these probabilities are even higher in the case of transboundary protected areas.

Transboundary protected areas in francophone Africa: some examples and considerations

Since 1992, when the 4th World Parks Congress took place in Caracas, Venezuela, the IUCN has asserted that transboundary protected areas are the future of conservation. Transboundary cooperation and management are, as such, promoted. In 2003, during the 5th World Park Congress in Durban, South Africa, the IUCN added a further provision to include regional networks and corridors of environmental protected areas. The target is that all protected areas should be linked into a wider ecological/environmental system on land and sea by 2015. Even if details on how these systems could be practically operationalized have not yet been given, documents mention that intergovernmental action should be fostered. Coordinated and consistent systems of management should be developed for these networks on a regional level. With such a global initiative, the IUCN intends also to promote peace and to facilitate cross-border mobility and trade of local populations within these cross-border protected areas. To this extent, social, economic, political, legal, and institutional cooperation are promoted worldwide, along with transboundary conservation. This trend has been rapidly developing in Africa since the 1990s, as peace and stability in sensitive regions of the continent are prioritized (Ramutsindela 2007).

The Niokolo-Badiar ecological complex is a cross-border park created in 1994 between Southern Senegal and Northern Guinea. It comprises the Senegalese Niokolo-Koba national park created by the French in 1954 (a UNESCO worldwide patrimony and biosphere reserve since 1981) and, on the Guinean side in the prefecture of Koundara, the Badiar national park. The Nikolo-Badiar complex includes these two protected areas as well as the *forêt classée* of Badiar South, the *forêt classée* of N'Dama and a peripheral area (or buffer zone), all three of which are located on the Guinean side. This ecological complex, which has included 1,409,723 ha since creation (Niokolo-Badiar project, 1996–97, Landsat TM satellite imagery) (Pellegrini 1996), benefited from intense scientific research, financed by the European Union Upper Niger and Upper Gambia River Basin Regional Management Program, 6th European Development Fund, by researchers and intern students from different Senegalese, Guinean, and Italian universities between 1995 and 1999. Among the questions that guided the research, the most important was certainly the difficult reconciliation between the economic activities of local communities (mainly fishing, hunting, agriculture, cattle breeding, and food gathering) and the conservation strategy.

At the time, in an attempt to avoid major conflicts, researchers advised the authorities to create three distinct zones: a central, integrally protected zone; a surrounding, partially protected zone in which economic activities would be allowed but regulated; and a transition zone in which cooperative efforts of economic development would be encouraged and sustained (Pellegrini 1996). Despite these attempts, conflicts were still reported during fieldwork at the end of the 1990s between local communities and park rangers: Land-management restrictions and rules imposed by environmental protection were not accepted as they affected agriculture and cattle breeding, and conflicts happened whenever rangers tried to sanction illegal behaviors. Furthermore, since the beginning of the new millennium, the situation has progressively degenerated due to lack of funding, following the withdrawal of the European Union from the project, and poor management. As management and leadership capacities were not built over time, local managers struggled to adapt to decreasing funding and worsening conditions on the ground: when the European manager supporting the Guinean manager left, the situation suddenly worsened. In the field, it became more and more evident that the ecological complex was destined to disappear and that the two remaining national parks were going to be managed by the respective states according to their national environmental legislation and capacities. The Badiar was still managed by state authorities (a *conservateur*) for some years but was ultimately afflicted by longstanding political turmoil in Guinea. Today, the park barely exists on paper and both development and conservation are at stake in this peripheral region far from Conakry. The Niokolo, which seemed destined to a better future, has had huge management concerns and, in 2007, UNESCO added it to the list of worldwide patrimony in danger. Ecotourism never produced the expected economic returns: The Simenti Hotel, the first touristic hotel built in the 1990s, and subsequent touristic structures, were in fact not enough or properly advertised and the road system has always been insufficient and poorly maintained. The local Mandingue peasants, scared by a possible lack of land, extended slash-and-burn agricultural practices (even illegally to protected land) and shortened the fallow period, in turn endangering the biodiversity of the region (Larrue 2002). Despite a multi-stakeholder meeting that took place in Saly Portudal, Senegal, in August 2007 and other attempts in 2011–2013 by the IUCN (attempts that included a planning workshop in January 2011 and a development project to sustain local communities in 2013), the park is now centrally managed by the DPN and is still a failure.

The system of protected areas W-Arly-Pendjari (SAP-WAP, Système d'Aires Protégées W-Arly-Pendjari) is a complex of twenty-four environmental protected areas covering about 3,000,000 ha (Casti and Yonkeu 2009), including the regional Park of W (a transborder protected area encompassing Benin, Burkina Faso, and Niger), the Arly national park in Burkina Faso and the Pendjari national park in Benin. The system was born in 2000 through the Tripartite Agreement, uniting preexisting parks and reserves. Among the challenges that remain unsolved, transhumant cattle farming has been identified as a crucial question, since the foundation of the W Park and pastoral land-tenure issues in and around the park could compromise environmental protection. More frequent drought events linked to climate change in the Sahel region, the spread of cotton production, and land conflicts between farmers and cattle breeders have pushed these cattle breeders to use park land for their transhumant grazing (Convers et al. 2007). The same problem has also been reported in the Arly national park, where the transhumance corridor amplifies the tensions linked to environmental regulations and restrictions (Casti and Yonkeu 2009). Slash-and-burn agriculture has also been considered as another important economic activity: The existing studies (Grégoire and Simonetti 2007) may help to better plan the future management of the area. Their major goal is to produce and constantly update a database including all the bushfires that have happened in the park from 2000 to today. According to the authors, this information, constantly transmitted to the park authorities, should allow them to monitor and measure the degree to which management plans are implemented and the areas where local communities threaten the implementation.

Village tourism is developing in the complex as an efficient way to try to reconcile environmental protection, cultural valorization of the territory, and economic development. A system of tourism is progressively emerging in the Arly national park (Casti and Yonkeu 2009), with different types of tourism in different areas and specialized vacations. Nevertheless, this development of the tourism industry is limited by structural problems, including a concerning infrastructure gap: Paths and banks see their conditions worsen due to poor maintenance and lack of funds. The core problem of the SAP-WAP complex, however, is that a unified management entity has never been set in place. The management has been ensured by the central national administrations in charge of the environmental protected areas in each of the three countries involved (Benin, Burkina Faso, Niger). Even if competent authorities were to manage in a concerted way, a unified political and administrative entity does not exist: Four separate and autonomous bodies (two for Burkina Faso), accountable to the respective states, manage the three national territories. As such, a transboundary protected area does not fully exist in this case.

In the previous examples, cross-border experiences are based on contiguous or proximate parks and reserves in the same region. In Central Africa, the Network of Protected Areas of Central Africa (RAPAC, Réseau d'Aires Protégées d'Afrique Centrale) was created in May 2000, linking eighty-two protected areas in eight countries (Cameroun, Congo, Gabon, Equatorial Guinea, Central African Republic, Democratic Republic of Congo, São Tomé and Príncipe, and Chad). The RAPAC is a direct consequence of the Yaoundé Declaration, signed on March 17, 1999, by the heads of state in the region, aimed at concerted action for the regional development of the forest system in Central Africa: Forests are at the heart of this process. Following the Yaoundé Declaration, the RAPAC, an independent regional inter-professional association, is in charge of the management of the environmental protected areas in Central Africa. The RAPAC includes both government and non-governmental stakeholders who share common technical and scientific goals. Given the size and the structure of this network, which includes parks and reserves far away from each other, a unique management scheme would be difficult to set in place for the short term. Nevertheless, the RAPAC has produced a Strategic Plan (www.rapac.org/index.php?option=com_content&view=article&id=247:plan-strategique&catid=91&Itemid=100043) to operationalize participative professional management of resources for both environmental protection and the development of the included protected areas. Knowledge management, concerted management, socio-economic development, and sustainable funding mechanisms are at the core of this plan. The document focuses on the need to build strategic partnerships among stakeholders to increase public awareness of the importance of environmental strategies. In addition, at the centralized level, the Yaoundé Declaration also encouraged the creation of the Conference of Ministers in charge of the Forests in Central Africa (COMIFAC, Conférence des Ministres en charge des Forêts d'Afrique Centrale) in June 2002 to coordinate all the institutions and initiatives in the forestry sector in the region. From the beginning, the COMIFAC has been handicapped by two main limitations, however: the lack of a unified legal framework and the need for a sustainable funding mechanism for its activities.

RAPAC and COMIFAC are principally intended to protect the forests, despite the large variety of landscapes that exist in Central Africa. This can be understood because of the anthropic pressure to which forests are subjected and because of their potential strategic role in the geopolitical peace and stability of the region. As resources at risk of disappearing by mismanagement, forests should become key resources of cooperation and socio-economic development. "Peace forests" here can be considered as the equivalent of the Peace Parks in Southern Africa: Integrated strategies are essential to this goal (Ramutsindela 2004). Forests are, nevertheless, more often spaces of conflict among different stakeholders with interests in different territorial resources. For the Kouffé Mountains in Benin, Gaston Akouehou (2004) identifies four levels of conflict between the state and local communities, native and nonnative stakeholders, farmers and transhumant cattle breeders, and local populations and forestry businesses. This can be generally considered true beyond this peculiar context. For different stakeholders with conflicting interests related to the forest, the territory, at the local scale, is a resource or a set of resources. For this reason, Gaston Akouehou suggests that, to solve these conflicts, a consensus among the concerned stakeholders is needed in order to reach a temporary compromise that may be renegotiated and adapted if the situation changes. The scale of this negotiation, according to the author, is inter-community cooperation, with the local level serving as the starting point of a wider cooperation process.

The local level is consequently very sensitive, exposed to conflicts, and crucial for mechanisms of cooperation. In official documents, such as its strategic plan, (www.rapac.org), the RAPAC claims to promote integrated and participative conservation and particular attention is given to ecotourism and alternative livelihood strategies for local populations. The vast majority of the ongoing projects and programs are nevertheless focused on biodiversity conservation. For this reason, human–elephant conflicts are still reported at the present time in the RAPAC, demanding that an attenuation strategy for these conflicts be developed. These conflicts, similar to others related to cattle breeding or to agriculture or to different economic activities elsewhere, signal that local populations struggle to acquire ownership of these processes. Local populations still see these transboundary protected areas primarily as conservation strategies and they are mostly interested in the biodiversity of these territories. Certainly, environmental protection and conservation are not the same, but are environmental protected areas really compatible with socio-economic development in francophone Africa? Under what conditions is this possible?

Environmental protection and development in francophone Africa: the impossible marriage?

As previously highlighted, environmental protection strategies are not easy to set in place and maintain along the same line without shifting to conservationist behaviors: Integrated and participative strategies truly concerned with socio-economic development of local populations are a challenge in francophone Africa, but also beyond (Rodary et al. 2003). Rules and imposed restrictions on the use of natural resources, what Amadou (2004) calls "external patrimonialisation," are more likely to create conflicts among stakeholders than territorial identities, understood as a sense of ownership and belonging through which local communities get involved in environmental protection and endorse it as a means to economic development. This is what Amadou talks about in the W Park where cattle breeders have felt dispossessed from their pastoral territories since the park's creation (Amadou 2004). Boissière and Doumenge (2008), using examples from DRC and Gabon, advocate for an agreement between local communities and "strong" actors of conservation (states, international NGOs, the private sector) to respect land rights and rights of usage of local populations as well as the territories of local communities. The examples cited above also emphasize that national parks and transboundary protected areas, which are expected to further extend their territories and their buffer zones according to global trends, are simply too large. For this reason, these huge territories are less likely to create territorial identity.

This trend is confirmed by the systematic and widespread use of geographic information systems (GIS) to create and manage large environmental protected areas. GIS is a computerized cartography using geo-referenced data, organized by thematic layers that can be selected and superimposed in various ways to produce screen or paper maps depicting multiple types of information at various scales. GIS are, in fact, used to support discourses of public participation although they hide digital imperialism. Digital imperialism, known and documented in Southern Africa, is also a reality in francophone Africa. Digital imperialism can be defined as the procedure by which the production and use of spatial digital data, obtained through GIS, increases the power of some stakeholders (namely park authorities, states, conservationist NGOs) through which they control communities, resources, and territories (D'Alessandro-Scarpari et al. 2008). As happens in the Peace Parks of Southern Africa, GIS have also been used in the Niokolo and in the Badiar from the beginning (the author can testify to this, having been present in the field) to support discourses of conservation with "scientific and irrefutable" proofs and to map in detail the entire area of the park to allow park authorities to better control it. The same can be asserted for the SAP-WAP complex, as GIS maps were produced by the Diathesis Cartographic Lab (University of Bergamo, Italy) for the W Park (included in the SAP-WAP) to better capitalize the information available on the park's buffer zones (Casti and Yonkeu 2009). In the W Park, GIS have always been used to map the use of slash-and-burn agricultural techniques and their seasonal changes, studies required by the park authorities to better control these activities (Grégoire and Simonetti 2007). Available documents also prove that participatory forest mapping of local communities in DRC, using GIS, has occurred in the Tshela Basankusu and Teturi forests, both of which are included in the RAPAC network (www.osfac.net). The GIS participatory cartography undertaken for these two community forests, eager to improve forest management by local protection of natural resources, does not have any direct effect on decision making; it produces a database of information on community forests, but real policy processes are not currently reported. GIS are used by park authorities (or state authorities) to gather constantly updated information on various issues of interest, recognizing that producing and using GIS analyses creates an advantage over other stakeholders (who don't have access or the necessary knowledge to do the same) in the event of a conflict or in a bid to control the park territory. Consequently, GIS do not directly influence land management, contribute to policy frameworks, or inspire decision-making processes in the RAPAC; nevertheless, better and consistently updated information on conflictual issues, such as land management, indirectly helps park authorities make decisions to minimize controversies with local communities and to better monitor sensitive areas.

This common use of GIS, even with its different meanings and scope in the different case studies mentioned here, is a sign of a deeper and more structural link in conservation between scientific research, a technical approach to park management, and state control over populations and spaces (Rodary 2008). This vision, antithetical to the exploitation of nature for social well-being, tends to transform these environmental protection processes in conservationist behaviors. For this purpose it benefits from a strong connection between scientific researchers and conservationist NGOs, hence presenting a pervasive presence in francophone Africa (Rodary 2011, 25–26).

This explains why livelihood strategies of local communities and economic development are not the main concerns in many environmental protected areas in francophone Africa. Ecotourism, viewed and presented by official discourses as the panacea to development concerns and the key driver of local economies in environmental protected areas, is, in reality, only a marginal activity in francophone Africa, in contrast with anglophone Africa, where game reserves and ecotourism have a longer history and better supporting infrastructure. In francophone Africa, ecotourism is still a mirage as it generally generates insufficient earnings for local communities. Better policies (especially related to land management), innovative funding mechanisms (including effective microfinance tools), and the improvement of public awareness and information access (through *ad hoc* campaigns) are needed to make ecotourism more economically attractive in francophone Africa. Other economic activities beyond ecotourism (craft industry, eco-certified productions, pharmaceutical, honey production, and more sustainable agriculture and fishing, etc.) are not even seriously considered or set in place. All the examples above can be used as a proof: Fragile or failed states, lack of basic infrastructure, non-existent or insufficient tourism infrastructure, and low levels of investment from the private sector may all explain the marginality of ecotourism in the region considered in this chapter. How then is development the complement of environmental protection in these parks? What should the development options of the populations living in or around environmental protected areas be in francophone Africa? Aren't conflicts among stakeholders more likely to happen when populations don't consider environmental protection as a means to improve their economic status?

Local experiences of environmental protection: peri-urban spaces and communities reserves

Environmental concerns are nowadays also a preoccupation in local spaces. This is even more evident and problematic in sensitive territories, where conflicts over natural resources are more likely to happen because of important demographic pressures, scarcity of resources, and competition among stakeholders, increased by global environmental change (Simon 2010). Peri-urban spaces are among these types of territories. They can be defined as the margins or edges of cities, the overlapping spaces between the "real" urban space and the hinterland, considered as the rural area. They question the contemporary reality and definition of what is rural, but they also show how urban realities are changing in their morphology and in their logics of functioning (Poulot 2008).

In Africa, peri-urban spaces are transitional territories in which a plurality of land uses (private, public/state, community/tribal, de facto), economic activities (horticulture, agriculture, construction of houses, commerce, investments in big-time ventures), and stakeholders (individuals and families, NGOs, city authorities, private small businesses, large multinationals) coexist, often in a problematic or conflictual way and frequently linked to widespread poverty and inequalities (Baker 1997). In Central Africa, peri-urban areas surround highly populated cities, with Kinshasa as the most extreme example. They are subject to a very significant demographic growth and placed under a hybrid structure of power between state power and traditional authorities. These territories experience an aggravated degradation of the environment, linked to various economic activities undertaken by "new" migrants in transit and by long-established households (Trefon and Cogels 2007). In this part of Africa, peri-urban spaces are a priority for natural resource management and for environmental protection. In Kinshasa, two peri-urban areas, Bateke Plateau and Bas-Congo, both major fuel-wood and charcoal supply zones, are subject to high land pressure and to overuse of forest resources, reflecting the fact that local management of land by traditional authorities (village chiefs) has failed. Ongoing negotiations on community-based land-management regulations testify that awareness is increasing locally about reforestation and environmental protection (Vermeulen et al. 2011). Peri-urban spaces, as territories that experience both conflict and compromise among different stakeholders, are hybrid, moving, and fluid zones that are more exposed to environmental degradation. Consequently, environmental protection, especially as this relates to land use for residential and agricultural purposes and access to infrastructure, can be difficult (Simon 2008).

In Western Africa, the city of Abidjan, in Côte d'Ivoire, is another interesting example, highlighting similar problems. Along the Gulf of Guinea, a spatial corridor with a strip of large cities has been developed on the coast since the colonial period and has grown even faster after independence. Abidjan is a paradigmatic case in this sense: Its important demographic growth and resulting negative impacts on the environment have been anticipated since the colonial era, precipitating the creation of the Banco National Park in the city itself and the *forêt classée* of Anguédédou in the northern periphery of the city. Despite these efforts, Abidjan is today a metropolis with more than three million inhabitants, and economic activities and housing construction in the peri-urban area are engendering a serious degradation of the environment and putting in danger these two environmental protected areas. The competition in peri-urban areas between agriculture (which has recently tried to enter the forest) and constantly growing residential areas is a strong concern that state strategies are failing to address effectively (Kouadio Oura 2012). Under the pressure of urban sprawl and increasing requests, the municipality grants building permits easily and land is given through informal procedures for housing purposes. This disorder brings environmental degradation and produces conflicts. In fact, the municipality, eager to try to get better earnings through building permits for housing, continually cuts agricultural land. The post-independence urban planning for a sustainable city has never been implemented: Housing problems and food security concerns are not properly taken into account as core issues for the urban population. Increasing levels of extreme poverty, hopeless individuals and households explain behaviors that damage the environment: firewood collection, for example, is the only way to cook and to heat the house for a vast majority of local citizens. Raphaël Kouadio Oura (2012) asserts that state authorities should encourage adapted measures for butane gas consumption to address the high prices of gas bottles that are currently unaffordable for most people and the reason why 80 percent of cooking activities use wood and charcoal.

Despite all these problems, it has to be acknowledged that the Ebrié living in Abidjan, traditionally a fishing ethnic group, fight collectively to protect the environment: The Ebrié lagoon is in fact seriously degraded by urban sprawl. Traditional authorities and groups of villagers have undertaken different actions (meetings, land-management attempts considering next generations) aimed at addressing their environmental concerns, although they tend to get obsessed and discouraged by the fact that state authorities do not relay their action to further levels and do not support it with adapted policies and legislation (Kouadio Oura 2012).

Improper use of forest resources affects peri-urban areas where demographic pressure, competition for land access, insecurity, and poverty are acute concerns, although this phenomenon is not limited to urban peripheries. It is also a sign of a deeper change in the relations between local communities and forest resources. The village of Popenguine, a town of about 3,000 people located approximately 70 km south of Dakar, Senegal, along the Petite Côte, is a good example of this trouble and a case study of applicable solutions. This village, like many others in Senegal, has a village forest that villagers use to handpick tree species and other resources, in accordance with a traditional user's regulation. These traditions fell progressively into disuse and, consequently, the village forest was mostly destroyed and destined to disappear: Villagers reported to the author that the forest was attacked by people from outside Popenguine who had come to destroy the village.

The Senegalese state, aware of this serious situation, established by decree the natural reserve of Popenguine in 1986 covering 1,009 ha. In 1988, an association of 129 women, the network of women of Popenguine for the protection of nature (RFPPN, Réseau des Femmes de Popenguine pour la Protection de la Nature), was locally created with support and training provided by some NGOs and media in order to restore the degraded forest in a participatory way and integrate it into a wider development strategy. Development was based on the creation of a tourism compound, Ker Cupaam: This economic activity then produced revenue that was invested to revitalize the forest. Progressively, the increasing and more consistent earnings have been used to maintain the compound with regular maintenance work, to reinvest in village infrastructure (a childcare facility was built in the village), and to finance retirement schemes for the association's members. The forest has become part of a "community natural space" (Ndiaye 1998) in which the two territories (the forest and the village) are complementary, working together to achieve the final joint goals of environmental protection and the socio-economic development of the local community.

Protracted field research from 1997 to today has allowed the author to observe that the experience of Popenguine, often idealized and considered as a textbook case for analogous experiences in Europe and South America, is not without problems in the longer term. The succession to the first generation of women who created the RFPPN appears very difficult,[3] and a lack of rules about the formal relation between the RFPPN and the reserve authorities responsible for decision making related to the forest has created an unclear legal situation. Legally, the *conservateur*, the reserve authority emanating from the Ministry of Water and Forests, is the only person allowed to manage and make decisions concerning the forest: In reality, however, he/she cannot ignore the RFPPN because it is a strategic stakeholder.

Nevertheless, the community natural space of Popenguine has created a trend in Senegal and beyond. Environmental protection tends to be a local reality, in which communities drive a process where the environment, when properly maintained, becomes a powerful tool of development that empowers local stakeholders in formulating a successful strategy adapted to the local context (Ndiaye 2010). The limits and achievements underlined in the case of Popenguine, but also in the other examples of local environmental protected areas, show that land governance, which starts from local territories and communities, is a key driver of a successful multiscalar process. Territories, and the relations within corresponding communities, are crucial to facilitating environmental protection based on socio-economic development. In francophone Africa, capacity gaps have to be reported which slow down and handicap land governance.

Land governance and capacities for environmental protection

Land governance approach

In the case of Abidjan, Raphaël Kouadio Oura (2012) refers to urban governance, emphasizing that, in this peculiar case, urban and peri-urban land use are at the core of urban land governance. He also makes explicit that city authorities, traditional communities, state authorities of environmental protection, and urban planners are part of this city governance.

In Central Africa, Trefon and Cogels (2007) use the expression "environmental governance," defining it in these peri-urban contexts as the way in which stakeholders exert power on natural resources. They add that stakeholders, resources, and spaces are key variables and that local factors are particularly important because legal frameworks often do not correspond to the realities that people experience in their ordinary lives. These two authors insist on the central role that must be given to local stakeholders and local communities in environmental protection strategies, although they also underline the numerous capacity gaps that exist at every scale (state authorities, local governments, communities, private sector, etc.).

Based on these insights into francophone Africa, it is possible to go more in depth into urban governance using Patrick Le Galès' insights (Le Galès 1995). This French urban sociologist, who follows an approach inspired by urban geography and urban planning, notes that city government includes various stakeholders: local authorities, private enterprises, public and semi-public agencies, various state authorities and agents, consultants, research and technical organizations, and civil society organizations. Urban governance then expresses an increased diversity in the way services may be delivered, their flexibility, and the variety of possible stakeholders, giving birth to a local democracy. According to Le Galès, local authorities are certainly important stakeholders of urban governance, although the same could be said for the state. Urban governance focuses not only on the action of every stakeholder but also on the motivations behind actions and the symbolic value of political action; it highlights networks of "local" stakeholders (stakeholders who act locally even if they are not locally present) where the local space is the common ground of a local territorial identity.

Land governance is a governance approach linked to a given territory and focused on land issues and concerns. Land governance is the interaction of various stakeholders intervening at the local scale in the territory as they try to defend their interests and views on land, natural resource management, and environmental protection. Every stakeholder has its strategies, its discourses, and its capacities, but land is always at the core of all action, either materially (by physically transforming it) or symbolically (by using it in discourses and to build *ad hoc* strategies). Land is also central because it is the object and final goal of environmental protection, meaning that land governance is environmental, and vice versa.

Land governance is not only a theoretical approach: It is more importantly an operational pattern for stakeholders to better understand situations and conflicts and to manage complex multiscale realities. Customary and indigenous land ownership not recognized by state laws engenders conflicts, environmental degradation, and land-management concerns (for instance, when large multinationals are responsible for extensive land-grabbing operations through state consent). A serious land-management gap is linked to the fact that most of the land (some say 90 percent of the total land available!) is still untitled in Africa: Without legal owners, the state can easily lease or sell it without even informing local communities. If statutory attempts to recognize customary land rights are reported in Africa, they are still mainly in anglophone Africa (Mozambique, Botswana, Tanzania) (Knight 2010).

Land governance is nevertheless an approach that needs precise and sophisticated capacities which most stakeholders lack, giving them a conspicuous disadvantage when compared to others who are better able to map the situation and the challenges on the ground or who possess financial and technical facilities to access such information.

Some capacity gaps for land governance in francophone Africa

In francophone Africa, the long history of imposed rules for environmental protection to which local communities have been subject contribute to explaining, with widespread poverty and social inequalities, the need to build technical and financial capacities for local communities. This poor level of local state authority capacity, in rural as well as in urban and peri-urban spaces, has been maintained, if not increased, by the inefficient decentralization of African states, by insufficient socio-economic development, and by policies and legislations maladjusted to national contexts. Corruption has contributed to worsen the situation in many contexts. States have consequently been unable to articulate national and local policies, resulting in local communities that are not provided with the fundamental capacities to take an active part in land governance, even when motivated and determined to act. The inefficient or insufficient action for environmental protection of local traditional actors in the case of Abidjan or, by contrast, the success of the RFPPN in Popenguine, confirms that ethnic prioritization is critical. Political ecology movements have in fact a limited capacity for action in Africa (Rodary 2011) and this is even more acute in francophone Africa where, compared to anglophone Africa, their presence is more limited and with less take-up on the ground: Local populations cannot rely on them.

For this reason, knowledge sharing is crucial for land governance aimed at protecting the environment from further damage. It is important to share success stories, common struggles, and difficulties at every level: Among neighboring villages in the same region, sharing similar preoccupations, as in the case of Popenguine, the first natural community space in Senegal, inspires others to follow. Civil society organizations are also crucial stakeholders raising awareness at every level on land issues. Sharing information allows also individual capacities to be built through the promotion of better leadership skills. Knowledge also has to be shared for environmental protection in francophone Africa because the schools training specialists in this sector are very limited in number (Mengue-Medou 2002). Sharing technical and scientific knowledge should also facilitate the creation of a participatory community mechanism to promote transparency, coordination, and consultation in local environmental resource management (Ndiaye 2010, 35).

When local territories are wider, as in the case of national parks or transboundary protected areas, land governance is more difficult because institutional mechanisms are not strong enough and territories are too vast in size to promote ownership among local populations. Often this institutional weakness is compounded by the absence of common legal frameworks at the national level, making implementation of environmental protection even more difficult. Legal and policy capacities able to incorporate land concerns in environmental protection strategies need to be built nationally and subsequently used as frameworks at the local and international level.

Conclusion

In the end, the alchemy between environmental protection and socio-economic development is very difficult in francophone Africa at every scale, although particularly with large-scale environmental protected areas. Even at the local level, a strong will, determination, and involvement of all the concerned stakeholders are needed to obtain real land governance, produce positive effects on the environment, and reverse damaging mechanisms and behaviors. Nevertheless, this is the best-case scenario, but what would be the consequences if, as Stéphane La Branche (2009) notes, local populations refuse or are reluctant to modify their behaviors and strategies for a better land governance for environmental-protection goals?

There is a serious risk that local communities are either marginalized (using discourses of public participation and integrated approaches) or that they are used with demagogic strategies (Boissière and Doumenge 2008) that benefit only "strong" stakeholders (states, international NGOs, and multinationals). Another threat for local communities is their relative role or progressive disappearance, in the name of global environmental concerns that cannot be considered at the local level, because they are part of a biodiversity cosmopolitics (Rodary 2008).

The examples cited have confirmed that local communities remain key stakeholders for land management: Their consensus and real participation in environmental-protection strategies have to be ensured and effective. To this extent, local civil society organizations are precious intermediaries, ensuring better local action and links with the national and international levels. At the same time, better national legal and policy frameworks are also needed: These frameworks need to find solutions that properly recognize customary and indigenous land rights in statutory instruments. Acknowledging that these legal questions are not easy to solve and adapting frameworks to specific national contexts is a very pressing issue in francophone Africa, where insufficient attention permits land-grabbing operations on a large scale.

Unsurprisingly, leadership capacities are at the core of this process for sustainable land management. Better leadership for national and local authorities, more capable park authorities and civil society organizations, better informed and capable local communities, more accessible technical knowledge, and an enhanced private sector together help reconcile ecotourism and other economic activities with environmental protection and serve as the fundamental measures to address land-management issues in environmental protected areas in francophone Africa.

Notes

1 See www.tbpa.net/.
2 Created in 1948, the IUCN is the largest and oldest global environmental network. It addresses environmental and development challenges, supports research, and manages field projects.
3 The women explained personally to me in 2007 that, despite some trials, they struggled to find successors locally: They also tried to involve some men, but without success. Some young women have subsequently been trained, but the concern is whether leadership capacities have been built sufficiently to ensure that the RFPPN survives.

References

Akouehou, Gaston S. (2004) "Environnement institutionnel et gestion traditionnelle des espaces forestiers: cas de la région des Monts Kouffé au Centre du Bénin." *Les Cahiers d'Outre-Mer*, April–September: 226–227, http://com.revues.org/526 (accessed May 11, 2016).

Amadou, Boureima (2004) "Aire protégée et construction de territoire en patrimoine: l'exemple de l'île de Karey Kopto (Niger)." *Les Cahiers d'Outre-Mer*, 226–227, http://com.revues.org/521 (accessed May 11, 2016).

Baker, Jonathan (ed.) (1997) *Rural-urban dynamics in francophone Africa*. Uppsala: Nordiska Afrikainstitutet.

Boissière, Manuel, and Charles Doumenge (2008) "Entre marginalisation et démagogie: quelle place reste-t-il pour les communautés locales dans les aires protégées?" *Les Cahiers d'Outre-Mer*, 244, http://com.revues.org/5476 (accessed May 11, 2016).

Caramel, Laurence (2013) "Pour sauver le parc congolais des Virunga, WWF porte plainte contre le pétrolier Soco." *Le Monde*, October 7, www.lemonde.fr/planete/article/2013/10/07/pour-sauver-le-parc-congolais-des-virunga-wwf-porte-plainte-contre-le-petrolier-soco_3490974_3244.html (accessed May 11, 2016).

Casti, Emanuela, and Samuel Yonkeu (2009) *Le parc national d'Arly et la falaise de Gobnangou (Burkina Faso)*. Paris: L'Harmattan.

Chartier, Denis, and Estienne Rodary (2007) "Géographie de l'environnement, écologie politique et cosmopolitiques." *L'Espace Politique*, 1, http://espacepolitique.revues.org/284 (accessed May 11, 2016).

Convers, Arnaud, Issa Chaibou, Aurélie Binot, and Dominique Dulieu (2007) "La gestion de la transhumance dans la zone d'influence du parc régional du w par le programme ecopas." *VertigO - la revue électronique en sciences de l'environnement*, 4, http://vertigo.revues.org/761 (accessed May 11, 2016).

D'Alessandro-Scarpari, Cristina, Gregory Elmes, and Daniel Weiner (2008) "L'impérialisme numérique. Une réflexion sur les Peace Parks en Afrique austral." *Géocarrefour*, 83, 1: 35–44.

Depraz, Samuel (2008) *Géographie des espaces naturels protégés. Genèse, principes et enjeux territoriaux*. Paris: Armand Colin.

Dudley, Nigel, and Sue Stolton (eds) (2008) *Defining protected areas: An international conference in Almeria, Spain, May 2007*. Gland: IUCN.

Giraut, Frédéric, Sylvain Guyot, and Myriam Houssay-Holzschuch (2004) "Les aires protégées dans les recompositions territoriales africaines." *L'information géographique*, 68, 4: 340–368.

Grégoire, Jean-Marie, and Dario Simonetti (2007) *Dynamique des brûlis dans le parc régional du W, le parc national de la Boucle de la Pendjari et la réserve d'Arly. Implication pour la gestion de ces aires protégées*. Luxembourg: European Commission Joint Research Centre.

Hannah, Lee (1992) *African people, African parks: An evaluation of development initiatives as a means of improving protected conservation in Africa*. Washington, DC: USAID.

Héritier, Stéphane (2007) "Les parcs nationaux entre conservation durable et développement local." *Géocarrefour*, 82, 4, http://geocarrefour.revues.org/2992 (accessed May 11, 2016).

Knight, Rachael (2010) *Statutory recognition of customary land rights in Africa. An investigation into best practices for law making and implementation*. Rome: FAO.

Kouadio Oura, Raphaël (2012) "Extension urbaine et protection naturelle: la difficile experience d'Abidjan." *VertigO*, 12, 2, http://vertigo.revues.org/12966 (accessed May 11, 2016).

Larrue, Sébastien (2002) "Le Parc National du Niokolo-Koba: un exemple de rupture entre le milieu et la société Mandingue (Sénégal Oriental)?" *Les Cahiers d'Outre-Mer*, 2018, http://com.revues.org/1076#tocto1n4 (accessed May 11, 2016).

La Branche, Stéphane (2009) "L'insoutenable légèreté environnementale de la participation: une problématisation." *VertigO - la revue électronique en sciences de l'environnement*, 9, 1, http://vertigo.revues.org/8346 (accessed May 11, 2016).

Le Galès, Patrick (1995) "Du gouvernement des villes à la gouvernance urbaine." *Revue française de science politique*, 1: 57–95.

Lévy, Jacques, and Michel Lussault (eds) (2003) *Dictionnaire de la géographie et de l'espace des sociétés*. Paris: Belin.

Locke, Harvey, and Philip Dearden (2005) "Rethinking protected area categories and the new paradigm." *Environmental Conservation*, 32, 1: 1–10.

Mengue-Medou, Célestine (2002) "Les aires protégées en Afrique: perspectives pour leur conservation." *VertigO - la revue électronique en sciences de l'environnement*, 3, 1, http://vertigo.revues.org/4126 (accessed May 11, 2016).

Ndiaye, Babacar (2010) *Gestion valorisée des ressources naturelles: le cas de la Réserve Naturelle de Popenguine*. Thiès: Institut Technique de Gestion de Thiès.

Ndiaye, Paul (1998) *La Réserve naturelle de Popenguine (Sénégal): une expérience de developpement durable basée sur la conservation de la biodiversité*. Workshop report to Scandinavian Seminar College.

Pellegrini, Alessandra (1996) *Proposition pour l'extension de la Réserve de la Biosphère du Niokolo-Koba (Sénégal) dans la Préfecture de Koundara (Guinea)*. Koundara: Centre de Recherche Ecologique Niokolo-Badiar.

Poulot, Monique (2008) "Les territoires périurbains: «fin de partie» pour la géographie rurale ou nouvelles perspectives?" *Géocarrefour*, 83, 4, http://geocarrefour.revues.org/7045 (accessed May 11, 2016).

Ramutsindela, Maano (2004) "Glocalisation and nature conservation strategies in the 21st-century Southern Africa." *Tidschrift voor economische en sociale geografie*, 95, 1: 61–72.

Ramutsindela, Maano (2007) *Transfrontier conservation in Africa: At the Confluence of capital, politics and nature*. Cape Town: University of Cape Town.

Ribot, Jesse (2001) "Historique de la gestion forestière en Afrique de l'Ouest. Ou: comment la "science" exclut les paysans", *Dryland Issue Paper*, F104, International Institute for Environment and Development, London, http://pubs.iied.org/pdfs/9071IIED.pdf (accessed May 11, 2016).

Rist, Gilbert (1996) *Le développement. Histoire d'une croyance occidentale*. Paris: Presses de Sciences Po.

Rodary, Estienne (2008) "Développer la conservation ou conserver le développement?" *Mondes en développement*, 141: 81–92. www.cairn.info/revue-mondes-en-developpement-2008-1-page-81.htm (accessed May 11, 2016).

Rodary, Estienne (2011) "Crises et résistants: les écologies politiques en Afrique." *Ecologie & Politique*, 42: 19–32.

Rodary, Estienne, Christian Castellanet, and George Rossi (eds) (2003) *Conservation de la nature et développement. L'intégration impossible?* Paris: GRET-Karthala.

Simon, David (2008) "Urban environments: Issues on the Peri-Urban fringe." *Environment and Resources*, 33: 167–185.

Simon, David (2010) "The challenges of global environmental change for urban Africa." *Urban Forum*, 21, 3: 235–248.

Sournia, Gérard (ed.) (1998) *Les aires protégées d'Afrique francophone*, Paris:Editions Jean-Pierre de Monza.

Toillier, Aurélie, and Georges Serpantié(2007) "Concilier conservation et développement: un nouvel enjeu pour l'aménagement du territoire? Le corridor de Fianarantsoa,

Madagascar." *Géocarrefour*, 82, 4, http://geocarrefour.revues.org/3202 (accessed May 11, 2016).

Trefon, Theodore, and Serge Cogels (2007) "La gestion des ressources naturelles dans les zones périurbaines d'Afrique central: une approche privilégiant les parties prenantes." *Cadernos de Estudos Africanos*, 13–14: 1–18.

Vermeulen, Cédric, Emilien Dubiez, Pierre Proces Simon Diowo Mukumary, Timothée Yamba Yamba, Shango Mutambwe, Régis Peltier, Jean-Noël Marien, and Jean-Louis Doucet (2011) "Enjeux fonciers, ressources naturelles et forets des communautés locales en périphérie de Kinshasa, RDC." *Biotechnologie, Agronomie, Société et Environnement*, 15, 4: 535–544.

Part III
Land management

8 Sustainable development of mineral commodities in Africa
Challenges and policies

Paulo de Sa

Introduction

Can Africa harness extractive industries for its development?

For resource-rich countries, the ultimate function of the development of their mineral resource endowment is to create a reliable long-term source of financial revenues that can be converted into sustainable economic activities through sound revenue management. This has traditionally been achieved through two main routes: exports of mineral commodities that can generate a sizeable amount of foreign exchange revenues, reducing constraints imposed by external factors on the overall economy, and taxation of extractive industries revenues, which have the potential of making a substantial fiscal contribution to the budget. Associated with sound financial management, these revenues are expected to provide governments with additional funds to create jobs and invest in infrastructure and other initiatives that can support the development and expansion of the national industrial base.

Without underplaying the importance of these two sets of financial flows, this chapter argues that increasingly a third (and complementary) route is available for governments to ensure that extractive industries contribute to the expansion of the national and local economies. We are referring to the maximization of the linkages that can be developed between extractive industries projects and other sectors of the economy in order to create new jobs and economic opportunities for local entrepreneurs. This requires active involvement of governments in the design and implementation of sound policies, since rich natural resource endowments will not automatically lead to a sustainable pattern of growth.

This chapter starts with a quick review of the recent economic performance of sub-Saharan Africa, highlighting key accomplishments from the adoption of sound government policies. It turns later to a discussion on how the production of mineral commodities can contribute to sustainable economic development, highlighting the importance of designing and enforcing balanced fiscal regimes and adopting prudent macroeconomic policies to avoid the so-called "resource curse."

The remaining part of the chapter explores ways to expand economic linkages from mining in order to reduce Africa's infrastructure gap and promote inclusive growth. We argue that, despite a weak track record in sharing benefits with local communities, mining and other extractive industries can be used as an instrument to harness economic growth through the promotion of value-added and local content around large projects.

Extractive industries' contribution to economic growth in Africa: the recent track record

The strong growth in Africa over the last ten years has been driven to a large extent by developments in the extractives and related industries. Sub-Saharan Africa (SSA) hosts about 30 percent of the world's mineral reserves in value terms, including 42 percent of the world's gold reserves, 55 percent of cobalt, and more than 60 percent of the platinum group of minerals (PMG) (United Nations Economic Commission for Africa 2011). The region produces more than sixty metals and mineral products, including gold, PMGs, diamonds, uranium, manganese, chromium, nickel, bauxite, and cobalt. It already depends highly on mining, with mineral products accounting for more than 20 percent of exports in fourteen countries and more than 40 percent in twelve countries in 2011.

While the extraordinary boom in SSA's mining sector during the last ten years is largely the product of the high mineral prices – driven by large increases in demand in Asia, most notably in China – the groundwork for this development was set by the modernization in the legal and regulatory frameworks in the 1990s and 2000s. The continent is expected to remain a world leader in the production of mineral commodities, but Africa now wants to focus more on the development agenda, namely increasing tax revenues and value-added, and improving the environmental and social management of extractive industries.

Recent developments on the macroeconomic front have also been favorable. In 2000–2010, Africa was the second-fastest-growing region in the world (McKinsey Global Institute 2013). SSA's Gross Domestic Product (GDP) growth rate was 4.2 percent in 2012.[1] Medium-term growth prospects for the area remain strong, with GDP expanding by 4.9 percent in 2013, and projected to increase by 4.5 percent in 2015. Growth was widespread in 2012, with about one third of the countries growing at or above 6 percent.[2] Consumer spending, which accounts for 60 percent of GDP, held up, supported by wage increases,[3] improved credit access, and steady flows of remittances.[4] Progress towards achieving the Millennium Development Goals has been significant, notably in primary education completion and the sharp decline in under-5 mortality. Poverty levels in the continent have also declined, with the share of people living on less than US$1.25 a day rate reduced by 10 percentage points between 1996 and 2010, from 58 percent to 48 percent.

Table 8.1 Growth rates in resource-rich countries

	1991–2000	1991–2010	2001–2010	2007–2011
Sub-Saharan Africa	2.3	3.6	4.9	4.6
Low- and lower-middle-income SSA mining	**1.8**	**3.4**	**5.1**	**5.3**
Low- and lower-middle-income SSA non-mining/-oil	3.2	3.5	3.8	4.3

Source: McMahon and Moreira (2014).

Of particular interest is the fact that since 2003, SSA's resource-rich countries have shown higher average growth rates than non-resource-rich countries, as seen in Table 8.1 (World Bank 2013a).

In addition, within the resource-rich country group, the gap in growth between oil and non-oil countries has narrowed. Oil, metal, and other mineral exports increased from US$56 billion in 2002 to US$288 billion in 2012, and oil exports alone accounted for over half of goods exports in 2012 (World Bank 2013b). Together, these commodities have contributed to over two thirds of total export growth during the period. As a result, the continent's share in world trade doubled to 8 percent.[5]

In spite of the substantial increase in mineral commodity exports, SSA's growth was achieved with a more diversified production mix, with manufacturing and services growing rapidly and absorbing labor, and agricultural productivity increasing. Looking forward, it is anticipated that the region's growth will continue to be supported by a combination of strong domestic demand and higher production in the mineral resources, agriculture, and service sectors.

SSA's growth has been helped by the implementation of better macroeconomic policies. Despite a challenging global economic environment, SSA countries have generally maintained prudent economic policies, namely bringing inflation under control, increasing tax collection, reducing wasteful subsidies, and redirecting government spending toward long-term investments in human capital, such as education and health. And in spite of an uptick in borrowing by many African countries, debt burdens remain, with few exceptions, moderate and broadly manageable.[6] The investment climate has registered sharp improvements. Among the fifty economies making the most progress in business regulations since 2005, seventeen are in Africa.[7] As a result, foreign direct investment to the region was sustained, helped by high commodity prices. In 2012, for instance, net private capital flows to the region increased by 3.3 percent to a record US$54.5 billion, notwithstanding the 8.8 percent decline in capital flows to developing countries (World Bank 2013b). New projects in resource-rich countries like Angola, Ghana, Mozambique, Uganda, and Zambia account for a great deal of the increase in foreign direct investment in Africa.

However, commodity prices are cyclical by nature, and a long-term structural decline in commodity prices represents an important source of vulnerability for resource-dependent countries. Global economic risks continue to hinder growth prospects as the global economy remains fragile and prone to policy uncertainty. Slower growth in China, for example, could pull down demand for and prices of African exports of metals and minerals.

Nevertheless, compared to their levels over a decade ago, and even taking into account recent weakness, prices of most commodities remain on a sustained path. The World Bank's energy price index and metals and minerals price index have risen by some 162 percent and 118 percent, respectively, between 2000 and 2013.[8] Commodity prices experienced substantial declines since 2013 and non-energy commodity prices in mid-2015 were down more than one third from their early-2011 high. Price decreases after 2013 are a result of technical breakthroughs in oil production, namely the so-called "shale" revolution in the USA, and efforts to overcome skill shortages and technical difficulties that led to increases in production capacity and to efficiency gains in the production processes. On the demand side, decreases of the metal intensity in the growth patterns of developing countries led to a moderate decrease of global consumption growth rates.[9] Looking forward, the World Bank expects that mineral commodity prices will slowly recover from their mid-2015 levels, sustained by a relatively strong global rate of demand (including metal-intensive large infrastructure investments).

In spite of the cautious optimism regarding future trends for commodity prices, vulnerability to commodity price cycles will continue to put the premium on governance, transparency, and accountability in managing resource riches. Job creation represents the major challenge, as most Africans continue to work in the informal sector.[10] Not enough productive jobs in the informal and formal sectors have been created to absorb the millions of young people entering the labor force each year. Infrastructure deficit, low human capital (characterized by poor learning outcomes, skills deficit, lagging health indicators), and limited economic and social inclusion will remain major drags on SSA's competitiveness and economic performance.

Can mineral commodities contribute to sustainable economic development?

The overall contribution to the economy

Mineral resources in most countries belong to the state and are typically developed through licenses or concession agreements which are intended to generate public revenues through royalties and taxes. The ultimate function of upstream mining and petroleum operations is to create, out of the geologically heterogeneous and geographically dispersed natural resource endowment of any given country, a reliable long-term source of financial flows that can be converted into sustainable economic activities through sound financial management.

This is usually achieved through two main routes. Exports of mineral commodities can generate a sizeable amount of foreign exchange revenues, reducing constraints imposed by external factors on the overall economy. In addition, revenues of extractive industries are often heavily taxed, generating (substantial) fiscal revenues for the budget. The existence of sizeable profits above normal returns on investment (also known as "rents") originating from mineral and petroleum activities is a key characteristic of extractive industries.

Given the potential existence of substantial rents, the extraction of mineral commodities cannot be considered like any other industrial sector of the economy and requires special treatment.[11] Upstream investments in the mining and petroleum industries combine a number of special features which have no exact parallel in any other type of industrial activity. These special features are to a large extent dictated by the geological environment. Each deposit is unique in a number of respects and, most significantly, mineral deposits are both fixed in location and non-renewable. Initially, the occurrence of minerals and petroleum can at best be predicted. Mineral deposits must be found and delineated before they attain any substantial economic value, which requires substantial know-how and investment. The amount of investment, even for individual projects, can be substantial and sometimes match the total size of a country's economy.

Because the development of mineral resources requires high initial investments with long and uncertain payback periods, the stability of the macroeconomic environment and of public policies is of paramount importance for the development of these activities. And because these resources are not renewable, the role of government policies is paramount in the transformation of this natural wealth into other forms of capital (financial, physical, social, human, etc.).

Without good governance and sound policies, a rich mineral resource endowment will not automatically lead to a sustainable pattern of growth in any country. For that to happen, governments need to properly address challenging problems often associated with natural resources-led growth. These include, among others: (i) dealing with the so-called "Dutch disease"; (ii) coping with macroeconomic issues associated with the volatility of commodity prices; (iii) deciding how much of the additional revenues generated by commodity booms are to be spent immediately of saved for future generations (to avoid excessive spending and over-borrowing); and (iv) avoiding capture of the natural wealth by vested interest by different modalities of corruption. We will return to these problems later in this chapter after discussing the instruments at the disposal of governments of resource-rich countries to capture a more substantial part of revenues from extractive industries in periods of commodity booms.

Extractive industries and the taxation of mineral rents

Because mineral resources are spatially confined to where they are found, it is commonly admitted that resource rents belong to the country where the mineral deposits are found. Governments use tax revenues to generate other economic opportunities but, because of the long gestation periods of projects, they need to calibrate carefully the overall tax burden imposed in the extraction of these deposits. In simple terms, if the enabling environment is not conducive and taxes are too high, the country will get little investment, and will not be able to develop its mineral endowment to its full potential. Conversely, if taxes are perceived as being too low, giving private firms ample opportunity to capture windfalls, tax revenues may be very slow to emerge. This will generate frustration among the population and could lead to nationalization of assets in periods of high commodity prices.

In any event, the production of minerals has become a global industry over time, and fiscal regimes have to be adjusted to the overall business climate of the country (the risk factor). They also have to be basically in line with what is practiced in countries with similar geological endowment competing in the world market for outlets of the same products.

When commodity prices are low, resource-rich countries compete to attract private investments. Governments might be tempted to forgo a part of the resource rents in exchange for job-creating investments and to try to capture and extend value from the construction of infrastructure and social and community development expenditures at least partly sponsored by mining companies. In contrast, during periods of commodity booms, governments tend to focus on getting a bigger share of the resource rents.

Tax collection in the mining industry was relatively low in the twenty years that preceded the boom in commodity prices that started around 2004. But the rise in commodity prices after 2004 led to generalized movement whereby governments sought a larger share of the mining sector's rents, notably through an increase of the fiscal take.

From 2004 on, many African countries moved from overall policies aimed at attracting foreign investment and job creation to more proactive measures targeted at capturing a bigger share of the mineral rents. This was the case of countries like Zambia, Ghana, and Tanzania, which introduced legislation that contemplated rises in the royalty rates and, in the case of the first two countries, resource rent taxes to capture the exceptional profit derived from the rise in commodity prices. More recently, Western and Central African countries like Guinea, Mali, and the Democratic Republic of the Congo also embarked on similar exercises. In many instances, these efforts were countered by mining agreements negotiated before the increase in prices that contained stability clauses sheltering these investments from further changes in the fiscal regime. In most of the countries mentioned, this led to a generalized movement to renegotiate the existing mining contracts.

Attempts to unilaterally increase the tax burden in periods of high prices faced steep resistance from mining investors. In some cases, the increase resulted in steep reductions in exploration and investment in the mining sector, which ultimately translated into fewer direct benefits from mining (fiscal or otherwise) over the long term.[12] The emerging trend is to introduce some sort of "flexible predictability" in mining fiscal regimes. This means progressive fiscal regimes that allow mining operations to remain competitive in periods of low prices but that would allow governments to capture an increasing amount of rents as prices increase. The most common instruments that, at least in theory, would allow for this to happen are sliding-scale royalties or windfall profit taxes, also known as resource rent taxes.

The most frequent form of sliding-scale royalties have the royalty rate increase as commodity prices go up. Mining companies have argued that periods of high commodity prices are also times that register steep increases in mining costs and that consequently higher royalty rates under sliding-scale royalties regimes should be triggered by increases in the operating margins, not by rises in prices. This debate, as well as the one that is associated with the introduction of higher income taxes when the project generates revenues for its shareholders that go beyond a certain level of profitability before taxes or an agreed internal rate of return on the investment,[13] underscores the overall issue of the low capacity of revenue authorities in most developing countries to collect mining-related taxes.

The overwhelming reality is that in most African countries tax authorities are not equipped to properly collect profit-based taxes and that some proposed new tax instruments, such as super-profit taxes, would be difficult to administer in many countries.[14] The rudimentary understanding of revenue collection authorities of the most basic principles of mining accounting has led some investors to benefit from tax loopholes in the form of overly generous depreciation regimes, poorly designed loss carry-forward incentives and some sort of transfer pricing.[15] The last of these may include, for example, transactions among related parts below market prices, ineffective control of grades of products sold, and also lack of proper accounting of sub-products contained in the main concentrate or metal.[16]

Zambia provides a widely discussed example of widespread tax avoidance by mining companies. In April 2012, a group of non-government organizations filed a complaint with Swiss and Canadian authorities against mining giant Glencore International AG and First Quantum Minerals for alleged tax evasion in Zambia, through their subsidiary Mopani Copper Mines Plc.[17] In 2009, the Zambian authorities, with support from the Norwegian government, commissioned an audit of Mopani Copper Mines Plc. by international accountants Grant Thornton and Econ Pöyry. Among the anomalies revealed in the audit were an unexplained increase in claimed operating costs in 2007, low reported volumes of extracted cobalt when compared to similar mining companies operating in the region, and manipulation of copper selling prices in favor of Glencore. The result of these anomalies was to reduce the taxable income of Mopani Copper Mines Plc. by an estimated US$700 million in the period 2003–2008 (Sikka and Willmott 2013).

The mining sector has in the past been affected by a lack of transparency as contracts or other fiscal agreements are often subject to confidentiality provisions aimed at providing incentives for investment or to adjust the legal framework to the specific characteristics of the deposit. Contract negotiation can be extremely time consuming and politically sensitive. The experience of West Africa, where contract negotiation remains popular in places such as Liberia and Sierra Leone as well as in many francophone countries, suggests that case-by-case negotiations of mining agreements often led to less satisfactory results than otherwise might have been achieved through a rigorous enforcement of a well-designed mining code.

More recently, there has been a marked trend to clearly state the basic conditions for the granting of licenses and development of mining operations in the legal and regulatory framework for the sector. Modern mining codes usually define standard types of mining licenses as well as the legal and fiscal obligations that are associated with the development of mining activities. Contracts might still be needed to provide stability to the provision of the mining code for a limited period of time, or to add specific conditions of the investment on areas indirectly related to the mining activity. This would be the case, for example, of specific conditions or incentives linked to the construction of infrastructure, special agreements aimed at developing the communities affected by the mining activity, or clauses that guarantee the provision of training and jobs to national citizens or the purchase of goods and services from local suppliers. But under no circumstances should these contracts provide derogations to the mining code or the overall tax regime.

In spite of noticeable progress, governance of natural resource revenues in many African countries remains in some cases non-transparent and subject to capture by political interests. Weak institutions and skills gaps remain major concerns, namely the limited capacity to negotiate investment agreements and monitor the enforcement of the legal and regulatory framework as well as specific contract arrangements. Another complicating factor, as pointed out by Collier (2007) and others, is the lack of modern geological data and overall knowledge of mineral potential that stands as one of the key barriers to improving the quality of resource deals.

In sum, it appears that a fiscal regime purely based on fixed rates will fail to realize the full contribution of the sector to government coffers in periods of high commodity prices. At best, it will lead to frequent contract renegotiations and negative knock-on effects for future investment. At worst, it could lead to conflict, at both national and local levels. It is important, however, that flexible regimes are transparent and stable, so that potential investors will know beforehand how rates vary with prices and/or profits. It is also crucial that the legislated taxes can be properly collected. This suggests that in low-income countries royalties will continue to play an important role in new fiscal regime models.[18]

Macroeconomic management: prudent fiscal policies to overcome the "resource curse"

The previous debate highlights the great responsibility that lies in the hands of governments regulating the development of extractive industries in their countries, as they must be able and willing to design and manage fiscal revenue frameworks efficiently, and allocate revenues in a manner that contributes to sustainable development. It is important to simultaneously build the capacity of government institutions to manage the large increase in revenues and overcome the political economy factors that will tend to drive the resources towards private hands. An important part of the natural capital should be transformed into entrepreneurial and human skills, as well as physical infrastructure, which often can be supported either through the construction of large mining ventures or clusters of smaller developments leveraging linkages to other sectors.

While companies, local governments, and other stakeholders (including civil society organizations) are primarily responsible for the social and environmental management and monitoring of mining operations, the sustainability of the economic benefits is primarily a macro problem related to governance improvements in a country. The national government has a fundamental role to play in ensuring that the development opportunities created by mining projects are captured and facilitated through sound macroeconomic policies, regional development planning, shared infrastructure, and capacity building for workers, small and medium enterprises, and local governments to facilitate the process. The national government is also responsible for ensuring that the financial capital captured in the form of fiscal revenues is sustainably converted into other forms of capital. Although Botswana is usually mentioned as the African country that has achieved most success in this this area,[19] significant efforts have also been made in countries like Ghana and Namibia, for example.

On the macroeconomic front, it is the primary responsibility of national governments to manage revenues accruing from extractive industries adequately, in order to avoid the risk of incurring in a loss of competitiveness in the overall economy caused by exchange-rate appreciation and the concentration of investments in only one sector of the economy, discouraging the development of other activities. This phenomenon is normally referred to as the "Dutch disease."[20] Simply put, the foreign exchange inflows resulting from exports of commodities appreciate the real exchange rate and increase the returns on investment of the products exported in relation to other tradable goods, attracting capital and labor to the natural resources sector from other parts of the economy. Higher spending leads to higher prices and output in the non-tradable sector, but increasing wages squeeze profits in economic activities that produce internationally tradable goods (such as manufacturing), resulting in a contraction or stagnation of other (non-natural resources) tradable sectors and an overall structure of the economy that is concentrated in the production of commodities. Zambia's economy's great dependence on copper illustrates this point.

Prices of mineral commodities are also extremely volatile because of rigidities in adapting supply to demand, at least in the short term. This can lead to instability in government revenues and spending, making macroeconomic management extremely complex. Vulnerability to sudden changes in commodity prices can cause large fluctuations in the real exchange rate, which can discourage investments in this and other sectors of the economy and inhibit growth. This in turn can lead to increased vulnerability and extreme dependence on the commodity sectors of the economy. Volatile fiscal revenues, often aggravated by procyclical government spending and over-borrowing, can reduce the efficiency of public spending and reduce overall growth.

More importantly, weak institutional capacity and poor governance in the management of extractive industries revenues may sometimes lead to an overall deterioration of the political and economic life in many countries, leaving them extremely vulnerable to internal conflict and external shocks that exacerbate the dependence on the industry. Decades of conflict in the Democratic Republic of the Congo seem to illustrate this point.

Two influential papers by Sachs and Warner (1995, 1997) looked at the relationship between growth and commodity exports' share of total exports or GDP, and concluded there was a negative impact of natural resources on economic growth. This perverse link was named the "natural resource curse."[21] In a more recent study published by the World Bank, Sinnott et al. (2010) concluded that, on balance, much of the literature on the links between resource dependence and growth has been overly pessimistic and that there is no consistent empirical support in favor of the "curse."[22] And although there are pitfalls to avoid in the development of extractive industries, commodities do not appear to be inferior engines of growth compared to other sectors of the economy. The authors suggest three major points of intervention to break the potential negative impacts between commodity dependence and growth: diversifying production, improving management of government revenues, and enhancing the quality of institutions.[23]

To conclude this section, it is worth referring to the good practices that can be deployed to overcome the resource curse as presented by Nigeria's former Minister of Finance (Okonjo-Iweala 2013):

- **Minimize procyclical government expenditure** by implementing prudent fiscal policies which insulate the national budget from fluctuations in commodity prices. Revenues accruing above a benchmark commodity price should be saved in a separate fund, as seen in the case of Chile, Ghana, and Nigeria.
- **Develop a rules-based stabilization fund**, creating a form of national public savings. The stabilization fund would provide savings to finance public expenditure programs when commodity prices decline. The most accomplished example is Chile's Copper Stabilization Fund, but a few African

countries like Zambia and Zimbabwe are now planning to introduce similar funds.
- **Aim at ensuring long-term income once natural resources are depleted**, by converting the natural resource into financial and physical assets. Resource windfalls may be partly invested in funds for future generations. Norway's oil "pension" fund provides a good example of this.
- **Focus on investments in productive physical assets** like public infrastructure (such as power plants, transport infrastructure), which reduce the costs of doing business for the private sector. It is essential to avoid prestige "white elephant" projects.
- **Invest in improving technical capacities and skills**, namely for the negotiation of fiscal regimes with extractive industries companies. As an example, the government of Liberia has brought in diaspora human resources to shadow extractives experts from other parts of the world, such as the US, for training purposes in various government ministries.
- **Improve tax administration capacities** to tackle tax-avoidance schemes such as transfer pricing practices by multinational firms.
- **Build strong institutions** which promote transparency and good governance, ensure property rights, support political stability, provide checks on the power of elites, and support participation of the majority of citizens in economic activity, as seen in the case of Botswana.

In sum, for extractive industries to have a sustainable impact on poverty, payments made out of these activities must be able to turn non-renewable capital into skills, infrastructure and economic opportunities. Governments have a key role to play in this. Extractive industries can have an impact on the long-run sustainable development of a country provided that governments engage in the design and implementation of policies that convert extractive sectors into an engine of growth adding value to other sectors of the economy through the spin-off of services and industries it creates, as well as by opening up opportunities to the development of non-dedicated infrastructure.

Factors contributing to the sustainable development of extractive industries

It is commonly admitted today that in any country, sound government policies are increasingly seen as a fundamental factor of success for the sustainable development of extractive industries, from the economic, environmental, and social point of views. This includes, among other things: (i) the establishment of a transparent and clear legal and regulatory framework for the sector, including, first and foremost, transparent and non-discretionary procedures in the allocation of exploration and production rights; (ii) the buildup of strong sector institutions, namely to negotiate investment agreements and monitor contract enforcement, but also in other related activities (like financial services, judiciary, etc.); (iii) the design and enforcement of adequate environmental management processes and practices; and (iv) the design and implementation of policies that are socially inclusive and enhance the contribution of the sector to inclusive economic growth.

A factor often neglected when designing good public policies is the need to foster the long-term competitiveness of the sector. This obviously entails a good geological endowment that is by far outside the control of governments. Public policies can nevertheless contribute to enhancing a country's geological potential through systematic development of its geological data (through geological surveys) and a carefully measured policy of openness to foster private-sector-led exploration.

The accurate knowledge of the existing and potential quantity of mineral resources in any given country based on credible geological data positively impacts the ability of governments to leverage their mineral resources in order to optimize sector benefits and outcomes. Evidence suggests that public investments in geo-scientific data collection can contribute to increasing the value of mineral properties through the auction process and can also deliver significant returns by stimulating private investments in the sector (Reeman et al. 2002). Analyses of known mineral resources by country combined with anecdotal evidence established that Africa is significantly "underexplored" in terms of subsoil assets as a result of lack of geo-data.[24] Thus, increasing the availability of good-quality geological data is crucial to obtaining these direct potential benefits to governments, the private sector, and ultimately, society at large. As pointed out by Collier (2007) and others, lack of modern geological data and overall knowledge of mineral potential is one of the key barriers to improving the quality of resource deals in Africa and elsewhere.

It is always important to remember that a good geological endowment is basically not enough to guarantee the expansion of mineral activity if it is not supported by more encompassing measures covering several areas of the economy. Sector policies are only one among several factors that can enhance the competitiveness of a country's extractives sector.

First and foremost, a country needs overall macroeconomic stability if it wants to develop its economy. At an intermediate level, a sound business climate and relatively open trade policies facilitating productive entrepreneurship are needed to expand overall economic activity. It is also widely recognized that business cannot prosper without a strong judiciary able to provide an overall enforcement of the rule of law. Attention should also be paid to enhancing competition in the sector, reducing barriers to entry and the power of oligopolies, improving labor markets, avoiding indiscriminate subsidies, and incentivizing research and development, to avoid the "Dutch disease."

Another important factor that has been previously mentioned is the ability to design and administer competitive fiscal regimes. A government's natural wish to increase its take of the mineral rent have to be balanced with reasonable incentives in order to provide adequate returns on investments to the private sector. In addition, extractives being global industries, fiscal regimes have basically to be in line with those of countries with similar geological endowments competing in the world market.

Since extractive industries are mostly driven by private investment, the existence of liquid financial markets is essential for a thriving sector. This includes not only access to long-term financing, but also the possibility of relying on capital markets to fund development projects as well as the early stages of exploration. In addition, as the recent boom in commodities has painfully shown, the human factor is essential for the success of a minerals industry. It takes many years of costly efforts to build the base of a competitive workforce in extractives industries, both at high levels of educations (geologists, engineers) and at intermediate levels, where the role of vocational training can never be over-emphasized.

Given that mineral deposits are located where they are found and mineral production needs to be brought to end-use markets, infrastructure also plays an essential role. A key factor in the development of the industry, especially when referring to more value-added downstream products, is the availability of reliable sources of energy at competitive prices. This is currently a major constraint in Africa. Mining operations need huge amounts of power, and power costs are often a big part of mining operations' cost structure, especially when it comes to processing and beneficiation. However, SSA's power deficit is huge and both households and companies pay a heavy price for this. A new database developed for the World Bank, the Africa Power-Mining Database 2013 – containing 455 mining projects in twenty-eight SSA countries, with the gross value of ore reserves assessed at more than US$250 million (World Bank 2013a) – provides an estimate of the demand for power and the range of possible power-sourcing arrangements for these projects.

Grid supply remains the dominant power-sourcing arrangement among African mining projects of the sample but self-supply, where the mining company develops its own source of power, has registered the most impressive increase in Africa over the last fifteen years (from 6 percent of the sample in 2000 to about 18 percent projected for 2020 in the study). Grid supply has been declining since 2000[25] because of the high costs of extending the transmission networks to reach new mines, low security of electricity supply, and high tariffs (especially where the grid is powered by expensive diesel or heavy fuel oil) (World Bank 2013a). As a result, and in order to ensure reliable supply, mining companies are increasingly willing to pay a higher cost for their own supply rather than sourcing power from the grid.

With proper policies, leveraging demand for power from the mining sector could transform power systems in SSA. Electric utilities could secure large revenues from creditworthy customers like the mining companies, which could in turn serve as anchor customers facilitating investments in generation and transmission. In Mauritania, for example, the government recently set up a public–private partnership that has allowed the development of offshore gas deposits to supply power for domestic use and the mining industry and even to export to neighboring countries. These investments could produce the economies of scale needed for large infrastructure projects that would benefit all consumers on the system. As mentioned before, for mining companies the direct cost of self-supply is generally higher than grid supply. Affordable and reliable grid supply would also reduce the burden of producing their own power and allow them to focus on their core business.

However, most public utilities are not viable partners for mining companies to invest in. Resource pooling among mines has proved to be difficult in the past given the sector's highly competitive environment. As a result, mining companies have invested substantial resources in building their own power generation capacity in the recent past and this suboptimal outcome is expected to increase in the future.[26] There is little incentive to construct power plants with greater capacity than one mine's own internal demand where there is an absence of regulatory and commercial incentives and a transmission network with spare capacity. The negative consequence is that power to local communities is typically overlooked unless mining companies integrate that as part of their corporate social responsibility commitments or are contractually required to do so.

Given that the demand for power in the refining and smelting processes is several times that of the extractive operations, availability of power at competitive prices is probably the biggest constraint for the development of a downstream minerals industry in Africa.[27]

Promoting value-added and local content around mining projects

It is a normal and desirable wish of governments of resource-rich countries to increase the value-added and percentage of local content input in the production of mineral commodities. The issue for these countries is that if examples abound of developed economies that have relied on their domestic mining industries to foster industrialization, this process seems not to happen endogenously in developing economies without a strong "push" from public policies. If left unattended, large minerals projects can at best turn into high-performance economic enclaves with few opportunities for the production of more diversified and upgraded products, and limited linkages and spillovers to the rest of the economy.

Of particular concern for developing countries is that very often misguided policies – sometimes pushed by strong-handed legislation dictated from the top without real consideration for the economic conditions of the country – have frequently led to frustration, having failed to produce any meaningful result.[28] At worst, these policies led to the construction of "white elephants" that destroyed value and overcrowded investment opportunities in other sectors of the economy (Tordo et al. 2013).

What is often overlooked is that vertical integration in mining needs to comply with the competitiveness constraint prevailing in the national economy. As such, opportunities for vertical integration may not be as much a function of the resource endowment of a particular mineral product as of the overall business climate and institutional environment of the country. Simply put, a rich mineral endowment does not translate automatically into a profitable downstream activity if other elements of competitiveness are not in place. Its location not being dictated by geology and depending foremost on transportation costs, production of downstream mineral products has tended to develop close to consuming centers, where it can adapt quickly to the demand of end-using industries both in terms of quantity and quality specifications. Trade barriers to the access to developed markets are another constraint that needs to be taken into consideration.

Downstream projects need to be carefully assessed and evaluated as to their financial implications if they are to produce any meaningful returns. A common pitfall to avoid is the generalized perception that more value-added means automatically more profitability. Downstream industries are subject to intense competition and the resource rents that are a structural feature of upstream extractive activities are nowhere to be found as production moves along the value chain. Sound financial principles require adequate returns on the investment in downstream facilities and point against providing subsidies over prolonged periods of time to uncompetitive downstream operations from the profits of extractive activities.

That does not mean that there are no opportunities for the producers of mineral commodities to integrate downstream. But these opportunities are better seized when these countries benefit from rising domestic (or sub-regional) consumption and can rely on other competitive advantages for the industrialization of their mineral products.

Contrary to the conventional wisdom, the production of mineral commodities is difficult to manage as it requires strong managerial skills in different areas (technical, financial, marketing, procurement, political, environmental, and social). A study by the World Bank (2009) shows that in a large sample of advanced and developing countries, total factor productivity growth is as high in commodity production as in the manufacturing sector. This has been essential for these activities to survive long periods of depressed prices. It also explains why the quantity of economically recoverable reserves has increased over time as a result of technical innovations in exploration and production.

Commodity sectors, especially in developing countries, tend to be easier to manage when developed in clusters (sharing infrastructure and know-how) and within networks of managerial competencies. Local opportunities for value addition are better perceived by national entrepreneurs that have a better reading of trends in the domestic market. This seems to suggest that the existence of strong national companies could be an important element when a country is trying to move along the production chain of mineral commodities. Economies can grow faster when domestically based firms move into higher value-added products through the identification of new economic activities in which they can profitably invest, incurring risks that they can manage. In another words, ownership could matter when a government tries to promote the industrialization of its mineral production.

In addition to overall measures aimed at improving the business climate, governments from resource-rich countries are increasingly involved in the design of policies that promote value-added coming from horizontal integration, trying to leverage the technological and managerial complexity as well as the infrastructure associated with the development of mineral commodities, while reducing at the same time the economic dependence of local populations on any individual project.[29] A current widespread trend is the adoption of measures aimed at fostering the availability in competitive terms of key goods and services for the industry sourced from local suppliers. These measures are commonly known as "local content" policies.[30]

Typical features of these policies include training to induce job creation (including managerial positions), both at the mine site and at associated activities, and training and capacity building to small and medium enterprises that can thrive as subcontractors of the mining operations. These policies often include a social dimension through the reinforcement of the capacity of local governments and civil society organizations for the improved delivery of social services and the provision of local (social) infrastructure. This can be accomplished either through direct investments funded by the budget or indirectly by the sharing of fiscal tax revenues through the government's general budgeting process, normally mandatorily linked to investment expenditures by sub-national governments, or more recently in some countries, through an earmarked portion of taxes statutorily mandated for affected communities, as seen, for example, in the Democratic Republic of Congo, Ghana, and Madagascar.

By voluntarily trying to avoid the generation of "enclave economies" around mining projects with reduced linkages to the rest of the economy, these policies also act as important elements of risk mitigation regarding conflicts with local communities affected by mining projects.[31] Communities that are impacted by extractive industries projects bear the brunt of their negative impacts but often fail to realize significant development benefits from them. Or where benefits are realized, they may not be sustainable once the extractive resource is depleted and the activity has closed.

A large investment in capacity building and training is required to take advantage of the opportunities enabled by large mining projects. Many new projects in developing countries include related provisions (sometimes referred to as community development agreements) through which the sponsor company commits to provide capacity building and training for that purpose, including to increase the percentage of local staff working in the mining operation.[32] One of the main motivations for companies to invest in public-sector infrastructure or services is to secure and maintain what is commonly known as their "social license to operate." Underlying these initiatives is obviously the expectation that government's capability to build state-of-the-art infrastructure and to provide services will be enhanced.[33]

In addition, many mining companies also make contributions, monetary and otherwise, to communities affected by their projects, and develop efforts to build the capacity of domestic small and medium enterprises to act as subcontractors to the mine. These companies do this willingly as part of their corporate social responsibility program,[34] partly to develop and keep good relations with their host communities, although some developing countries are developing legislation to make this sort of contribution mandatory in all new mining projects. Foundations, trusts, and funds can also be good vehicles for companies and governments aiming at sharing the benefits of mining operations with communities. To succeed, however, they must be properly integrated in their local context and must have a corporate structure adapted to their vision, funding, and capacity.[35]

In conclusion

As discussed in this chapter, resource-rich countries in Africa have in general benefited from the recent commodities boom to achieve high growth rates and have managed to achieve better macroeconomic outcomes than during previous times of high commodity prices. Growth has been sustained by the implementation of better macroeconomic policies, bringing inflation under control, increasing tax collection, reducing wasteful subsidies, developing stabilization funds, and redirecting government spending toward long-term investments in infrastructure, health, and education.

The extraction of mineral commodities cannot be treated like any other industrial sector of the economy given that it requires high initial investment with long and uncertain payback periods, and it creates opportunities for the capture of potentially substantial rents. Because of the long gestation period of investment projects, extractive industries have a different risk profile than most other economic activities. The stability of the macroeconomic environment and of public policies is of paramount importance for the development of these activities.

Prices of mineral commodities are also extremely volatile because of rigidities in adapting supply to demand, and this generates a lot of uncertainty regarding the potential volume of rents that might be captured at any point in time through the fiscal regime. Therefore, fiscal regimes need to be calibrated to reflect the overall business environment of the country and be flexible enough to adjust to changes in commodity prices. In addition, the global production value chain for mining resources is highly fragmented, with individual activities taking place in different countries according to comparative advantage. This creates opportunities for profit shifting to less tax-intensive jurisdictions, making it difficult for the tax authorities of resource-rich countries to properly collect the appropriate amount of taxes.

Many African countries still need to refine the design of their fiscal policies for the sector if they are to realize the full potential of mining to the economic development of the country. More important, a huge investment needs to be made at the level of the tax authorities of resource-rich countries to ensure compliance of private operators with the fiscal aspects of the law.

214　*De Sa*

Although a lot of progress has been achieved in Africa in terms of managing the macroeconomic effects of minerals development, more needs to be done on the microeconomic front to fully realize the economic impacts of a country's resource endowment.

Although, as discussed in this chapter, true opportunities for downstream processing still appear limited, beyond the pure fiscal contribution, the provision of economic opportunities and jobs through the local provision of goods and services, infrastructure, and community services associated with large mining projects is increasingly seen by the governments of some resource-rich countries as an important way of promoting sustainable development.

Mineral developments today can no longer take place in enclave fashion. In order to be successful, they have to better integrate with the affected communities and increase the number of linkages to other economic sectors, either directly through the generation of new economic opportunities or through a better integration of associated infrastructure with the rest of the economy.

Notes

1 Key macroeconomic indicators in this section were extracted from World Bank (2013a).
2 The GDP growth rate for 2007–2011 for the fourteen resource-rich countries mentioned above was 5.1 percent and for the twelve was 5 percent.
3 Real monthly wages increased by 18 percent in Africa in 2000–2011 (International Labor Organization (2013).
4 In 2012, an estimated 30 million African migrants sent US$60 billion in remittances to support more than 120 million family members (The Africa-EU Partnership 2013).
5 According to the World Trade Organization (WTO), Africa accounted for 4 percent of world exports and 3 percent of world imports. For more on the WTO report, please see www.wto.org/english/news_e/pres13_e/pr688_e.htm.
6 SSA countries now carry the lowest external debt burden in thirty years. This is a big change from the mid-1990s, when some countries' debt overhangs rose to unsustainable levels (Jacquelain 2013).
7 Of the seventeen countries, eight are mining dependent and two oil dependent (The World Bank and the IFC 2013).
8 The World Bank monitors major commodity markets important to the developing countries. Monthly prices for over seventy series are published at the beginning of each month. Price forecasts for the next ten years are published on a quarterly basis. A comprehensive review of commodity markets is published four times a year, January, April, July, and October.
9 See Canuto and Giugale (2010). According to the authors, four global trends have begun to unlock the potential of developing countries and are expected to continue in the medium term: (i) the vertical decomposition of the global production chain across frontiers allows less advanced countries to insert themselves in supply chains by specializing in single, simpler tasks; (ii) the expansion of "South–South" trade increases the availability of technologies that have been tested and adapted to developing countries' settings; (iii) information and communication technology gets ever cheaper and more widely embraced; and (iv) as a middle-income class grows in emerging economies, local technological adoptions begin to break even.

Sustainable development of mineral commodities   215

10 In SSA, the share of informal-sector employment is around 54 percent among the sixteen countries with available information, with some countries (e.g. Côte d'Ivoire, Kenya, Mali, and Rwanda) having reached rates above 70 percent (International Institute for Labour Studies 2013).
11 For a discussion on why natural resources are different, see Collier and Venables (2010).
12 Global mining giant BHP Billiton's exit from Guinea following that country's acceptance of new mining codes in 2011 is a good example of this. Another example was the widespread announcement of new investment freeze in Zambia following the introduction of a resource rent tax. The new tax was ultimately repealed.
13 A resource rent tax is applied only when the accumulated cashflow from the project is positive. In the early years, the net negative cashflow is accumulated at an interest rate that, at least in theory, is equal to the company's opportunity cost of capital adjusted for risk, or discount rate. The resource rent tax kicks in once the company has earned this threshold rate of return and captures a share of the resource rent, which is the return over and above the company's opportunity cost of capital. For a discussion on resource rent taxes, see Daniel et al. (2012).
14 Countries like Ghana and Zambia have drafted legislation regarding the introduction of super-profit taxes but have delayed their enforcement.
15 According to the Africa Progress Panel (2013), "Africa Progress Report: Equity in Extractives", transfer pricing costs the continent US$34 billion annually, more than the region receives in bilateral aid.
16 While there is an abundance of literature concerning the objectives and principles of fiscal policy for extractive industries, information is relatively scarce about the issues and practices associated with the administration of mining taxation. For a discussion on how to improve mining tax administration and collection frameworks, see Guj et al. (2013).
17 SHERPA (France), the Center for Trade Policy and Development (Zambia), the Berne Declaration (Switzerland), l'Entraide Missionnaire (Canada), and Mining Watch (Canada) filed a complaint on April 12, 2011, against Glencore International AG and First Quantum Minerals Ltd. before the Swiss and Canadian National Contact Points (NCP) for violating the OECD guidelines for multinational enterprises. See www.actionaid.org.uk/tax-justice/glencore-tax-dodging-in-zambia#5ieZFID1FvjgCTUw.99.
18 For a comprehensive discussion of royalties for solid minerals and metals, see Otto (1995).
19 Botswana's government since independence has designed and implemented conditions of governance that have ensured stability and social and economic progress. Dutch disease was avoided by government investment in public goods and infrastructure. Volatility was overcome by unlinking public expenditure from revenue. The government set up a savings fund and avoided typical "procyclical" behavior and real exchange rate volatility. As a result of its prudent fiscal policy, Botswana has benefited from relative macroeconomic stability and avoided the boom-and-bust cycles that affect many resource-rich countries (Lewin 2011).
20 For a comprehensive description of the effects of the "Dutch disease," see Eastwood and Venables (1982). For a more recent discussion on policies to deal with the "Dutch disease," see also Brahmbhatt et al. (2010).
21 For a comprehensive discussion of the "resource curse" in the oil sector, see also Gelb and Associates (1990).
22 Lederman and Maloney (2007) have also challenged the Sachs and Warner findings on measurement and econometric grounds, and they found natural resource abundance to have positive effects on growth.

23 In his studies on the theory of rent cycling, Auty highlights the existence of institutional quality thresholds below which natural resource discoveries harm a country's development path (Auty 1993).
24 See Collier (2007). Gelb et al. (2012) present a very interesting discussion on the process of discovery for mineral resources. They conclude that, spurred on by technology change and strong market conditions, the value of discovered reserves is high relative to the costs of exploration, particularly when low social discount rates are used to value potential production in the future. This difference may justify policies adopted by governments to encourage exploration, including through the provision of geo-scientific data to create incentives to discovery as well as competition among extractive companies.
25 From 60 percent of the sample in 2000 to about 50 percent now.
26 According to World Bank (2013a), over 2000–2012 mining companies invested around US$1.3 billion in generation capacity for 1,590 MW in arrangements with some form of self-supply. Looking to 2020, around 10,260 MW is expected to be added to meet mining demand. Of this, self-supply arrangements will represent 1,753 to 3,091 MW. This will cost between US$1.4 bilion and US$3.3 billion and represent 21–30 percent of the total generation capacity needed to meet mining demand in 2020.
27 According to World Bank (2013a), mines could benefit from US$640 million in operating costs savings in Guinea and US$990 in Mauritania by moving from self-supply to a reliable scheme of grid supply.
28 The Democratic Republic of the Congo, for example, has had to suspend the export ban on concentrates for lack of power to process them domestically.
29 The Republic of South Africa and Ghana have been at the forefront of this movement in Africa.
30 The Africa Union's African Mining Vision 2050 outlines a resource-based industrialization and development strategy for Africa, based on downstream, upstream, and sidestream linkages, and both ECOWAS and WAEMU have developed mineral-development strategies. National governments are also increasingly looking for ways to maximize benefits derived from investment in mining. For a description of local content policies in the mining sector in West Africa, see World Bank (2012a). The report argues that there is a compelling economic argument to support local content policies in West Africa as they can bring about significant benefits to a wide range of stakeholders. Mining companies can minimize their logistics costs, reduce their lead times, increase security of supply, and enhance their corporate social responsibility work. Local businesses, entrepreneurs, and communities can benefit from better economic opportunities, stability and diversity of markets, and improvement of business capabilities. Wider benefits include increased employment and skills, increased domestic and foreign investment, technology and knowledge transfers, exports and foreign exchange, and increased government tax revenues.
31 Aragon and Rud (2009) have conducted a detailed evaluation of the revenue flows in a Peruvian gold mine and found rather extensive linkages through the use of local labor and purchases of inputs.
32 For a review and analysis of the global experience in community-development agreements (voluntary or regulated), see World Bank (2012a). The study attempts to extract from current practice the key building blocks for a successful community development and to develop a methodology through which the approach to mining community development could be improved and results measured on the ground. See also O'Faircheallaigh (2013).
33 Crowson (2009) lists the following benefits accruing from companies' investments in physical and social infrastructure associated with mining projects: (i) to enable

the profitable exploitation of a resource through creating infrastructure; (ii) to secure adequate supplies of appropriately qualified manpower and other resources; (iii) to maintain the health of employees and their families; (iv) to defuse tensions that might arise between local communities affected by the basic investment and national government priorities; (v) to protect the basic investment against the effects of weak governance; (vi) to gain access to opportunities for future investments in exploration for, or the exploitation of natural resources; (vii) to allow entry into markets; (viii) to compete effectively with other potential investors; and (ix) to protect or enhance the company's reputation.
34 Investments in public-sector infrastructure should not be confounded with initiatives taken by companies under their corporate social responsibility programs, although they may sometimes overlap. Activities that fall under corporate social responsibility programs usually require companies to behave ethically, minimize their impact on the environment (broadly defined), and have proper regard to the wellbeing of their workers, their customers, and the wider communities within which they operate (Crowson 2009).
35 For a comprehensive review of the experience of foundations, trusts, and funds as instruments to share benefits with local communities, see Wall and Pelon (2011).

References

The Africa-EU Partnership (2013) *Migration and Development - Why Strengthen the Links Between Migration and Development*. Available from: www.africa-eu-partnership.org/areas-cooperation/migration-mobility-and-employment/migration-and-mobility/why-strengthen-links.

Africa Progress Panel (2013) *Africa Progress Report - Equity in Extractives: Stewarding Africa's Natural Resources for All*. Geneva, Switzerland: Africa Progress Panel.

Aragon, F. M., and Rud, J. P. (2009) *The Blessing of Natural Resources: Evidence from a Peruvian Gold Mine*, Working Paper Series DT, 2009–015 (December). Lima, Banco Central de Peru.

Auty, R. (1993) *Sustaining Development in Mineral Economies: The Resource Curse Thesis*. New York: Taylor & Francis.

Brahmbhatt, M., Canuto, O., and Vostroknutova, E. (2010) *Dealing with Dutch Disease*. Economic Premise Note 16, June. Available at www.worldbank.org/eonomicpremise.

Canuto, O., and Giugale, M. (2010) *The Day After Tomorrow: A Handbook on the Future of Economic Policy in the Developing World*. Washington, DC, World Bank.

Collier, P. (2007) *The Bottom Billion: Why the Poorest Countries Are Failing and What Can Be Done About It*. Oxford, Oxford University Press.

Collier, P., and Venables, A. J. (2010) "International Rules for Trade in Natural Resources". *Journal of Globalization and Development*, 1(1), Article 8.

Crowson, P. (2009) Adding Public Value: The Limits of Corporate Responsibility. *Resources Policy* 34: 105–111.

Daniel, P., Keen, M., and McPherson, C. (eds) (2012) *The Taxation of Petroleum and Minerals: Principles, Problems and Practice*. Washington, DC, International Monetary Fund.

Eastwood, R. K., and Venables, A. J. (1982) The Macroeconomic Implications of a Resource Discovery in an Open Economy. *Economic Journal*, 92 (366): 285–299.

Gelb and Associates (1990) *Oil Windfalls: Blessing of curse? A Comparative Study of Six Developing Exporters*. Oxford, Oxford University Press.

Gelb, A., Kaiser, K., and Viñuela, L. (2012) *How Much Does Natural Resource Extraction Really Diminish National Wealth? The Implications of Discovery*, Working Paper 290. Washington DC, Center for Global Development.

Guj, P., Bocoum, B., Limerick, J., Meaton, M., and Maybee, B. (2013) *How to Improve Mining Tax Administration and Collection Frameworks: A Sourcebook*. Washington, DC, World Bank.

International Institute for Labour Studies (2013) *World of Work Report 2013: Snapshot of Africa*. Available from www.ilo.org/INST.

International Labor Organization (2013) *Global Wage Report 2012/2013*. Geneva, International Labour Office.

Jacquelain, V. (2013) *Toward a Sustainable External Debt Burden in Sub-Saharan Africa*. Ideas for Development, April 16, 2013. Available at: http://ideas4development.org/en/toward-a-sustainable-external-debt-burden-in-sub-saharan-africa/.

Lederman, D., and Maloney, W. F. (eds) (2007) *Natural Resources: Neither Curse nor Destiny*. Washington, DC, World Bank, and Stanford, CA, Stanford University Press.

Lewin, M. (2011) *Botswana's Success: Good Governance, Good Policies, and Good Luck*, ICES- Information Centre for the Extractives Sector. Nairobi, Kenya African Development Bank.

McKinsey Global Institute (2013) *Africa at Work: Job Creation and Inclusive Growth*. London, MGI.

McMahon, G., and Moreira, S. (2014) *The Contribution of the Mining Sector to Socioeconomic and Human Development*. Extractive Industries for Development Series, Washington, DC, World Bank.

O'Faircheallaigh, C. (2013) 'Community Development Agreements in the Mining Industry: An Emerging Global Phenomenon'. *Community Development*, 44(2): 222–238.

Okonjo-Iweala, N. (2013) *Good Governance of Natural Resources*. High-level Panel Working Papers Series, prepared for the third HLP meeting in Monrovia, Liberia, Jan. 29–Feb. 1, 2013.

Otto, J. M. (1995) 'Legal Approaches to Assessing Mineral Royalties', in Otto, J. M. (ed.) *Taxation of Mineral Enterprises*. London: Graham & Trotman.

Reeman, A. J., Calow, R., Johnson, C. C., Piper, D. P., and Bate, D. G. (2002) *The Value of Geoscience Information in Less Developed Countries*. Keyworth, Nottingham, British Geological Survey.

Sachs, J. D., and Warner, A. (1995) 'Economic Reform and the Process of Global Integration'. *Brookings Papers on Economic Activity* 1: 1–95.

Sachs, J. D., and Warner, A. (1997) *Natural Resource Abundance and Economic Growth*. Cambridge, MA: Center for International Development and Harvard Institute for International Development.

Sikka, P., and Willmott, H. (2013) *The Tax Avoidance Industry: Accountancy Firms on the Make Centre for Global Accountability*. University of Essex, UK. Available at: https://www.essex.ac.uk/ebs/research/working_papers/WP2013-2_Corporate_Governance.pdf.

Sinnott, E., Nash, J., and De La Torre, A. (2010) *Natural Resources in Latin America and the Caribbean: Beyond Booms and Busts?* World Bank Latin America and the Caribbean Studies, Washington, DC, World Bank.

Tordo, S., Warner, M., Manzano, O. E., and Anouti, Y. (2013) *Local Content in the Oil and Gas Sector, a World Bank Study*. Washington, DC, World Bank.

United Nations Economic Commission for Africa (2011) *Africa Review Report on Mining* (Executive Summary). Addis Ababa, Ethiopia, UNECA.

Wall, E., and Pelon, R. (2011) *Sharing Mining Benefits in Developing Countries: The Experience with Foundations, Trusts, and Funds*. Washington, DC, World Bank.

World Bank (2009) *Global Economic Prospects: Commodities at the Crossroads*. Washington, DC, World Bank.

World Bank (2012a) *Increasing Local Procurement by the Mining Industry in West Africa*. Washington, DC, World Bank.

World Bank (2012b) *Mining Community Development Agreements Sourcebook*. Washington, DC, World Bank.

World Bank (2013a) *Africa Pulse*, Volume 8, October 2013. Washington, DC, World Bank.

World Bank (2013b) *Africa Pulse*, Volume 7, April 2013. Washington, DC, World Bank.

World Bank (2014) *The Power of the Mine: A Transformative Opportunity for Sub-Saharan Africa*. Washington, DC, World Bank.

The World Bank and the IFC (2013) *Doing Business: Smarter Regulations for Small and Medium-size Enterprises*. Washington, DC, The World Bank.

9 Future land-grab solutions?

The evolution and potential impact of public and private governance initiatives at the global level

Kathryn Anne Brunton, Anni-Claudine Bülles, and Matthew Gaudreau

Introduction

Land has become a critical topic of debate as lagging governance models have failed to recognize and protect vulnerable populations within an increasingly liberalized and globalized land market. While national policy, legislation, and enforcement offer a means to regulate this evolving transnational market, there are real limits to state-level regulation. Inter-country power dynamics, the proliferation of implicated corporations, and state-level corruption demand a global approach.

Although the majority of global land governance mechanisms are driven by and cater to the private sector, some of the most recent proposals have integrated significant public-sector elements (Goetz 2013; Seufert 2013; Stephens 2013). Private governance theorists Mayer and Gereffi (2010) have analyzed this development in other transnational markets and argue that complementary public mechanisms are in fact a necessary condition for effective global governance.[1] They hypothesize that while global private governance initiatives can be effective under certain political-economic circumstances,[2] there are limits that "will likely spur renewed attention to public governance and to new forms of public and private governance interaction" (p. 3). The latter prediction offers important insight in the land debate where the most recent large-scale global governance initiative attempts to leverage these public–private synergies.[3]

The Committee on World Food Security (CFS), a UN body housed within the Food and Agriculture Organization (FAO), is working with a variety of public and private stakeholders to develop a global set of voluntary guidelines for responsible agricultural investment.[4] From November 2013 to March 2014, the Committee conducted regional and electronic consultations, which will contribute to the preparation of the final draft of the Principles for Responsible Agricultural Investment (CFS-RAIs), set to be endorsed in October 2014.[5]

According to preliminary documentation on the CFS-RAI framework (CFS 2013b), the creation and targeting of the principles will be shared within the private and public realms. In light of this and the more general evolution towards increased public–private interaction in the governance of global issues (Mayer and Gereffi 2010), we think that analysis and reflection on this model are warranted. Specifically, are there unique circumstances that must be addressed in the governance of land compared to other transnational markets? How might an effective governance formulation incorporate these land-specific issues?

This chapter will first present the problems caused by poor land governance, analyzing the drivers, actors, and impacts of land grabs, specifically in countries of sub-Saharan Africa (SSA). We will then introduce Mayer and Gereffi's (2010) analytical framework of private governance to build the reader's understanding of the political-economic context that transnational governance mechanisms must operate within. The next section will offer a general review of the tools currently available at the national level to govern the global land market. This overview will again focus on SSA, using case examples from Ethiopia due to the prominence of land acquisition in this country (Sassen 2013, 30). In the fifth section, we will summarize the evolution of governance mechanisms at the global level and provide further details on the CFS-RAI framework. We will then use Mayer and Gereffi's (2010) framework to analyze the potential for effective governance of land by private or public–private mechanisms at the global level and conclude by offering some suggestions for further research on this topic.

Land grabs

For the purpose of this chapter, we define "land grabs" in relation to the most recent global land rush (Arezki et al. 2011), where large tracts of agricultural territory have been bought or leased by foreign and domestic investors through transactions that are notably unjust to the supplier.[6] Although land grabbing is a global problem, countries throughout Africa have been frequent targets.[7] The *Land Matrix*, a global and independent land-monitoring initiative, notes that of the 228.1 million hectares (ha) of large-scale land acquisitions worldwide, approximately 161.7 million ha are located in Africa (Anseeuw 2013; Anseeuw et al. 2012).

A confluence of domestic and external factors drives this phenomenon. Looking inwards, some African countries are attractive to large-scale foreign investors due to their low production costs and the alleged widespread availability of land and water, as well as "geographic proximity and climatic conditions for preferred staple crops" (von Braun and Meinzen-Dick 2009, 1). Additionally, many developing countries in this region depend heavily on foreign investment and receive aid from institutions that encourage national policies that are conducive to large-scale land acquisitions.[8] This disempowers national governments by adding the constraint of meeting investor demands in order to secure aid and further investments.

Externally, growing food crop and biofuel markets have had a drastic impact, as some estimate that the vast majority of large-scale investments made in

African countries are directed towards the production of these two resources (Anseeuw 2013; Byerlee 2011). For instance, Vermeulen and Cotula (2010, 2) note that a general increase in the global price of energy and commodities has resulted in "highly publicised large-scale land deals" for biofuel crops.[9] This demand has resulted in the widespread sale of land for both speculative purposes and investments in sugar and Jatropha curcas for biofuel production (Hall 2011, 197).

Looking beyond the structural drivers, "competing claims between various groups of local and long-distance actors" (Zoomers 2010, 441) also drive land grabs.[10] These include national and local governments, private organizations, financial institutions, and the real-estate sector. Anseeuw (2013) provides a framework that identifies three types of actors involved in these kinds of investments:

1. Western food-producing, processing, and exporting companies;
2. land- and water-scarce, populous, and capital-rich countries;
3. financial actors, commercial banks, investment/pension/hedge funds, and asset management companies.

The first group represents private Western investors, who focus on securing access to primary production and profit-making cash crops, meaning any high-value export commodities (Anseeuw 2013). The second group of investors originates from countries such as China, South Korea, and the Gulf States, and focuses on large-scale foreign investments through "government involvement, state-owned enterprises or sovereign wealth funds" (Anseeuw 2013, 164). The third group reflects indirect private investors who engage in speculative financial transactions and who hold a high degree of control over capital flows (Anseeuw 2013, 164).[11]

Land-grab actors can also be categorized geographically based on the origin or destination of the investment. Although land grabbing is often perceived as a North–South problem, it is also a product of South–South, and even South–North investment deals (Franco 2012; Zoomers 2010). In the case of SSA, land grabs are typically North–South and South–South in nature, although there is a significant diversity of countries, which is depicted in the graph below.

Although investment dollars often originate out-of-country, it is important to note that local governments also play a role in the transactions taking place. For instance, national policies, such as investment licenses or tax incentives, have an important impact on the type of investors a country attracts and permits. While discretion over investment policy allows governments to achieve agricultural and other land-related objectives, policy choices also influence the welfare of vulnerable populations (Lavers 2012a, 120–121). Proponents of large-scale land acquisitions focus on the potential benefits these transactions offer to rural populations. For instance, benefits can include the creation of employment opportunities, development and improvements of rural infrastructure, and new sources for knowledge-transfer (Zoomers 2010; von

Future land-grab solutions? 223

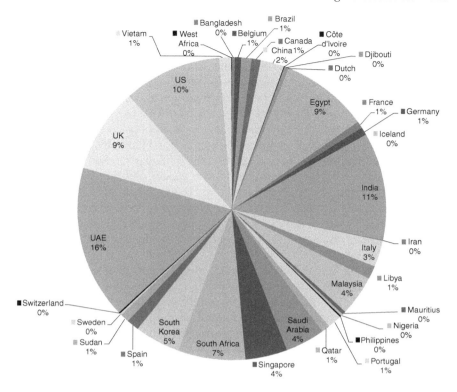

Figure 9.1 Breakdown of hectares in land-grab deals in SSA by country of origin.

Braun and Meinzen-Dick 2009). These transactions are also said to provide an opportunity for farmers to sell their land in order to make new and more economically viable investments (Zoomers 2010, 441).

While proponents promote large-scale land acquisitions as a win–win situation, the extent to which these types of investments are mutually beneficial is questionable. In addition to the dispossession of land and water assets, land grabs often entail the expropriation of livelihoods and human rights. This is especially true in SSA, where most rural communities are highly dependent on land not only for shelter but for money, food, and water as well.[12] Land is a means to survival in these communities where crops and livestock are the principal source of income and sustenance. As a result, when a community is forced to move, its members often suffer increased hunger and poverty as it can be challenging to adapt to different agricultural conditions that require unfamiliar farming techniques and tools (Oakland Institute 2013a, 10). As such, land grabs can infringe on the human right to shelter, food, water, and even life.[13] According to Anseeuw (2013, 169), the cost for local populations is simple, "the poorest members of agrarian societies risk losing their only major assets, namely land, water and housing." Although local populations are sometimes promised compensation or employment opportunities from either government or implicated corporations, land transactions are rarely at market value – making it difficult to acquire other land – and newly created jobs are often given to "better qualified and cheaper migrants" (Zoomers 2010, 441).

Additionally, if added employment or production contracts are provided, local elites are often the ones to benefit (Vermeulen and Cotula 2010, 9–10). Consequently, Shepard and Mittal (2009) note a disconnect between increasing transnational agricultural investments in developing countries and the aim to reduce poverty and secure food supplies for vulnerable populations. The environmental impacts of land grabs amplify this gap when commercial monoculture agricultural production is the end goal. Shifting from subsistence to commercial monoculture farming methods has broad consequences for the surrounding communities, such as land degradation, overuse of fresh waterways, heavy use of fertilizers and pesticides, and increased emissions due to dependence on fossil fuels for machinery (Vermeulen and Cotula 2010; Anseeuw 2013).[14]

Despite these consequences, many governments and local elites continue to welcome harmful types of large-scale land acquisitions intended for industrial production. While various levels of corruption drive some of this support, many countries also emphasize the potential development opportunities for the agricultural sector and rural populations (von Braun and Meinzen-Dick 2009; Grant & Das 2015). Although we do not wish to negate all possibility of positive impacts from these types of transactions, our aim is to highlight the vital need for guidance for both governments and large-scale investors in engaging with the communities where land is being acquired.

Analytical framework

In looking at guidance from a global perspective, we begin by noting that while private governance initiatives are relatively new, they have increased in both scope and reach in recent decades (Jenkins 2001). While regulatory initiatives had previously been undertaken by national governments, in the 1990s private-sector actors[15] became more heavily involved in the governance of transnational corporate activity.[16]

In light of this, private governance theorists Mayer and Gereffi (2010) introduced a set of hypotheses regarding the determinants of successful private governance initiatives.[17] They point to four principal factors, defended through case examples, which act as conditions for private governance to have any effect. In their most basic form, these factors are that effective private governance is dependent on:

1. the structure of the particular global value chain in which production takes place;
2. the extent to which demand for a firm's products relies on its brand identity;[18]

3. the possibilities for collective action by consumers, workers, or other activists to exert pressure on firms; and
4. the extent to which commercial interests of lead firms align with social and environmental concerns.

(Mayer and Gereffi 2010, 1)

When combined, these four interrelated points identify potential conditions under which private governance initiatives are likely to be successful.

The authors provide a strong argument that the potential for effectiveness is increased when (1) lead firms have leverage over smaller suppliers, (2) products and firms are highly sensitive to their brand names, (3) there is mobilized "societal pressure" acting to influence business behavior, and (4) there is an alignment of interests between these firms and social actors (Mayer and Gereffi 2010). There are several prominent examples of transnational markets where these conditions have been satisfied, leading to improved governance in specific production networks.[19]

Given the high specificity of Mayer and Gereffi's (2010) hypothetical conditions, however, and in consideration of the shortcomings of private governance initiatives, the authors expand to note two additional hypotheses dealing with the relationship between private and public governance. These indicate that with the concentration of production in "larger emerging economies" comes an expectation of strengthened public governance in these countries, which will "reinforce rather than replace private governance" (Mayer and Gereffi 2010, 15, 17). Thus, Mayer and Gereffi advocate for a stronger role for states in the formulation of private regulation initiatives.

This framework will provide an important base of comparison for understanding land grabs as they relate to common conditions under which private governance initiatives have previously been effective. Given the current surge in global land-grab governance initiatives, such an assessment will be valuable in better conceptualizing ways forward. However, before providing such a comparison, we must first review the current governance tools and initiatives that are being used to regulate them.

National-level governance mechanisms

Land governance is an integral part of the national development process and requires the alignment of multiple policies, including those related to development, environment, tenure, and labor. Additionally, while land reforms should be appropriate for unique national circumstances, greater alignment is also needed among neighboring countries to counteract the emergence of "race to the bottom" type policy environments that occur as a result of competition for investment. Using Ethiopia as a case example, the following section analyzes some of the tools available to states to produce effective governance.

Legal frameworks

In the case of Ethiopia, the 1995 Constitution and the Rural Land Administration and Land Use Proclamation No. 456/2005[20] provide the legal framework for land acquisition. These two documents cover the transfer and redistribution of land, the removal of holding rights, and matters concerning land administration and security (Alemu 2011, 9). By cementing land policy in a legal framework, the government openly communicates that the rules surrounding land will not easily be changed or weakened (Gebreselassie 2006, 4). As a result, smallholder farmers and other vulnerable populations know what to expect in terms of future land access, allowing them to evaluate risk and invest in their land if the opportunity is available.

In practice, this approach has done little to aid smallholder farmers in Ethiopia, as the national government's application of the constitution is highly selective. In the Gambella region, for example, pastoralists follow a traditional land administration system based on boundaries determined by local customs (Human Rights Watch 2012, 71). Although Article 40(5) of the Ethiopian constitution recognizes customary rights, stating that "Ethiopian pastoralists have the right to free land for grazing and cultivation as well as the right not to be displaced from their own lands," the constitution also allows the state to enact laws concerning the utilization of land. Consequently, the government ignores Gambella's customary rights by referring to the land as "unused" and/or "underutilized" (Human Rights Watch 2012, 71).[21] As a result, tenure security is low and land grabs are very common in both Gambella and other regions of Ethiopia (Abbink, 2011; Grant & Das 2015).

Land certification programs

The World Bank publication *Securing Africa's Land for Shared Prosperity: A Program to Scale Up Reforms and Investment* presents the registration of land as another approach to promote tenure security, and notes Ethiopia, Tanzania, and Rwanda as having recently introduced such an approach (Byamugisha 2013). Proponents of land certification programs argue that they provide various benefits, such as a public record for easy access to information on land ownership and sale costs, which diminishes tenure insecurity (Deininger et al. 2008b, 4).

In 2003, the Ethiopian government introduced a land certification model with the aim of reducing tenure insecurity and its negative impact on farmer investment. Five years later, it was deemed one of the largest land administration programs carried out in Africa (Deininger et al. 2008b). According to a study by the World Bank, the Ethiopian model has demonstrated that possessing a land certificate carries substantial benefits for its holder. Unlike traditional certification programs, Ethiopia's program promotes gender equality with joint spousal ownership, and is adjudicated through a participatory and decentralized process (Deininger et al. 2008a). It therefore addresses some of the typical challenges encountered with the content and implementation of land certification programs.[22]

Despite these advancements, the Ethiopian government has not attempted land registration in some important regions, such as Gambella, due to a lack of state capacity and the logistical challenges presented by pastoralists and recently resettled farmers. Ethiopia's certification scheme therefore further marginalizes these populations by making it difficult for them to prove that they have historically occupied or used the land (Lavers 2012b). Deininger et al. (2008b, 16) also note that the Ethiopian government's disregard for land certificates in some of its activities, such as "urban expansion, outside investors, or internal redistribution," is undermining this certification scheme. As a result, although certification programs offer improvements in tenure security, they are difficult to implement, and without strict adherence, easily undercut.

Land-tenure policy

In 1975, the Ethiopian state (under a previous socialist regime) enacted the "Public Ownership of Rural Land Proclamation," which nationalized all rural land (Crewett et al. 2008, 1).[23] The subsequent regime upheld this policy in the 1995 constitution, and as a result, the current government owns all land and administers it to the Ethiopian population through a leasehold tenure model. The Ethiopian Economic Association (EEA) and many donor agencies have lobbied for the privatization of property rights as they view state ownership of land as a hindrance to the development of land markets and farmer investments (Crewett et al. 2008).[24] Other private property proponents note the missed opportunity of accessing capital through mortgage-based credit, which is especially important for impoverished or vulnerable populations in developing countries such as Ethiopia (de Soto 2003). The Ethiopian government argues, however, that public ownership serves to protect rural peasants by preventing them from selling under desperate and vulnerable circumstances (Crewett et al. 2008). Selecting effective tenure policy based on the unique socio-economic and cultural determinants of a society is therefore a complex endeavor. As the Ethiopian system demonstrates, a leasehold model is beneficial in the social security it offers by "guaranteeing some form of livelihood through granting free access to a piece of land" (Gebreselassie 2006, 4). It presents economic deterrents, however, as some see the inability to sell or mortgage land and the insecurity of finite access rights as crucial roadblocks to greater economic growth and development.

The Framework and Guidelines on Land Policy in Africa

Each state in SSA is highly context specific in terms of its investment, legal, and regulatory environments, and under the Constitutive Act of the African

Union, each member state has the right to decide its own policies (African Union 2000). As a result, until recently, there has been no pan-regional push for coherence of land-related policy approaches across SSA countries. The *Framework and Guidelines on Land Policy in Africa* (Framework and Guidelines, hereafter), finalized in 2009 as a non-binding normative framework,[25] and provides African member states with guidance[26] on strengthening land rights, enhancing productivity, and contributing to secure livelihoods (AUC-ECA-AfDB Consortium 2010).

Although the Framework and Guidelines provides little guidance in terms of foreign direct investment (FDI), it does recommend the drafting of adequate policies to manage or avoid the risk of uncompensated land loss (Ibid.). It also advocates for land policy reform that addresses marginalization based on race, class, and gender (AUC-ECA-AfDB Consortium 2010, 23). Although African countries recognize the need for land policy reform, discrepancies exist on the focus and direction of reform. The Framework and Guidelines therefore act as an important starting point for pan-African land policy alignment.

In sum, governance mechanisms at the national and regional level have experienced fleeting success, hence the growing prevalence of global governance mechanisms. The subsequent section will provide an overview of these global mechanisms in order to better understand why and how the CFS-RAI initiative was developed.

Global-level governance mechanisms

The most recent insertion of land governance into the international public agenda occurred as a result of the International Conference on Agrarian Reform and Rural Development (ICARRD), convened by the FAO in March 2006.[27] The aim was to mobilize national governments and the greater international community in "securing tenure rights and access to land and other natural resources [for] the poor" (FAO 2005). While the FAO made progress through the final conference declaration, the 2008 world food price crisis[28] propelled the objective even further as land-related FDI became a matter of public knowledge and concern (Margulis et al. 2013, 7).

Although the FAO was already conducting discussions in the public realm through initiatives such as ICARRD, subsequent intergovernmental initiatives were slow and fragmented. As a result, in the years following the world food price crisis when civil society called for increased governance of transnational land markets,[29] an absence of public initiatives propelled the private sector to address these requests themselves. As such, commercial initiatives related to agricultural production chains and broader transnational investment directives, such as those outlined in the Table 9.1, became the first iteration of global land governance mechanisms.

Despite the proliferation of these types of private-sector initiatives, civil society remains highly critical of their effect on the land investment market

Table 9.1 Land-grab-related private governance initiatives

Initiative	Year	Content/context
The Equator Principles	Launched 2003, revised 2006, 2012	• Industry self-regulation • Developed by 9 international banks • 10 principles for financial institution investments (including land), using IFC's performance standards
The Principles and Criteria for Sustainable Palm Oil Production	Adopted 2005, finalized 2007	• Certification scheme • Developed by plantation companies, manufacturers, and retailers of palm oil products, environmental non-government organizations (NGOs) and social NGOs • 8 principles (including one specific to land investments)
The Principles for Responsible Investment in Farmland	Launched 2011	• Self-regulation scheme • Developed by institutional investors (banks, insurance companies, pension funds, hedge funds, investment advisors, and mutual funds) • 5 principles focused exclusively on farmland investments

Source: (CFS 2013a).

since they are untargeted, fragmented, or untested. For example, although the number of financial institutions that subscribe to the Equator Principles rose from four in 2003 to seventy-seven in 2012, its impact has been minimal due to the vagueness of the framework's principles and its lack of external accountability (Goetz 2013). Additionally, despite a growing member base, the Principles and Criteria for Sustainable Palm Oil Production address only a fragment of the land governance issue as palm oil represents one niche sector for land investments. Finally, while the Principles for Responsible Investment in Farmland offer a more comprehensive approach, having launched in late 2011, they are currently being implemented (Clapp, 2016). Consequently, much like national public approaches, global private initiatives have yet to fill the governance deficit for global land markets.

In 2012, the CFS entered into debates with its stakeholders[30] to create the terms of reference (TORs) for the CFS-RAI Principles,[31] which informed the initial draft of the Principles. The TORs emphasized that agricultural investments s to be based on "coordination, cooperation and partnership" among private and public sector stakeholders (2013b, 2). As such, the CFS engaged a mix of private and public actors in consultations on its preliminary "zero draft" of the Principles, including governments, companies, civil society organizations (CSOs), and intergovernmental institutions. The members of the CFS's Open Ended Working Group (OEWG)[32] – a mixture of private- and public-sector actors as listed below – then used these discussions to revise the draft for final negotiations:[33]

1. UN agencies and other UN bodies;
2. civil society and non-governmental organizations, particularly organizations representing smallholder family farmers, fisherfolks, herders, landless, urban poor, agricultural and food workers, women, youth, consumers, and indigenous people;
3. international agricultural research institutions;
4. international and regional financial institutions such as the World Bank, the International Monetary Fund, regional development banks and the World Trade Organization;
5. private-sector associations and philanthropic foundations.

(CFS 2014a)

The final CFS-RAI framework, endorsed in October 2014, advocates that agricultural investment is to be based on transparent and inclusive government structures with a multitude of private and public elements embedded in its implementation (20014a). In addition to drawing on these consultations, the content of the CFS-RAI Principles reference binding international agreements in an effort to highlight the existing public governance mechanisms that can be applied in the land-grab context (e.g. the Universal Declaration of Human Rights and its stated right to food). Although the CFS-RAI framework is be voluntary in nature, it is applicable to all stakeholders with equal focus on the public and private sectors. "In particular, they are meant to encourage investors at all levels to make provisions to invest responsibly, and identify key areas where States and other actors should focus their efforts to put in place an enabling environment for responsible investment" (CFS 2014b, 2). According to the final draft, all stakeholders, public and private, also have a key role in promoting, monitoring, and reporting on the implementation of the Principles. Therefore, from development to execution, both public and private actors in deliver the CFS-RAI framework (CFS 2014a).

Is the incorporation of the public realm within a private mechanism effective in the land governance context? The next section will attempt to analyze the global land governance landscape described above in the context of six conditions that have proven to enable effective governance in other global markets. In doing so, we will shed light on the potential of purely private models, and whether public–private models like the CFS-RAI Principles are necessary alternatives.

Analysis

As Margulis et al. (2013, 2) indicate, the nature of contemporary global land grabbing is closely related to economic globalization in terms of "flows of capital, goods, and ideas across borders." Hundreds of transnational corporations are engaging in this new form of global land investment, affecting an increasing volume of people and territories. As the case of Ethiopia illustrates, some national governments are responding to these changes, though the impacts are unclear. As a result, measures at the global scale have been a prominent direction in international policy discourse (Borras et al. 2013).

Should land grabbing receive the attention of global governance actors? Held's (2002) notion of subsidiarity sheds light on this question. Unlike nationally based issues, where authority to address a particular policy arrangement lies strictly within the borders of a specific country, land grabs spill over between states. Further, there are highly uneven power relations between states in which land grabs occur. As discussed above, developing countries that depend on foreign governments and companies for development assistance and investment, and that compete with other countries for these financial tools, often feel compelled to offer weak land policy requirements to attract and retain investors. Additionally, states may not represent their poorer or more marginalized populations – particularly in the case of non-democracies. Even with a democratically elected government, as in the case of Ethiopia, certain land rights are ignored, demonstrating that the scale of governance necessary for these issues surpasses an isolated focus on nation-states. Having determined that global governance arrangements, despite previous failures, are one appropriate scale at which to address this issue, we turn now to our analytical framework introduced above to gain insight into reasons for failure, as well as if and how the CFS-RAI framework overcomes these obstacles.

Condition 1: The more economic leverage large lead firms have over smaller suppliers in their value chains, the greater is the potential impact and scope of private governance

In the global land market, there are few, if any, lead firms that might hold adequate leverage to satisfy this condition. As indicated above, there are a multitude of actors grabbing land, originating from various countries. A review of GRAIN's (2012) land-grab database also reveals that out of 416 recorded cases there are no less than 250 firms involved, originating in over fifty countries, representing six sectors, and producing multiple products. These numbers are an early indication that the value chains into which these firms are integrated are disparate. While some can be traced back to large lead firms in certain sectors, many cannot.

This fact places an early limitation on effective private-sector-led governance, as larger firms looking to lead regulation initiatives are not typically in a position to harness the required leverage to influence smaller firms into following suit. While this condition is more appropriate in industries such as multinational textile companies or in the more integrated agricultural production networks of large Western conglomerates (Dauvergne and Lister 2012), recorded land-grab networks are typically much less centralized in terms of lead firms from specific countries (Borras et al. 2013).

Additionally, when analyzing the economic leverage of the typical groups victimized by land grabs, such as smallholder farmers and pastoralists, rarely are they powerful enough to challenge the companies, foreign governments, or domestic elites acquiring land. Therefore, in addition to a lack of leverage to regulate smaller firms in the production network, all firms also face very weak opposition when sourcing land. Consequently, there is a further imbalance between the power afforded to disparate firms engaging in land grabbing and those local landholders often dispossessed by these transactions.

Although they offer little impact in terms of creating an environment of lead firms and downward leverage in the production chain, the CFS-RAI process made a point of highlighting and addressing the lack of power held by smallholder producers (CFS, 2013b). This group was provided with a strong role during consultations, as well as a seat at the table for negotiations of the final draft of the principles. Also, by engaging a wide array of government stakeholders in consultations and negotiations, the CFS-RAI process is set up to invoke broader state ownership of and support for monitoring and prosecuting firms engaged in land acquisitions both at home and abroad. This governance framework, which requires government stakeholder engagement, therefore lessens the need for lead-firm leverage within private regulation schemes, as the public realm would shoulder more of the regulatory responsibility of the production network.

Condition 2: Private governance is most likely for highly branded products and firms

Unlike many of the better-known private governance initiatives and certification schemes, the industries directly involved in land grabbing are often not highly visible. As such, they typically do not rely on brand name credibility, and are not held to account in the same way by their consumers.

There are, however, promising exceptions to this rule. Examples of brand name targeting can be found in land-grab-related campaigns by international non-government organizations (INGOs). For example, Oxfam International has targeted transnational soft-drink companies involved in sugar-related land grabs and was successful in influencing Coca-Cola to adopt an anti-land-grab policy (Oxfam 2013). Further, brand name visibility has induced improved measures in other realms of environmental governance (cf. Dauvergne and Lister 2012). Despite these specific cases and campaigns in which brand names are associated, they are in the minority. Overall, the potential use of brand name reputation in the context of land grabbing is weak, and does not provide adequate leverage in wider governance initiatives.

The CFS-RAI process counteracted this shortcoming by emphasizing the need for investor responsibility and by maintaining investor engagement in the consultation process. In retrospect, the CFS-RAI framework was born out of the CFS's refusal to endorse another set of principles[34] which promoted a more investor-friendly approach to agricultural investment.[35] When

Future land-grab solutions? 233

the CFS announced that it would develop the CFS-RAI Principles instead, part of its aim was to uphold the need for investors to be held responsible in their decisions and transactions. Therefore, building on the need for government stakeholder engagement in monitoring mechanisms mentioned in the analysis of Condition 1, the CFS-RAI framework, through its provisions for large-scale investors will lessen the need for brand recognition as a motivating factor for responsible investor behavior.

Condition 3: Effective private governance is most likely in the face of effective societal pressure, which, in turn, depends on the relative ease of mobilizing collective action

Land grabbing has generated tremendous societal concern. The 2008 world food crisis, which was most acutely felt in developing countries, was a major catalyst for social organization related to land grabs. In only four to five years, networks of local CSOs, INGOs, and academics have raised this issue to prominence.[36]

The polycentricity of land-grab value chains has presented limitations, however, as the nature of these networks, in terms of both geographic location and the number of companies, means it is difficult for civil society to mount traditional campaigns highlighting the victimization of developing countries by a few developed world actors. Unlike the multinational textile production chain, for example, where a major Northern-based company like Levi Strauss[37] or a major Northern country like the United States is perpetrating human rights violations, there are a multitude of actors in both Northern and Southern regions of the world involved in land-grab networks.

Although the CFS-RAI framework cannot change the structure of land-grab networks, it does address the challenge of civil society involvement by ensuring civil society has equal footing in the OEWG negotiations of draft versions of the CFS-RAI framework and by offering explicit support for the more marginalized sections of civil society. For example, the "Guidelines for Participation in CFS Open Ended Working Groups" singles out "smallholder family farmers, fisherfolks, herders, landless, urban poor, agricultural and food workers, women, youth, consumers and indigenous people" (CFS 2014a, 1) as the most important civil society groups to be represented within the drafting of the Principles.[38] Significant inclusion of civil society stakeholders in the CFS-RAI process will likely ensure the CFS-RAI framework is more effective, since they were given direct and equitable access to the negotiation table.

Condition 4: Private governance is most likely to be adopted when commercial interests align with social or environmental concerns

The issue of land grabs can be framed in such a way that commercial interests do in fact align with the social pressures identified in previous sections. As the managing director of one of Coca-Cola's largest bottlers once stated, "land purchases which ignore the interests of local communities and the local landscapes are both morally wrong and commercially short-sighted" as these kinds of land deals "fuel opposition to all outside investment" (Oxfam 2013). Where there is a lack of support from community stakeholders because they have been displaced from their land, resistance behaviours, such as protests and destruction of crops and machinery are more likely (Rahmato, 2011). Thus, there are long-term benefits to companies like Coca-Cola to ensure their value chain partners are acquiring farmland ethically and with the thought of supporting local communities in mind. Oxfam International's campaign against soft drink companies similarly capitalizes on a company's concern for long-term growth by framing the issue of land grabs in a way that focuses on the risk they pose to a company's brand (Oxfam, 2013). As one Oxfam report (2013) notes "as rising demand for commodities has driven an unregulated rush for land, the risk that food and beverage companies face that their ingredients or operations will be linked to land grabs has also grown" (7).

The CFS-RAI process has further sought to address this need for commercial alignment by engaging private-sector associations and investment-focused multilateral institutions in consultations and negotiations of the final draft of the Principles. As such, it is possible that an additional overlap of interests will appear, and that there will be an increased alignment between commercial and social or environmental concerns as the CFS-RAI framework is implemented.

Condition 5: The more production becomes concentrated in the larger emerging economies, the more we should expect public governance in these countries to strengthen

Agricultural production is dispersed widely, and is not typically concentrated in larger emerging economies. This is true along the value chain, both at the level of the actual land grab and also within the investing firms. As Borras et al. (2013) indicate, there have been tremendous shifts in the global food regime, which has shifted power over production to a more polycentric regime. That is to say, whereas in the recent past, power was concentrated in a US-led food system, the rise of BRICS and middle-income countries has led to actors from multiple states gaining increasing roles in global food systems and land grabs (Borras et al. 2013; Margulis and Porter 2013).

This diffusion can be seen more concretely in reference to GRAIN's (2012) land-grab database. The land grabs recorded here have occurred in over fifty countries, by companies originating in more than fifty countries. This geographic and corporate diversity is an indication of a general lack of concentration in terms of both countries that headquarter land-grabbing firms or governments and countries in which land grabbing is happening. Given the lack of concentration, it is unlikely that a push for public governance in key emerging countries will appear in the short term.

The CFS-RAI process attempted to address this lack of public governance at the national level in multiples ways. As mentioned previously, the CFS-RAI process engaged a wide array of government stakeholders. While the CFS was originally embraced by mostly member states of the G77, member states of the G8 and G20 have recently come on board (McKeon 2013, 114–115). This broad acceptance could serve as a catalyst in motivating states to build or revise national legislation so that it is in line with the CFS-RAI framework. Secondly, in referencing existing binding international agreements, this governance framework could also serve as a reference point for local legal claims, forcing resistant states to acknowledge and confront the need for strong public governance.

Condition 6: Stronger public regulation in developing countries will reinforce rather than replace private governance, and will promote multi-stakeholder initiatives involving both public and private actors

Strong public regulation for global land markets, both by governments of the countries in which investors originate and governments of the countries where the land acquisitions take place, have yet to emerge. As a result, it is difficult to argue that stronger public regulation has appeared in developing countries, thereby precipitating multi-stakeholder, public-private initiatives. Developing countries did, however, gain enough power on the world stage, through organizations such as the G77, to challenge the development of a top-down, investor-friendly, governance initiative from the World Bank on agricultural investments. The CFS-RAI framework, a multi-stakeholder initiative involving public and private actors was developed in response to this challenge.

The ample challenges for purely private governance mechanisms, demonstrated by our analysis of global land markets through Mayer and Gereffi's (2010) framework, highlight the need for this public–private governance approach. With no lead or highly branded firms in most agricultural sectors and few main actors for civil society to target, there is little hope for the purely private global mechanisms that currently exist. The CFS-RAI framework, on the other hand, offers a hopeful alternative in that it addresses some of these limitations through its integration of the public realm and broad inclusion of varied stakeholders.

The Although the CFS-RAI Principles have been approved, they are not binding and their future success will thus depend on voluntary public and private commitment and participation. While the Principles lay out not only the roles and responsibilities of each stakeholders, they also emphasize shared responsibilities, such as balancing stakeholder interests and mutually agreed decision-making (2013b). An initial concern during the CFS-RAI consultation process was that the involvement of a broader array of actors may result in contentious and possibly fractious negotiations. For example, late in the negotiation process, the Canadian government sought to exclude any mention of the need for "free, prior and informed consent" (FPIC) with respect to indigenous peoples, despite objections from almost all other stakeholders.

It will be important to monitor these types of debates more closely now that the Principles have been endorsed and are in the process of being implemented. Additionally, in light of their voluntary nature, further discussions regarding specific monitoring and enforcement mechanisms will be just as, if not more important than the simple endorsement and implementation of this framework.

Conclusion

While the structure of global land markets differs from the more typical production chains presented by Mayer and Gereffi (2010) in the application of their framework, the six conditions offer significant insight for the land-grab issue. From the effects of a polycentric value chain to the alignment of social and commercial objectives through investment risk framing, the framework enables a greater understanding of the unique circumstances faced by global governance advocates when tackling transnational land markets. The framework also allowed us to offer a preliminary analysis of the CFS-RAI Principles in terms of how they may address these land-specific issues through the integration of public elements and a broader inclusion of civil society.

In completing our analysis, however, we realize that some of Mayer and Gereffi's (2010) conditions could be expanded in light of the changing global political-economic order. For example, as consumer markets continue to expand in emerging economies and outgrow their Western counterparts, Western-centric perceptions of brand recognition may no longer accurately reflect true brand reputation vulnerability. In the specific case of global land markets, we feel that determining whether implicated firms have locally based high-profile brand names in countries such as China or Brazil will be an important next step. Further, it is important to distinguish between state-owned and private/public companies to assess whether there are differences in behavior.

Mayer and Gereffi's (2010) framework could also be expanded to account for the ability to frame a social issue in a way that maximizes public support in addition to commercial alignment. As the technological means for disseminating social messages allows for an increasingly broad reach, the need for a flexible message becomes more crucial in attracting and retaining this wider audience. For example, since human rights "resonate with basic ideas of human dignity common to most cultures" (Sikkink 1998, 520), campaigns that can translate local issues to this or a similar contextually appropriate frame, engender greater resonance among transnational audiences. With wider support, these counter-movements are then better able to invoke meaningful private governance responses. Greater analysis of Oxfam International's campaign against soft-drink companies offers an important starting point in the case of land grabs (Oxfam 2013).

Therefore, while Mayer and Gereffi's (2010) framework offers an important starting point for the analysis of transnational issues, greater examination of the land-grab issue through the expansion of these conditions is needed. Additionally, in light of the fact that the implementation of the CFS-RAI Principles has only recently begun and our analysis thus far has been mostly theoretical in nature, follow-up research on the progress of this governance initiative, using this expanded framework, will be helpful in determining the effectiveness of the public–private model in practice.

Notes

1 Although Mayer and Gereffi's paper focuses on production networks, their analytical framework offers important parallels and is equally relevant in shedding light on regulation of the land investment market.
2 These conditions will be reviewed in greater depth later in this chapter.
3 The most recent initiative is the Principles for Responsible Agricultural Investment (CFS-RAIs) which are set to be submitted for endorsement by the CFS at its 41st session in October 2014.
4 Although it is difficult to assess the level of support from governments and regional bodies at this point, many big players, such as the World Trade Organization (WTO), the G8, the G20, the United States, and the World Bank, have come on board since consultations began (McKeon 2013).
5 Feedback from regional consultations will aid the CFS in deciding how the CFS-RAI framework will be used and implemented by different stakeholders.
6 While the term "land grab" can refer to large-scale land acquisitions initiated by domestic investors, this chapter will focus mostly on those initiated by foreign investors.
7 According to GRAIN's (2012) database, in SSA, Sudan, South Sudan, Ethiopia, Tanzania, and Mozambique have been particularly susceptible to land grabs.
8 For example, the International Financial Corporation (IFC) promotes policy reforms in developing countries to eliminate policy barriers to foreign direct investment (FDI) (Shepard and Mittal 2009, 6).
9 While the European Union (EU) was partially behind this rush for biofuels, demanding at least 10 percent of EU transport energy being met through renewable resources by 2020 – biofuels being a top option (Bailey 2008, 6) – some African countries also increased production for domestic purposes.
10 Zoomers (2010) uses the term "long-distance actors" to refer to landownership by foreign investors who are not from the local community.
11 While this push for foreign investment is beneficial for large-scale farm operations, Shepard and Mittal (2009) note that small-scale local farmers are often squeezed out in the process.
12 Approximately 60 percent of people in SSA depend on land for their livelihoods (McIntyre et al. 2009).
13 Ethiopia is one example where land grabs have resulted in discussions of human rights violations. For example, in order to free occupied land for foreign investors, the Ethiopian government has introduced villagization programs which involve the "clustering of agropastoral and/or shifting cultivator populations into more permanent ... settlements" (Human Rights Watch 2012, 11). Although the Ethiopian government describes these programs as "voluntary," the resettlement of indigenous people from their homeland is often forceful and has led to human rights abuses (Oakland Institute 2013a, 7) with respect to the right to life and freedom of movement.
14 To illustrate, approximately 428,000 ha of land surrounding the Gambella National Park in Ethiopia have been awarded to investors without proper Environmental Impact Assessments. The Saudi Star Agriculture Development Plc is one such investor who is using the land for large-scale rice farming, which has resulted in deforestation and the loss of fertile farmland (Oakland Institute 2011).
15 Private-sector-led initiatives include the International Organization for Standardization (ISO) (Clapp 1998), as well multilateral and public–private efforts through international organizations such as the Organisation for Economic Co-operation and Development (OECD) or United Nations (UN) (Clapp 2005).
16 This suited the "prevailing liberal ideology of most states" (Clapp 1998, 312), which continues to emphasize restricting the size of the state and delegating regulatory functions to non-state actors (Fuchs and Kalfagianni 2010).

17 Literature on private governance initiatives has been growing since the late 1990s (Cashore 2002). Indeed, there has been particular focus on environmental governance, including land-based activities such as agriculture, forestry, and mining (Cashore 2002; Grant and Taylor 2004; Pattberg 2006; Dauvergne and Neville 2010; Fuchs and Kalfagianni 2010). In addition, these activities have been placed within global production networks, emphasizing the transnational nature of contemporary production systems (Gereffi et al. 2005; Dauvergne and Lister 2010, 2012).

18 In the case of global land markets, firms can refer to both private companies and parastatal organizations.

19 Levi Strauss was one of the first transnational companies to promote its own corporate code of conduct (Mayer and Gereffi 2010, 6). As a lead firm with a highly visible brand, and a commercial disinterest in continuing production in China as NGO campaigns were starting to highlight poor labor conditions in global supply chains, Strauss was primed to self-regulate. The resulting code of conduct included provisions against employing forced and child labor (Jenkins 2001; Mayer and Gereffi 2010) and spawned many other codes of conduct in the transnational apparel industry.

20 The stated aim of Proclamation No. 456 is to "increase tenure security, improve productivity and avoid expectations of land re-distribution" (LANDac 2013, 3).

21 One possible reason for this classification is the ecological wealth of the "unused" or "underutilized" land, and its potential value if converted to a commodity for the government.

22 See Deininger et al. (2006) for information on how certificates are obtained.

23 Land was redistributed to local farmers with the aim of abolishing the tenure system of the previous imperial regime, which had allowed landlords to exploit their agricultural tenants (Crewett et al. 2008, 1).

24 The main differences between private property and leasehold tenure regimes is that the latter does not encompass the right to sell or mortgage land, nor does it offer indefinite access rights.

25 Commitment to the Framework and Guidelines was reaffirmed at the High Level Forum on Land-Based Foreign Direct Investments in Africa in 2011.

26 This non-prescriptive approach is important as Diao et al. (2013) note that the success of land reform depends on recognizing the diversity in tenure systems, ultimately rejecting "one-size-fits-all policy prescriptions" (p. 20).

27 The FAO hosted ICARRD in Brazil from March 7 to 10, 2006, with the intent of exploring new approaches to sustainable development and agrarian reform. Almost one hundred governments signed the resulting final declaration of this conference, which highlighted the "fundamental importance of secure and sustainable access to land, water, and other natural resources" (Seufert 2013, 182).

28 In 2008, a variety of factors, such as an increasing global demand for biofuels, coalesced to cause a major peak in prices for important cereal crops. Low-income groups in developing countries were the hardest hit as prices for some food crops almost tripled between 2005 and 2008 (Mittal 2009). This event had far-reaching implications, one of which was highlighting the importance of access to agricultural land and fresh water.

29 NGO campaigns include Oxfam International's campaign against soft-drink companies that had sourced sugar from suppliers complicit in land grabs (Oxfam 2013) and the Oakland Institute's campaign against universities that had made endowment fund investments in companies accused of land grabbing (Oakland Institute 2013b).

30 The CFS website provides an up to date list of members www.fao.org/cfs/cfs-home/cfs-about/cfs-members/en/.

31 Although the CFS had already worked to facilitate voluntary guidelines for the governance of tenure of land, fisheries, and forestry, the CFS-RAI framework represented their first land-centric governance initiative.

32 The CFS website outlines how the OEWG operates within these types of projects: www.csm4cfs.org/files/2/guidelines_for_participation_in_vg_oewg_meeting_en.pdf.
33 This revision and negotiation process has been scheduled to begin on April 29 2014 when the OEWG meets in Rome for their first post-consultation discussion on the zero draft. They will have roughly 5 months to complete this process in order to submit the final draft for endorsement by the CFS in October 2014.
34 The *Principles for Responsible Agricultural Investment* (PRAIs) were developed by the World Bank, FAO, UN Conference on Trade and Development (UNCTAD) and International Fund for Agricultural Development (IFAD) in 2009.
35 The PRAIs received little support outside of a handful of state governments, the G8 and G20, and the private sector (McKeon 2013).
36 See note 33.
37 See note 19.
38 These groups also have a dominant presence in the International Planning Committee for Food Sovereignty (IFC), which facilitates the engagement of civil society with the CFS (McKeon 2013).

References

Abbink, Jon (2011). "Ethnic-based federalism and ethnicity in Ethiopia: Reassessing the experiment after 20 years." *Journal of Eastern African Studies* 5, no. 4: 596–618.
African Union (2000). *The Constitutive Act*. Addis Ababa: African Union.
Alemu, Getnet (2011). *Rural Land Policy, Rural Transformation and Recent Trends in Large-Scale Rural Land Acquisitions in Ethiopia. European Report on Development*. http://erd-report.eu/erd/report_2011/documents/dev-11-001-11researchpapers_alemu.pdf.
Anseeuw, Ward (2013). "The rush for land in Africa: Resource grabbing or green revolution?" *South African Journal of International Affairs* 20, no. 1: 159–177.
Anseeuw, Ward et al. (2012). "The state of large-scale land acquisitions in the world: Features and determinants." *LAND Matrix Partnership*. www.cde.unibe.ch/v1/CDE/pdf/state.pdf.
Arezki, Rabah, Klaus Deininger, and Harris Selod (2011). *What Drives the Global Land Rush?* CESifo Working Paper Series No. 3666.
AUC-ECA-AfDB Consortium (2010). *Framework and Guidelines on Land Policy in Africa. Land Policy in Africa: A Framework to Strengthen Land Rights, Enhance Productivity and Secure Livelihoods*. www.pambazuka.org/aumonitor/images/uploads/Framework.pdf.
Bailey, Robert (2008). *Another Inconvenient Truth: How Biofuel Policies Are Deepening Poverty and Accelerating Climate Change*. Oxfam Briefing Paper No. 114.
Borras, Saturnino M. Jr., Jennifer C. Franco, and Chunyu Wang (2013). "The challenge of global governance of land grabbing: Changing international agricultural context and competing political views and strategies." *Globalizations* 10, no. 1: 161–179.
Byamugisha, Frank K (2013). *Securing Africa's Land for Shared Prosperity: A Program to Scale Up Reforms and Investments*. Washington, DC: World Bank Publications.
Byerlee, Derek (2011). *Rising Global Interest in Farmland: Can It Yield Sustainable and Equitable Benefits?* Washington, DC: World Bank Publications.
Cashore, Benjamin (2002). "Legitimacy and the privatization of environmental governance: How non-state market–driven (NSMD) governance systems gain rule-making authority." *Governance* 15, no. 4: 503–529.

CFS (2013a). *Consultancy Output 1: Summary of International Initiatives that Provide Guidance on Responsible Investment: Key Characteristics.* CFS. www.fao.org/fileadmin/templates/cfs/Docs1314/rai/CFS_RAI_Sum_Int_Init_EN.pdf.

CFS (2013b). *Terms of Reference to Develop Principles for Responsible Agricultural Investment.* www.fao.org/fileadmin/templates/cfs/Docs1314/rai/CFS_RAI_ToRs.pdf.

CFS (2014a). *Guidelines for Participation in CFS Open Ended Working Groups.* CFS. www.csm4cfs.org/files/2/guidelines_for_participation_in_vg_oewg_meeting_en.pdf.

CFS (2014b). *Background Document on Principles for Responsible Agricultural Investment (Rai) in the Context of Food Security and Nutrition Zero Draft.* CFS. www.csm4cfs.org/files/News/115/background_document_on_principles_for_responsible_agricultural_investment_in_the_context_of_food_security_and_nutrition_zero_draft.pdf.

Clapp, Jennifer (1998). "The privatization of global environmental governance: ISO 14000 and the developing world." *Global Governance* 4, no. 3: 295–316.

Clapp, Jennifer (2005). "Global environmental governance for corporate responsibility and accountability." *Global Environmental Politics* 5, no. 3: 23–34.

Clapp, Jennifer. "Responsibility to the rescue? Governing private financial investment in global agriculture." Agriculture and Human Values Online First, (2016): 1–13.

Crewett, Wibke, Ayalneh Bogale, and Benedikt Korf (2008). *Land Tenure in Ethiopia: Continuity and Change, Shifting Rulers, and the Quest for State Control.* International Food Policy Research Institute (IFPRI) Report No. 91.

Dauvergne, Peter, and Jane Lister (2010). "The power of big box retail in global environmental governance: Bringing commodity chains back into IR." *Millennium-Journal of International Studies* 39, no. 1: 145–160.

Dauvergne, Peter, and Jane Lister (2012). "Big brand sustainability: Governance prospects and environmental limits." *Global Environmental Change* 22, no. 1: 36–45.

Dauvergne, Peter, and Kate J. Neville (2010). "Forests, food, and fuel in the tropics: the uneven social and ecological consequences of the emerging political economy of biofuels." *The Journal of Peasant Studies* 37, no. 4: 631–660.

Deininger, Klaus, Daniel Ayalew Ali, and Tekie Alemu (2008a). *Impacts of Land Certification on Tenure Security, Investment, and Land Markets: Evidence from Ethiopia.* Washington., DC: World Bank.

Deininger, Klaus, Daniel Ayalew Ali, Stein Holden, and Jaap Zevenbergen (2008b). "Rural land certification in Ethiopia: Process, initial impact, and implications for other African countries." *World Development* 36, no. 10: 1786–1812.

Deininger, Klaus, Daniel Ayalew Ali, and Jaap Zevenbergen (2006). "Assessing the Certification Process of Ethiopia's Rural Lands." Proceedings of Symposium *Les frontières de la question foncière – At the frontier of land issues*, May 17–19, Montpellier.

de Soto, Hernando (2003). *Mystery of Capital: Why Capitalism Triumphs in the West and Fails Everywhere Else.* New York: Basic Books.

Diao, Xinshen, Adam Kennedy, Ousmane Badiane, Frances Cossart, Paul Dorosh, Oliver Ecker, et al. (2013). *Evidence on Key Policies for African Agricultural Growth.* IFPRI Discussion Paper 01242. *International Food Policy Research Institute.* http://citeseerx.ist.psu.edu/viewdoc/download?doi=10.1.1.278.6653&rep=rep1&type=pdf.

FAO (2005). *Concept Note: International Conference on Agrarian Reform and Rural Development: New challenges and options for revitalizing rural communities.* FAO. www.fao.org/docrep/meeting/009/AE899E.htm.

Franco, Jennifer C. (2012). "Global land grabbing and trajectories of agrarian change: A preliminary analysis." *Journal of Agrarian Change* 12, no. 1: 34–59.

Fuchs, Doris, and Agni Kalfagianni (2010). "The causes and consequences of private food governance." *Business and Politics* 12, no. 3.

Gebreselassie, Samuel (2006). *Intensification of smallholder agriculture in Ethiopia: Options and scenarios*. Future Agricultures Policy Brief. www.future-agricultures.org/publications/research-and-analysis/policy-briefs/133-intensification-of-smallholder-agriculture-in-ethiopia-1.

Gereffi, Gary, John Humphrey, and Timothy Sturgeon (2005). "The governance of global value chains." *Review of International Political Economy* 12, no. 1: 78–104.

Goetz, Ariane (2013). "Private governance and land grabbing: the Equator Principles and the Roundtable on Sustainable Biofuels." *Globalizations* 10, no. 1: 199–204.

GRAIN (2012). "GRAIN releases data set with over 400 global land grabs." *GRAIN* February 23. www.grain.org/article/entries/4479-grain-releases-data-set-with-over-400-global-land-grabs.

Grant, E. and Das, O. "Land grabbing, sustainable development and human rights." Transnational Environmental Law 4:2 (2015): 289–317.

Grant, J. Andrew, and Ian Taylor (2004). "Global governance and conflict diamonds: The Kimberley Process and the quest for clean gems." *The Round Table* 93, no. 375: 385–401.

Hall, Ruth (2011). "Land grabbing in Southern Africa: The many faces of the investor rush." *Review of African Political Economy* 38, no. 128: 193–214.

Held, David (2002). "Law of states, law of peoples: Three models of sovereignty." *Legal Theory* 8: 1–44.

Human Rights Watch (2012). *Waiting Here for Death: Displacement and "Villagization" in Ethiopia's Gambella Region*. www.hrw.org/sites/default/files/reports/ethiopia0112webwcover_0.pdf.

Jenkins, Rhys (2001). *Corporate Codes of Conduct: Self-Regulation in a Global Economy*. UNRISD Technology, Business and Society Programme Paper Number 2. www.unrisd.org/80256B3C005BCCF9/search/E3B3E78BAB9A886F80256B5E00344278?OpenDocument.

LANDac (2013). *Ethiopia: Food Security and Land Governance Fact Sheet*. Utrecht: Netherlands: LANDac. www.landgovernance.org/system/files/Ethiopia%20Factsheet%20-%202012.pdf.

Lavers, Tom (2012a). "Land grabs development strategy? The political economy of agricultural investment in Ethiopia." *Journal of Peasant Studies* 39, no. 1: 105–132.

Lavers, Tom (2012b). "Patterns of agrarian transformation in Ethiopia: State-mediated commercialisation and the 'land grab'." *Journal of Peasant Studies* 39, no. 3–4: 795–822.

McIntyre, Beverly D., Hans R. Herren, Judi Wakhungu, and Robert T. Watson (2009). *Agriculture at a Crossroads. International Assessment of Agricultural Knowledge, Science and Technology for Development (IAASTD): Global Report*. Synthesis Report. Washington, DC: Island Press.

McKeon, Nora (2013). "'One Does Not Sell the Land Upon Which the People Walk': Land Grabbing, Transnational Rural Social Movements, and Global Governance." *Globalizations* 10, no. 1: 105–122.

Margulis, Matias E., and Tony Porter (2013). "Governing the global land grab: Multipolarity, ideas, and complexity in transnational governance." *Globalizations* 10, no. 1: 65–86.

Margulis, Matias E., Nora McKeon, and Saturnino M. Borras Jr. (2013). "Land grabbing and global governance: Critical perspectives." *Globalizations* 10, no. 1: 1–23.

Mayer, Frederick, and Gary Gereffi (2010). "Regulation and economic globalization: Prospects and limits of private governance." *Business and Politics* 12, no. 3.

Mittal, Anuradha (2009). *The 2008 Food Price Crisis: Rethinking Food Security Policies*. Washington, DC: United Nations.

Oakland Institute (2011). *Understanding Land Investment Deals in Africa: Saudi Star in Ethiopia*. Land Deal Brief. www.oaklandinstitute.org/sites/oaklandinstitute.org/files/OI_SaudiStar_Brief.pdf.

Oakland Institute (2013a). *Unheard Voices: The Human Rights Impact of Land Investments on Indigenous Communities in Gambella*. Briefing Paper. www.oaklandinstitute.org/sites/oaklandinstitute.org/files/OI_Report_Unheard_Voices.pdf.

Oakland Institute (2013b). *Vanderbilt University Divests from "Land Grab" in Africa*. Oakland Institute, February 13. www.oaklandinstitute.org/vanderbilt-university-divests-land-grab-africa.

Oxfam (2013). *Oxfam Media Briefing: Nothing Sweet About It: How Sugar Fuels Land Grabs*. Oxfam, October 2. www.oxfam.org/sites/www.oxfam.org/files/nothingsweetaboutitmediabrief-embargoed2october2013.pdf.

Pattberg, Philipp (2006). "Private governance and the South: Lessons from global forest politics." *Third World Quarterly* 27, no. 4: 579–593.

Rahmato, Dessalegn. Land to investors: Large-scale land transfers in Ethiopia. No. 1. African Books Collective, 2011.

Sassen, Saskia (2013). "Land grabs today: Feeding the disassembling of national territory." *Globalizations* 10, no. 1: 25–46.

Seufert, Philip (2013). "The FAO Voluntary Guidelines on the Responsible Governance of Tenure of Land, Fisheries and Forests." *Globalizations* 10, no. 1: 181–186.

Shepard, Daniel, and Anuradha Mittal (2009). *The Great Land Grab: Rush for World's Farmland Threatens Food Security for the Poor*. Oakland: The Oakland Institute.

Sikkink, Kathryn (1998). "Transnational politics, international relations theory, and human rights." *PS: Political Science and Politics* 31, no. 3: 517–523.

Stephens, Phoebe (2013). "The principles of responsible agricultural investment." *Globalizations* 10, no. 1: 187–192.

Vermeulen, Sonja, and Lorenzo Cotula (2010). "Over the heads of local people: Consultation, consent, and recompense in large-scale land deals for biofuels projects in Africa." *The Journal of Peasant Studies* 37, no. 4: 899–916.

Von Braun, Joachim, and Ruth Suseela Meinzen-Dick (2009). *"Land grabbing" by foreign investors in developing countries: Risks and opportunities*. Washington, DC: International Food Policy Research Institute.

Zoomers, Annelies (2010). "Globalisation and the foreignisation of space: Seven processes driving the current global land grab." *The Journal of Peasant Studies* 37, no. 2: 429–447.

10 Winners and losers

Contestation over land in the advent of oil exploration in Uganda

Winifred Aliguma, Roberts Muriisa, Medard Twinamatsiko, and Pamela K. Mbabazi

Introduction

Globally, there is an upsurge in land acquisitions by individuals, organizations, and countries. This exercise has been referred to variously as: land acquisitions (Deininger et al. 2011), land deals (Anseeul et al. 2012; Cotula et al. 2009), land grabs (GRAIN 2008; Kachika 2010), and large-scale land acquisitions (World Bank 2011), among other categorizations. The rush for investment especially in oil exploitation in Uganda has been more profound in the last five years and is becoming a force to reckon with, as communities lose their land to the government, the major oil companies, and unscrupulous individuals. There is considerable evidence that local communities rarely benefit equitably when major extractive activities occur in any locality and this impacts negatively on the livelihoods and cultures of such communities (Sawyer and Gomez 2008). In South Africa, for instance, the colonial invasion of 1652, and the wars of land dispossession waged against the indigenous people to seize land for the extractive use of its natural resources by the white settlers, alienated the blacks from land ownership and totally configured the society there, right up until today (Chisoro et al. 2007).

Although the rush for land in the world has been going on since colonial times, the speed, scale, and nature of land acquisition since 2008 is most worrying. The phenomenon of land acquisition in the world became more tense with the 2007–2008 global food and energy crisis, in which world commodity prices rose precipitously, sparking fears among many net-food-importing countries about the security of their food and energy supplies. In 2009, the International Food Policy Research Institute (IFPRI) estimated that deals of 15–20 million hectare of farmland in developing countries were under negotiation between 2006 and 2009 (Cotula et al. 2009). This might have been an under-representation (Hall 2011). The World Bank's report on *Large-Scale Land Acquisitions* of 2010 suggests that the scale is bigger, 56 million hectare were announced before the end of 2009, and more than 70 percent of it was in Africa (Deininger et al. 2011, xiv). The Land Matrix report (Anseeuw et al. 2012) estimates the land deals at 83.2 million hectares in developing countries. Now with the fuel prices plummeting to an all-time low and with much of the land across the countries and regions of Africa already appropriated by governments, foreign companies, and unscrupulous individuals, the future of many peasant farmers across the continent seems too ghastly to contemplate.

It is important to note that while land acquisition has gained prominence and been widely popularized by media reports and other researches such as GRAIN, the international land deals and their impacts on the local populations remain under-represented. This under-representation is largely due to limited data on the scale, who is involved, and the nature of the land deals taking place, especially in Africa (Kachika 2010; Deininger et al. 2011; Anseeuw et al. 2012). Although there is incriminating evidence of a glaring increase in the rush for land that was formerly of no interest to any investment, most of the land acquisitions taking place today remain opaque and invisible to the public (Kugelman 2009). There is limited information on the nature, scale, and location of such deals, and the conditions under which these deals have been made remain obscure. The specificities surrounding these land deals have often been left to media speculation and have remained largely unclear. Indeed, as Anseeuw et al. (2012) point out, many of the large-scale land deals take place in a non-transparent manner, making it difficult to report the nature and the scale of these deals with accuracy. As Kachika (2010) also argues, accessing accurate data on land grabbing is challenging because governments and investors often have different data regarding the size and scale of the same investment.

Uganda has been a victim of land deals and land appropriation, but this is not clearly understood since it its existence is denied by the government.[1] In Uganda, large-scale land acquisitions are generally a sensitive matter and attract a lot of controversy and threats to investigators. Much of the controversy surrounding large-scale land acquisition in Uganda and the subsequent tensions that have emerged as a result of the discovery of oil have been sustained by the government's limited willingness to release important information regarding land deals relating to oil exploitation and production in the oil-rich region of south-western Uganda.

The discovery of oil in Uganda has dramatically escalated already existing tensions between groups and exacerbated the land question in Uganda. New tensions have been created and this could easily spark localized land conflicts. International Alert (2009) notes four oil-wealthy sub-regions along the Albertine Rift Valley where land conflicts have been escalating largely because oil exploration is forcing localized displacement. Furthermore, the rights to land are being bought up by Ugandans from all across the country as well as foreigners, and traditional land rights are being largely ignored. These challenges are further complicated by high population growth rates[2] and increasing land scarcity. As groups position themselves to reap the benefits from oil, land tensions are also increasing, which makes the future of the oil industry in Uganda even more ghastly to contemplate.

Given the above background, this chapter argues that the manner in which land deals relating to Uganda's emerging oil industry are being made is highly invisible. It is not at all clear how this land acquisition takes place, who exactly is acquiring the land, and the impact this is having on the local population, as there is scanty and limited information regarding this. Even in the few instances where certain incriminating data has come out, it is often denied by government and threats have been made to those releasing such data. A recent threat by the government to close or deregister the Uganda Land Alliance, one of the civil society organizations in Uganda which advocates for land rights, is one example of the sensitivity of this topic locally.[3] In this instance, the government called on anybody to come up with evidence that there is land grabbing in Uganda.

This chapter therefore tries to unravel the dynamics and impact of recent land acquisitions in Uganda, particularly focusing on the oil-rich region, and tries to identify the invisible hand behind these deals and who the winners and losers are. The paper focuses on four main key objectives, namely: (a) to identify the existing forms and nature of land deals in Uganda's oil-rich region; (b) to identify the key drivers of land deals in Uganda; (c) to assess the impact of land appropriations in the oil region on rural livelihoods and (d) to describe the land governance challenges in Uganda today. Without understanding the scale, the nature, and the dynamics involved in these land acquisitions one cannot state with certainty the extent to which land deals for the growing extractive industry in Africa can impact on rural livelihoods of the majority poor in developing countries.

Understanding land grabbing

In this chapter, land grabbing is considered to be any form of land acquisition where there are limited consultations with the local people by government, the investor, or the new land owners, where people are dispossessed of land they have used for ages, and where contracts between locals have been questioned, and where there are few benefits accruing from land contracts. Uganda's land law requires that transfer of land ownership should be agreed upon by the land owner and the bona fide occupants and that the new owners should respect the bona fide occupants (Government of Uganda 2010).

Analysis of the literature indicates that the theory surrounding land grabbing has foundations in globalization and power relations; it is power relations that drive land grabbing. In the case of Uganda, due to an emerging power differential reflected in the growing middle-class and the increase in foreign direct investments, particularly with the recent discovery of oil, those with influence and financial resources take the lead in land grabbing. The poor cannot afford to pursue land rights, and consequently the powerful exploit the poor and grab their land.

As we have stressed, precise information is hard to find; nevertheless there is evidence that significant land grabbing does take place in Uganda (see, for example, Anseeuw et al. 2012; Oxfam 2011; Zeemeijer 2011), although there are limited details on how it takes place and who the perpetrators are. As noted earlier, the practice remains highly invisible and may easily go unnoticed.

In this next section, we present data on the nature of land deals mainly in Ssembabule and Buliisa districts where we carried out an investigation.

The nature of land deals in Uganda: The case of Buliisa and Ssembabule

To determine whether land grabbing does exist and understand its nature we investigated the process of land acquisition in Uganda: how land is acquired, who is involved in the land acquisition, and whether the law is followed when people are acquiring land.

Processes of land acquisition

During our investigations, we found that land acquisition in parts of our study area is through buying, concessions, and forced entry. Most of the land existing in the oil-rich districts and mostly under contention is Mailo land. The 2009 Land Amendment Act stipulates that land may be sold to a willing buyer at free will, but it also recognizes that bona fide occupants should be given first opportunity before land is sold to another person. We found that land buying is more or less a closed deal, which takes place between the buyer and the seller without consulting the bona fide occupants as prescribed by the constitution and subsequent Land Amendment Act (see Government of Uganda 2010). This is clearly a violation of the local people's land rights. We found that district land officials, the local council chiefs, and the area land boards are never consulted when land deals are negotiated and executed. According to one highly placed government official in Buliisa District:

> The way people buy land in Buliisa leaves a lot to be desired. How land is acquired is only known by the seller and the buyer and maybe, by the land officer who issues the title, since many come carrying titles claiming that they are the new owners of land. We only get to know about any land transfers and acquisitions when there are problems with squatters.
>
> (Interview with district official)

Many people have been occupying land without knowing that it belongs to someone else or without knowledge that there is a title on the land. As required by law, anyone who has a title should consult the people (bona fide occupants) before transferring land. However, people are often surprised when they see someone claiming he has bought land and wants them to vacate it. In Buliisa District, people were forced to leave land where they had stayed for more than two decades, and their property was destroyed. People claim that they were not aware that the new landowner had acquired the land.

One day someone came to our place, he told us he had bought land, he instructed us to vacate the place. We wondered how he had got the land. We later learned that he had got land after paying the bank. Later we also learned that he had sold the land to a certain army man who does not want anybody living on the land. We do not know this new person. We are now being forced to leave the land to clear way for the new owners.

(Focus group discussion in Buliisa)

Again in Buliisa, some people claimed that they bought land, but we found that the people who were purported to have sold that land either do not exist or never owned the land in question. In an interview with the local council chairman of Kasenyi, where the Kasemene oil well belonging to the Tullow Oil Company is located, it was revealed that when the community land was sold, the community was not involved, but people who had previously settled on the land were said to have sold the land, and attempts to investigate the sale by communities were met with hostility and violence. According to the chairman:

Kahwa, a rich Mugungu who stays in Kampala, claims he bought land from two Congolese, who never owned the land but had been resident in Buliisa having fled from Congo because of insurgency in Congo. Kahwa later sold to Tullow Oil. In both cases, there were no witnesses or local council officials. A month later, I received a letter from Buliisa Town council informing me to inform villagers that they were coming to inspect and fence Kahwa's land. The letter further requested me to mobilise the villagers for a meeting over this matter. In May 2012, the official arrived for the meeting. Soon after the meeting had begun, a group of people arrived with sticks, bows and arrows and started beating people and dispersing them. Shortly after, the police and other government officials also arrived and they joined in the beating and some arrests were made. It was a horrible experience. I was arrested for five days, after which I was taken to Masindi and released on bail. The case was later dropped. We now fear to go to the police because they are all Kahwa's agents. We feel very insecure.

(Interview with LC I chairman)

This testimony by the LC I chairman confirms the fact that many communities in Uganda's oil-rich region experience insecurity of tenure. Land tenure in much of Buliisa is overwhelmingly customary, and it is local leaders who allocate to families the right to use this land. Those rights can be inherited by new generations in a family, but occupants do not have land titles and they are not entitled to sell.

Land speculation is certainly rife in the oil-rich areas of Buliisa, and local entrepreneurs have been buying up plots from individual farmers, perhaps on behalf of even wealthier families from elsewhere and with the assistance of the District Land Board, which has jurisdiction over land titles and is independent of central government control. The NRM Member of Parliament for Buliisa County whom we interviewed has been waging war on land speculation in Bunyoro for several years claims that:

> Around 30 families "from Kampala" have been using local agents, including Franco Kahwa to buy land along the whole Albertine Graben.

He alleges that he has also been harassed and intimidated by local security chiefs and police because of his efforts to expose this land-grabbing racket. He revealed that many local district officials and security personnel are involved and are facilitating the land grabbing in his area. The MP noted that on December 2, 2010, he officially complained to parliament that the officer in charge of Buliisa Police, a one Edison Muhangi, had shot at him three times (interview with the Hon. MP, July 2012) because of his trying to protest against and curb land grabbing in his constituency. The MP claimed that his investigations and outcries prompted President Museveni to announce a ban on further land transactions in the area, in a bid to calm the situation. (interview with the MP, July 2012).

Several respondents elsewhere in Buliisa frequently mentioned Kahwa's name in connection to dubious land deals, and a Paris-based regional publication, *The Indian Ocean Newsletter*, has also linked Kahwa to land deals in Buliisa on behalf of senior Ugandan politicians, which goes to exemplify the invisible nature of land deals in Uganda. Its December 2010 issue reported:

> The current minister for information and former Chairperson of the National Resistance Movement parliamentary group, Kabakumba Masiko, is high on the list of landowners who hope to see their land increase in value when the oil exploration comes under way. She is believed to have obtained the land through cooperation with another land owner, a certain Kahwa Franco, who supervised the transaction in collusion with Fred Lakumu, the head of Buliisa District Council. Among the other landowners in this zone are the Second Deputy Prime Minister Henry Kajura as well as some DRC Nationals who have obtained land deeds from Uganda Land Commission, like Rapheal Soriano, a wealthy businessman from Katanga.
>
> (Indian Ocean Newsletter 2010)

From the above data and testimonies of land-grabbing victims, one can deduce that land grabbing in Uganda is a reality, but in the areas we investigated, it is clear that land is being appropriated by wealthy locals, who seem to be enjoying police (and arguably government) protection to terrorize the helpless peasants.

In Ssembabule, Rwendahi sub-county, which is a neighboring district, according to respondents, people woke up one morning and were told to vacate the land because it had been bought. We followed people who had been evicted and who were staying in another location, and one respondent told us how they had lost land they had lived on for three decades;

> My father migrated from Bukimbiri Kisoro district, we stayed on Mailo land for 30 years. Joseph [not real name] bought land neighbouring us, one day he came and told us, that he no longer wants to see any other person on the land we were staying; that he had bought the land. You are now illegally staying here so you should move, this is my land, he told us. We knew we were staying on Mailo land whose owner we had never known and never met. We do not know how Joseph acquired the land.
> (Interview with respondent living in Chabi, having migrated from Rwendahi – names withheld for security reasons)

We probed our respondents further and found that in some areas of Bunyoro, people are given first opportunity to stay on the land upon payment of a price which they cannot afford, a condition which forces them to leave and to sell to the new landlord. In an interview with one of the respondents, he revealed that compensation is only determined by the buyer not the seller.

> We are asked to pay one million Uganda Shillings (about US$400) per acre of land if we want to stay, but if we opt to leave and get compensation, we are told we will be paid five hundred thousand Uganda Shillings (about US$200).
> (Interview with respondent in Ssembabule District)

In Rutunku and Rwendahi sub-counties of Ssembabule – which are the areas mostly affected by land grabbing – people were forced to leave, even when they resisted. A key informant told us:

> Mafenda had to leave for Kiboga without compensation after resisting for so long, Manirageza is now in Gomba with no land. These people put up a strong fight, but they were eventually overpowered and they had to leave without anything. Banyenzaki, the only Mukiga who managed to pay his way and is still staying in Rwendahi, is living under threat and is contemplating selling under intense pressure of animals grazing his crops, but we doubt whether he will get the compensation he deserves. It will be on the basis of take what I offer basis since now he is the one demanding to leave, we wait to see.
> (Key informant in Lutunku – Ssembabule District)

It was reported that the compensation received by most landowners is still minimal or sometimes not there. The majority of the local people interviewed reported that the money given to them as compensation by landowners is not comparable to their land and other investments on it. In most cases, people are forced to leave and are offered compensation that is not worth the land and the property or investments on land. In Manyogaseka, Mubende district, people were given 200,000 Uganda Shillings (less than USD$100) as compensation, and some were defrauded and left with no compensation at all.

In some instances, people are lured into signing documents, which are eventually forged to appear as if they were agreements of compensation. In an interview with people who are still living on the land under contention and whose property was destroyed purportedly by people sent by one landowner, we learned that:

> After several trials and notices to evict us without success, George (not real name) sent his men to tell us to go for our compensation so that we leave the land. We were told that each will receive Uganda shillings two million (2,000,000) almost 700 USD. When we arrived at his house, he made us sign an agreement that he had compensated us. After signing he told us that he had miscounted the money and he can only offer us 200,000, and the rest will be paid later. It is this agreement he insists that it is evidence that he paid us our compensation.
> (Focus group discussion with people still stranded on the land in Manyogaseka)

The evidence above is corroborated by evidence from interviews with other key informants. One of the respondents put it thus:

> We signed an agreement and were paid Uganda Shillings 200,000. After three years he came back with police from Mubende under leadership of Musisi (Sergeant), and burnt houses. His foremen first came and cleared all our plantations, he enquired how much money I wanted, I told him I wanted 30 million, after three days he came and cut the plantation. He stood with army men side by side.
> (Interview with key informant in Mubende)

We traced one person who, after the scare, fled the land and is staying in Kigando. Jane, 39 years old, a widow with five children, formerly resident of Manyogaseka, informed us that:

> In 1999, June, we saw land surveyors on the land we had lived on for three decades. We sent them away. In 2002 we saw a man George [not real name] coming and he told us that he had bought the land from the bank and wants us to leave his land. After this notice, he left only to come in 2004 this time with a gun. People reacted and refused to vacate, and he called in police and people were arrested. We called the area Member of Parliament to rescue us but he told us that he would not get into conflict with George [not real name] and instead he advised everyone to find his/her way out. We were harassed and intimidated until 2009 when George

brought cows which would be released into our gardens at night to destroy them. Later, after failing to get us out by harassing us, we were told that we were not supposed to get food from our gardens since the land did not belong to us. We remained defiant and continued to get food from our garden. Finally, on 14/08/2009 George's cows ate all my gardens, 3 hectares of banana plantation, 1 hectare of cassava. Five families were affected including mine. When we found the cows in our gardens, we held seven of them hostage and called the chairman LC 1. Realising this, George's workers cut one of them, and reported the matter to police. Police came, we were beaten by the officer in charge of police, and we were tied together, bundled on a police truck and taken to Mubende police. We were kept in police cells for four days and the local council chairman and other people came and bailed us out on condition that we report to the police twice a week. After a week it became costly for us, we paid 400,000 shillings each and the matter was dismissed. He again came and instructed us to leave his place, he paid people 200,000 UGX. I was given 350,000 UGX. I had nothing to do but leave his land. On the day I was leaving, people with guns and machetes came and destroyed our property. Houses were destroyed including mine, plantations cut and no one remained with a banana plantation in the village. The pressure had become too much, the law we trusted was no longer on our side. I decided to leave. Only about three families still stay on that land, others like me fled this terror.

(Interview with Jane, a victim of land grab)

Jane's story is repeated by those who stayed and have since abandoned their plantations in fear of them being cut down again. We met three of the remaining families whose stories are similar to Jane's.

The stories and testimonies of the victims presented above show the fraudulent process by which land acquisition takes place.

Uganda's land governance challenges

In Uganda there are four types of land-tenure system recognized by the constitution: mailo, leasehold (public), freehold, and customary land-tenure systems. There is limited knowledge of how the land-tenure system operates in Uganda and people buying or grabbing land exploit people's ignorance. Our findings in Buliisa show that a large number of people do not know the forms of land-tenure systems and which land-tenure system does exist in the places of their residence. As many as 80 percent of the local people whom we surveyed did not understand the operation of the tenure system.

The Ugandan constitution provides for security of tenure, but people do not know that there is a land law, they are not aware of their rights and how to secure them. The 1900 Buganda agreement created a stream of absentee landlords. This was repealed by subsequent land laws, such as the 1975 Land Decree (Government of Uganda 1975), allowing other people to occupy land at will. Also, the 1995 constitution recognized the rights of occupancy by the bona fide occupants. According to the Land Amendment Act 2010, bona fide occupants can be evicted only when they fail to pay ground rent. We found, however, that people were ignorant of the law. We asked respondents to indicate whether they knew the law based on the statement, "on a scale of 1–10 (whereby 1 represents less knowledge and 10 represents highly known), please determine the transparency and the practice of the land law in Uganda." It was found that 60 percent of the citizens are aware of the law, 20 percent practice the knowledge of the law, and 10 percent do not know the law. It is ignorance of law that has made land wrangles and land grabbing a key phenomenon in Uganda today.

According to the constitution of Uganda, a person can be evicted from land which he/she previously occupied through failure to pay the ground rent – *busulu* – which is prescribed by parliament. Subsequently, districts enacted laws governing this rent and the amount to be paid. In the areas of our investigation, it was revealed that each tenant is supposed to pay 200,000 Uganda shillings (less than US$100) as annual fee from ground rent, irrespective of the size of land she/he occupies. Against this background it was found that one of the triggers of land grabbing is the low price for land in terms of ground rent. Owing to the low ground rent, landlords will always opt to sell the land to whoever can take the risk of dealing with the bona fide occupants. In Buliisa and Ssembabule we learnt that the biggest challenge is the land conflicts between the new landlords and the bona fide occupants. Most of the land being grabbed is that where absentee landlords exist and purportedly sell to other people without giving bona fide occupants an opportunity to buy, as prescribed by law. The new landlords are subsequently evicting people on their terms, and not in recognition of the law. During our key informant interviews, one local leader had this to say:

> One of the major problems we have here in Buliisa is not the law but the ignorance of the law which landlords are using to evict people. They prescribe the compensation they want to give and do not in any way consider bona fide occupants as prescribed by the law. Bona fide occupants do not know their rights either and believe that they are at the mercy of the landlord. Yet this is not the case. In many areas of Buliisa, the problem has been that of absentee landlords. Most people were *bibanja* owners and did not have any clue who the owner was and what rights they have on land, until one day one rich man came and told the whole village that he had bought the land on which they lived, and therefore must vacate. Some vacated without any resistance, because they believed they had no rights at all.
> (Chairman LC II, Buliisa district)

Furthermore, in Buliisa district we found that people mainly owned land on a customary basis but did not know that they needed to have a certificate of customary ownership for them to have claim over the land. In the neighboring district of Hoima, we interacted with four family members who claimed that their land had been grabbed by other clans; further interaction revealed that they had nothing to show that the land in question ever belonged to them. The Abaseka clan in Kyaruboija, Buhimba sub-county, led by Kahwa, Rugiretima, Kiiza, and Arinda (we requested their consent to use their names in our report and they agreed) narrates their loss of land:

> We have owned land for generations, we were born on this land, our fore fathers lived here, but one day in 1990s, four other families (names withheld- efforts to reach these families fell on deaf ears we could not collaborate this evidence) ganged together and grabbed our land. We reported the matter to court which ruled in our favour. In 2007, after most of our elders had died, the group ganged together again and took over the land again, they grazed their animals on our gardens, destroyed our property and we came together as clans and fought back. Beyagira and Alinda sustained injuries and were hospitalised, the police did not arrive on time to save the situation. Today we are still, battling the matter in court but it is very expensive to continue
> (Focus Group Discussion with Kahwa, Rugiretima, Kiiza, and Arinda of the Abaseka clan)

We asked them whether they had evidence that the land in question belonged to them, and they indicated that they had no registered title to the land and no certificate of occupancy. This complicates the matter, as communal land in this sub-region seemed to be taken over on the pretext that it belonged to nobody. The above discussion indicates how people can exploit a weak system of land governance and utilize it for their selfish interests.

Data gathered from Buliisa and Ssembabule indicates that while there is a clear law about land access and land rights, the same law is not well understood and evidently not practiced. The constitution provides for rights of access, but people's land rights are not protected. People are aware of the law but their understanding of it is not clear. Of the 60 percent of respondents interviewed who claimed they were aware of the existence of the law, a majority of these did not know its application. Indeed, interpretation of the law is still a challenging factor; moreover, the law is silent on certain key aspects, such as payment of rent in case tenants fail to locate the holder of the title. It is such loopholes and challenges that provide a conducive milieu for land grabbing to thrive in the different parts of Uganda.

In the areas of our research, we found that land governance is far from being transparent. Local people have limited access to records. We made a survey on the statement "On a scale of 1–10, where 1 is non-transparent at all and 10 is very transparent, rate the transparency of the land system in your district." In response, 70 percent of the respondents indicated that the land system is not transparent at all, 10 percent indicated that the land system is transparent, and 20 percent indicated that the system is fairly transparent.

We used qualitative data to corroborate this data. In Mubende (a district neighboring Ssembabule), it was indicated that the system favors Baganda more than any other people. As one respondent noted:

> There is a native factor – Baganda versus other tribes – it may take a year before land application forms are processed by the land board if you are not a Muganda and less than 2 weeks if you are a Muganda.
> (Interview with government official Mubende District)

We interviewed one person who has been applying for a land title since 1996, even after paying lease offer fees, and the respondent lamented, "I have failed to get a land title because the process is so slow and unfair." According to the documents carried by the respondent, he applied for a lease in 1984, which offer was given under Minute ULC min8/3/84a. Payment of premium fees of Uganda shillings 500,000 was made on receipt no. 476713 on 11/08/1986 in respect of 200 ha at Kanyirunga, Mubende. To date, the applicant has not received a title to the land. Instead, in 1987, some other person came and occupied the land. He indicated he had been following up the case with the President's Office after the district land board failed to resolve the issue, but there has still been no progress.

Land records are vital for land governance, and access to such records by legitimate inquirers such as the land rights holders is an important indicator of a transparent land governance system (Deininger et al. 2012). However, we found that districts in our research lack record systems that can facilitate access to land records. Uganda has a central registry of land and records exist at district land offices. Over time, Uganda has undergone divisions involving creating new districts out of the old ones. For example, Ssembabule district was created out of Masaka, Mubende out of Mityana, Buliisa out of Masindi. Creation of these districts, however, has not been followed by effective creation of land registries in the new districts. We found that the new districts did not hold land records; instead, the old districts still held them, making record access and verification difficult for the land officers and people concerned. We interviewed the land officer of Mubende district and he lamented that lack of records was hampering land management and governance in the district:

> Mubende district is a new district prone to land conflicts; we in the land registry have almost no records, most land records are still in Mityana. We have received many people who claim to be tenants wanting to know whose land they occupy, since they have never seen their land lord, yet they have to pay rent. We cannot help them. We refer them to Mityana. This is failure on our part.
> (Land officer, Mubende district)

In the areas where we held interviews, local leaders also indicated the challenge of tracing mailo land owners. When asked how they are handling the issue of people who come into the area claiming that they are the owners of mailo and the threat of eviction of bona fide tenants, one of the respondents had this to say:

> We are mobilising people to find the true owners of the land where they are living, but in the land office, it is not easy to trace the land owner. Whenever you go to the land office, it is not easy to trace the owner of the title.

According to the Chief Administrative Officer (CAO) Ssembabule district:

> There are limited proper land records, we tried to establish a land office at the district, but the transfer of records from Masaka has not been done. The district does not have a lands officer, we advertised for the post but there were no applicants with qualifications we wanted for the office. The district still utilises the services of Masaka District.
> (Interview with CAO Ssembabule District)

Evidently, access to land records is a big problem for new districts. This has hampered the operations in these districts with respect to land management. According to the CAO, most of the land wrangles existing in the district result from lack of records of land.

One other factor related to the land governance challenges in Uganda is the system of transfer of land from one party to another. Land in Uganda can be transferred in different ways: through purchase (willing buyer–willing seller), through inheritance, where land is held on customary basis, and through leasing (especially with public land). The system of land transfer seems very clearly laid down. However, rarely is the system followed. We found that although influence, peddling, and power remain highly invisible, they play a large role in land transfers. This is manifested in the indirect manner of land purchases and the approach that land grabbers use. Through focus group discussions in Buliisa, Ssembabule, and Mubende it was found that most land grabbers use their power and influence to buy land. The approach they use is to ensure that people are left with no choice but to sell their land. They do this by exposing the people to risks and vulnerable situations, such as crop damage by cattle, or by allowing them priority to buy land at a price they cannot afford. Land grabbers who use power and influence include military officers, powerful politicians, and the relatives of those in power. In most cases, when land is grabbed, the victims fear to take the matter to court, largely because they are poor and cannot stand the challenge the rich land grabbers pose.

Asked whether they were interested in taking cases to court, local residents who are victims of land grabbing mentioned the challenge of their poverty situation, which makes them incapable of handling court cases as advanced by top district leaders. Two local residents in Mubende had the following to say:

> The way they buy land here leaves a lot to be desired. This is not a case of willing buyer and willing seller but forced buying and forced selling. People have lost their land to the outsiders without any choice. Most of them are very poor that they cannot take cases of grabbing to court. Some even fear going to court because they know court cases are always bought in favour of the rich who have influence and are educated to buy lawyers. When you talk about compensation, I do not understand you well because, you cannot compare 2 acres of land and someone giving you just 200,000shs. This is not comparable.
> (Interview with Balya Yowesi, Kashambya LC I, Mubende district)

Another respondent had this to say:

> Army men harass local people here. They do not compensate them when they take ownership of their land. In cases where they decide to do it, they do not do it genuinely. They are the ones to determine how much to pay the squatters. In general the process of land acquisition is not transparent; you cannot know how people get land titles. The law provides a process through which people should get land titles, but these are not followed at all.
> (Sub-County Chief Kigando Sub-County, Mubende District)

Most of the people interviewed for this study do not like the way their land is being taken over, and some have resisted, although with limited success, as noted by one resident:

> Brigadier Lutaya in 1981 made claimed that he wanted to survey public land. He surveyed even my land in the public land he surveyed. He asked me if I had documents and took me to lands office. In 1981, he forced me to get out of my land without success. He would get police and soldiers to scare us. We are about 30 people and on another side of Mubende they were 60 residents.
> (Mzee Eriya Kanyaruju Kiyonga Parish, Kigando sub-county)

Power and influence also seem to play in the area of Buliisa. It is believed that the acquisition of land in Buliisa is related to the power which people hold and how they relate with the powerful men in government. The discovery of oil in the region has made it possible for people to rush for land in Bunyoro, and in Buliisa in particular, in the desire to position themselves so as to benefit from the oil. Since most of the land in Bunyoro is held under customary tenure, the land is not registered to one single owner but is held communally. In Hoima, a certain army officer was named in a complex land dispute in

Kisukuma village, Kigorobya sub-county, where local residents were arrested after resisting forceful evacuation of the land they occupied. From key informant interviews, it is alleged that the army officer bought 1,205 hectares of land from a Bunyoro teachers cooperative savings and society, and yet this organization had acquired the title fraudulently. People who dared take the matter to police or to the resident district commissioner were arrested and this scared away others.

Conclusions

We have discussed how land grabbing is a global phenomenon which has also affected Uganda. We have shown that the nature and character of large-scale land acquisition in Uganda can only be described as land grabbing. This is based on the understanding that any land acquisition which leads to violation of people's rights, in which people are discontented with the compensation they receive, and which involve dispossession of people of their rights to land, should be considered as land grabbing. Indeed we found that land grabbing is a feature characterizing the districts of Buliisa, Ssembabule and Mubende. We also found that the nature of land acquisition and the processes involved leave a lot beneath the eye for it to easily be recognized as land grabbing. We thus conclude that land grabbing in Uganda largely remains highly invisible and may easily pass as genuine land acquisition, and that the winners are the unscrupulous individuals who obtain land at giveaway prices while the local residents and farmers are losing out. We found that land grabbing in Uganda has affected rural development and the lives of the people; people have lost property, they are not adequately compensated, and are not employed by the new land owners. We thus conclude that land grabbing in Uganda has not in any way contributed to rural development.

We conclude, however, that while land grabbing is a feature that spells doom for Uganda's rural development strategies, increased sensitization and dissemination of information regarding people's land rights can make land deals in Uganda beneficial to the local communities. We therefore conclude that making people aware of their rights to land can lead to a win–win situation in the event that land is taken away from the bona fide occupants, since they can be adequately compensated. Assurance of adequate compensation would therefore make people utilize the land and not leave it fallow. We further conclude that informing people of their land rights can make land grabbing visible, making it possible to prevent it or to make better use of it by making genuine claims and demanding better compensation. Once people are well compensated, they can easily relocate and maintain good lives. In addition, proper policies and their implementation and follow-up would make the land grabbers fulfill their obligations as stated in land deal agreements, thus allowing people and communities to benefit from the investments.

The final conclusion we would like to emphasize is that much as large-scale land appropriations in the oil-rich region of Uganda might have potentially positive effects on rural agrarian transformation, the benefits of this investment do not always translate into tangible outputs that can benefit the largely rural communities of Uganda, unless there is a deliberate effort to ensure that the majority rural peasants also enjoy some positive outcomes. We conclude that improving the process of knowledge creation about the existing land law will increase the benefits of land grabbing, and there is need for further research on how to actualize this.

Notes

1 *The Independent* newspaper on May 6, 2012 reported that "On Thursday April 26th 2012, the Internal Affairs Minister, Hillary Onek, under whose docket the NGOs fall, summoned representatives of the two NGOs to explain an anti-land campaign they are involved in. He wanted to know what land grabbing they are campaigning against and whether it exists in Uganda." (See www.independent.co.ug/coverstory/5726-museveni-angry-over-ngo-report-on-land-grabbing, accessed May 2012.)
2 With a population growing by 1.2 million every year, Uganda has one of the highest population growth rates worldwide and therefore competition for resources is stiffer. At an annual growth rate of 3.2 percent per annum, Uganda's population is projected to double in the next few years, spelling more doom for a country whose population is largely youthful and unproductive. This is one of the biggest challenges to Uganda's development. (For more details see www.nbs.ug.)
3 See www.farmlandgrab.org/post/print/20419 (accessed May 13, 2016).

References

Anseeul, Ward, Boche, Mathieu, Breu, Thomas, Giger, Markus, Lay, Jann, Messerli, Peter, and Nolte, Kerstin (2012) *Transnational Land Deals for Agriculture in the Global South: Analytical Report Based on the Land Matrix Database*. CDE/CIRAD/GIGA, Bern/Montpellier/Hamburg.

Chisoro, Clever, Del Grande, Lisa, and Ziqubu, Ndabe (2007) *The Rise and Fall of Social Economic Land Rights in the Province of Kwazulu – Natal, South Africa – A Case Study*. South Africa, Association for Rural Advancement.

Cotula, Lorenzo, Vermeulen, Sonja, Leonard, Rebecca, and Keeley, James (2009) *Land Grab or Development Opportunity? Agricultural Investment and International Land Deals in Africa*, London/Rome, FAO, IIED and IFAD.

Deininger, Klaus, Byerlee, Derek, Lindsay, Jonathan, Norton, Andrew, Selod, Harris, and Stickler. Mercedes (2011) *Rising Global Interest in Farmland: Can It Yield Sustainable Benefits?* Washington, DC, World Bank.

Deininger, Klaus, Selod, Harris, and Burns, Anthony (2012) *The Land Governance Assessment Framework: Identifying and Monitoring Good Practice in the Land Sector*, Washington, DC, World Bank.

Government of Uganda (2010) *Land Amendment Act of 2010*, Kampala, Uganda.

Government of Uganda (1975) *Land Reform 1975 Decree, No. 3*, Kampala, Uganda.

GRAIN (2008) *Seized! The 2008 Land Grab for Food and Financial Security*. GRAIN Briefing Note, October 2008.

Hall, Ruth (2011) "Land grabbing in Southern Africa: the many faces of the investor rush," *Review of African Political Economy* Vol. 38, No. 128, 193–214.

Indian Ocean Newsletter (2010) *Uganda: Land Grab in the Oil-Bearing Zone*, Business Circles No. 1299. www.africaintelligence.com/ION/business-circles/2010/12/18/land-grab-in-the-oil-bearing-zone,86837285-ART?createok=1#2 (accessed May 13, 2016).

International Alert (2009) *Harnessing Oil for Peace and Development in Uganda: Investing in Peace*, Issue no. 2, September 2009, www.internationalalert.org/sites/default/files/publications/Harnessing_Oil_for_Peace_and_Development_Uganda.pdf (accessed, May 24, 2016).

Kachika, Tinyande (2010) *Land Grabbing in Africa: A Review of the Impacts and Possible Policy Responses*, Oxford, Oxfam International Pan African Programme.

Kugelman, Michael (2009) "Introduction," in Kugelman, Michael and Levenstein, Susan (eds) *Land Grab? The Race for the World's Farmland*, Washington, DC, Woodrow Wilson International Center for Scholars.

Oxfam (2011) *Land and Power: The Growing Scandal Surrounding a New Wave of Investing in Land*. Oxfam briefing paper no. 151, www.oxfam.org/sites/www.oxfam.org/files/bp151-land-power-rights-acquisitions-220911-en.pdf (accessed on May 13, 2016).

Sawyer, Suzana and Gomez, Edmund Terence (2008) *Transnational Governmentality and Resource Extraction: Indigenous Peoples, Multinational Corporations, Multilateral Institutions and the State*. Geneva: United Nations Research Institute for Social Development.

World Bank (2011) *Rising Global Interest in Farmland: Can It Yield Sustainable and Equitable Benefits?* Washington, DC: World Bank.

Zeemeijer, Ilse (2011) *Who Gets What, When and How? New Corporate Land Acquisitions and the Impact on Local Livelihoods in Uganda*, Utrecht, Leiden International Development Studies Department of Human Geography, Utrecht University.

Part IV
Foreign policy

11 Canada and China
Accepting Africa's rise?

Joseph K. Ingram

Introduction

A defining characteristic of the twenty-first century is the unprecedented growth of what most people refer to as the "global middle class." This explosive growth is creating extraordinary demand for consumer products and the natural resources needed to produce them. Sub-Saharan Africa, one of the last continental regions with relatively unexploited natural resources, has become the focus of intensified global attention – and not just from its former colonial masters. Investors are attracted to its abundant mineral wealth, vast agricultural land, and increasingly skilled labor force. This attractiveness is reflected in consistently high GDP growth rates in the region, exceeding in the past decade even those of the so-called "Asian tigers."

Canada and China, both trading nations with growing demand for good investment opportunities, have increased their investments in sub-Saharan Africa – albeit for somewhat different reasons. This growing engagement is driven by distinct strategies which use varied combinations of public and private policy instruments. This chapter seeks to identify and compare the strategies and policy instruments deployed by both countries, while revealing the extent to which their approaches "accept" Africa's rise. ("Accepting Africa's Rise" was the title of a conference hosted in September 2012 by the International Development Research Center and the University of Alberta's China Institute, for which a brief oral version of this chapter was presented by the author.) It will specifically examine the extent to which the engagement of Canada and China responds to the region's need for more equitable and sustainable forms of economic and social development. Such an analysis also adds to the limited academic literature comparing and contrasting the engagement of different bilateral donors with sub-Saharan Africa.

The interface of globalization and extractives

The second half of 2012 witnessed three significant developments in three parts of the globe, which together have had profound implications for Canada's and China's pursuit of their distinct strategic foreign policy objectives with respect to sub-Saharan Africa.

In August of that year, a labor dispute over higher pay and better working conditions resulted in 34 deaths at a platinum mine in Marikana, South Africa, owned by Lonmin – one of the world's more profitable mining companies. The South African government had a difficult time containing the unrest, which quickly spread to other South African mining operations. Consequently, South Africa's prospects for sustained economic growth in the long term were seriously constrained. The country's GDP growth fell following the August events from a relatively anemic 3.2 percent across the first three quarters of 2012, to 1.2 percent in the last quarter. Economists have attributed this slowdown largely to the dramatic production declines in the platinum and gold sectors (allAfrica.com 2012).

South Africa is not alone in having to deal with the consequences of increased labor strife. The recent increases of labor unrest in Asia's and Latin America's mining communities broadly suggest that miners in developing economies want a fairer share of the substantial financial benefits generated by the growing global demand for natural resources. As two of the world's leading investors in the extractive sectors of developing economies, Canada and China would be greatly affected if this trend continues and their companies became bigger targets for such demands.

The second significant development was the US Securities and Exchange Commission's decision, in late August 2012, to implement Section 1504 (known as the Cardin-Lugar Amendment) of the Dodd-Frank Act – a financial reform package that in 2010 was signed into law by the administration of US President Barack Obama. This legislation was adopted in an effort to level the global playing field by improving transparency in the extractive sector. The legislation was intended to contribute to setting global standards for the behavior of extractive companies and their host governments. Specifically, it requires all US-listed companies – including over 100 Canadian companies – as of September 30, 2013, to disclose the payments they make to foreign governments. Similar European-wide legislation, intended to improve accountability and transparency in the extractive sectors of EU countries, was adopted by the European Parliament in June 2013.

At the time of writing, Canada had no comparable legislation in place, though at the 2013 G8 meetings held in the UK, Prime Minister Harper announced that draft legislation tightening accountability with respect to the extractive sector was being prepared (this was in the form of amendments to Bill S-14, "The Corruption of Foreign Public Officials Act" for which in June 2013, this author was invited to testify before the House of Commons Standing Committee on Foreign Affairs and International Development). Absent, however, was legislation seeking to enhance transparency on the part of Canadian mining companies, a logical and seemingly necessary precursor to greater accountability, and something remarked upon critically by the African Union's "Africa Progress Panel for 2013." In fact, previous to these proposed amendments, the federal government had resisted efforts to tighten regulatory requirements on the country's mining sector. An attempt was made in October 2010 through the preparation of Bill C-300 – a private member's bill submitted to Parliament by an opposition member. The bill was narrowly defeated following an intense government-supported lobbying effort by the Canadian mining industry. Only members of the opposition parties voted in favor of the bill. The bill had sought to tighten disclosure requirements and increase the transparency of Canadian mining companies, seeking partially to emulate the intent of the Cardin-Lugar Amendment in the United States. It would also have prevented Export Development Canada (EDC) and other government agencies from funding companies engaged in human rights violations. Unexpectedly, however, in September 2012 the mining industry, through the Mining Association of Canada and independent of the federal government, suggested that it was prepared to support new regulations similar to those adopted in the United States and being prepared in Europe. The association's vice president of sustainable development stated: "We kind of realized the writing was on the wall. We agree with the concept. We thought it was time to be proactive and help shape what this would look like and be part of the solution instead of providing opposition" (Munson 2012a).

In the case of China, its government has also been subjected to criticism by African public authorities and civil society organizations for a lack of accountability and transparency, especially regarding its investments in the extractive sectors. A growing sensitivity to such criticism, however, combined with the realization that China's commercial brand is a significant determinant of its longer-term global competitiveness, led the Chinese government to tighten regulatory legislation with respect to the behavior of Chinese investors. In February 2011, the Standing Committee of China's National People's Congress adopted the Eighth Amendment to the Criminal Law of the People's Republic of China, which makes it a criminal offense to effect payments to foreign public officials and officials of international public organizations for any "illegitimate commercial benefit." Not only does the new law have extraterritorial application, but it also affects non-Chinese companies in Chinese-organized joint ventures and non-Chinese companies with representative offices in China (Mark and Bullock 2011). Further research is needed on the application and enforcement of this new Chinese law, as well as whether payment disclosures are required. Significant, nonetheless, is that China too seems to be moving in the direction of increased regulation, accountability, and transparency with respect to commercial payments outside of as well as within China.

Africa stands to benefit the most from these new regulatory trends with extraterritorial application. Encouraged by international efforts to increase transparency, African leaders adopted the Africa Mining Vision in 2009, which established how mining could better contribute to local, national, and regional development through "transparent, equitable and optimal exploitation of mineral resources to underpin broad-based sustainable growth and socio-economic development" (ACF 2013, 1). Although still in its formative state, the Vision signals a paradigm shift towards greater ownership for African parliaments,

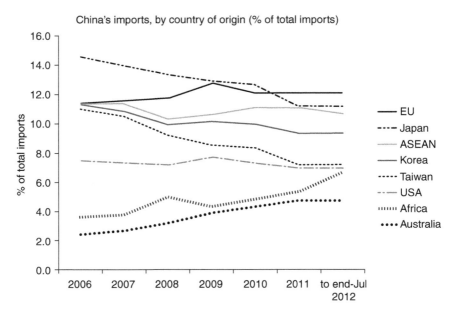

Figure 11.1 China's imports, by country of origin.
Source: Allen 2012.

citizens, and civil society. Stronger disclosure requirements could allow its mining communities to gain increased access to information about how much was paid to whom and by whom. Such access is vital for the continent's economic health – Africa being one of the "two largest remaining unexplored frontiers" with regard to resources (UNECA 2011). The African continent is considered to be the last significant source of oil and gas reserves not already dominated by major Western companies, meaning that those reserves are available to Chinese and other emerging economies' investors. Consequently, as noted earlier, resource extraction has intensified in Africa more than anywhere over the past decade. Africa's share of expenditures, as a percentage of global commercial exploration, has increased from 12 percent in 2000 to almost 16 percent in 2008, notwithstanding that during the first five years of this century the share of new mining projects in Africa was constant (UNECA 2011).

The third significant development was the release of Chinese trade data in September 2012, revealing that the share of China's imports from Africa had more than doubled from less than 4 percent in 2006 to slightly less than 8 percent in 2012 – a period when Chinese imports from all other trading partners had remained flat or fallen (see Figure 11.1). Driving this unprecedented jump in African imports was China's insatiable demand for minerals (Allen 2012).

During this same period, Canada shifted its foreign policy priorities away from Africa and its numerous Commonwealth and "Francophonie" member states. Instead, in 2007 it turned its attention to a largely unproductive "Americas-First Strategy" that engaged Latin America and the Caribbean (see DFAIT 2011), and then within several years, "pivoted" towards East Asia – particularly China. Canada's links to sub-Saharan Africa became marginal at best. The continent's share of Canada's overall trade only rose from 0.59 percent in 2005 to 1.79 percent in 2011, with most of the increase in the form of energy imports to Canada: namely crude oil and minerals, totaling approximately $13 billion. Over 85 percent of the imports came from just four countries: Algeria, Nigeria, Angola, and South Africa. Canada's exports to Africa totaled about $2.5 billion, resulting in a trade deficit of over $10 billion in 2011 (CIDP 2012).

An emerging Africa: Reality or illusion?

Before discussing the significance of these three global developments for Canada and China, it is necessary to focus specifically on Africa's nuanced development challenges and its progress to date.

It is important to recognize that the prevailing narrative about Africa has been changing from one that emphasizes a lost cause to one of a hopeful continent: phrases used are "Africa rising" (*The Economist* 2011), and "emerging Africa" (Radelet 2010). Seventeen African countries are defying the negative stereotypes associated with past decades – another six are on the verge of doing so. Following annual per capita economic growth of just above 0 percent between 1975 and 1995, the continent's annual growth between 1996 and 2008 increased to 3.2 percent, which is equivalent to 5 percent growth in overall GDP (Page 2012). The IMF's *World Economic Outlook Updates* for 2012 and 2013 projected GDP growth for Africa to be 5.3 percent and 5.5 percent respectively. As seen in Figure 11.2, Africa experienced increases in labor productivity at an annual rate of 2.8 percent between 2000 and 2008, outpacing the United States (1.5 percent) and Europe (1 percent) (BCG 2010).

Researchers have identified five principal drivers of this economic growth in Africa. First, there was an increase in the number of democratic and accountable governments: From 1989 to 2008 the number of countries categorized as democratic increased from three to twenty-three – almost half the countries on the continent (although the importance of democratic systems in improving governance is acknowledged in academic literature, studies examining resource-rich democratic states suggest that democracy often leads to increased corruption (Collier 2010)). Second was the implementation of more sensible economic policies initiated in the late 1980s, including structural reforms supported by international financial institutions. Third, debt-reduction programs begun in the 1990s by global financial institutions such as the World Bank and the IMF eased budgetary burdens on those African low-income states that demonstrated improving governance. Fourth, the information technology revolution created new economic opportunities for millions of people who previously had few or none. For example, in 2010 over 60 percent of adults

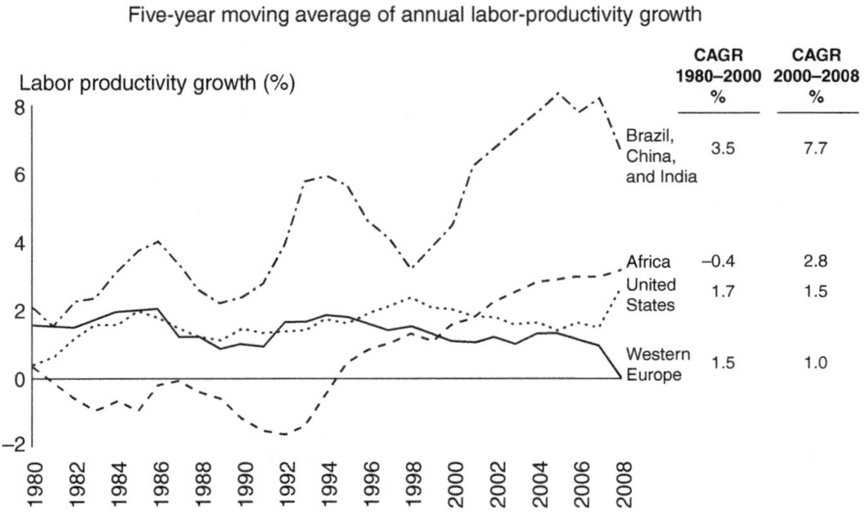
Five-year moving average of annual labor-productivity growth
Labor productivity growth (%)
CAGR 1980–2000 %
CAGR 2000–2008 %
Brazil, China, and India 3.5 7.7
Africa –0.4 2.8
United States 1.7 1.5
Western Europe 1.5 1.0
8
6
4
2
0
–2
1980
1982
1984
1986
1988
1990
1992
1994
1996
1998
2000
2002
2004
2006
2008

Figure 11.2 Africa is outperforming the United States and Western Europe in productivity gains.

Source: Groningen database, BCG analysis.

in Nigeria, Botswana, Ghana, Kenya, and virtually all households in urban Tanzania used cell phones. Finally, a new more experienced and educated generation of leaders emerged in both the public (see The African Capacity Building Foundation Report 2011) and private sectors (see BCG 2010).

Yet there is no room for complacency, despite the mentioned positive indicators. Nor is there much room for the conclusions of those people who talk of "dead aid" (Moyo 2009) and see only private-sector investment and free trade as the panaceas for Africa's development challenges. The picture is much more nuanced. Virtually all development experts acknowledge that private investment and trade are critical growth drivers, and both have dramatically increased in Africa over the past decade. The fact is, however, that the bulk of foreign direct investment (FDI) and private investment in Africa has historically been concentrated in a handful of resource-rich countries. Although FDI has increased as a share of gross fixed capital formation at a rate twice the global average over the past decade, "a large share of FDI goes to extractive industries in a limited group of countries and attracting investment into diversified and higher value-added sectors remains a challenge for Africa" (AfDB et al. 2011).

Commodity exports currently account for over 30 percent of Africa's GDP, and between 2000 and 2009 about 75 percent of FDI to Africa went to a handful of oil-exporting countries. Collier notes that "Africa is distinctive in being more dependent upon commodity exports than other regions, aside from the Middle East" (Collier 2010, 42). Significant amounts of private capital have not flowed to those countries in what Collier calls "the poverty trap" (Collier 2007). Moreover, contrary to the view of those who see private-sector investment on its own as the key to African economic development, according to recent analysis from South Africa's North-West University (Claassen et al. 2012), the link between FDI and economic growth/employment is weak or virtually non-existent, *unless human capital and infrastructure are upgraded*.

Private investment in Africa as a whole remains low relative to other regions of the world, and FDI is largely concentrated in mining and energy. A recent study of Africa's industrial and manufacturing progress noted that exports have remained largely composed of agricultural products with little local value-added, despite successes with cut flowers in East Africa, back-office services in West Africa, and textiles in Madagascar and Lesotho (AfDB et al. 2012). Africa's share of global manufacturing value-added (excluding South Africa) actually fell from 0.4 percent in 1980 to 0.3 percent in 2005 (AfDB et al. 2012). In the medium term, therefore, many African countries will need to continue relying on aid and public investment to help create the structural basis for sustained economic growth and for catalyzing private investment.

To address these issues the evidence clearly demonstrates that aid programs should shift their focus from the overwhelming emphasis of the past several decades on social services and primary schooling, to higher education and critical infrastructure. International initiatives such as the global Aid for Trade initiative have infrastructure financing and trade facilitation investments at their core. Along with a more educated labor force, investments in infrastructure are recognized as basic factors that successfully generate private investment – both foreign and domestic – and thereby create much-needed employment opportunities for Africans. Because Africa will have the world's youngest population in the coming years, the reduction of youth (aged 15–24) unemployment and underemployment is emerging as one of its critical challenges. Although theoretically advantageous for improving economic productivity (if industrial processes accelerate in tandem with rapid urbanization), Africa's youth bulge, if unaddressed, will result in unrealized expectations, social unrest, and instability – potentially with global consequences.

Examples across Africa demonstrate some of the complex challenges facing high-growth African countries. Ethiopia typifies them. The country saw 10 percent GDP growth in 2010, with serious income distribution problems reflected in an urban unemployment rate of almost 25 percent, with its large youth cohort experiencing even higher levels of unemployment and underemployment (ILO 2012). Recent estimates from other countries reveal similar challenges. South Africa, considered the continent's most prosperous economy, has a youth unemployment rate close to 50 percent. Nigeria, Africa's leading energy producer, with a GDP growth rate of about 8 percent in 2011, is challenged by a youth unemployment rate of almost 38 percent, as well as social indicators that generally fall below the average for sub-Saharan Africa (Ushie 2012).

So, high GDP growth notwithstanding, sub-Saharan Africa remains the world's most impoverished area as measured by social indicators, despite poverty declining in absolute terms. Thirty-three of the world's forty-nine low-income economies are in Africa, and the region is furthest from achieving the targets of the Millennium Development Goals. Some 400 million Africans – almost half the continent's population – live in extreme poverty, defined as less than $1.25 per day, and one in four is malnourished. Recent droughts and the global financial crisis have made conditions worse. Moreover, with the exception of Uganda and Ethiopia, those countries where GDP growth has been high have seen income inequality, as measured by the Gini coefficient, increase. Progress on reducing hunger, improving health outcomes (particularly for rural women and children), and improving access to clean water and sanitation has been especially slow. Add to this the fact that climate change will have negative consequences for health, migration, and infrastructure on the continent, conceivably reversing some of the gains already made, and it is clear that private investment, trade, and aid programs need to focus much more on improving the quality of growth rather than just increasing growth rates (UNDP 2012).

Failure to support Africa in developing its human capital and infrastructure will cause income gaps to widen further and existing social consensus to erode. Joseph Stiglitz, among others, has observed that "widely unequal societies do not function efficiently, and their economies are neither stable nor sustainable in the long run" (Stiglitz 2012, 83). Another possible consequence of inadequate investment in human capital is the continued emergence of fundamentalism of all sorts. The presence of al-Qaeda in the Maghreb, typified by the takeover of Northern Mali by the al-Qaeda-linked Islamic Maghreb, and Al Shabab in parts of East Africa, seems to be growing. Countries with significant Muslim and Christian communities – Nigeria, Kenya, Cameroon, and until recently the Ivory Coast – have also been experiencing religiously inspired violence. The faith-based political agendas of several elected governments emerging from the Arab Awakening, such as in Egypt and Tunisia, are also fueling domestic conflict. Should these trends of poor job growth, widening income gaps, and unmet economic expectations continue, economic and social development in Africa will not be sustained. Political instability and the emergence of more failed states will intensify the challenges both for the continent and across the globe including increased flows of economic migrants to Europe and North America and heightened risk of terrorism and insurgency. This is not the direction in which Canada or China, as globally linked economies, want Africa to move.

Africa and globalization

Given Africa's development challenges, it is in the self-interest of both Canada and China not only to accept but to actively support its rise. The increased incidence of community unrest associated with resource extraction, the push in key developed economies and China for stronger regulation of the extractive sectors, and the growing demand for Africa's natural resources, can all be approached in various ways. This chapter now turns to identifying the Canadian and Chinese governments' current strategies and soft-power instruments – trade, investment, and aid – employed to achieve their objectives in Africa in the light of these major developments.

Canada is the world's primary investor in mining, accounting for almost half the world's mining activities (Fantino 2012). However, this position is slowly eroding in Africa (Robert 2012). In 2007, Canada was the leading mining investor on the continent. Five years later, it had fallen to fourth after China, South Africa, and Australia dramatically increased their investments in Africa's mineral wealth (UNCTAD 2012). More concerning, however, is the fact that the apparent loss of competitiveness in mining investments is consistent with Canada's overall loss in market share of world exports during the 2000–11 period. Mark Carney, Governor of the Bank of Canada, recently announced that "we've dampened our [2013] forecast of [Canadian] exports because we're seeing a competitiveness challenge – a productivity issue. Even with that, the export performance has been lower on average than we have expected" (Friend 2013). Among the Group of Twenty (G20) countries, eight lost market share. As illustrated in Figure 11.3, among the gainers were China, with an increase in market share of about 170 percent, and Australia with a gain of about 50 percent (Carney 2012). Canada lost almost 38 percent of market share, behind only the United Kingdom, which lost close to 50 percent. As noted by the Conference Board of Canada, the past decade has effectively been "a lost decade" for Canadian exports, with "no growth in volumes … [Canada has] lost export market share to emerging markets in a wide variety of products, including Canadian stalwarts like wood and paper products" (Ai and Burt 2012, 2).

For Canada, a country whose economic health depends on external trade, and whose principal trading partner, the United States, has seen its growth stagnate and debt balloon, reversing this loss of global competitiveness requires strategic vision, a more diversified set of trading partners, and a more strategic use of certain policy instruments. In the face of unrelenting competition from China and other emerging economies, can Canada regain its competitive position in Africa and, ultimately, in the world? To answer this question, this chapter will now examine China's and Canada's grand strategies with respect to Africa, and the soft-power instruments that they currently deploy to achieve their strategic priorities.

China's strategic presence in Africa

The economic growth and social stability of Canada and China ultimately depend on their success as trading nations – both are global mercantilists. For China, Africa's natural resource wealth is critical to sustaining its own economic growth, and it has made no secret of this. Since the establishment in 2000 of the Forum on China–Africa Cooperation (FOCAC), Chinese–African trade has risen from US$2 billion to US$160 billion, which makes

272 *Ingram*

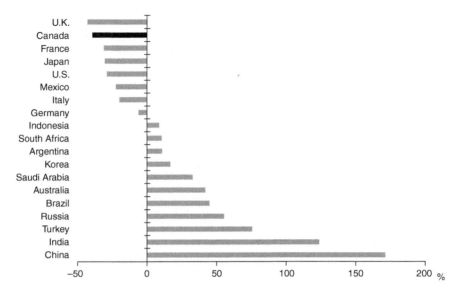

Figure 11.3 Percentage change in share of world exports for G20 countries, 2000–2010.
Source: Groningen database, BCG analysis.

China Africa's largest trading partner (Cissé 2012). Establishing global competitive dominance over the long term is China's primary strategic goal. The prevailing concern of the Chinese government is that if it cannot sustain gross domestic product rates above 8 percent, social instability could result as the Communist party may not be able to retain control over the rural poor and an increasingly restive urban population (Ncube and Fairbanks 2013).

Failure by China to contribute to more equitable patterns of African growth will likely erode the former's competitive position over the long term, since African governments and their informed and often unsatisfied populations will resist the substitution of their historical colonizers by a new colonial presence from the emerging economies. During the China–Africa Forum held in Beijing in July 2012, South African President Jacob Zuma emphasized: "Africa's commitment to China's development has been demonstrated by supply of raw materials, other products, and technology transfer. This trade pattern is unsustainable in the long term. Africa's past economic experience with Europe dictates a need to be cautious when entering into partnerships with other economies" (Hook 2012).

More concretely, in 2011, the Zambian government and human rights organizations took action against Chinese mining companies in Zambia's copper mines, where low wages, long working hours, and dangerous practices had become prevalent (BBC 2012). The significance of these criticisms, however, has been contested, with union leaders and others suggesting that virtually all mining companies in Zambia have been abusing miners' rights and that the action against China in Zambia's case was politically motivated by a highly pro-Western government to "perpetuate Western racist stereotypes about China's 'neo-colonial' expansion in Africa" (Sautman and Hairong 2011).

Yet, perhaps as a result of expressed concerns, China's conduct in Africa appears to be changing. China has largely seen Africa as a strategic ally – for instance, it pushed for greater African representation in international organizations, including the UN – but now it is combining support at the political level with more investment in infrastructure, including dams, airports, wind farms, and light manufacturing. Between 2003 and 2008, Africa became the third largest recipient of Chinese FDI at 7 percent, ahead of Europe, Oceania, and North America (Claassen et al. 2012, 11583–79). Despite some decline in total investment in the continent in 2010–12 because of uncertainty related to the "Arab Awakening" and instability in Libya and Egypt, Chinese FDI in Africa increased by 46 percent per year since 2001, according to the Chinese Ministry of Commerce (Renard 2011).

During this same period, the destination and the composition of Chinese investments were broadened. China invested in forty-five of Africa's fifty-four countries, a contrast to the concentration of most other foreign investments going to resource-rich countries (as has been largely the case with Canada's investments). For the most part, China's investments were aimed at diversified, medium-growth economies (65.4 percent of Chinese FDI) – rather than oil- and single commodity-dependent economies (16.2 percent of Chinese FDI), with South Africa attracting the largest share of China's African FDI (Claassen et al. 2012, 11589). Since around 97 percent of all Chinese FDI flows between 2003 and 2008 went to countries that could consistently grow their GDP at 3 percent per year, China appears to be interested in investing in Africa to gain long-term access to larger markets for its products and to gain experience in establishing and managing its brand (Claassen et al. 2012). In terms of the composition of investments, China's strategy when investing in extractive sectors involves offering interest-free loans, especially for the development of needed infrastructure, and having the loans repaid with the windfalls from the resource extracted. In addition, Chinese investments in agriculture increased substantially over the same period due to concerns about rising food prices and food security (Hallam 2009).

Concerns about China's brand seem to be resonating with Chinese investors. A recent study of chief executive officers of twenty-five major Chinese companies suggests that Chinese investors are cognizant that putting China's brand at risk through poor corporate behavior and a single-minded focus on extractives will damage their long-term competitiveness in Africa (Zadek et al. 2009). Although the study's sample is small, what is striking in its results is the acknowledgment that behavior in accordance with principles of corporate social responsibility (CSR) is increasingly perceived as key to improving the Chinese brand against the backdrop of increasing competition from other emerging economies and the West, Canada included.

But the introduction of CSR "à la chinoise" risks adding to what is already a scattergun approach to CSR and voluntary regulation by companies investing in Africa. Adam Sneyd (2012, 144) argues:

> While Africa's official development partners have attempted to harmonize their efforts and align their aid disbursements with the principle of country ownership through the Paris Declaration on Aid Effectiveness and the Accra Agenda for Action, efforts have not yet been made to harmonize or align overlapping approaches to CSR. The evident profusion of divergent responsibility systems appears to be fuelling an emerging competition between prospective non-sovereign governors.

Despite what appears to be growing sensitivity to local standards in an effort to enhance its brand, China's absence from the Organisation for Economic Co-operation and Development (OECD) and its reluctance to conform to the broader standards that OECD member countries would normally adhere to (exceptional is Canada's emphasis on voluntary CSR rather than more regulatory requirements) means that investors' approaches continue to diverge and the global playing field remains uneven.

Through mechanisms for South–South cooperation, such as the absence of explicit policy conditionality, China stresses that it is providing African economies with greater economic autonomy than traditional donors have allowed – particularly in relation to terms of development financing, a sector focus on productive investments, project aid rather than program aid, budgetary support, and support for industrialization (Poon 2012). The increased proportion of Chinese investments in Africa's services, financial, tourism, and agricultural sectors and in local value-added manufacturing suggest that the prescriptions of Harvard University's Dani Rodrik and former chief economist of the World Bank Justin Yifu Lin are being reflected in Chinese policy (Rodrik 2011; Lin 2010). Kaname Akamatsu's "flying-geese paradigm" (Akamatsu 1962 quoted in Lin 2011) points to the fact that due to rising labor and transport costs in China, as well as the Chinese government's ambition to move into high-technology production, economic space is being opened for African economies to move from natural resource extraction and rural-based activities into the production of more labor-intensive manufacturing – adding more local value while slowly moving up the global value chain (Hille and Jacob 2012). Using the provisions of the European Union's Cotonou Agreement with the African, Caribbean, and Pacific Group of States, Chinese investors are increasing the establishment of joint ventures with local African investors – especially in agriculture, agribusiness, textiles, and light manufacturing – and in the process helping to build local capacity, boost technology transfers, and raise export levels for many of the forty-five countries in which they are investing. Here at least, Dambisa Moyo (2009), in promoting the value of Chinese investments with Africa, has got it right.

Canada's strategic presence in Africa

Since the Conservative government of Prime Minister Stephen Harper came to power in 2006, there has been little academic analysis of Canada's economic relations with Africa. Moreover, the continent is pretty much absent from the government's formal foreign policy strategies. In 2007, the Harper government adopted an "Americas-First Strategy" that made Latin America and the Caribbean its top international priority, with the intention of "reinforcing bilateral relations ... strengthening regional organizations ... bolstering Canadian partnerships ... [and] expanding Canada's presence" – all with a view to diversifying Canada's trade relationships and reducing its overwhelming dependence on the US market (DFAIT 2011). Indeed, the region remains an apparent priority according to DFAIT's most recent policy documents, though since 2010 the reorientation toward Asia has increasingly dominated the government's rhetoric.

Recent statements by Canadian government officials that Africa is a Canadian priority are not only belated, but also come without specific strategic content, at least until the time of writing. Indeed, what is most striking in reviewing DFAIT's policy paper on strategic priorities for 2012–13 is the virtual absence of Africa as an articulated priority – the continent is mentioned in only one brief paragraph of the twenty-four-page document, and emphasis is primarily on security, stability, governance, and human rights, not trade or commerce (DFAIT 2012–13).

And African governments seem to be noticing that Canada's engagement with Africa is unpredictable. Although Canadian public assistance to Africa doubled in volume between 2005 and 2010 to meet commitments made at the G8 Gleneagles Summit in 2005, total foreign aid was limited to twenty "countries of focus," with only seven African countries among them; Senegal, Mali, Ghana, Sudan, Ethiopia, Tanzania, and Mozambique – down from a total of fifteen African states prior to 2009. Also, in stark contrast to China, Canada has closed several of its African diplomatic and trade missions on the continent since the Harper government came to power – today Canada has fourteen embassies covering fifty-four countries. The virtual absence of African support for Canada's 2010 bid for a temporary seat on the UN Security Council suggests that African governments had taken the closures as part of a larger message.

And Canada's strategies regarding economic relations seem to have had as little success in Latin America as in Africa. Despite Canada's continued emphasis on the "Americas-First Strategy," a recent report by DFAIT concluded that the strategy has not proven to be highly successful. Additionally, a report by the Canadian International Council indicates that there is controversy in addition to uncertainty:

> [T]he evidence is ... clear that Canadian direct investment in Latin America, investment that in the words of the Canadian government is the "face of Canada" in the region, has become increasingly controversial.

> There are legitimate concerns about the impact of such investment on local workers, on the environment, and on the regulatory capacity of the host governments. The meagre contribution of Canadian direct investment on the national economies of Latin America's host countries [has also been remarked upon].
>
> (Randall 2010, 21)

Alongside this seemingly limited strategic success in Latin America, and as a result of the acknowledged need to diversify its trading relationships following the global financial crisis, as noted, the Canadian government's strategic focus since 2010 broadened to include Asia. Negotiating membership in the Trans-Pacific Partnership, a free-trade zone among eleven countries that would contribute to Canadian export diversification, has been at the top of the priority list. Canada formally joined the Partnership in October 2012 and participated in a round of trade negotiations in December of the same year. Increased exports of Canadian energy products and extractives to China, as well as the initiation of free-trade negotiations with India, have been other prominent Asia-focused initiatives.

Yet, as noted earlier, Africa appears to be largely marginalized in Canada's foreign policy strategy. During the June 2012 Africa Day event in Ottawa, it was stressed that Canadian support for Africa's development was going to be pursued through intensified trade and commerce. No mention was made of increased aid to Africa, or the reopening of diplomatic or trade missions. Indeed with respect to aid, the Center for Global Development in Washington, DC, in its "2012 Commitment to Development Index 2012", ranked Canada's aid performance eleventh out of twenty-seven, with one of its major weaknesses being the fact that it provides a "significant share of aid to less poor and worse-governed recipients." This suggests that Canada's ambitions may be driven more by mercantilist strategies, irrespective of the quality of host country governance, than by the desire to alleviate poverty and support broad-based development through investments packaged in "Canadian values." In the same index, Canada's aid volumes also ranked poorly (14th out of 27) because it provides a "moderately low net aid volume as a share of the economy." With respect to the internationally established aid target of 0.7 percent of gross national income (GNI), Canada provided only about 0.33 percent of GNI in 2012, making it among the poorer performers in terms of aid volume (CGD 2012). More recent cuts will certainly reduce the percentage (as of the time of writing, the impact on aid to Africa resulting from the dissolution of the Canadian International Development Agency (CIDA) and its integration into the Ministry of Foreign Affairs is unknown).

The two sectors in which Canada's private sector is an acknowledged global player are the extractive sector, especially energy and mining, and the financial services sector. Over 1,000 Canadian companies are currently active in mining, while Canadian financial institutions are only beginning to invest outside of Canada, mainly in the United States and increasingly in parts of

Asia. Some 70 percent of global mining investors are listed on the Toronto Stock Exchange. Yet Canadian mining investors appear to be losing their competitive position in Africa. Canada's mining brand has taken serious hits over the past several years. Widely reported violent incidents in Tanzania, the Democratic Republic of the Congo, Peru, and Mongolia, among others, have contributed to the tarnishing of Canada's brand. As documented in a 2009 study by the Canadian Centre for the Study of Resource Conflict (CCSRC) on the incidence of violence linked to mining, of the 171 companies identified in mining and exploration-related violence since 2000, 34 percent were Canadian, a figure that is triple that of its closest peer, Australia (CCSRC 2009).

Additionally, Canada may be increasingly viewed globally as the odd man out for failing to play a leadership role in setting standards for the extraction of natural resources in Africa, and for failing to itself comply with accountability mechanisms such as the Extractive Industries Transparency Initiative (EITI). The US Securities and Exchange Commission's adoption of rules defined in the Cardin-Lugar Amendment will nonetheless require all US-listed mining companies (including Canadian companies listed on US exchanges) to disclose payments that they make to governments on a country-by-country and project-by-project basis. With the EU's recently adopted legislation, China tightening its legislation in 2011 to apply extraterritorially, and the African Union tightening regulations and transparency requirements through the Africa Mining Vision adopted in 2009, Canada indeed does risk appearing as insensitive to and/or unaware of Africa's real development needs – a risk not without potential implications for Canada's presence in Africa and its own long-term economic interests.

An alternative approach, with benefits for both Canadian companies and African economies, would be to have Canadian companies, supported by the Canadian government, provide leadership in setting global standards for the extraction of natural resources, in strengthening governments' capacities to regulate their extractive sectors, and in supporting local economic development through value-added and job-producing investments in Africa. In doing so, they would need, among other things, to take environmental, social, and human rights impact assessments seriously and negotiate impact and benefit agreements that truly benefit local communities. In supporting Canadian mining investors, the Canadian government would be following global best practice in asking host governments at the outset "whether the proposed extractive project is the best economic alternative for the specific site and area in the first place, or whether some other economic activity might be better suited" (Weitzner 2011, 35). Should the fact that a Canadian company is operating in Africa, or elsewhere abroad, give it license to hold itself to lower disclosure, human rights, or environmental standards than it would in Canada (see Ingram and Lissakers 2012)? Being perceived as seeking short-term competitive advantages for Canadian companies by not seriously integrating longer-term economic and social concerns into Canada's national and corporate strategies will not only continue to erode Canada's long-term competitive prospects in the extractives sector, but it will also fail to contribute to equitable and sustainable economic development in Africa.

Conclusions

This chapter began by describing three developments in different parts of the globe in 2012 that have considerable significance for the future economic and political well-being of Canada, China, and the continent of Africa. These developments were the deaths of South African miners that illustrated the increased global incidence of community unrest associated with resource extraction, a growing push in the United States, Europe, China, and Africa for the stronger regulation of natural resource extraction, and the release of Chinese trade data that demonstrated a growing demand for Africa's resources, as evidenced by the significant increase of Africa's exports to China. The chapter then compared how China and Canada have addressed Africa's economic and political rise, especially in light of these three developments.

What has emerged from this comparison is that, while both the Canadian and Chinese governments are in part driven by similar strategic objectives, the soft-power instruments of trade, investment, and aid they use to achieve them are distinct and produce significantly different outcomes for them and for African development.

From public rhetoric alone, it is difficult to draw conclusions about the precise motives underlying Canada's and China's strategies toward Africa, though there is some consensus in the academic literature based largely on the behavior of the two countries' governments. In the case of Canada, David Black of Dalhousie University has sketched out a framework that suggests Canada's "foreign policy towards the global South has been guided by inertia, or a foreign policy of drift" (Black 2009, 41). Others have reached similar conclusions (see Joe Clark's recent book *How We Lead* (2013), on the failure of the Harper government's foreign policy, and Michael Harris's *A Party of One* (2015)).

In China's case, while the creation of FOCAC in 2000 signaled its strategic intention to increase its presence in Africa with mercantilist and geopolitical objectives prioritized, it did so with "FOCAC policies targeted to Africa's practical needs and urgent issues, and to resolving problems to the benefit of African development" (Anshan et al. 2012, 56). At the same time, it was clear in China's deployment of a combination of instruments that "for countries lacking in resources and markets, there will be more assistance, but for countries rich in both, there will be more international trade and investment" (Anshan et al. 2012, 57).

Irrespective of each country's strategic motives, the extent to which the two countries appear to contribute to Africa's development can be contrasted. China's presence in Africa is driven both by economic need (its large and growing middle class has a high demand for minerals) and geopolitical ambitions (it values support from Africa's fifty-four governments within the United Nations and other multilateral bodies).

Canada's strategic motives for its presence in Africa are less discernible. In spite of government officials' recent public statements claiming that Africa is a strategic priority and that Canada will support Africa's development primarily through the increased presence of Canada's private sector, the government's strategic motives have not yet been systematically articulated, at least not publicly. Canada's volume and distribution of aid and FDI flows – limited as they are to a handful of countries and sectors – falls far short of its rhetoric. Regarding aid, the former Canadian International Development Agency's list of twenty "countries of focus" that was introduced in 2009 resulted in aid being cut off for eight of fourteen previously supported African states. Black (2009, 43) points out "the net effect of these shifts was to reduce the concentration of bilateral aid resources in countries experiencing the highest levels of poverty."

Additionally, a comparison of China's use of soft-power instruments with Canada's, and the extent to which each country responds to Africa's most pressing development needs, is also striking.

China's aid and investment flows to the continent unsurprisingly dwarf those of Canada, while China's distribution by country and by sector is much more extensive. Chinese investments have broadened from natural resource extraction to manufacturing and services. China, as a developing country itself, often gives explicit recognition to job creation as a critical priority for Africa. At the same time, China's aid programs are concentrated in building the infrastructure and human capacity necessary for sustained economic growth and social stability. Apparently, China is more responsive to the "reality" of Africa's rise than to the new narrative about high GDP growth rates in Africa's emerging economies.

In contrast, Canada's recent statements that it will shift its support for African development from past reliance on aid to more trade and investment through the private sector, especially in extractives, may prove to be less comforting to African governments, especially in light of empirical evidence accumulated over the past several decades about the extractive sector's contributions to growth and job creation. While investment in energy and extractives may produce higher GDP growth and improved trade balances in the shorter-term, empirical evidence has shown that such investment does not create the job numbers nor the quality of jobs that Africa desperately needs today and will need tomorrow. President Jacob Zuma recently warned Western companies that "they must change their old 'colonial' approach to Africa or risk losing out even more to the accelerating competition from China and other developing powers" (Russell 2013).

It is also empirically demonstrated that unless there is parallel investment in infrastructure and building of human capacity, investment in energy and extractives generally has perverse effects economically, politically, and in terms of social stability (recall the pervasive "resource curse"). In contrast to Chinese policy, Canadian policy suggests an acceptance of the "illusion" of broad-based African development based on the GDP growth of Africa's fastest-growing economies. Africa's political and economic elites, as well as its growing and often restive civil society, however, can distinguish between the reality and the illusion.

Failure on the part of the Canadian and Chinese governments to recognize Africa's real development needs and close the gap between public rhetoric and actual presence on the continent could prove costly both in terms of their countries' branding and competitive strengths in the long term. Today, China's presence is clearly more responsive to Africa's needs than Canada's is. As a developing country, China understands that broad-based development and social stability require more than just high GDP growth and private foreign investment in extractives. To produce mutual long-term benefits for itself and Africa, Canada needs to do the same.

References

ACF (Africa-Canada Forum). 2013. *The African Mining Vision: A Transformative Agenda for Development*. Backgrounder. Ottawa: The Canadian Council of International Cooperation and the Canadian Network on Corporate Accountability.

African Capacity Building Foundation. 2011. "*African Capacity Indicators 2011: Capacity Development in Fragile States.*" South Africa: Ultra Litho (PTY) Ltd.

AfDB, BI, AGI, and UNWIDER. 2012. *Learning to Compete: Accelerating Industrial Development in Africa.* www.theigc.org/wp-content/uploads/2014/08/John-Page-Industry-AGF2013.pdf.

AfDB, OECD, UNDP, and UNECA. 2011. *African Economic Outlook 2011*. Paris: OECD Publishing.

Ai, Lin, and Michael Burt. 2012. *Walking the Silk Road: Understanding Canada's Changing Trade Patterns*. Briefing. Ottawa: The Conference Board of Canada.

Akamatsu, Kaname. 1962. "A Historical Pattern of Economic Growth in Developing Countries." *The Developing Economies* 1 (s1): 3–25.

allAfrica.com. 2012. "South Africa: GDP Eases to 1.2 Percent in Third Quarter." November 28. http://allafrica.com/stories/201211280440.html.

Allen, Kate. 2012. "Just How Special Is China's "Special Relationship"?" *FT Data* (blog), *Financial Times*, August 30. http://blogs.ft.com/ftdata/2012/08/30/chinas-special-relationship.

Anshan, Li, Liu Haifang, Pan Huaqiong, Zeng Aiping, and He Wenping. 2012. *FOCAC Twelve Years Later: Achievements, Challenges and the Way Forward*. Discussion Paper No. 47, Nordiska Afrikainstitutet, Uppsala.

BBC. 2012. "Zambian Miners Kill Chinese Manager During Pay Protest." August 5. www.bbc.co.uk/news/world-africa-19135435.

BCG (The Boston Consulting Group). 2010. *The African Challengers: Global Competitors Emerge from the Overlooked Continent*. Boston: BCG.

Black, David. 2009 "Out of Africa? The Harper Government's New "Tilt" in the Developing World." *Canadian Foreign Policy* 15 (2): 41–56.

Carney, Mark. 2012. "Exporting in a Post-Crisis World." Remarks to the Greater Kitchener-Waterloo Chamber of Commerce, Waterloo, April 2. www.bankofcanada.ca/2012/04/speeches/exporting-in-a-post-crisis-world.

CCSRC. 2009. *Corporate Social Responsibility: Movements and Footprints of Canadian Mining and Exploration Firms in the Developing World*. Revelstoke: CCSRC.

CGD. 2012. "2012 Commitment to Development Index.". www.cgdev.org/section/initiatives/_active/cdi/.

CIDP (Canadian International Development Platform). 2012. "Canada's Trade Patterns: A Quick Review." The North-South Institute, http://cidpnsi.ca.

Cissé, Daouda. 2012. *FOCAC: Trade, Investments and Aid in China–Africa Relations*. Policy Briefing, May. Stellenbosch: Centre for Chinese Studies.

Clark, Joe. 2009. Canada's Assets in a Changing World. Allan J. MacEachen Lecture in Politics, St. Francis Xavier University, Antigonish, October 22.

Clark, Joe 2013. *How We Lead: Canada in a Century of Change*. Canada: Random House Canada.

Claassen, Carike, Elsabé Loots, and Henri Bezuidenhout. 2012. "Chinese Foreign Direct Investment in Africa: Making Sense of a New Economic Reality." *African Journal of Business Management* 6 (47): 11583–97.

Collier, Paul. 2007. *The Bottom Billion: Why the Poorest Countries Are Failing and What Can Be Done About It*. Oxford: Oxford University Press.

Collier, Paul. 2010. *The Plundered Planet: Why We Must – and How We Can – Manage Nature for Global Prosperity*. Oxford: Oxford University Press.

DFAIT (Foreign Affairs and International Trade Canada). 2011. *Evaluation of the Americas Strategy: Final Report*. Ottawa: DFAIT.

DFAIT (Foreign Affairs and International Trade Canada). 2012–13. *Report on Plans and Priorities 2012–13*. Ottawa: DFAIT.

The Economist. 2011. "The Hopeful Continent: Africa Rising." December 3. www.economist.com/node/21541015.

Fantino, Julian. 2012. "Reducing Poverty - Building Tomorrow's Markets." Keynote address to the Economic Club of Canada, Toronto, November 23. www.acdi-cida.gc.ca/acdi-cida/ACDI-CIDA.nsf/eng/NAT-1123135713-Q8T.

Friend, David. 2013. "Canada Faces Exports Challenge: Carney." *Canadian Press*, February 25.

Hallam, David. 2009. "Foreign Investment in Developing Country Agriculture – Issues, Policy Implications and International Response." Paper presented at the Organisation for Economic Co-operation and Development's Eighth Global Forum on International Investment, Paris, December 7–8.

Harris, Michael. 2015. *A Party of One: Stephen Harper and Canada's Radical Makeover*. Canada: Penguin.

Hille, Kathrin, and Rahul Jacob. 2012. "China: Beyond the Conveyor Belt." *Financial Times*, October 14. www.ft.com/intl/cms/s/0/53358d5e-1452-11e2-8cf2-00144feabdc0.html#axzz2Jf3wTWRa.

Hook, Leslie. 2012. "Zuma Warns on Africa's Ties to China." *Financial Times*, July 19. www.ft.com/intl/cms/s/0/33686fc4-d171-11e1-bbbc-00144feabdc0.html#axzz2JwSLdOye.

Ingram, Joseph, and Karin Lissakers. 2012. "Mining's Golden Rule: Transparency." *Globe and Mail*, September 24. www.theglobeandmail.com/commentary/minings-golden-rule-transparency/article4560624.

ILO. 2012. *Africa's Response to the Youth Employment Crisis: Regional Report*. Geneva: ILO.

Lin, Justin Yifu. 2010. "Industrial Policy Comes Out of the Cold." *Project Syndicate*, December 1. www.project-syndicate.org/commentary/industrial-policy-comes-out-of-the-cold.

Lin, Justin Yifu. 2011. "From Flying Geese to Leading Dragons: New Opportunities and Strategies for Structural Transformation in Developing Countries." World Institute for Development Economics Research annual lecture, Maputo, May 4.

Mark, Renee, and Peter Bullock. 2011. "From May 1st New China Anti-Corruption Laws Follow Long Arm Jurisdiction Trend." Pinsent Masons Asia, May 30. http://thebriberyact.com/2011/05/30/from-may-1st-new-china-anti-corruption-laws-follow-long-arm-jurisdiction-trend/.

Moyo, Dambisa. 2009. *Dead Aid: Why Aid Is Not Working and How There Is a Better Way for Africa*. New York: Farrar, Straus and Giroux.

Munson, James. 2012a. "Mining Industry Decides More Rules Are the Way to Go." *iPolitics*, September 6. www.ipolitics.ca/2012/09/06/mining-industry-decides-more-rules-are-the-way-to-go.

Ncube, Mthuli, and Michael Fairbanks. 2013. "How Could Africa use China for Development?" *FT Data* (blog), *Financial Times*, February 21. http://blogs.ft.com/economistsforum/2013/02/how-could-africa-use-china-to-spur-economic-development/.

Page, John. 2012. *Aid, Structural Change and the Private Sector in Africa*. Working Paper No. 2012/21, United Nations University World Institute for Development Economics Research, Helsinki.

Poon, Daniel. 2012. *South–South Policy Space Dimensions*. Working paper, The North-South Institute, Ottawa.

Radelet, Steven. 2010. *Emerging Africa: How 17 Countries Are Leading the Way*. Washington, DC: Center for Global Development.

Randall, Stephen J. 2010. "Canada, the Caribbean and Latin America: Trade, Investment and Political Challenges." *Foreign Policy for Canada's Tomorrow*, no. 9. Toronto: Canadian International Council.

Renard, Mary-Françoise. 2011. *China's Trade and FDI in Africa*. Working Paper No. 126, African Development Bank Group, Tunis.

Roberts, Chris. 2012. "Canada's Hidden Role in China's Rise in Africa: Canadian Leverage at a Tipping Point." Paper presented at the China and Canada in Africa: Interests, Strategies and African Perspectives conference, Ottawa, September 20–21.

Rodrik, Dani. 2011. "The Future of Economic Convergence." Paper presented at the Jackson Hole Symposium of the Federal Reserve Bank of Kansas City, Jackson Hole, August 25–27.

Russell, Alec. 2013. "Zuma In "Colonial" Warning to West" *Financial Times*, March 4.

Sautman, Barry, and Yan Hairong. 2011. "Barking up the Wrong Tree: Human Rights Watch and Chinese Copper Mining in Zambia." *Pambazuka News*, Issue 563, December 14. www.pambazuka.org/en/category/features/78660.

Sneyd, Adam. 2012. "Governing African Cotton and Timber through CSR: Competition, Legitimacy and Power." *Canadian Journal of Development Studies* 33 (2): 143–63.

Stiglitz, Joseph E. 2012. *The Price of Inequality: How Today's Divided Society Endangers Our Future*. New York: W. W. Norton & Co.

UNCTAD (United Nations Conference on Trade and Development). 2011. *The Least Developed Countries Report 2011: The Potential Role of South–South Cooperation for Inclusive and Sustainable Development*. New York and Geneva: United Nations.

UNCTAD (United Nations Conference on Trade and Development). 2012. *World Investment Report 2012: Towards a New Generation of Investment Policies*. New York and Geneva: UNCTAD.

UNDP. 2012. *Africa Human Development Report 2012: Towards a Food Secure Future*. New York: UNDP.

UNECA (United Nations Economic Commission for Africa). 2011. *Minerals and Africa's Development: The International Study Group Report on Africa's Mineral Regimes*. Addis Ababa: UNECA.

Ushie, Vanessa. 2012. *Political Decentralization and Natural Resource Governance in Nigeria*. Working Paper, The North-South Institute, Ottawa.

Weitzner, Viviane. 2011. *Tipping the Power Balance: Making Free, Prior and Informed Consent Work; Lessons and Policy Directions from 10 Years of Action Research on Extractives with Indigenous and Afro-descendent Peoples in the Americas*. Ottawa: The North–South Institute.

Zadek, Simon, Chen Xiaohong, Li Zhaoxi, Jia Tao, Zhou Yan, Kelly Yu, Maya Forstater, and Guy Morgan. 2009. *Responsible Business in Africa: Chinese Business Leaders' Perspectives on Performance and Enhancement Opportunities*. Working Paper No. 54, John F. Kennedy School of Government, Harvard University, Cambridge, MA.

12 Russia's geostrategic vision of African natural resources

Leonid Fituni

Until very recently, effective governance of the global system was a prerogative of a select group of world powers. Through centuries, with the exception of irregular short periods of revolutions and seditions, Russia had been among them. At the beginning of the new millennium, the country is trying to find a new *modus vivendi* in the changed geopolitical environment of a globalized world, in which Moscow's global *economic* power rests almost exclusively on its natural resources endowment.

The defeat in the Cold War, territorial disintegration, and the disastrous results of the economic liberalization and market reforms of the 1990s have seriously undermined the former Soviet high-tech and manufacturing capabilities. Post-Soviet Russia has turned into a natural resource-based economy.[1] The dominant part of Russia's mining production is exported: oil, over 60 percent; phosphates, 90 percent; non-ferrous, rare metals and stones between 90 and 100 percent. The overall share of mineral materials in exports in 2013 was 83 percent.[2] This data and the figures in Note 1 testify that, in Russia, the primary sector's main functional purpose is no longer to supply the domestic economy with raw materials but to serve as a source of revenues for the national budget and to replenish the treasury with foreign currency. It is widely believed that industrial development in commodity-exporting low- and middle-income economies is disadvantaged as a direct consequence of the exploitation of natural resources, that is, that such economies suffer from a resource curse (Kaplinsky 2011, v).

At the same time, the prospects for enhancing socio-economic development, ensuring stability of the world economy and international security, and raising the standard of living depend on the availability of the necessary natural resources. The increasing global shortage of resources is one of the reasons for the escalating local, regional, and global crises of the new millennium. As the events of the beginning of this millennium have shown, one of the most important vectors in government policy worldwide is the striving to control the declining supplies of natural resources or gain reliable access to them.

After the break-up of the Soviet Union, key deposits of some vitally important resources (manganese and uranium, to name a few) remained outside the new Russian borders. Moreover, though deposits of some now undersupplied minerals were discovered as far back as the 1940s, their extraction may be commercially unviable under the existing level of technological development or due to the extremely harsh conditions of exploitation. That is why Russia is very much interested in both the global resource governance agenda and in cooperating with African countries on resource issues. In the African direction, Moscow's interest is twofold. On the one hand, Russia attaches much significance to securing the import of lacking raw materials, while on the other, the Kremlin works to form cooperative alliances (or at least optimal cohabitation arrangements) with the main exporters of the commodities Russia supplies to the world markets.

Moscow preserves much of the residual political influence in the world – primarily thanks to its status as a permanent member of the UN Security Council and an outstanding military potential. However, Moscow's vision of the dynamics and fundamental contradictions of contemporary international relations focuses on the intensifying global competition for natural resources,[3] which enfeebled Russia now re-enters from unfavorable positions. The Kremlin strives to embrace the realities, ideas, concepts, and beliefs of the post-modern world but is still limited in its ability to secure a worthy place and its bygone influence in it. Consequently, Moscow simultaneously holds two conflicting viewpoints in accepting and trying to play an important role in global governance (through UN Security Council, G8, G20, BRICS (Brazil, Russia, India, China and South Africa), etc.), while at the same time being cautious and reluctant to cede its sovereign rights in the sphere of natural resource governance.

This turns out not to be an easy task, since two contradictory trends have been shaping the new world system and its economic foundations. On the one hand, the *existing* paradigms of both industrial and post-industrial development, together with the recent economic advancement of large and populous developing countries (China, India, Brazil, Mexico, Indonesia, etc.), have engendered a relative deficit of natural resources, which has resulted in acute competition between now multiple centers of economic power, nearing confrontation in such regions as Africa. On the other, the deepening trend towards global governance and supranational regulation limit the possibility of practical use of natural resources as an instrument of projecting power for commodity producers, be they Russia, Australia, Canada, or South Africa. Such nations have to adjust their national practices of exploitation of those resources to international "rules of the game" and abide by externally imposed constraints – in certain cases even limiting or ceasing the use of their sovereign natural endowment.

In this chapter, the author introduces a theoretical interpretation (a *Concept of models of global economic development – MGEDs*) of how and why such "rules of the game" undergo regular transformations, and what implications this has for the formation of various systems of both global and natural resource governance. This concept is presented against the historic background of Russia's involvement in the creation of national systems of resource governance in various African countries. It is worth mentioning here that although this chapter often refers to Russia's "African policy," the latter has never been a separate and/or a singular political line. Moscow has always been careful to adequately address the diversity and plurality of African realities and to demonstrate individual attention to the countries of the continent.

The Kremlin's cognitive dissonance

Today, Moscow's international policy line and behavior proceed from the assumption that new transborder threats and challenges increasingly dominate the international agenda, rising in proportions and becoming more diversified in form and geography. Russia's main strategic document in the diplomatic sphere, the newly adopted *Concept of the Foreign Policy of the Russian Federation* (2013), provides a broad list of such dangers, singling out, among other, "scarcity of essential resources, demographic problems, global poverty, environmental, sanitary and epidemiological challenges, climate change and threats to information and food security."[4]

In particular, as seen from the official documents, the Kremlin is concerned with the fundamental changes "taking place in the energy sector, which is related, *inter alia*, to the use of innovative technologies to develop hard-to-recover hydrocarbon reserves. At a time when it becomes increasingly important for the states to diversify their presence in the world markets in order to guarantee their economic security, we [Russians] are witnessing imposition of various unjustified restrictions and other discriminatory measures."[5] According to the Russian Ministry of Economy, despite the country's full membership in the World Trade Organization (WTO), seventy-two restrictive measures targeted Russian produce (as of April 1, 2013) in nineteen countries. The largest number of restrictions in relation to Russian goods existed in the USA, the EU, the Ukraine and Belorussia.[6]

The above quoted *Concept of the Foreign Policy* provides no concrete sources for such unfair restraints. However, most likely, the document means both various formally autonomous state and non-state actors often acting in unison to such a degree that their efforts might be qualified as systemic and universal. Geographically, they include not only such distant parts of the world as Africa but the immediate Russian neighborhood in Europe, Asia, and the Arctic.

One of the main vectors in international economic relations in the twenty-first century will be the leading nations' concerted efforts to acquire natural resources, including those in Africa. In so doing, the struggle for sales markets, which is still going on and essentially becoming aggravated, will undergo significant changes in form and intensity. Information warfare has been gaining more and more importance as a salient element of this.[7] Non-state actors will increasingly become involved, either intentionally or unwittingly, working for both supranational and national interests and causes. Asymmetrical responses to the moves of perceived rivals or competitors are to be expected on a much wider and more frequent scale than today.

These evolutions represent a logical consequence of globalization entering the mature phase as well as of the ensuing increase in the importance of the "world market" over the "national market." Many restricting elements inherent in the national market (customs tariffs and, in particular, non-tariff regulation of import and export, and so on, at the national level) are proving to be less influential today than before (owing to supranational governance, WTO regulations, the composition of international trade agreements, internal links and flows in transnational corporations, and so on).

Raw mineral reserves are distributed very unevenly throughout the planet and, as a rule, the largest consumers of such reserves are far from the leading producers. Acknowledging the existing disproportion between the level of socio-economic development of the countries and the percentage of resources they consume, on the one hand, and the size of their population and the natural resource reserves in their territory, on the other, is important for understanding the key problems of global development in the twenty-first century.

It will be no exaggeration to claim that the desire to ensure control over resources at the global, regional, sectoral, or branch level continues to be one of the main motives for re-examining geopolitical reality. The latter can be achieved by military or peaceful means. In the nuclear age, the use of the military option on the global scale may be suicidal, therefore other means, including regulatory and normative instruments, will have to be used to obtain the desired results. Global governance in key spheres may be a solution, provided one group of players is capable of advancing and imposing its set of the "rules of the game" as universal norms. It would be naive to assume, however, that all the other groups of players would only be happy to have those rules imposed upon them or to cede their current rights and privileges to others. This holds true for both "old" and "new" centers of economic power in the contemporary world. The former groups would like to preserve (and even expand) their current dominant positions in the hierarchies of the current world order by defining the normative framework of the global governance in accordance with their visions and values. Meanwhile, the "newcomers" would be happy to preserve only those bits of the existing world order and of the global governance system which reinforce their newly acquired (or regained) might, while "improving" those parts that assure the "old" players' dominance.

Further below, the author will provide a conceptual interpretation of this phenomenon within his theory of successive change of models of global economic development (MGEDs). Here, however, it is important to emphasize that the described dilemma constitutes a key point in understanding the current Russian position vis-à-vis the concept of global governance in general and that of resource governance in particular. As a "residual element" of the group of "old" global powers and a founding member of BRICS, a club of emerging global leaders still in search of self-identification, Russia is bound to experience a cognitive dissonance between the old "vertical/hegemonic" power relationships of the twentieth century and the emerging "rules of the game" of a new polycentric world.

While Moscow remains in limbo between the "old" and "new" players, the final decision as to what camp the country will ultimately join depends on what place Russia may be offered within either of them and on what set of arrangements are recognized as the Kremlin's legitimate rights and powers within a given system of governance. Taking into consideration the current state of the Russian economy and the cumulative weight of the post-Soviet societal disarray, it would be fair to say that, to a very significant extent, those prospects are defined not by the Kremlin but by other players of the "old" and "new" camps. Such a tug-of-war situation is pregnant with extremely serious challenges to international security.

From the geopolitical and geo-economic points of view, the situation is delicate indeed, since joining the club of old players and ultimately converging with the system of global governance favored by the rich world on terms acceptable to Moscow is dependent more on external factors and foreign interests than on Russia itself. Meanwhile, the decision-makers in the old camp are reluctant to offer Russia an equal place within their ranks, while Moscow is unwilling and unable to accept the role of underdog there.

In contrast, the new world order and a corresponding system of governance under creation by new players (BRICS, in particular) is largely a product of Moscow's own design. By default, a respected and influential place seems to be guaranteed within it; though not without some jostling and elbowing with China.

Advancing universal norms in such areas as resource governance may prove to be a long and complicated way of achieving these goals, especially in the case of strategically important resources. Moreover, the anticipated outcome cannot be guaranteed. Recent history shows that some players are inclined to military solutions on the regional scale in order to guarantee the necessary "change of the rules" or preservation of the existing ones.

The global demand for raw materials may grow, according to various forecasts, from 25 to 50 percent by the middle of the century.[8] The increase is expected to be caused mainly by the combined effect of the rise and assertion of many developing economies, on the one hand, and increased consumption in the rich world, on the other. Besides that, technological progress is likely to create additional demand (poorly assessable now) for minerals and other natural resources currently considered to be of low priority (as was the case with strontium, which in the 1960s had a very limited use but now is a backbone of a global multimillion-dollar market).[9]

Keeping in mind the growth in such countries as China, India, Brazil, Mexico, Turkey, Indonesia, etc., even cyclical slumps in the world economy and significant price fluctuations will not hinder an increase in fuel and raw-material consumption. For example, according to the estimates of the US Energy Information Administration, even if the higher prices return (the level reached in the first half of 2008), the consumption of liquid fuel types will increase to 99 million barrels a day by 2030 (in 2005, it amounted to 84 million barrels a day).[10]

In these conditions, the African continent, with its still not fully developed and largely untouched rich deposits of fuel and raw materials, will become the arena of a desperate fight among the three main players – the US, the EU, and China – in the next few years. However, it would be more correct to classify all the countries of the informal BRICS group collectively as the third player in the battle over resources. Naming the big three does not mean that other competitors, like Canada, Japan, South Korea, Iran, Turkey, Saudi Arabia and, in fact, many others, will stand idle aside.

The peaceful introduction and spread of generally accepted norms of natural resource governance can hardly be achieved without the understanding that the emergence of new powers, particularly BRICS (but also of several other dynamic and rapidly growing actors in Africa, Asia, and Latin America), is an objective process, which stems from the transformation of the current model of global economic development (MGED).

The concept of MGEDs

A MGED can be described as a definite arrangement of "stable and repetitive international paradigms of social and economic relations of production, exchange, distribution and consumption in the world, which exist at a given historical stage of development of mankind and reflect a concrete balance of forces in the global economy under a given level and type of technological and economic development."[11] Being a complex system, MGED incorporates a number of autonomous elements (sub-models), which jointly determine its character and qualities. Each sub-model determines an important set of characteristics that delineate the peculiarities of a given set of social and economic relations and "rules of the game" in a given field or sector – financial, industrial, commercial, demographic.

Each MGED would have a particular kind of governance relationship, specific only to it. In this connection, a particular type of governance of global resources is characteristic to each individual MGED. Sub-models do not remain in stasis, they evolve and acquire a number of new features necessary for fulfillment of the tasks and challenges of their contemporary world. With time, the quantity of new features reaches a point when a new quality is born. Likewise, the renovation of a qualitatively sufficient number of sub-models produces the emergence of a new MGED. The sub-models do not change simultaneously in unison. In some, the pace of evolution is very slow (e.g. demographic sub-models, which are based on generational behavior stereotypes), in others, on the contrary, it may be relatively rapid (financial sub-models, also known as global financial systems). History shows that the pace of change in the sub-model of global resource governance is somewhere in the middle, but closer to the slower side.

Thus, MGEDs have defined life cycles, whose duration is determined by the pace of change within the constituent sub-models. They are born (formed), expand, mature, decline, and die (give way to new ones). Each MGED is governed by its own specific set of relations of dominance and subjugation, cooperation and competition. It establishes its own rules of the game and mechanisms of power. A change of MGED is accompanied by shifts in the world balance of power, by shake-ups of hierarchies, and by global governance reforms. Each period of transition from one MGED to another is usually accompanied by an increase in contradictions, instability, and conflict, since the old declining powers struggle to preserve their privileged positions in the existing governance systems and transpose them into a new nascent system, while the new rising powers vie to acquire a bigger share of the limited global resources needed for their development and expansion and create a set of rules for a new system that is optimal to the "newcomers."[12]

Within the period of the last 150–200 years (from approximately the first third of the nineteenth century to date), one can clearly isolate and identify qualitatively specific periods of global development which produced individual MGEDs: (1) the period of mature industrial capitalism and formation of colonial empires (approximately till the end of the nineteenth century); (2) the period of fierce imperialist rivalry (beginning of the twentieth century till the end of the Second World War); (3) the Cold War period (roughly, till the incorporation of Eastern Europe into the EU; and (4) the current stage of formation of a polycentric world system.

As mentioned above, the new MGED under formation in the twenty-first century is characterized by an increased global influence of large and populous developing countries, whose economies have been growing at a significantly higher pace than the world in general. This higher pace of development allowed some of the nations to narrow the gap in GDP and the standard of living between them and the advanced economies of the world.[13]

A few rising nations have outrun some of the Organisation for Economic Co-operation and Development (OECD) members in a number of respects, including the value of their industrial production, their share in global trade, percentage of high-tech goods in their exports, and the number of new international patents issued. Since 2012, China has been ahead of all OECD nations in terms of exports (by value).[14] In 2011, China was second in the world (after Japan but ahead of the USA) by application of patents and third (after both Japan and the USA) by granted patents.[15] In 2012, for the first time, residents of China accounted for the largest number of patents filed throughout the world.[16]

However, despite all these achievements, the real influence of even those successful countries in global governance remains limited. Furthermore, rich nations with smaller economies, declining population, inferior economic performance, and increasing social problems continue to cling to the levers of the old power mechanisms and to restrict, either willingly or unconsciously, the possibilities for further development and growth of the new rising actors. Many examples of such diversity and, at times, conflicts of interest constitute the core of still unresolved issues of reforming and modernizing such global governance institutions as the World Bank and the International Monetary

Fund (IMF), and collective negotiations within the WTO, on environmental protection and climate change or on information technologies and electronic communications.

The Soviet legacy in African resource governance

The change of the MGED will be inevitably accompanied by a change of the sub-model of governance, including the governance of resources. Since the break-up of the global system of colonialism in the middle of the twentieth century, the governance of natural resources has been predominantly the responsibility and the right of national governments. Both historically and legally, the concepts of *anti-colonialism* and *national governance of natural resources* were intrinsically interconnected, while Moscow spearheaded both the anti-colonial and national sovereignty movements within the United Nations (UN) and beyond. The question of a declaration on the granting of independence to colonial countries and peoples was initially proposed for inclusion in the agenda of the General Assembly by Nikita S. Khrushchev, the Chairman of the Council of Ministers of the USSR, during his address to the Assembly on September 23, 1960.

On December 14, 1960, the UN General Assembly adopted Resolution 1514, better known as The Declaration on the Granting of Independence to Colonial Countries and Peoples. The next day, Resolution 1515 was adopted, which recommended that the sovereign right of every state to dispose of its wealth and its natural resources should be respected.[17] Finally, the adoption of General Assembly Resolution 1803 (XVII) of December 14, 1962 turned the principle of "permanent sovereignty over natural resources" into international law.[18] The further Declaration on the Establishment of a New International Economic Order and the related Programme of Action (Resolutions 3201 (S-VI) and 3202 (S-VI) of May 1, 1974), and the Charter of Economic Rights and Duties of States (Resolution 3281 (XXIX) of December 12, 1974) provided an inevitable legal linkage between self-determination, and its goal of decolonization, and a postulated new international law-based right of freedom also in economic self-determination.[19]

For the Soviet Union, economic assistance and cooperation in the sphere of natural resources was an important element of asserting its influence in what was then called the Third World. Being practically self-sufficient in nearly all kinds of fuel, mineral, and other natural resources, the USSR pursued such cooperation not so much out of commercial or business interests, but as an important element of global competition between socialism and capitalism. Africa was the primary field for such competition.

The USSR contributed a great deal to the development of the material base of natural resource exploration in Africa. Soviet organizations provided assistance in setting up national geological prospecting, design, research, and other entities in Algeria, Angola, Egypt, Congo (Brazzaville), Ethiopia, Guinea, Ghana, Libya, Mali, Morocco, Mozambique, Nigeria, Senegal, Sudan,

Tanzania, and other African countries. Their contribution to the governance of natural resources in Africa consisted of assisting in the establishment of national institutions in these spheres after the departure of the former colonial administrations. A systematic survey of mineral deposits on the territory was performed in fourteen countries, broad programs of prospecting for ferrous, non-ferrous, rare and precious metals, rock products, and other minerals was developed for the above-named countries. The Soviets rendered assistance in preparing and expanding the mineral raw-material base for such metals as lead, zinc, mercury, antimony, tin, tungsten, iron, and gold, as well as barium and rock salt.

In Algeria, Soviet entities discovered, expanded, or helped to reconstruct lead and zinc mines in El Abadia, tungsten deposits in the Hoggar Uplands,[20] antimony-polymetallic deposits near Hammam N'bails, rich mercury deposits in Ismail, Mrasma, Guenicha, and Fendek. On the basis of the Ismail deposit, a mining and metallurgical integrated plant was built at the beginning of 1973 with Soviet assistance, its initial capacity being more than 300 tons of mercury a year. As a result, Algeria has become one of the leading producers of mercury.

The USSR provided assistance in the establishment, development, and management of national oil industries in Algeria, Libya, Egypt, Congo (Brazzaville), and Angola. This was a time when newly established African national oil companies often encountered fierce pressure from the large transnational oil corporations, which had previously been the sole masters of local oil and gas. Soviet companies per se never owned oil or gas fields in Africa but provided the technologies and equipment for the extraction of hydrocarbons.

Soviet geologists have discovered mineral deposits of international importance in Guinea (bauxites in Kindia, Goual, Dian Dian), Morocco (combustible shales, phosphates, cobalt), and Congo (Brazzaville) (zinc, lead in the middle Hiari region, polymetallic ores in Gengile, gold placers in Sunda Kakamoeka, polymetallic ores in Yanga Kibenga) and established an ore-dressing enterprise in M'Vouti in Mali (limestone Bafoulabe-Kai, gold in Kalama), and many others.[21]

Along with the fieldwork, the USSR also brought the Soviet approach to resource governance. Elements of planning were introduced in resource exploitation and management. The state sector became the backbone of national extractive industries in many African countries of so-called *socialist orientation*. Ironically, long after the demise of the Soviet Union and its planned economic system, many elements of the system of resource governance implanted in Africa with the help of Soviet specialists continue to exist and even deliver stable inflows of hard currency, much needed for economic development. It is important to stress that the discovered deposits, constructed mines or factories and other sites and projects of Soviet-African cooperation were never owned by the Soviet state or companies, but from the beginning became the property of national African states. As such, those enterprises contributed directly to the state budget revenues. Local natural resource management systems, and geological services, water management, and irrigation, in particular, still incorporate many of the initial elements established with the assistance of the Soviet Union, and the staff includes many African graduates of Soviet education and training institutions.

By the mid-1980s, the Soviet Union had signed hundreds of agreements in economic, cultural, and other fields with African countries. An estimated 25,000 Africans were trained at Soviet universities and technikons, and thousands graduated from military and political schools. Among such alumni are the current presidents of Angola (Jose Eduardo dos Santos), Mozambique (Armando Guebeza), Ghana (John Mahama), and South Africa (Jacob Zuma). In addition, at least 200,000 specialists were trained by the Soviets on African soil. The Soviet Union had agreements with thirty-seven African states on technical and economic assistance, and with forty-two African states on trade.[22]

During the years of Gorbachev's *perestroika* and Yeltsin's market reforms, Russia withdrew from Africa almost completely. The state of the Russian economy and the political uncertainty did not allow adequate attention to be paid to a part of the world so remote from Moscow. It was only at the beginning of 2000s that the domestic situation improved enough to renew external economic expansion and diplomatic activity.

Still, since the collapse of the Soviet Union, Russia's re-emergence as an important player at the African chessboard has been repeatedly compromised by the above-mentioned cognitive dissonance and the Kremlin's inconsistency and indecisiveness in this seemingly peripheral area of global competition. Between 1992 and 2012, Moscow undertook a number of half-hearted attempts to recover some of the economic and political positions it had enjoyed on the continent during the Cold War years, only to retreat soon after from the regained bastions. Although the concrete reasons for such retreats were very diverse, the basic one was, evidently, that the country's economy had not yet fully recovered from the disastrous effects of the transition to the market economy and liberalization of the l990s. At the same time, it would be fair to say that each new attempt began from a somewhat better position and resulted in limited but real (re)gains.

Russia's Africa policy: Does one exist?

The initial attempt was undertaken in the wake of the Gleneagles G8 Summit, in 2005. For that meeting of the leaders of the eight leading powers, the British government set the priorities of supporting Africa's economic development (by agreeing to write off the debts of the poorest countries and to significantly increase aid) and of moving forward initiatives to research and combat global warming. President Putin, who at that time had cordial relations with the then UK Prime Minister Blair, was one of the main supporters of the new initiatives. The Kremlin also decided to activate cooperation with other G8 partners in the African direction, in particular in the fields of debt relief, capacity building, and human security. Moscow contributed to joint efforts by writing off over $20 billion of African debt to Russia, far more than any other G8 nation.[23] Several groups of specialists on fighting tropical diseases as well as numerous means of transport (helicopters, planes, road vehicles) were mobilized for the needs of joint efforts with other G8 countries. Surprisingly, not all of the latter were equally interested in developing the African direction of G8 activity. Since then, G8's attention to the African agenda has been uneven – at times it had higher priority, but at other times less.

In 2006, Putin visited Algeria, Morocco, and South Africa, bringing back important agreements and contracts whose execution started in 2007. The follow-up visits by the Russian Foreign Minister prepared the ground for expanding the geography of close cooperation with other African nations. The next president, Dmitri Medvedev, paid visits to Egypt, Nigeria, Namibia, and Angola in 2009 and to Algeria in 2010. The significance of those visits was twofold. First, they reconfirmed Russia's willingness to rekindle multifaceted cooperation with African countries. Second, multiple agreements were signed by the two Russian presidents, covering areas as diverse as economy, science and technology, culture, education, defense, fishing, atomic energy, prevention and management of plant disease, sports and tourism, health protection, mass communication, and parliamentary exchanges. Unfortunately, the events of the "Arab spring," which happened soon after President Medvedev and his ministers had signed contracts in Egypt and Libya, prevented the realization of several projects in the spheres of oil and gas, pipeline construction, building of railways, and environmental protection in those countries.

Despite the turmoil in the Arab world, relations with Morocco and Algeria have continued without interruption since the mid-1950s and early 1960s, respectively. In 2001, Russia and Algeria signed the Declaration on Strategic Partnership. During Mr. Medvedev's 2009 visit, six contracts were signed with Algiers (on technical-military cooperation and on oil and gas, an intergovernmental agreement on maritime transport and memorandums on cooperation in the oil and gas sphere, energy, and standardization). Russian company Gazprom signed a cooperation agreement with the Algerian state oil and gas corporation Sonatrach.[24] During Mr. Putin's visit to Morocco, over a dozen agreements were signed. One of them, On Marine Fishing and Fisheries, is of key importance: twelve Russian vessels received the right to conduct annual pelagic (deep-sea) fishing in the Moroccan economic zone. Their annual quota is 120,000 tons of fish. One of the provisions of the agreement envisages that crews shall incorporate Moroccan nationals for training.[25] Morocco is the largest trading partner of Russia in Africa and the Arab region. On a visit to Moscow in June 2014, Moroccan Foreign Minister Saad Dine El Otmani underscored that both countries are driven by the same will to boost bilateral cooperation. The recently expanding areas of cooperation include air transportation, tourism, and the fight against terrorism.[26]

With Namibia, the emphasis was on the exploration and extraction of mineral resources, as well as the development of the energy, fisheries, transport, and tourism sectors. A number of important bilateral documents were signed as a result of the Namibian leader's visit to Moscow in 2010, including the intergovernmental agreements on cooperation in fisheries and tourism, a memorandum of understanding between the two governments on intentions in the development of cooperation in geological and uranium exploration on the territory of Namibia, and a memorandum on cooperation between the ministries of education.[27]

In Angola, the following bilateral agreements were signed in 2009: intergovernmental agreements on air services; on the promotion and mutual protection of investments; on cooperation in the fields of geology and higher education; a program of economic, scientific, technical, and commercial cooperation for 2009–2013. Contracts have been signed for the establishment and financing of the joint project of Angolan satellite communication and broadcasting, Angosat.[28]

In 2009, Russia and Nigeria's presidents Dmitri Medvedev and Umaru Yar'Adua signed six agreements. Russian state-owned energy giant Gazprom and the Nigerian National Petroleum Corporation (NNPC) agreed to cooperate and make deals on capital investment protection, extradition, and nuclear power, as well as in Africa's biggest oil and gas sector, including the natural gas and space spheres. The two countries created a new company Ni-Gaz, a 50/50 joint venture between Gazprom and NNPC, aiming to build refineries, pipelines, and gas power stations throughout Nigeria.[29]

Still, despite the seemingly abundant bumper crop of agreements, the overall activity in the African direction has been sporadic and retroactive. The Russian Federation does not have a particular "Africa Policy" that is fundamentally different from the policy line towards other developing countries. Moreover, although the understanding of Africa's increasing importance and the general willingness to develop ties with African countries is undoubtedly present, many within the ranks of the Western-leaning factions of the Russian elite doubt that Moscow objectively needs such a separate policy. At the same time, it would be fair to acknowledge the existence of definite policy lines vis-à-vis individual African nations. For various reasons, the relations with some countries have become particularly dynamic in recent years. Among these are South Africa, Egypt, Algeria, Morocco, Nigeria, Angola, and Namibia, but the list of close partners is by no means limited to these countries.

In my view, there are two important factors that speak for the necessity to be still more active on the African arena. The first is Moscow's interest in a broader political dialogue with Africa as an influential force in the global diplomatic arena. The continent is the home to nearly a quarter of the voting UN member nations. African countries, in general, have a very positive attitude toward Russia. They remember Moscow's crucial positive role in their obtaining of independence – sometimes against military counter-efforts of their former colonial masters. Besides, quite often, African nations perceive Russia as a possible effective counterbalance to the pressure and aggressive expansion of other stronger global players.[30]

The second factor in favor of Russia's comeback to Africa is purely economic. Due to the obvious unwillingness on the part of the West to engage in deep economic cooperation with Moscow on a level basis, Russia has been increasingly opening to the East and the South. In this, BRICS and Africa are the two most obvious partners. Both possess vast internal markets that welcome Russian products, in particular, the manufactured goods to which Western markets are virtually closed. Cooperation with BRICS and Africa is perceived in Moscow as almost the only way to overcome the raw materials dependency of Russian exports.

African countries, on their part, discovered new export opportunities in Russia after the division of the USSR and the disappearance of the COMECON (SEV) deprived Moscow of many traditional suppliers of both manufactured goods and raw commodities. As shown below, this is especially true in relation to several types of mineral resources (manganese, chromium, etc.). Deposits of almost all the well-known types of minerals have been discovered in Africa. The continent occupies first place in the world in terms of manganese, chrome, iron ore, bauxite, gold, platinoids, cobalt, vanadium, diamonds, phosphate rock, and fluorspar supplies. It is second in terms of copper ore, asbestos, uranium, antimony, beryllium, and graphite reserves, and third in terms of oil, gas, mercury, and iron ore supplies; it also has large amounts of titanium, nickel, bismuth, lithium, tantalum, niobium, tin, wolfram, and precious gems.

In the past few years, the level of Russian–African relations has risen. Investment activity has become animated and foreign trade turnover has increased somewhat, though it is still very low, even in comparison with other BRICS partners. Official data on the current Russian investment in Africa is absent. The debt problem was essentially removed from the agenda of Russian–African relations when Russia wrote off Africa's $20 billion debt under Soviet loans.

Nevertheless, the great potential of Russian–African relations is evidently not being fully tapped. In particular, they clearly lack scope, singleness of purpose, institutional complexity, and a sufficient set of tools. Russia's economic and trade cooperation with the states of the African continent, its volume and results, despite some animation in the 2000s, remain rather modest. The volume of Russia's foreign trade circulation with Africa in 2010 amount to US$8.66 billion, of which the North African countries accounted for 80 percent.[31] On average, during the last five years, the annual trade turnover between Russia and the countries of Africa remained around US$4–5 billion dollars. In 2012, trade with some countries (the Republic of South Africa, Egypt, Morocco, Ghana, Ethiopia) became more active, but in 2013 it recoiled and the overall turnover with Africa returned to the US$8 billion level. As for the sub-Saharan countries, the trade volume with them is no higher than US$2 billion. In a number of states (Guinea, Ghana, Angola, the Republic of South Africa, Nigeria, Madagascar) Russian companies made considerable investments in domestic measures. Some leading Russian

Russia's vision of African natural resources 297

corporations (Rusal, Alrosa, Renova, Lukoil, etc.) have large African assets in the form of investments in oil production, bauxites, uranium raw materials, and so on. Russia's assets in Africa are estimated at a total of US$3–3.5 billion. The 750 state stipends Russia grants the Africans every year are usually not used in full.[32]

In return, Russia mainly receives aluminum ore (imports cover 65 percent of Russia's needs) and tropical agricultural products (primarily coffee, cocoa, fruit, and vegetables) from Africa. African investments in the Russian economy are no higher than US$500 million and mainly come from South Africa.

Tourism is the only sphere of Russian–African cooperation that is developing quickly. In 2010, more than 2.5 million Russians visited Africa.[33] They mainly went to Egypt and Tunisia, but they also visited several countries of East and Southern Africa. East African tourism has experienced an unprecedented growth since the developments of the "Arab spring."

On the whole, Russia's economic position is growing slowly. In other words, Russia's so-called return to Africa announced in the 2000s has clearly been delayed, mainly due to the combined negative effect of the global financial and economic crisis and political instability, which by strange coincidence began exactly in those countries which manifest their preparedness or that were already actively involved in economic engagement in Russia (among recent examples are Egypt, Tunisia, Libya, Côte d'Ivoire, Mali, Sudan). Some Russian analysts tend to interpret such twists of fate as an intensification of the competitive struggle for influence in Africa between the old and new players (Vasiliev 2011; Vasiliev, Abramova et al. 2008; Fituni 2011, 18–19).

Although Russia possesses extremely rich supplies of natural resources, domestic capabilities for fully meeting industry's needs for high-quality raw material and at competitive prices are shrinking. Many profitably exploitable deposits have been exhausted or are on the brink of exhaustion. After the collapse of the common Soviet economic space, Russia has been experiencing a visible shortage of several of the most important minerals, including almost 100 percent of manganese, 80 percent of chromium, 60 percent of bauxite, and so on (see Table 12.1). As mentioned at the beginning of the chapter, although some of the undersupplied minerals are physically present in the Russian soil, their extraction under present conditions is often economically unviable. New Russian deposits of many important minerals are largely found in the northern latitudes and their development is associated with large investments and long introduction into service. According to the estimates of the Institute for African Studies of the Russian Academy of Sciences, from the commercial point of view, it would be more profitable to use commodities imported from Africa. At the same time, a strong lobby of local producers argue that any deliveries from overseas increase Russia's dependency on foreign suppliers, carriers, and on the political will of foreign governments. Ironically, the same arguments are often used by Western politicians in relation to EU dependence on Russian oil and gas supplies.

The exhaustibility of profitably exploitable supplies is becoming an increasingly urgent problem. Experts of the national geological agency Zarubezhgeologia note that the exploitable supplies of manganese ore were essentially exhausted in 2010, chromium by 2012, and wolfram by 2016, while oil and bauxite will run out by 2025. The increment in known supplies of chromium ore is fourfold lower than the recovery of this resource, 15 percent of molybdenum recovery is covered by the increment in explored reserves, 60 percent of metals in the platinum group, only 9.4 percent of zirconium, and so on.[34] It stands to reason that, in the interests of Russia's security, some resources should be saved rather than being depleted to the limit. The US has been following this strategy for decades.

In these circumstances, the potential for international cooperation in the raw mineral sector, particularly with the African countries, must be tapped. Developing partnerships with the African states in the exploitation of mineral resources presents opportunities not only for overcoming the difficulties that have arisen but also for reducing the load on the mining industry, as well as for meeting Russian industry's growing needs for raw materials on advantageous conditions. No exact calculations on the potential effect of substituting expensive local raw materials with cheaper African ones exist. However, Table 12.1 gives a general idea about the areas where the import of African minerals may be crucially important.

At present, Russia imports raw materials extracted in Africa by Western corporations but it is also beginning to invest in the development of extractive industries on the continent. Russian companies, which, compared to their Western competition, are quite young and, on average, lack the financial potential, diplomatic underpinning, and historic foothold in Africa, are operating there on a limited scale.

Russian big business in Africa

In recent years, Russian companies have made perceptible efforts to expand their positions in the development of Africa's natural resources. Eighteen large Russian companies are implementing forty projects. The most significant prospective projects are as follows: diamond production in Angola (Alrosa), building the Nigeria–Algeria gas pipeline (Gazprom), nickel production in Botswana (NorNickel), developing the oil field in the coastal zone of Côte d'Ivoire and Ghana (Lukoil), developing deposits of manganese and vanadium in South Africa (Renova, Evraz), and oil production in Equatorial Guinea (Gaspromneftegaz). Most of these projects are at the execution stage.

Comprehensive information on Russian investment in the development of African natural resources is lacking. A general idea of the scope of investment and major projects can be obtained from Table 12.2 (in Annex) based on the research of the African Development Bank (AfDB) and updated by the author.

Table 12.1 Russia's mineral resource shortage and potential of Africa's mining sector (according to data at the end of 2008)

Raw mineral	Russia				Africa	
	Production	Shortage,%	Russia's provision with supplies in% based on a 10-year cycle	Supplies	Production	
Manganese ore	17,000 tons (0.05%)**	97.0	2.4	1,326m tons (22.1%)**	10.63m transport (31.5%)**	
Uranium ore	3,600 tons (9.2%)**	82.0	18	433,200 tons (16.7%)**	6,000 tons (15.4%)**	
Tin ore and concentrate	814 tons (0.3%)**	61.7	47	415,000 tons (7.5%)**	15,000 transport (4.8%)**	
Chromium ore	733,000 tons (3.0%)**	60.3	40 (based on an annual ore import of 1.01 mln tons)	1,839,200 tons (48.4%)**	10,470,000 (43.4%) **	
Titanium concentrate	82,000 tons (0.7%)**	59.2	38.7	435.8 (44.6%)**	2.389 (20.0%)**	
Aluminum in bauxite	5.3m tons (2.6%)**	50.0	37.6	7464.0 mill. tons (42.6%)**	20.9 m transport (10.5%)**	
Zinc ore and concentrate	337,500 tons (2.9%)**	27.8		17040.0 thou. tons (7.1%)**	284,400 transport (2.4%)**	
Molybdenum ore and concentrate	5,400 tons (2.4%)**	19.5	88	19.0 (0.1%)**	0.0	
Wolfram ore and concentrate	4,220 tons (7.5%)**	4.3	97 (with imports of concentrates of up to 3,040 tons and production of 6,500 tons a year)	6,000.0 tons (0.2%)**	160.0 transport (0.3%)**	
Niobium (manufactured only at the Solikamsk plant)		70				

Sources: *Government Report on the State and Use of the Russian Federation's Raw Mineral Resources in 2008*, Ministry of Natural Resources, Moscow, 2009; *Statistics Guide Mineral Resources of the World*, Mineral Information and Analytical Centre, Moscow, 2009.

Notes: * – only confirmed supplies in category ABC_1.
** – in percentages of world statistics.

In 2008, ARMZ Uranium Holding Co., together with VTB Capital Namibia (Pty) Ltd. and Arlan Invest Holdings, established a joint venture – SWA Uranium Mines in Namibia. ARMZ owns part of the project via Runex Uranium (Pty) Ltd., a daughter company formed on a parity basis with VTB Capital Namibia (Pty) Ltd. The results of fieldwork completed in 2008 point to potentially prospective uranium mineralization structures in the south-eastern and eastern parts of the EPL 3850 property. This, in turn, has allowed SWA Uranium Mines to target priority areas for exploratory drilling. The joint venture plans to carry on with exploratory works.[35]

In 2010, ARMZ Uranium Holding Co. consolidated a 51.4 percent controlling stake in Uranium One Inc., a Canada-based publicly traded uranium mining company with a diversified portfolio of projects located in Kazakhstan, the USA, and Australia. In June 2011, ARMZ Uranium Holding Co. closed a deal to acquire a 100 percent shareholding in Australian-based Mantra Resources Limited, a publicly traded company. Mantra Resources Limited's largest project is Mkuju River in Tanzania, with a total mineral resource base of about 45,900 tons of uranium. The operator of the Mkuju River project is Uranium One Inc.[36] The Tanzanian government expects to generate direct and indirect cashflows exceeding US$640 million during the span of the new uranium mining starting in 2013.[37]

In 2007, Renova, a major private Russian business group became the first Russian investor that has been able to come to an agreement with OAO Tekhsnabexport on a uranium project. Renova received a 50 percent share in several joint ventures with the state company for geological exploration and production of uranium in Africa.[38]

As part of its participation in the 2013 BRICS summit, the Renova Group of companies has signed four strategic cooperation agreements with its South African partners in alternative energy, telecommunications, construction of marine ports, and mining. According to the agreement reached during the summit, Majestic Silver Trading, a consortium of South African investors that is already a partner of the Renova Group in UMK, Renova's South African mining company, will acquire a share in the capital of Transalloys (RAS), a ferroalloy facility. The goal of this cooperation is to expand value-added manganese ore processing. In particular, Transalloys will be used as a platform for creation of a state-of-the-art ferroalloys production facility (with the construction of two new high-capacity furnaces), with the output of silicomanganese to double to 360k tons as from 2015. The parties also intend to set up a joint US$100 million investment fund in order to diversify into other areas of resource mining.

Renova's African interests are not limited to mining. It is developing innovative industries and technologies there. In the field of alternative energy, the Renova Group has entered into a MoU with South African Inyanga Energy Investments. The document suggests joint effort in the construction of solar PV parks in South Africa and other African countries with overall capacity of at least 200MW. Moreover, Renova will supply to South Africa solar PV modules manufactured by Hevel, a Russian solar PV panel manufacturer (Renova's joint venture with a Russian high-tech corporation OJSC Rusnano). The scope of export to South Africa is expected to be around 100MW per annum. Akado Group, a member of the Renova Group, will develop telecommunication business together with South African Factostep. The companies intend to cooperate in developing broadband in South Africa and Mozambique. In its partnership with OJSC MDB Compass and South African Guma, the Renova Group is planning to establish and develop marine and river port infrastructure in South Africa. The construction of these facilities will be based on the mobile ports know-how of MDB Compass.[39]

Another prominent Russian metal ore producer Evraz also operates in South Africa. Vertically integrated steel and vanadium producer Evraz Highveld Steel and Vanadium Limited (Evraz Highveld) is South Africa's second-largest steelmaker and the primary producer of medium and heavy structural sections. Steel and vanadium slag are produced at the integrated steelworks situated in eMalahleni, Mpumalanga, with ore for the steelworks obtained from the Mapochs Mine in the Roossenekal area, Limpopo. In 2012, Evraz Highveld produced 144,000 tonnes of plate, 98,700 tonnes of coil, 204,500 tonnes of sections and 43,000 tonnes of vanadium slag.[40]

In Liberia, another important African producer of metal ores, the government continued actively to seek investment in the redevelopment of the country's vast iron ore deposits in partnership with Russian companies. Projects to improve mining-related infrastructure included the joint venture of African Aura Mining Inc. of Canada and OAO Severstal Resources of Russia to develop the Putu iron ore project in Grand Gedeh County. In September 2010, the government granted OAO Severstal (61.5 percent) and African Aura (38.5 percent) an MDA for the Putu iron ore project. The twenty-five-year agreement provides for the construction and development of the project. Inferred mineral resources were estimated to be 1.08 billion metric tonnes of ore with an average grade of 37.6 percent iron. A definitive feasibility study was expected to be completed in 2014. The project would require the construction of a 130 kilometer railway line to the coast and a new deepwater port.[41]

Russian companies are also demonstrating interest in developing Africa's aluminum ore deposits. Africa is the most promising partner in the Far Abroad with respect to this mineral due to historic ties and the high quality of African bauxites. This primarily concerns Guinea, which ranks first in the world in terms of bauxite supplies. Furthermore, the quality of bauxite in Guinea is very high. Guinea was expected to meet a quarter of the world demand for bauxite in 2015.[42] It was the Soviets who discovered the deposits and helped to organize production in Guinea. Since then, Russia has been the leading importer of Guinean bauxites.

Russia is also a major player in the diamond market. Expanding cooperation with the African countries is seen as an important prerequisite for strengthening Russia's position in the world market of this raw material.

Alrosa's Projects in Africa Development Strategy was worked out in 2012. The company's plans to intensify the implementation of its geological exploration projects are aimed at the creation of new diamond-mining enterprises. Angola is considered to be the priority partner. According to Alrosa, "The Company will also use this country as a springboard for the implementation of the new projects on the continent."[43]

In Angola, Alrosa became a co-founder of Catoca Ltd. Mining Co. with a 32.8 percent share in the authorized capital. Every year, Catoca mines and sells rough diamonds worth some 6.7–6.8 million carats. Catoca Ltd. Mining Co. in its turn is also a majority founder of Luemba company (Angola), with the Tchiuzo pipe, another large primary diamond deposit, located on its concession territory. Russia's Yakutniproalmaz Institute developed the technical design for the development of this pipe and conducted the feasibility study for investments. The second priority country is Botswana. In August 2013, affiliated companies of Alrosa and Botswana Diamonds Plc. signed an Agreement on the Establishment of a Joint Venture to be engaged in geological exploration aimed at discovering primary diamond deposits and subsequent obtaining of the rights for their exploitation. Alrosa is also eyeing Zimbabwe for the geological exploration and, possibly, for the establishment of joint diamond-mining enterprises. At the end of 2012, Alrosa's geological service and Zimbabwe's DTZ–Ozgeo reached an Agreement on Technical Cooperation aiming to choose promising areas and assess their resource potential. This work may result in the establishment of a joint diamond-mining enterprise.[44]

Russian–African cooperation in the oil and gas sphere will acquire special significance in the twenty-first century. In order to retain its influence in the world oil and gas market, Russian companies are taking steps not only to develop new deposits in the Russian Federation but also to extend the geographic framework of their activity by organizing oil production in other, more favorable regions of the planet, including Africa. By 2021, Russia's largest independent crude producer, Lukoil, plans to invest around US$10 billion in its existing shelf projects. Lukoil is also interested in new initiatives in West Africa and is speeding up geological exploration projects in Africa in order to proceed quickly to the production stage. Overall spending on exploration was US$144 million. Lukoil Group has carried out geological exploration work in four African countries – Egypt, Côte d'Ivoire, Ghana, and Sierra Leone. The earliest agreement was signed with Egypt, where the company operates in the Meleiha block in the Western Desert and in the WEEM block located in the eastern part of the Eastern Desert, 8 kilometers west of the city of Hurghada. In Côte d'Ivoire, Lukoil has the rights for Blocks CI-101 and CI-401 on the continental shelf. In Ghana, Lukoil's Cape Three Points deepwater block is located on the continental shelf. In 2011, Lukoil acquired a 49 percent interest in an exploration and development contract at the offshore deepwater Block SL-5–11 in territorial waters of Sierra Leone from the company Oranto Petroleum.[45]

Russia's main producer of natural gas, Gazprom, has operation agreements with Algeria, Libya, and Nigeria, as described above, although stable industrial production is now maintained only in Algeria. Gazprom EP International is operator of the El Assel project in partnership with the Algerian State Oil and Gas Corporation Sonatrach. Gazprom and Sonatrach hold 49 percent and 51 percent stakes in the project, respectively. A 3D seismic survey has been performed over the area of 1,100 square kilometers out of the projected 2,700.[46]

On April 17, 2008, Gazprom and Libya's National Oil Corporation (NOC) signed a Memorandum of Cooperation. Pursuant to the Memorandum, the parties studied the possibilities of implementing joint projects in the energy sector. Before that, in December 2007, based on the bidding results, Gazprom obtained exploration rights for licensed blocks No.19 and No.64. In addition, following the asset swap deal with BASF, Gazprom acquired a 49 percent stake in Libya's oil concessions C96 and C97.[47] Since the fall of the Qaddafi regime, the company has been struggling to return to normal operation.

In Nigeria, Gazprom and the Nigerian National Petroleum Corporation set up a joint venture in 2009 concerned with the construction of gas transport and power generation infrastructure in Nigeria, the design and development of an associated petroleum gas gathering and processing system as well as building the Nigerian part of the Trans-Sahara gas pipeline.[48]

Social aspects of resource governance

The new stage of Russia's economic engagement in Africa is characterized by increased attention to the social components of natural resources governance and business ethics. In many ways, the current corporate social responsibility (CSR) policies of modern Russian corporations (both state and private) echo the approaches of Soviet enterprises that operated in Africa in the 1960–1980s, which were described earlier in this chapter. As a rule, major Russian companies strive to integrate social, environmental, ethical human rights, and consumer concerns into their business operations and core strategy in close collaboration with their stakeholders. Even the advent of capitalism in Russia has not changed the stand on the property issue in relation to projects of social nature. Social objects created by Russian corporations operating in Africa become the property of African states or local communities. Such projects include construction and operation of educational, medical, and community centers in Nigeria, Guinea, Angola, and other countries.

One of the leaders in this respect is Severstal. The company has recently joined two of the most renowned sustainability organizations in operations and sourcing, the United Nations Global Compact (UNGC) and the Conflict-Free Sourcing Initiative (CFSI). This effort allows Severstal to take its existing purchasing practices to the next level and become an industry leader in transparent and sustainable sourcing standards among Russian companies operating in the sphere of natural resources development in Africa.[49]

Other Russian companies operating in Africa are also part of the UNGC. Among them are: UC Rusal, Sistema JSFC, Rosneftegazexport, JSC Russian railways, Lukoil, Renova group, Polimetal, and Rosneft Oil Company JSC.[50] In 2008, UC Rusal commissioned an Economist Intelligence Agency Report, with the support of PwC in Russia and the UNDP, entitled "From Russia with Love: A national chapter on the global CSR agenda," which provides a detailed picture of the company's progress in CSR. A significant part of it is dedicated to Rusal's CSR achievements in Africa.[51]

In South Africa, the Russian metal producer launched Evraz Highveld eMalahleni Community Forum, seeking to benefit the most vulnerable members of local communities. The forum primarily focuses on social development, education, and health. Evraz also supports hydroponics and agricultural projects, which combine realistic alternative work opportunities for local people while also improving access to basic nutrition.[52]

UC Rusal, the world's largest producer of aluminum and alumina, launched an extensive social investment program designed to support development of the local communities of UC Rusal Alscon, the aluminum smelter in Ikot Abasi, Akwa Ibom State. UC Rusal Alscon has committed to providing support in such areas as education, healthcare and wellbeing, and supply of water and electricity. The parties are jointly developing an Ikot Abasi Local Government Area Development Plan, which contributes to the Local and State Economic Empowerment Development Strategies (LEEDS and SEEDS). This plan calls for joint programs focused on health, education, power generation and distribution, and water treatment. According to the terms of signed agreements, UC Rusal is creating committees responsible for overseeing various areas of the program's implementation, including conciliatory committees, the Memorandum Compliance Control Committee, and the Human Resources Committee.[53]

In partnership with Group 5, the Ibom Power Company, the Power Holding Company of Nigeria and local government, UC Rusal Alscon has put in place the infrastructure necessary to release 5MW of power to the Power Holding Company of Nigeria to supplement the national grid. In addition, UC Rusal Alscon is partnering with the Water Company of Nigeria to rehabilitate the water distribution network in Ikpa Ibekwe wards 1 and 2.[54] An occupation health unit is being refurbished and standards raised to meet those of Rusal. The hospital facilities at the Alscon site are being upgraded to provide secondary services as part of the company's social program. These include neurology and physiotherapy, cardiology and therapy, dentistry, ophthalmology, gynecology, and ear, nose and throat facilities. The laboratory unit and ultrasound facilities are being upgraded, making this facility a center of excellence in the region able to offer mentoring services as well as back-up facilities to local health practitioners. UC Rusal Alscon also supports the development of education in Ikot Abasi, through the granting of various scholarships as well as the repair, expansion, and equipping of municipal nurseries and schools, the setting-up of vocational technical schools, and organization of different training courses.[55]

UC Rusal Alscon's activities in partnership with the state government and local community groups are aimed at establishing a locally owned and managed community-based organization dedicated to implementing the Ikot Abasi Local Government Area Development Plan. This model, developed with the support of Pro-Natura International (Nigeria), is already operating in the neighboring regions of Opobo/Nkoro and Eastern Obolo and has been recognized by the UN and the World Bank as one of the most effective models for community development in the Niger Delta.[56]

Achieving an optimal combination of the interests of Russian business and the African partners is an important condition for successfully promoting the interests of Russian mining companies in Africa. Africa (like Russia) is extremely dependent on raw materials for its livelihood. The mining complex is currently and will be for the next few decades the most important and, for many African countries, the only source of budget revenue and investment. In this respect, the Africans are resolutely organizing the deepest possible processing of the raw material they produce, right down to putting out end products in situ. They are insisting on adherence to the established industrial standards in CSR. This means that the foreign investor must assume responsibility for creating road and social infrastructure, training national employees, and so on.

Conclusions

In the twenty-first century, the national interests of Russia and of many African nations are intersecting with the interests of the leading players in the world market of natural resources. A graphic example of such interests is the striving of the old centers of economic power in the world to prevent states with large supplies of raw minerals and fuel from forming strategic alliances. The matter primarily concerns Russia and several states of the African continent. The West often interprets the very fact that Russia is establishing partnerships and intensifying economic cooperation with these countries as a threat. The actual underlying reason for such accusations is the increased global competition for access to the depleting supplies of natural resources and raw materials, a significant amount of which can be found in Russia and Africa. Consequently, the world economic role of the latter as the leading players in the global raw-material market is growing. Meanwhile, difficult cooperation and competition relations are developing between Russia and the African countries.

The strengthening of the position of Russia and the African countries in the world economy of the twenty-first century will largely depend on whether Russia and Africa will be able to take advantage of the favorable situation in the world raw-material markets to modernize their national economies. Only in this event will both Russia and Africa be able to act not simply as suppliers of raw materials but as leading players in the world market of depleting natural resources.

Today and in the foreseeable future, Africa will play a particular role in the emerging polycentric world order. In the twenty-first century, the continent has become a place where the interests and also the risks of both the old and the new world power centers intersect. This is where the contradictions in the transformation occurring in the global world order are intersecting in a specific way – the struggle of the new and old power centers for resources and markets, for retaining or acquiring economic and political positions on the continent, but at the same time the growing responsibility for resolving Africa's most acute socio-political, environmental, and other problems, which have global dimensions.

The struggle on the African continent for political and economic influence will mainly be waged among three centers – the European Union (headed by the former metropolises), the US, and the new power centers (the BRICS countries). Furthermore, the old centers – the EU and the US – will largely act from similar positions, competing for supremacy with the new players in the African space, primarily with China, India, and Brazil. However, within the Western camp itself, specific processes will develop related to the existence of internal multidirectional vectors and competition. This includes both consolidating factors (overall military-strategic goals and ideological unity) and divisive aspects (national interests and strategies for ensuring them, historical rivalry, the interests of individual transnational corporations). China, India, and other new power centers will consistently build up their presence in Africa and push out the West in various spheres.

Africa's resource potential is a vital factor in the continent's influence on the world economy. In light of the depletion of many types of fuel and raw materials that are vital for the development of the real sector of the world economy, Africa is still one of the few resource-abundant regions of the world in terms of many types of minerals. This means that the fuel and other raw minerals of the African continent are acquiring new value in the twenty-first century. Opportunities are appearing for the African countries to take advantage of their favorable situation in the world raw-material markets to modernize their national economies and societies. Taking advantage of these opportunities depends both on the ability of the Africans to resolve their internal conflicts and find an efficient model of socio-economic development and on the position of non-African actors.

In contrast to the previous period, African countries are no longer inarticulate raw-material appendages of the developed world and are quite capable of occupying an active, rather than subordinate, position in the global fuel and raw-material markets, while effectively defending their own interests. Given the new changes in the balance of forces in the world arena and the planet's depleting raw material and fuel potential, rational use of resources could turn the African states into a viable entity of the changing world economy.

Annex

Table 12.2 Major Russian investment projects in African natural resources (1992–2013)

Russian investor	Host country/ company	Industry	Type of investment	Value	Year
Norilsk Nickel	South Africa Gold Fields	Gold mining and processing	M&A (acquired 30% of Gold Fields)	US$1.16 bn	2004
Norilsk Nickel	Botswana Tati Nickel	Nickel mining and processing	M&A (acquisition of Canada Lion Ore Mining gave it 85% stake in Tati Nickel)	US$2.5 bn	2007
Sintez	South Africa, Namibia, Angola	Oil, gas, diamonds and copper exploration	"Greenfield" investment	US$10–50 m	2006
Lukoil	Côte d'Ivoire, Ghana	Oil exploration	M&A (acquired interest in 10,500 km^2 deepwater blocks)	US$900 m	2010
Rusal	Nigeria Alscon	Aluminum refining	M&A (acquired majority stake in Aluminum Smelter Company – Alscon of Nigeria)	US$250 m	
Severstal	Liberia	Iron ore	M&A (acquired control of iron ore deposit in Putu Range area of Liberia) US$40 m invested in the feasibility study for the Putu project (greenfield)	US$40 m + US$50 m and US $40 mln	2008 2012 2013
Gazprom	Algeria Sonatrach	Natural gas exploration	Joint exploration and development projects by debt write-off agreement and arms deal	US$4.7 bn and US$7.5 bn	2006
Alrosa	Angola, Namibia, DRC	Diamond mining, and hydroelectricity	Greenfield investment	US$300–400 m	1992
Rosatom	Egypt	Nuclear power	Ongoing negotiations to build Egypt's first nuclear power plant	US$1.8 bn	2010
ARMZ	Tanzania	Uranium	ARMZ acquired the Mkuju River project when it bought Mantra Resources. Toronto-listed Uranium One is the operator of the Mkuju River project, which is owned by the Canadian uranium producer's majority shareholder, Russia's JSC Atomredmetzoloto (ARMZ).	Around US$1 bn	2011–13

Source: This version updated by the author is based on AfDB (2011, p. 4). Due to the complexity of transactions and the lack of clarity about the jurisdiction of the ultimate investor, this AfDB table does not provide a full coverage of Russian investments. On the other hand, some of the figures included in the table, though announced by the companies, may have failed to be invested in full.

Notes

1 Calculations based on the data of Russia's State Committee of Statistics show that in 2012, the share of the primary sector in the GDP was 15 percent, which roughly equalled that of manufacturing. The shares of the secondary sector (i.e. manufacturing plus construction, production of electricity, etc.) and that of the tertiary were 25 and 60 percent, respectively. However, the key indicator of the resource exports dependency – the primary commodities exports to GDP ratio in Russia – rose from 0.10 in 1972 (for RSFSR Republic within USSR) to 0.21 in 2012 (for comparison, Canada's and Australia's ratios in 2012 were just slightly higher than that of the communist Russia in 1972 – 0.11 each).
2 Calculated on the basis of Goskomstat current figures www.gks.ru/wps/wcm/connect/rosstat_main/rosstat/ru/statistics/ftrade/ (accessed June 28, 2014).
3 *Concept of the Foreign Policy of the Russian Federation* (2013) Approved by President of the Russian Federation V. Putin on February 12, 2013. www.mid.ru/ns-osndoc.nsf/1e5f0de28fe77fdcc32575d900298676/869c9d2b87ad8014c32575d9002b1c38?OpenDocument (accessed May 4, 2013).
4 Ibid.
5 Ibid.
6 Statistics of the Ministry of Economic Development of the Russian Federation. Department of Coordination, Development and Regulation of External Economic Activity. *Ogranichitelnye mery v otnoshenii Rossiyskih tovarov: statistika* http://pasmi.ru/archive/84277 (accessed January 9, 2014) (in Russian).
7 The term *information warfare* (IW) is widely used in international academic and other analytical publications to describe the concept of the use and management of information and communication technology in pursuit of a competitive advantage over an opponent.
8 Forecast figures by specialists from the US and Russian government geological agencies (US Geological Survey, USGS and Zarubezhgeologia, respectively) vary considerably. But in both cases, a huge increase is anticipated. (See: Kesler 2007; Bezhanova 2013).
9 Kesler (2007, p. 55).
10 World Trade Organization (2010, p. 3).
11 Fituni and Abramova (2012, p. 3) and Abramova et al. (2007, p. 29).
12 Fituni and Abramova (2012, p. 4).
13 Between 1990 and 2010, the GDP growth in developing countries (DCs) exceeded, on average, 5–6%, i.e. it was twice as high as in developed countries. In 2010, the DCs produced more than 45% of global GDP at purchasing power parity. The share of the DCs in world imports had risen to 38% by 2010; in exports it had exceeded 40%. All the while, trade among the DCs was growing both in absolute and relative terms (43% of foreign trade turnover in 2010). The share of the DCs in manufactured exports rose from 12% in 1960 to 70% in 2010, while the share of foreign direct investment (FDI) in the DCs increased from 26.8% in 2007 to 45% in 2010. DCs are becoming increasingly important exporters of capital. In 1985, the share of FDI originating in the DCs did not exceed 6% of the total, whilst in 2009 this indicator reached 21%. In 1995, the DCs accounted for only 1.1% of foreign assets of the largest 2,500 transnational corporations (TNCs), but in 2010 this figure reached 9% (http://unstats.un.org/unsd/snaama/dnltransfer.asp?fID=2, accessed January 12, 2014).
14 According to UN statistics, in 2012, China was the second-largest economy in the world by GDP (ahead of Japan, Germany, France, and the UK), followed by Brazil and Russia, which occupied respectively the 7th the 8th places (ahead of Italy). India ranked 10th (slightly ahead of Canada), Indonesia was 16th, and Turkey 17th (ahead of the Netherlands) (http://unstats.un.org/unsd/snaama/dnltransfer.asp?fID=2, accessed January 12, 2014).

15 www.wipo.int/ipstats/en/statistics/country_profile/countries/cn.html (accessed January 12, 2014).
16 In addition, the Chinese State Intellectual Property Office (SIPO) accounted for the largest number of applications received by any single intellectual property office. Residents of China filed 560,681 patent applications; this compared with those filed by residents of Japan (486,070) and residents of the United States of America (460,276). Similarly, the SIPO received 652,777 applications, compared to 542,815 for its US analogue (the USPTO) and 342,796 for the Japan Patent Office (JPO) (*World Intellectual Property Indicators*, 2013, Geneva. p. 7).
17 Resolutions adopted by the General Assembly during its Seventeenth Session (1960): Res. 1514 (XV) 14 December 1960, Declaration on the Granting of Independence to Colonial Countries and Peoples and Res. 1515 (XV) 15 December 1960, Concerted Action for Economic Development of Less Developed Countries www.un.org/documents/ga/res/15/ares15.htm (accessedMay 6, 2013).
18 Resolutions adopted by the General Assembly during its Seventeenth Session (1962). Res. 1803 (XVII) 14 December 1962, Permanent Sovereignty Over Natural Resources. www.un.org/documents/ga/res/17/ares17.htm (accessed May 6, 2013).
19 McWhinney (2013).
20 Tarabrin (1977, p. 196) (in Russian).
21 Fituni and Abramova (2010, pp. 103–105).
22 Arkhangelskaya and Shubin (2013, p. 6).
23 Vladimir Putin, President of Russia: *Speech at meeting with heads of African states.* Durban, South Africa, March 27, 2013. English transcript at: http://eng.kremlin.ru/transcripts/5184 (accessed May 16, 2016).
24 www.algerie.mid.ru/sob_1.html (accessedJanuary 13, 2014).
25 www.iimes.ru/?p=4914 (accessed January 13, 2014).
26 www.maroc.ma/en/news/morocco-russias-largest-trading-partner-arab-world-africa-fm (accessed June 28, 2014).
27 www.rusemwhk.mid.ru/index_ru.html (accessed January 13, 2014).
28 http://kremlin.ru/news/4626 (accessed January 13, 2014)).
29 http://gazprom-international.com/ru/operations/country/nigeriya?overlay=true (accessed January 13, 2014).
30 Besides the author's own first-hand "on the ground" experience of such attitudes expressed by African politicians, academics, students, businessmen, and representatives of many other strata of African societies during my visits in at least two dozen African countries, concrete evidence of African nations remembering and being thankful for Russian help in gaining independence may be seen also in regular official statements, letters, and addresses by African leaders and prominent politicians commemorating memorable events in the historical relations between the countries of Africa and USSR/Russia. In certain cases, the memory of such support is scientifically documented and preserved for current and future use by researchers and public. For example, the "enormous role of the Soviet Union" in supporting the struggle of African peoples against colonialism and apartheid has been thoroughly documented by the South Africa-based international Nelson Mandela Foundation (NMF). Some of the historical documents of such support are displayed at the NMF website www.nelsonmandela.org/aama/country/category/soviet-union (accessed June 26, 2014).
31 Russian Federal Customs Service: www.customs.ru/index.php?option=com_content&view=article&id=13858&Itemid=2095 (accessed June 28, 2014).
32 www.gks.ru/wps/wcm/connect/rosstat_main/rosstat/ru/statistics/ftrade/ (accessed January 15, 2014).
33 www.rstnw.ru/statistika-poseshheniya-rossijskimi-grazhdanami-zarubezhnyix-stran.html (accessed June 26, 2014).

34 Here and hereafter, the data on work materials were kindly supplied by OAO Zarubezhgeologia.
35 http://armz.ru/eng/companies/projects/namibia/ (accessed May 16, 2016).
36 www.armz.ru/eng/companies/Foreign_assets/ (accessed May 16, 2016).
37 Deodatus Balile, "Tanzania Poised to Become Leading Uranium Producer," AllAfrica, April 26, 2013: http://allafrica.com/stories/201304290915.html (accessed May 16, 2016).
38 www.kommersant.com/p735629/r_529/Renova_Tekhsnabexport_uranium/ (accessed May 16, 2016).
39 Ibid.
40 www.evraz.com/products/business/constructional/evraz_highveld/?sphrase_id=96458 (accessed May 16, 2016).
41 African Aura Mining Inc. (2010a, p. 48); African Aura Mining Inc. (2010b, p. 4).
42 Bulleten *'inostrannoy kommercheskoy informatsii* [Bulletin of Foreign Commercial Information] – BIKI, 08.07.2006.
43 http://eng.alrosa.ru/operations/african-projects/ (accessed May 6, 2013).
44 Ibid.
45 *The Moscow Times* www.themoscowtimes.com/business/article/russia-abroad-rosneft-nears-african-pipeline-deal/469716.html#ixzz2SgXRRaNo (accessed May 6, 2013).
46 www.gazprom.com/press/news/2010/march/article86632/ (accessed May 6, 2013).
47 Ibid.
48 *Gazprom – a Flexibility Test*, statement by the Chairman of the Management Committee of OAO Gazprom Alexey Miller at the Annual General Shareholders Meeting on June 26, 2009, www.gazprom.com/press/news/2009/june/article66793/ (accessed May 6, 2013); Gazprom and Nigerian National Petroleum Corporation Sign Agreement on setting up joint venture, www.gazprom.com/press/news/2009/june/article66613/ (accessed May 6, 2013).
49 www.severstal.com/eng/media/news/document11390.phtml (accessed January 14, 2014).
50 UNDP Russia. *United Nations Global Compact Network Russia. Corporate Social Responsibility Practice* www.undp.ru/download.phtml?$1404 (accessed May 5, 2013).
51 See: www.rusal.ru/docs/FromRussiaWithLoveRUS.pdf (accessed January 15, 2014).
52 www.evraz.com/sustainability/charity/ (accessed January 15, 2014).
53 www.metalinfo.ru/en/news/25274 (accessed May 5, 2013).
54 Ibid.
55 Ibid.
56 Ibid.

References

Abramova, I., L. Fituni, and A. Sapuntsov (2007) *Voznikayushchie in nesostoyavshiesia gosudarstva v mirivoy ekonomike i politike* [Emerging and Failing States in the World Economy and Politics]. Moscow: INAFR (in Russian).

African Aura Mining Inc. (2010a) 2009 *Annual Report and Accounts*, Vancouver, British Columbia, Canada: African Aura Mining Inc.

African Aura Mining Inc. (2010b) Granting and Ratification by the Government of Liberia of the Mineral Development Agreement for Putu Iron Project. Vancouver, British Columbia, Canada, African Aura Mining Inc. Press Release, September 15.

AfDB (2011) *Africa Economic Brief*, Vol. 2, Issue 7.

Arkhangelskaya, Alexandra and Vladimir Shubin (2013) *Russia's Africa Policy*. SAIIA. Occasional Paper No.157. Johannesburg.

Bezhanova, M.P., and L. I. Strugova (2013) *Resursy, zapasy, dobycha I potreblenie vazhneyshih vidov poleznyh iskopemykh.[World Resources, Reserves, Output and Demand of Major Fuels and Minerals]* Moscow: Vniizarubezhgeologia (in Russian).

Fituni, L. (2011) Arabskie revolutsii nanesli oshchutimy udar po rossijskim biznes-interesam. *Generalny Direktor* No. 7, pp. 18–19.

Fituni, Leonid and Irina Abramova (2010) *Resource Potential of Africa and Russia's National Interests in the XXIst Century*. Moscow: INAFR.

Fituni, L., and I. Abramova (2012) Zakonomernosti formirovania i smeny modeley mirovogo economicheskogo razvitia [Laws of formation and succession of global economic development models], in *Mirovaya ekonomika i mezhdunarodnye otnoshenia [World Economy and International Relations]*, No. 7, Moscow (in Russian).

Kaplinsky, Raphael (2011) *Commodities for Industrial Development: Making Linkages Work*. UNIDO Working Paper No. 01/2011, Vienna.

Kesler, Stephen E. (2007) Mineral Supply and Demand into the 21st Century. Proceedings of the *Workshop on Deposit Modeling, Mineral Resource Assessment, and Sustainable Development*. http://pubs.usgs.gov/circ/2007/1294/reports/paper9.pdf (accessed May 16, 2016).

McWhinney, Edward (2013) *The Declaration on the Granting of Independence to Colonial Countries and Peoples*. Washington, DC: UN. Available at: http://legal.un.org/avl/ha/dicc/dicc.html (accessed May 16, 2016).

US Chairman of the Joint Chiefs of Staff (2000) *Joint Vision 2020: America's Military Preparing for Tomorrow*. Washington, DC: Institute for National Strategic Studies, National Defense University. Available at: www.dtic.mil/dtic/tr/fulltext/u2/a526044.pdf (accessed May 16, 2016).

Vasiliev, Alexey (2011), Tsunami revolutsii. *Asija I Afrika segodnia*, No. 3.

Vasiliev, A., I. Abramova et al. (2008) *Strategicheskoe sopernichestvovedushchih ekonomik mira za afrikanskie resursy* http://inafran.ru/node/48 (accessed May 16, 2016).

World Trade Organization (2010) *World Trade Report 2010: Trade in Natural Resources*. Geneva: WTO.

Index

2009 recession 142 *see also* global downturn, global economic crisis

Africa Mining Vision xvii, 2, 13, 15, 27–28, 83, 114, 162, 265
African agency 2
Algeria 49, 98–100, 138, 267, 291–292, 294, 295, 298, 303
Angola 49, 72, 75, 81, 83, 85, 101, 115, 138, 157, 159, 166, 199, 267, 291–298, 302–304
Australia 67, 118, 173, 266, 271, 277, 285, 300

biodiversity 115, 177, 179, 181, 190
Botswana 20, 40, 48–49, 53, 76, 81, 111–113, 118, 120, 144, 149–150, 173, 188, 205, 207, 268, 298, 302
BRICS 1–2, 4, 42–43, 46, 56, 234, 285, 287–288, 296, 300, 306
Burkina Faso 81, 84, 177, 179–180
Burundi 81

Cameroon 82, 100, 270
Canada xvii, xxi, 3, 67, 85, 263, 271, 275–278
Chad 71, 82, 175, 176, 180
China xviii, 1, 8, 14, 16, 42–43, 47, 64, 81–85, 96, 101, 145, 173, 198, 200, 222, 236, 263–280, 285, 288–290, 306
Cold War 284, 290, 293
colonization 171, 173–174, 176, 291
commodities super cycle 31, 33–34, 82–83 *see also* commodity boom
commodity boom 14, 46, 82, 95, 112, 144, 157, 201 *see also* commodities super cycle

commodity exports 100, 105, 118, 142, 199, 206, 268
corporate social responsibility xvii, xxii, 4, 43, 45, 71, 210, 213, 273, 303–305
corruption 20, 48, 54, 112–114, 121, 150, 156, 160, 188, 201, 220, 224, 267

democracy 112, 118, 120, 187, 267
diversification 4, 26–30, 95, 110–111, 119, 121, 144–146, 165, 276; economic 16, 45, 71, 158, 161, 166
Dodd-Frank Act 23, 47, 56, 85, 264
Dutch disease 7, 20, 102–107, 110–111, 117, 149, 201, 205, 208 *see also* resource curse

economic transformation 6, 16, 35, 65–66, 71–72, 75, 85, 141
environmental protection 171, 174, 291
Eritrea 81, 84
Ethiopia 16, 24–26, 81, 97, 147, 221, 225–227, 231, 291, 296
Extractive Industry Transparency Initiative (EITI) xx, 23, 44, 46, 56, 82, 85–88, 114, 162, 277

foreign direct investment 2–3, 20, 27, 42, 76, 101, 199, 228, 245, 268 *see also* foreign investment
foreign exchange revenues 197, 201
foreign investment 4, 96, 117, 148, 202, 221, 273, 280 *see also* foreign direct investment

Gabon 49, 81, 85, 138, 175, 180, 182
Ghana xv, xviii, 2, 7, 32, 43, 47, 49, 64, 72, 75, 79–81, 97, 100, 157, 165–167,

Index   313

199, 201, 205–206, 212, 268, 275, 291, 296, 298, 302
Global competition 285, 290–3, 298, 305, 306
global downturn 98 *see also* global economic crisis, 2009 recession
global economic crisis 82 *see also* global economic crisis, 2009 recession

industrial development 16, 85, 104, 156, 284–285 *see also* industrialization
industrialization 7, 14, 16–18, 27–28, 34–35, 64–65, 71, 73, 83, 102, 109–111, 118, 145, 156, 158–159, 162, 173, 210–211, 274 *see also* industrial development
inflation targeting 143–144
investment-trade nexus 159

Kenya xviii, 33, 49, 84–85, 139, 140, 149, 268, 270

Lagarde, Christine 157
land acquisition 8, 221–224, 226, 232, 235, 243–246, 251, 256–257 *see also* land grab, large-scale land acquisition
land governance 172, 187–189, 220–221, 225, 228–230, 245, 251, 253–255
land grab 8, 221–226, 230–234, 236, 243–246, 248, 252–258 *see also* land acquisition, large-scale land acquisition
land-tenure systems 251
large-scale land acquisition 221–224, 243–244, 257 *see also* land acquisition, land grab
liberalization 64, 67, 79–80, 82–87, 100, 138, 140, 284, 293
Liberia 42–43, 48, 54, 72, 74, 81–82, 115, 204, 207, 301
local content 5, 7, 14, 20, 26–27, 71, 80, 156–167, 198, 210–212

Madagascar 24, 82, 177, 212, 269, 296
Malawi 140
Mali xv, 75–76, 80–81, 84, 175, 202, 270, 275, 291, 297
Mauritius 145, 149
models of global economic development (MGED), Concept of, 285, 287, 289–91

Mozambique xviii, 19, 22, 32, 43–44, 49, 56, 64, 75, 81, 157, 188, 199, 275, 291, 293, 301

Namibia 49, 81, 205, 294–295, 300
national content 159
nationalization 15, 27, 67, 76, 202
Natural Resource Charter xv, xvi, xx, 3, 44, 160
Niger 176
Niger Delta xxii, 42, 112, 158, 305
Nigeria xix–xxiii, 6–7, 42, 48–49, 65–66, 70, 75–81, 84–85, 112, 121, 138, 144, 147, 149, 157, 159–160, 163–167, 206, 267–270, 291, 294–298, 303–305

Ottawa Forum 1, 5

poverty alleviation 3, 64, 85–86
price volatility 26–27, 116, 138
private governance 8, 220–221, 224–225, 229, 231–236
privatization 3, 67, 81–82, 100, 114, 140, 227

regional coordination 65
regional integration 7, 15, 27, 34, 46, 116, 121, 146–147
resource curse xvii, 6–7, 20, 39–40, 66, 68, 76, 83–84, 86–87, 96, 102–103, 107–108, 110–114, 117–120, 149, 156, 197, 206, 279, 284 *see also* Dutch Disease
Resource Governance Index 160
resource nationalism 19, 33, 64, 66, 76, 83–84
revenue management 197
rural communities 39, 58, 223, 258
Russia 1, 8, 42–43, 142, 284–305
Rwanda 49, 81, 84, 97, 226

Senegal 173, 175–176, 178–179, 186–187, 189, 275, 291
Sierra Leone 42–43, 72, 74, 81, 115, 204, 302
social licence 15, 34, 160, 212
South Africa xviii, 1, 19, 70, 75, 81–82, 84–85, 101, 145, 147, 149, 176, 178, 243, 264, 267, 269, 270–273, 278, 285, 293–301, 304
sovereignty vs. global governance 285–291
state intervention 65, 85, 159

structural deficiencies 16, 19
Sudan 43, 56, 71, 81, 84, 149, 275, 291, 297
sustainable growth xvi, 1, 13, 15, 265

Tanzania xviii, 32, 48, 64, 72–73, 75–78, 80–81, 84–85, 100, 146, 188, 202, 226, 268, 271, 277, 292, 300
tariff protection 27
tax revenue xxii, 2, 18, 112, 198, 202, 212
Tunisia 99–100, 148, 270, 297

Uganda xviii, 8, 49, 64, 72, 81, 84, 97, 144, 199, 243–258, 270

value chain 14, 24, 26, 46, 54, 56–57, 64, 158, 165, 211, 213, 224, 231, 233–234, 274
value maximization 68–69, 71, 76, 79, 82–84

youth unemployment 161, 269

Zambia xv, xviii, xxii, 19, 25, 43, 46–47, 76, 79, 81, 84, 111, 138, 140, 199, 202–203, 206–207, 272
Zimbabwe 25, 75, 81, 84–85, 99, 138–140, 150, 207, 302